South Asian Feminisms

South Asian Feminisms

ANIA LOOMBA and RITTY A. LUKOSE, editors

Duke University Press　Durham and London　2012

© 2012 Duke University Press
All rights reserved
Printed in the United States of America on
acid-free paper ∞
Designed by Nicole Hayward
Typeset in Minion Pro by Keystone
Typesetting, Inc.
Library of Congress Cataloging-in-Publication
Data appear on the last printed page of this
book.

Contents

ANIA LOOMBA AND RITTY A. LUKOSE

South Asian Feminisms
Contemporary Interventions

THIS COLLECTION OF ESSAYS, originating in a conference held at the University of Pennsylvania, presents recent interventions in key areas of feminist scholarship and activism in South Asia.[1] Over the last four decades, the various nations in this region— India, Pakistan, Sri Lanka, Bangladesh, Nepal, and Afghanistan —have been the location as well as the focus of important feminist work that has contributed to rethinking colonial and postcolonial history and literature, law, culture and the nation-state, domesticity and the family, religious and ethnic identities, sexualities, and labor relations. *South Asian Feminisms* builds upon this legacy as it engages complex new challenges to feminist theory and activism that have emerged in recent years. Our contention is that such feminist engagements in this region (with its long-standing and cross-cutting histories of colonialism, nationalism, and women's movements, as well as contemporary struggles around sexuality, religion, human rights, war, peace, globalization, and contemporary iterations of empire and the exploitation of labor) can productively enrich the larger horizon of feminist theorizing. Thus the volume attests to the specificity of diverse South Asian locations and concerns, while also staging a dialogue with other attempts to rethink the central question of "difference" within contemporary feminist theory and praxis.

Recent developments in postcolonial South Asia have resulted in a crisis of feminist thinking and organizing, through which some vital perspectives have emerged—perspectives that can be salutary beyond the region. Threats to women's freedom (in the holistic sense of the term) have escalated, posed by the rise of religious fundamentalisms within and across national boundaries, on the one hand, and intensifying state repression and militarism, on the other. The most recent phase of globalization has led to sharper conflicts over land, water, and resources, as well as to increasing disempowerment and forced migration for large sections of postcolonial populations in the region. It has also produced new conditions and types of employment for women and new arenas and sites for articulating gender and sexual identities. The last few decades have also been marked by the appropriation of feminist vocabularies and agendas by local and national governments, NGOs, and international funding organizations, which readily speak of women's "empowerment" and participation, but in ways that blunt the edge of feminist critiques, offering patronage instead of a fundamental redistribution of resources, or envisaging individual advancement while disabling collective opposition.[2] This has, in turn, resulted in some disenchantment on the part of feminists with their own previous agendas, such as the advocacy of legal reform or rights-based agitations. At the same time, however, new forms of feminist activism have also sprung up, such as those centering on sex work and sexual equality, against militarism, and against oppressive forms of globalized labor. Such new formations have resulted in more vital and dynamic interconnections between theory and activism, and between "South Asia" and "the West," which this volume explicitly highlights.

Accordingly, we have organized the book to highlight dialogues across different locations in South Asia, as well as between scholars and activists. Given the diversity of issues and histories involved, no single volume can aspire to comprehensive coverage. Nor can it be free of the geopolitics within the region (hence the predominance of essays on India). Nevertheless, this volume foregrounds a diverse and dynamic set of contributions to feminist theorizing and activism. It is in recognition of such diversity, and the fact that there are necessarily enormous debates and divergences between feminists in the region and beyond, that we use the word "feminisms" in the book's title and in this introduction. At the same time, we also sometimes use the word "feminism" in the singular when we wish to indicate particular aspects of this larger plurality, or when we refer to the idea of

ANIA LOOMBA AND RITTY A. LUKOSE

feminism as a general concept or horizon of hope and desire, or when we indicate a terrain shared by various groupings or locations. Indeed, it is only in the vibrant interaction between such specificities and differences on the one hand, and shared desires and endeavors on the other, that feminist futures can be imagined.

The sixteen essays included here are grouped into six sections. The first deals with the challenge of religious fundamentalism and secularism for feminist work in both India and Pakistan, and examines how religion shapes the agency of both Hindu and Muslim women. The second section engages with the challenges for feminist labor organizing in the wake of recent forms of globalization in India and Sri Lanka. The next offers feminist critiques of militarization and state repression in Sri Lanka and India, and evaluates some recent forms of peace activism and resistance that have emerged there. The fourth section takes up the question of representations —literary as well as historical—and the questions they pose to feminists today in Bangladesh and India. The fifth section considers the histories and challenges of organizing sex workers in India and Bangladesh, including queer approaches to sex worker activism. The final section interrogates the limits as well as potential of taking South Asia as the grounds for new theoretical work in feminism. Together, they testify to the fact that in South Asia, it is not possible to imagine that one has entered a postfeminist age, or a time beyond politics; as a result, feminist engagements in the region eschew both complacency and despair as they highlight critical new challenges that face them.

In this introduction, we discuss key features of these political and ideological developments and elaborate on some concerns crucial to this book. We first highlight feminist rethinking with respect to two issues that have hitherto been central to postcolonial feminists everywhere, but especially in South Asia: first, the historical recovery of the precolonial and colonial past, and second, the postcolonial formation of the nation-state. We show how such rethinking, along with significant new developments in the region and globally, has revised the relationship between "theory" and "praxis," a question that we turn to more explicitly in the third section of this introduction. Here, we elaborate how the different essays contribute to critically rethinking feminist praxis across different sites of intervention. These revisions, we suggest, are in continuous (if often unacknowledged) dialogue with other challenges to mainstream feminism in the global North. Finally, we turn to the institutional and disciplinary histories and developments that shape the interaction between feminist inquiry and the entity called "South Asia," in the academy and beyond.

THE BURDEN OF HISTORY

Feminist scholarship about South Asia was in its earlier stages understandably preoccupied with undoing the legacy of colonial epistemologies and knowledges, and offering insights into nationalism and the postcolonial state; thus interrogations of histories of the colonial past, decolonization, and the making of postcolonial nations were its major burdens. Maitrayee Chaudhuri argues that in India it was "feminist *historical* research" that "laid the grounds for theorizing feminism."[3] In other parts of South Asia as well, new understandings about female agency, the workings of patriarchy, and possible agendas for postcolonial feminism emerged through feminist reevaluations of the place of gender in anticolonial nationalisms, in colonial constructions of gender and sexuality, and in the creation of the different nation-states of the subcontinent.

For example, Kumari Jayawardena's now classic *Feminism and Nationalism in the Third World* (1986) traced the deep historical roots of feminism in Asia and parts of the Middle East by examining feminism's relations with nationalist movements. This book argued that feminism was not a Western import, but emerged organically in many parts of the once-colonized world through anti-imperial struggles. Another pioneering and enormously influential work was an edited collection, *Recasting Women* (1989), that analyzed colonial and indigenous constructions of Indian women from the so-called Vedic past to the heyday of anticolonial activity. The fact that *Recasting Women* offered rewritings of colonial *history*, even though its two editors, Kumkum Sangari and Sudesh Vaid, were trained in English literary studies, testifies to the hospitality of literary and cultural critique to early feminist scholarship in South Asia, much as it had been in the West.[4] Such work explicitly demanded a questioning of established disciplinary protocols, which may explain the "sanctioned ignorance" on the part of mainstream Indian historians to feminist interventions that has been noted by Janaki Nair.[5]

Of course, South Asian feminists simultaneously offered major revisions of other scholarly disciplines and areas of inquiry, most notably

ANIA LOOMBA AND RITTY A. LUKOSE

literature, law, economics, and sociology, and they also intervened in established modes of activism and organizing.[6] But history has continued to be disproportionately central to feminist scholarship in South Asia, in part because of the nature of postcolonial politics in the entire region.[7] The spectacular rise of communalism, sectarian violence, and militarism has necessitated a continued feminist engagement with histories of religious identity, community, and social memory. Thus Urvashi Butalia's pathbreaking investigation into the gendered aspects of the communal violence of the 1947 Partition of British India into India and Pakistan was catalyzed, she explains, by the horrific escalation of such violence in the 1980s, and specifically the anti-Sikh riots that erupted in Delhi after the 1984 assassination of Prime Minister Indira Gandhi by her two Sikh bodyguards.[8] Feminist historians had to engage anew with the long lineages of Hindu cultural nationalism following the destruction of the Babri Mosque in 1992 by Hindu fundamentalists, an event that ushered in an era of heightened anti-Muslim rhetoric and practices.[9] Analogously, Neloufer de Mel writes that her account of the gendered history of Sri Lankan nationalism was impelled by contemporary "ethno-nationalism [that] has produced one of the harshest ethnic wars of South Asia in which thousands of lives have been lost, property destroyed, welfare, education and health programs have been neglected and a culture of violence taken root."[10] In contrast, the long lineages of anticolonial or nationalist history have occupied less space in the writings of Pakistani feminists, who have been far more engaged, for good reasons, with the role of Islam in women's struggles in independent Pakistan, especially since they were "jolted into action by the Islamization process started by Zia-ul-Haq in 1979."[11]

Feminist engagements with history were impelled by contemporary South Asian politics and were prone to be evaluated through the lens of such politics. Take, for example, Lata Mani's extremely important essay on *sati* or widow immolation. Mani showed how this practice became a "site" for colonial authorities and Indian nationalist men of different persuasions to engage with each other, marginalizing women's voices and obscuring their desires. She suggested that perhaps female agency could be located as much in some widows' desire to die on their husbands' pyres as in other women's desire *not* to do so.[12] While this essay became especially visible in the West because it dovetailed with critiques of colonial discourse and questions of subaltern speech and agency that were being raised by postcolonial theory, it became very controversial in the subcontinent itself, where the revival of incidents of actual widow immolation demanded immediate feminist intervention.[13]

Today, the need for historical reevaluation remains as important as ever, and feminists are increasingly turning to innovative ways of engaging with history. Here, Mrinalini Sinha assesses the adequacy of established historical tools for understanding gender formations at the end of the twentieth century in India; Anjali Arondekar comments on the nature of historical records as they pertain to the figure of the *devadasi* (variously understood as temple dancer, prostitute, or sex worker); Atreyee Sen and Amina Jamal evaluate the uses of history among religiously inflected women's organizations (the right-wing Hindu Shiv Sena in India and the Muslim Jamaat-e-Islami in Pakistan, respectively). All of these essays are self-consciously interested in the methodological, theoretical, and political insights such engagements with history can offer contemporary feminists. Thus, Arondekar shows how in recent years the devadasi has been recast as a figure who possesses artistic, juridical, economic, and sexual agency. Such a figure, Arondekar observes, can function as an anachronistic backward projection of the contemporary feminist critic's own desires for a sexually radical and economically autonomous subject. Arondekar examines the investments that contemporary sexuality studies in the region have in such a figure by attending to the history of the Gomantak Maratha Samaj, a devadasi community in western India. By tracing the colonial and postcolonial histories of the Samaj, the essay both reframes the question of the history of devadasis and illustrates the ways in which contemporary Indian feminism is being reshaped and reconfigured through the more consolidated emergence of sexuality studies. This essay is in productive conversation with three others in the book—those by Firdous Azim, Toorjo Ghose, and Ashwini Sukthankar—that deal with the challenges of organizing sex workers today.

It is also significant that the two essays in this volume that revisit the relationship between Western and South Asian feminisms do so by rereading history. Ratna Kapur describes the ways in which the postcolonial feminist movement in India has arrived at an impasse, one that is shared by left and other progressive movements, because of its ongoing attachment to liberal-colonial notions of historical progress, "rights," and "equality." She suggests that only by abandoning such a narrative can South Asian

ANIA LOOMBA AND RITTY A. LUKOSE

feminists both engage with postcolonial theory and look back anew at their own historical and philosophical traditions, which are capable of yielding radical ways of conceptualizing gender, identity, and freedom. Mrinalini Sinha revisits well-known accounts of late nineteenth- and early twentieth-century Indian women to ask whether we unthinkingly continue to interpret non-European contexts and histories through Eurocentric understandings of gender identities, which were themselves produced by the positing of binary differences between men and women. Drawing on recent ethnographic and historical work that demonstrates the pluralities of gender in South Asia, she suggests that it is time to see whether the specificities of South Asia can yield alternative views of the conceptual categories of gender and sexuality, such as those suggested by Afsaneh Najmabadi in the case of Iran.[14]

These essays depart from earlier feminist writings by suggesting that both historical and feminist methodologies are in need of simultaneous revision.[15] In other words, we cannot use self-evident feminist insights to scrutinize history. Both Kapur and Sinha also urge us, albeit in very different ways, to take very seriously what is offered by the specific histories and philosophical traditions of the region. As opposed to earlier feminists, they are less squeamish about asking for a renewed engagement with local "pasts" and the articulation of local differences that can be useful for feminist rethinking about identity, although both are careful to distance such a plea from the nativist insistence on the "special/essential" nature of a unique and untranslatable local history or culture. Indeed, both urge South Asian feminists to engage with feminists elsewhere—Kapur with a "postcolonial feminism" critical of the "liberal project" that has stymied some South Asian feminists, and Sinha with African, Iranian, and Western feminists who are currently rethinking categories of gender analysis. In other words, both suggest that the specificity of South Asia, in conjunction with a breadth of vision, might allow us to expand the contours of feminist theory and escape the stranglehold of ideas that have emerged from a liberal-colonial history, while also providing resources for confronting the contemporary challenges of feminisms. An analogous engagement with feminists elsewhere also marks other essays in this volume, notably those by Flavia Agnes, who draws on the notion of intersectionality as articulated by the African American legal theorist Kimberlé Crenshaw to suggest ways in which Indian feminists need to think about religious difference alongside gender difference; Malathi de Alwis, who finds Judith Butler's notion of the political useful for thinking about the contributions of feminist peace activists in Sri Lanka; and Laura Brueck, who draws upon Sharon Marcus's notion of a "rape script" to draw attention to the fiction of contemporary Dalit women. These essays make clear that today, feminists are in a position to reevaluate not just the failures of the postcolonial state, or the legacies of colonialism and nationalism, but also their own earlier presuppositions about feminism. Such a reevaluation does not worry overly about an opposition between feminism in South Asia and in the West, although it certainly articulates *differences* that it hopes to arrive at through a dialogue with other feminists, regionally, in the global South, and beyond.

THE NATION, SOUTH ASIA, AND BEYOND

In exploring divergent ways through which feminisms in South Asia can both reinvigorate themselves and become exemplary beyond their own locales, many contributors signal a second distinctive feature of *South Asian Feminisms*—a departure from the boundaries and constrictions of the nation-state, within which most feminist scholarship on the region has hitherto been confined. Such departures, we suggest, also mark the possibilities of further dialogues between feminist work on South Asia and feminist scholarship that has, from other locations, queried the politics of national borders and scrutinized the histories of migration and the constitution of diasporic communities, especially as these dovetail with the uneven histories of colonialism and contemporary global politics.[16]

The religious and ethnic violence that accompanied the very formation of postcolonial nation-states in South Asia only deepened in the late twentieth century; therefore it is not surprising that the nation and its discontents, margins, and exclusions have been the persistent focus of feminist inquiry in South Asia. Feminist scholarship in the region has extensively scrutinized the relationship of women to religious nationalism and communalism, reflecting on the differences as well as shared concerns across different nation-states. In Pakistan and Bangladesh the emphasis has been on deepening Islamicization, in India on the aggressive expansion of the Hindu Right, and in Sri Lanka on the violence marking the strife between Sinhala and Tamil nationalisms.[17]

ANIA LOOMBA AND RITTY A. LUKOSE

While it is understandable that South Asian feminists were largely preoccupied with how nationalist political and legal frameworks enabled or retarded feminist praxis, there remains the danger that such preoccupations can result in inward-looking analyses, both at the level of the nation-state and at the level of particular regions, ethnicities, or religious identities. In South Asia, anticolonial policies/politics developed in crucibles of distinctive regional and linguistic affiliations and cultural formations that were entrenched by colonial rule. So, for example, Bengali nationalists would not necessarily include their counterparts in Maharashtra or Punjab in crafting a cultural vision of the Indian nation for which they were fighting; nor would most Hindu nationalists include Muslims. In studying such partial conceptions of the nation, however critically, we run the risk of replicating their exclusions by letting the part we study stand in for the whole we wish to theorize. Thus, for example, the gendered dynamics of colonial Bengal have tended to become the basis for theorizing anticolonial nationalism in general. Within Bengal itself, the Hindu family and Hindu nationalism have been the dominant objects of scrutiny, and it is important not to use them as shorthand for "Indian" familial formations. For feminists, it is particularly important to be wary of reinforcing, even if unconsciously, the very national, religious, or communitarian asymmetries that they seek to analyze in the past as well as in the contemporary moment.

Flavia Agnes was one of the first to point out that in trying to assert its difference from the West, and "in order to establish [its] 'Indianness,' " the feminist movement "relied on Hindu iconography and Sanskrit idioms denoting female power, thus inadvertently strengthening the communal ideology [for which] Indian, Hindu and Sanskrit are synonymous."[18] When feminists concentrate on exposing the workings of communalism or casteism, the unwitting result can be the continued projection of Muslims, Christians, Dalits, and others as simply marginalized objects; as subjects, they can tell stories that may surprise feminists. This is what Agnes suggests in her essay for the present volume. She writes that since the passage of the controversial Muslim Women's Act in 1986, which debarred Muslim women from seeking alimony in court, the Indian media has relentlessly projected a "Muslim woman" victimized by Muslim patriarchy. But as a lawyer Agnes has found that Muslim women have continued to seek alimony, and surprisingly, the courts have continued to award it to them. Agnes probes this apparent contradiction by tracking what actually happens in specific court battles, and suggests that media insistence on Muslim women's oppression, often underscored by feminists as well, has blinded us to the actual struggles and victories that are now taking place.

If in India the Hindu majoritarian violence that permeates the public sphere also shapes feminist vocabularies and visions, similar nationalist-religious tendencies are rehearsed by the feminist movement in Pakistan, even if historic parallels are not exact.[19] Amina Jamal's essay in this volume scrutinizes the religiosity of Muslim women in the Jamaat-e-Islami today, placing it in the context of a vexed relationship between the religious and the secular in Pakistani nation-state formation. Jamal argues that such religiosity has been shaped by a long and specifically South Asian tradition of Islamic piety and social action that is now rapidly being transformed by contemporary Western military and discursive assaults on Muslim societies through the so-called War on Terror (which has a specific salience for Pakistan).

How women's agency has been enabled by religiosity is also addressed by Atreyee Sen, who examines the militancy of women affiliated with the Hindu right-wing organization, the Shiv Sena. In Mumbai slums, such women reach out to and mobilize the poor by narrating stories of past heroes and heroines. Sen suggests that such appropriations of history by right-wing women challenge feminists to think anew about contemporary forms of agency. As a spate of recent publications testifies, this is an urgent question for feminists in all the regions of South Asia.[20] If women are not just "victims" of right-wing ideologies, but also articulate and enforce them, what does this say for the feminist desire to unify all women and mobilize them against the workings of patriarchy? Examining Muslim and Hindu women's identities as they appear in different national contexts, these essays not only track the continued and transformed power of religious nationalisms in South Asia, but also critically examine the secularist agenda of feminists in different nations. These questions also emerged out of feminist work on the 1947 Partition of British India, as well as on contemporary communal violence, which has shown that women are not just targets of violence but also passionate advocates of the ideologies of community, honor, shame, revenge, and masculinity that shape such violence.[21]

While there are strong parallels between the situations in different South Asian nations, we cannot forget that there are also enormous asymmetries *among* them. As Niloufer de Mel has pointed out, "It is perhaps proof of

ANIA LOOMBA AND RITTY A. LUKOSE

India's dominance in the region" that while "Sri Lanka's history cannot be narrated without the Indian factor, the reverse is not true."[22] There are important differences also in attitudes to Partition: whereas in India it is viewed as an internal rupture, the cutting off of limbs of a national whole, in Pakistan it marks the birth of the nation. Similar differences inform the secession of Bangladesh from Pakistan in 1971. Such differences necessarily shape us as feminist activists and scholars, whether we work in South Asia or abroad. The Indian state's big-brotherly attitude toward Sri Lanka and Nepal is often uncomfortably replicated in the asymmetries that structure the category of South Asia, particularly as it is deployed in the Western academy, and which we discuss in the final section of this introduction.

Thus, it is not enough for feminists to be critical of their respective nation-states or even national cultures—they must work harder to think through both the shared histories and cultures of the region and the differences among them. In bringing together writings of activists and scholars from across the region, this is, in part, what *South Asian Feminisms* seeks to do. Despite important exceptions, including the pioneering work of scholars such as Kumari Jayawardena, until recently much of the most influential feminist scholarship tended to remain within the borders of the nation-state, especially in the case of India.[23] It can be argued that this focus was the necessary result of particular institutional histories, as well as of the dynamics of the early years of independence from colonial rule. But it is also testimony to the power of nationalist ideologies and the nation-state that even as feminists critiqued them, it was not easy to step outside their confines.

Feminist scholarship on the multiple partitions of the subcontinent represented the most sustained attempt to break through such borders, at least by providing a sustained critique of the gendered violence through which India and Pakistan were subdivided in 1947, and Bangladesh came into being in 1971.[24] It showed how "women, their bodies and their honor, are [crucial] to creating national borders, physical and conceptual," but at the same time that women's legal and emotional rights are repeatedly and swiftly denied in the so-called interests of the nation."[25] During these partitions, Hindu, Sikh, and Muslim women were kidnapped as badges of honor. Often it was not women who moved—the boundaries of the nation did, making women "alien" in their own homes. Hindu women found themselves in Pakistan, or Muslim women in India, and were forcibly repatriated when "rescued" by the new postcolonial state to which they were deemed to belong. But, as already mentioned, women were often the bearers of the very patriarchal, familial, and nationalist ideologies that subjected them to violence.

Such histories remind us that women are understood as both the heart of nation and community, and the permeable borders of these spaces. In Sri Lanka, the protracted civil war made most painfully obvious this process of simultaneous belonging or disaffiliation on the part of women. Feminists there have been combating militarization and managing conflict and postconflict situations for some time, as these issues have become increasingly urgent in every part of the region.[26] With the formation of the Women's Action Committee, women's groups both intervened in, and reflected, larger political divisions. In Pakistan, where the military (generally backed by the United States) has been directly in power for several of the six decades of the nation's history, feminists have been consistently pointing to the connections between the entrenchment of antiwoman laws and militarization. According to Sara Suleri, "It is not the terrors of Islam that have unleashed the Hudood Ordinances on Pakistan, but more probably the U.S. government's economic and ideological support of a military regime during that bloody but eminently forgotten decade marked by the 'liberation' of Afghanistan."[27] The militarization of India and Pakistan is a direct consequence of their rivalry, particularly over Kashmir; even apart from that state, India has had no dearth of state-driven and separatist violence within its postindependence territorial borders and boundaries, particularly in the northeast.[28]

Feminist attention to such issues is relatively sparse, despite the fact that women have been at the forefront of movements against militarization in these areas. They have also forcefully articulated the nexus between patriarchal violence and militarization, the most dramatic instance being the naked protest staged in Manipur on July 15, 2004, by fourteen women who carried a banner that read "Indian Army Rape Us."[29] In Manipur, too, an extraordinary woman, Irom Sharmila Chanu, has been on a political fast unto death since 2000, demanding the withdrawal of an Armed Forces (Special Powers) Act that has enabled the Indian state to flagrantly abuse all human and civil rights there.[30] Maoist insurgencies involving and arming women have also been escalating in the region, from Nepal to large areas of

ANIA LOOMBA AND RITTY A. LUKOSE

India, inviting the wrath of a militarized state, as in the case of the Liberation Tigers of Tamil Eelam (Tamil Tigers, or LTTE) in Sri Lanka.[31]

In this volume, Vasuki Nesiah and Malathi de Alwis contend, in different ways, with the war and its aftermaths for feminist praxis in Sri Lanka. Nesiah highlights the complicity of a particular form of institutionalized, multilateral global feminism (what she calls "international conflict feminism") with global governance and empire as it affects the management of "peace" and Sri Lankan feminist organizing. Critically evaluating the role of the "international community" in adjudicating conflict in the country, she draws attention to the complex and difficult relationship between Sri Lankan and global feminist configurations. De Alwis examines the limits and possibilities of a radical feminism in Sri Lanka in the context of the massive NGOization that has been enabled by the conflict. Critically reevaluating some of her own earlier formulations, she wonders whether in the aftermath of war, grief and mourning can be enabling tools for Sri Lankan feminists. Angana Chatterji examines gender, violence, and nationalism in India-administered Kashmir, exploring the critical labor of fact-finding and documentation via a citizen's tribunal as a possible avenue for feminist witnessing and praxis. Whereas the idea of an international community (shaped by United Nations dictates) has come under criticism in the Sri Lankan context, Chatterji argues for the productive possibilities of such a community (rooted in citizen action and uniting local and international citizenry) in relation to Kashmir.

The most obvious redefinition of national belonging may be what emanates from the global transformation of older patterns of migration and labor.[32] Economic globalization also has an uneven history in the region. Sri Lanka, for example, has had free trade zones for a longer period of time and in a more sustained way than India. In this volume, two essays attest to these differences. Sonali Perera examines the literary writings of working-class women belonging to a collective within free trade zones in Sri Lanka, using these writings to chart the changing relationship between feminism and labor activism as NGOs rather than unions emerge as the dominant model for mobilizing in the country. Indeed, a persistent and pervasive theme that runs through several essays on such issues as militarization, conflict, sex work, and labor is a critical interrogation of the contemporary rise and role of NGOs, particularly for feminist politics in the region. From a very different perspective, Anannya Bhattacharjee offers a unique take on the question of globalization, labor, and feminism. She shows how her own coming of age as a feminist activist was shaped by her migrations between the United States and India. Bhattacharjee now organizes workers in Gurgaon, India, a city that has been transformed by the influx of global capital. She explores the connections and tensions between feminism and labor organizing in these disparate spaces, and examines how both these forms of activism are shaped by larger forces of economic globalization.

The essays by Perera and Bhattacharjee, and indeed the volume as a whole, exemplify Chandra Mohanty and Jacqui Alexander's observation that while "grounding analyses in particular, local feminist praxis is necessary, . . . we also need to understand the local in relation to larger, cross-national processes."[33] Precisely because the contemporary processes of globalization and transnational migration are not new phenomena but build upon the terrain carved by older histories of colonialism, race, empire, and nation, feminists see history and contemporary affairs, the local and the global, as necessarily interconnected. Thus, the regional framework of this volume reminds us that we must go to locales that are both larger and smaller than the nation precisely when we scrutinize the politics of national agendas and imaginaries, nation-state formations and international relationships.

THEORY, POLITICS, AND FEMINISM(S)

The first two sections of this introduction have already outlined some ways in which feminist theoretical and activist rethinking have increasingly prompted one another in South Asia. Historical inquiry and contemporary political interventions, we suggested in the first section, are deeply enmeshed. And, as we outlined in the second section, attempts to rethink the contours of the nation have been provoked by challenges faced by feminists working on the ground, who have had to rethink nationalist verities in order to intervene in contemporary problems. But there is no denying that the question and status of theory and theorizing within feminism, to which this volume hopes to contribute, has always been vexed and contested. Much feminist scholarship, in a variety of disciplines across the academy, emerged as a reaction to and argument against dominant modes

ANIA LOOMBA AND RITTY A. LUKOSE

of theorizing. Very often, the particular and the specific, the subjective and the relational, were pitted against "universalizing theory." Working within and alongside a tradition of critical theory, feminist scholars across the disciplines sought to produce alternative frameworks for analysis as they scrutinized the relationship between knowledge production and feminist agendas.

This larger politicization of theory on the part of feminist scholars has not, however, resolved the contested place of theoretical writing within feminist scholarship. The question of who produces theory, from what location, and for what purposes has been a cornerstone of much criticism from women of color, as well as Third World and postcolonial feminist perspectives.[34] Challenges to the international division of labor that underwrites knowledge production have gone hand in hand with critical engagements with Western theoretical traditions and concepts (particularly, testing them for their applicability to and resonance with non-Western contexts). An important and growing body of scholarship has queried the marginalization of women of color and Third World women from women's studies and feminism in the West. This body of work, which has taken shape at least since the early 1980s, queries the easy assertion of a global sisterhood and also reconfigures new alliances of feminists across geographic and racial borders.[35]

Since at least the 1980s, feminists in South Asia have offered analogous insights as they analyze the place of gender in South Asian history and society, and debated their relationship with Western feminism. However, Maitreyee Chaudhuri argues that there is "a very rich body of writing on women's activism but a sparseness of *theoretical* writing on feminism" in India, a gap that, in her view, "may be explained by the existing international academic division of labour which presumes that theorization is the preserve of western concern and expertise."[36] In her essay for this volume, Ratna Kapur argues that South Asian feminists' concern with present-day realities has put pressure on scholarship to speak only to the most immediate struggles of women. Kapur suggests that this has resulted in a fear of critical theories that might challenge fundamental "liberal" categories of analysis. Janaki Nair has offered a different reading, suggesting that "feminist scholarship's debt to the critical political event serves not to highlight a deficiency . . . but a particular institutional and pedagogical practice within which the effects of western theory have been slighter.

Consequently, the mode of feminist theorisation in India has been quite different from those of what we might poorly describe as the global west."[37] It is true that even where the catalyst has not been the critical "event" as such, South Asian feminists' deep engagements with the colonial and pre-colonial histories of the nation, and particularly with the different forms taken by patriarchy and the family in the region (to take but one example), have allowed them to offer major revisions to, inter alia, issues of female agency, the limits of the archives, and the discourse of rights.[38] Still, there is no denying that in South Asia, as elsewhere, there has been an embattled relationship between feminist theorizing and activism. Debates among feminists have in the past often centered on the influence of "Western" scholarship or the supposed "distance" from realities "on the ground" on the part of the activist-scholar.[39]

Today, many of the most compelling feminist voices in and about South Asia do not inhabit such divides, seeking a more organic connection between theory and practice. Thus, many scholars are participants in actual campaigns and struggles, while activists have produced salient pieces of scholarship. Others, such as lawyers or social workers, straddle these domains. Of course, the mode in which any individual writes is necessarily shaped by her own history and training, institutional and disciplinary location, as well as the audience she seeks to reach. These differences and convergences are visible in this volume. Some of our contributors—such as Bhattacharjee—are primarily organizers who work within India and the United States, while Agnes, Sukthankar, and Kapur combine legal work, scholarship, and activism within India and beyond. Ghose, Azim, Nesiah, de Alwis, and Chatterji are scholars with academic and other organizational interests within Bangladesh, India, and Sri Lanka but also, more often than not, beyond these national locations. Ghose is also a social worker, and all of them write out their concrete political engagements. Others in this volume, such as Jamal, Brueck, Sinha, Perera, Karim, Arondekar, and Sen, write from more straightforward academic locations—anthropology, sociology, English, and history—within the United States, Britain, and Canada.

The multiple, cross-cutting, and diverse locations and positions of the contributors to this volume reflect our sense that the most vital feminist theorizing, engagement, and praxis are becoming more interconnected.

ANIA LOOMBA AND RITTY A. LUKOSE

This is particularly visible in this volume's section on sex work. The relationship of feminist politics to the contemporary emergence of sex worker movements in the region has entailed a thoroughgoing and critical interrogation of feminist assumptions about women, sexuality, agency, modalities of mobilization, politics, and organizing. Azim examines the uses and limits of the discourse of rights for sex workers' movements in Bangladesh. Charting the interactions between brothel workers and Naripokkho, a middle-class feminist organization, Azim traces which issues garnered public response and sympathy, and which remained occluded, even for the feminists involved. She shows how the movement challenged middle-class feminist assumptions about women's sexualities and identities. In another essay, Ghose turns to the better-known instance of Durbar, a long-established sex workers union in Sonagachi, Calcutta, one of the busiest red-light districts in Asia. He places this organization in the context of national and global health initiatives addressing HIV/AIDS at the same time that he considers how Durbar functions within the power structures of the Communist Party–led state government of West Bengal. These two contexts allow Ghose to explore the implications of the sex workers' mobilization for current theories of civil and political society, especially those articulated by Partha Chatterjee. In a third essay on sex work, Sukthankar incisively explores the solidarities and dissonances between feminist, queer, and trade union approaches to sex work in Bangalore. She places the particular histories of local organization within international as well as specifically Indian debates about sex work, the history of attitudes to the state in India, and the global sex trafficking discourse abetted by the administration of President George W. Bush. These essays show that sex worker mobilizations in South Asia are necessarily situated on the constantly shifting terrain of larger national and global policies on sex work and the trafficking of women. They also pose acute questions for feminist understandings of the categories of woman, her agency, and her politics.

These categories are also destabilized and enriched by the question of feminist writing, which has been of abiding concern for feminist scholarship in the region.[40] Lamia Karim examines the politics surrounding the Bangladeshi writer Taslima Nasreen, whose critique of Islamic fundamentalism resulted in her exile to Europe and to India. Blasphemy and free speech have, over the past few decades, acquired a particular resonance given the West's engagements with Islam. Decentering such approaches, Karim unpacks how and why Nasreen received little feminist sympathy in Bangladesh while being heralded by feminists in India. Karim contextualizes this controversy within complex histories: the fear of Indian hegemony in the region, the aftermath of the war of 1971, long-standing and newer configurations of Hindu-Muslim relations within and across borders, and different formations of middle-class sensibility across the two nations. In doing so, she shows how such a transnational, regional framing enables a deeper and more complex appreciation of Nasreen, a figure who all too easily could be folded into a highly problematic global discourse polarized between Islam and the West. Such an approach displaces the West as the primary route or node through which internationalism and transnationalism can be thought, while engaging anew with the shifting and different understandings of "feminism" in the region.

The deconstruction of the presumed universal feminist subject, "woman," has been a cornerstone of many debates within feminist theorizing over the last several decades, which have resulted in major analyses of gender essentialism and the constitution of feminist agency. In India the question of a uniform civil code—presumed to be a secular code that would regulate marriage and family practice across various religious communities—has deeply divided feminists. As Agnes's essay explains, the question of caste has been equally explosive in relation to the question of affirmative action for women.[41] In 2001, Dalit groups insisted that caste should be discussed by the United Nation Conference against Racism in Durban, leading to heated debates about whether casteism is a species of racial discrimination. Whatever stance we take on that question, it is beyond dispute that both racial and caste discrimination are equally meshed with questions of gender and sexuality. Dalit women, for instance, are vulnerable to blatant sexual exploitation by high-caste men, as well as to patriarchal oppression by their own men. Brueck's discussion of the Hindi Dalit feminist writer Kusum Meghwal helps us understand how Dalit feminists are radically rewriting the trope of the raped Dalit woman, which has for decades animated mainstream fiction and cinema. While even otherwise radical writers represent the Dalit woman as the eternal victim of sexual violence, Dalit feminists are today boldly making a very different claim, offering images of women who react, often violently, against their rapists. On one level, such actions might dovetail with the vigilante scenarios offered in mainstream cinema, or with

ANIA LOOMBA AND RITTY A. LUKOSE

the images of avenging goddesses that have been part of Hindu culture, but in these narratives they work to a very different end by reworking what Brueck identifies as the "rape script" of Dalit women.

Religion and caste are just two of the categories that have catalyzed fundamental rethinking about the problem of "difference" and its relationship to definitions of the feminist subject. The volume as a whole demonstrates the pressure that is put on the category of woman vis-à-vis other categories (worker, sex worker, Muslim, Hindu, slum dweller, Dalit, mother, temple dancer). In this way, across the essays, we find critical interrogations of such identities and their implications for feminist politics. The analogies between these categories and those of racial difference and immigrant identities are useful, if not exact. In South Asia today, the problem of "difference" is refracted through reinvigorated identitarian movements— particularly through violent, militaristic, religious, and ethnic nationalisms, which are escalating across the region. In such situations, feminist analyses of new forms of gender violence are desperately necessary, but at the same time, some basic feminist assumptions about secularism, as well as a leftist antipathy to maternalism, are thrown into crisis. How should feminists think about women's agency when it is manifested through religious beliefs or through sex work? Is "the maternal" (or motherhood), with its essentialized assumptions about women's nature, a useful rubric for organizing women against war and militarization?

In sum, the fundamental question is, what constitutes progressive and radical feminist politics today? This volume offers a variety and diversity of critical insights. For example, while Agnes urges feminists within India to interrogate their universalizing and secular assumptions when confronted with the politicized figure of the "Muslim woman," Jamal eschews the generalized critique of Western secularism that is gaining ground today, instead urging attention to the dense connections between nationalism and secularism in Pakistan, and secularism's relationship to South Asian Islamic traditions. This is an essay that resonates with Karim's argument that Taslima Nasreen's history should be contextualized within the complex web of relations between India and Bangladesh instead of being too easily conscripted into a global discourse about Islam and the West. While Nesiah worries about the ways that "international conflict feminism" and its manifestations in Sri Lanka deploy notions of women's peaceful nature, de Alwis wonders whether the dismissal of the "maternalism" of the Mothers' Front by Sri Lankan feminist and peace activists was too hasty. While Azim scrutinizes the difficulty middle-class women's organizations in Bangladesh had in reaching out to sex workers, Sukthankar critically appraises middle-class and queer investments in the figure of the sex worker in the Indian context (an appraisal that resonates with Arondekar's discussion of the critical stakes that sexuality studies in India have in the figure of the devadasi).

What progressive feminist politics looks like has, of course, animated debates about the impact of postmodernist frameworks on feminism. But the essays assembled here suggest that this discussion cannot be divorced from the problem of the appropriation of feminist vocabularies by the mainstream, nor can it be divorced from the way issues of gender and sexuality circulate in neoliberal discourse, global capital, and new forms of empire. How do we rethink feminist organizational politics in the wake of the proliferation of multinational funding organizations, or the many international organizations that aim to monitor conflict in the region? Where is the space for oppositional action in a world where the liberal state and world political and economic order seem to appropriate radical discourse, and where government-funded NGOs seek to replace grassroots political organizations? Are rights-based approaches to gender justice, drawn from liberal discourse and appealing only to the existent practice of the law, bankrupt ideas today? Whether it is by invoking the impact of NGOs, the international donor and United Nations community, global capital, or even the increasing activism of women within right-wing movements, several of the essays contend with the difficulties of articulating radical feminist visions and modes today.

Again, a diversity of critical insights are offered here. While Bhattacharjee articulates a revitalized organizational and movement-based understanding of labor activism within the globalized spaces of labor and capital in India, Perera draws attention to the nonunitary and unfinished revolutionary subject of working-class literature in her analysis of free trade zone women workers in Sri Lanka. While de Alwis and Nesiah are critical of the NGOization of feminist activism in Sri Lanka, Perera urges us to pay attention to the articulation of feminist and labor subjectivities within NGO spaces. While Nesiah is highly critical of the workings of the international community and the ways that it has transformed feminist politics in Sri Lanka in the aftermath of the civil war, Chatterji wonders about the political possibilities of a citizen-based international community for combating militarization and state-sponsored violence in India-administered Kashmir.

It needs to be emphasized that contributors to this volume critically reflect upon and complicate long-standing debates about the feminist subject and the constitutive features of progressive feminist politics, not just by scrutinizing epistemological frameworks but also by paying attention to the exigencies and challenges of feminist praxis. They interrogate the limits and possibilities of different forms of feminist organizing—their inclusions and exclusions, their assumptions and reformulations, their rigidities and generosity, and their histories of uneven and unequal interconnection with other social movements in the region and globally. But these essays offer little evidence of despair, or of nostalgia, or indeed of inwardness, even as they produce searching, often searing self-critique and engage in an intense scrutiny of feminist frameworks and methods. Thus, taken as a whole, these interventions suggest ways in which feminism continues to be a vital political language of contemporary struggle in the region.

FROM WHERE WE SPEAK

The conference that provided the starting point of this volume was funded largely by the University of Pennsylvania's South Asia Center and Women's Studies program; it seems apt to conclude by briefly considering some aspects of the intersection between "South Asia" and "feminism" in the U.S. academy and beyond. "South Asia" is a term whose shifting connotations reflect the changing geographical, historical, cultural, and political ties, as well as tensions, between the different nation-states and populations of a vast region, in tandem with shifts in colonial and postcolonial global relations. The South Asian Association for Regional Cooperation (SAARC) was established in 1985 by the governments of Bangladesh, Bhutan, India, the Maldives, Nepal, Pakistan, and Sri Lanka. In 2007, Afghanistan became part of the organization; now Iran, China, and Burma have expressed interest in joining it, underlining the fact that even the physical contours of this region are not self-evident or unchanging. The SAARC configuration has made this "area" into a more pervasive unit of analysis, generating several studies on gender and women's development in particular (especially on health, education, violence, and sexual trafficking) from

UNIFEM (United Nations Development Fund for Women) and other international organizations, as well as from different bodies within the nations involved.[42] Many groupings of women in the region, or focused on it but located elsewhere, have taken shape over the years.[43] Such groups either follow the SAARC logic or extend it, but it is worth pointing out that Afghanistan is relatively marginalized within them, despite many feminists' interest in extending support to women there and establishing connections with Afghan feminists.[44]

The study of South Asia in the West has been shaped by colonial knowledge production; the British Association for South Asian Studies was a reworking of the colonial Asiatic Society, while "area studies" were institutionalized in the United States after the Second World War through Cold War imperatives. As they developed, South Asian studies were largely derived from the study of India. One of the effects of this peculiar history was that "civilizations" were primarily defined in terms of religious groupings, which in the case of South Asia meant the privileging of Hindu and Sanskritic traditions. It also meant that ancient histories, languages, literatures, and culture were privileged over their contemporary manifestations, though a significant body of work in anthropology, political science, and history sought to understand contemporary social, political, and cultural change under the rubric of "modernization." Both these features were of course not new, because they had existed within earlier traditions of Orientalist scholarship, but they were now simultaneously strengthened and sometimes reconfigured to speak to issues of "new nations" and their developmental trajectories.

This is not the place to analyze such histories in detail; we invoke them only to emphasize some of the institutional and disciplinary protocols of "South Asian" studies, which feminist scholarship has to work within and against. It needs to be emphasized, too, that the seemingly arbitrary geographical divisions central to both Orientalist scholarship and area studies; their simultaneous and often silent privileging of particular national, religious, and political histories; and their marginalization of certain kinds of knowledge are features they share with the institutional histories of other disciplines. In these ways, they have also shaped feminist scholarship and its institutional homes in the academy. Women's studies in the Western academy is, as an area of institutionalized scholarly inquiry, putatively interdisciplinary; but, like area studies, its institutional history has

ANIA LOOMBA AND RITTY A. LUKOSE

also privileged particular methodological approaches and certain kinds of scholarship. In both area studies programs and women's studies, scholarship by women of color and by those from developing or Third World countries was long marginalized in the field. Despite major changes in some universities, this continues to be the case in most places. If women's studies and feminism, as areas of inquiry in the university, were the direct result of women's activism, the entry of South Asians in large numbers into area studies is also fast reconfiguring South Asian studies in the Western academy. Of course, these situations are *not parallel*, but it is the uneven and often unwieldy terrain upon which they overlap that allows us the vantage point from which to scrutinize the place of South Asia within women's studies, feminist studies, and studies of sexuality, as well as the place of feminist thinking in South Asian studies.

Here we might wish to remember an important institutional detail: there is no such thing as "South Asian studies" *in* South Asian universities. The place of feminism in "South Asian studies" is therefore a question that in a literal sense pertains largely to the Western academy. Nevertheless, it is deeply connected with the development of feminist work in South Asia, as well as with an important and growing body of scholarship that queries the institutionally sanctioned ignorance of the work produced by women of color and Third World women within women's studies and feminism in the West. Feminist attempts to think about transnational connections and asymmetries can be very useful in reconfiguring some existing problems with area studies programs that have, in the past, privileged the study of dominant social formations of religion and tradition in ways that have disconnected the region from wider sociocultural and geopolitical processes. To make gender and women central to the study of any geographical area is the necessary flip side of the effort to internationalize women's studies and make it more responsive to non-Western perspectives and experiences.[45]

Scholarship by Third World and women-of-color feminists coined phrases such as "feminism without borders," "transnational feminism," "relational and multicultural feminism," and "international feminism" to capture the ferment of new approaches to feminisms globally.[46] Such scholarship also asks us to rethink the value of "difference" as an analytic category for feminism, an issue that we have already commented upon at some length in the previous section. Ella Shohat argues that forms of multiculturalism and internationalism within global feminist formulations use a "sponge/additive" strategy that depends on reductive and ghettoized notions of identity and culture.[47] She points out that "Eurocentric versions of global feminism assume a telos of evolution toward a reductive identity practice" that "reproduce[s] Eurocentric notions of culture under the sign of global feminism."[48] "Diversity" and "multiculturalism" can often strengthen instead of challenge Euro-American norms of gender, sexuality, and women's identities; global diversity within these categories can then only be understood as difference from such Euro-American norms. Feminist writing can be salutary when, as in the case of this volume, it neither assumes such norms nor offers itself as evidence of a singular "difference." It is our contention that a sustained focus on the dense histories, interconnections, and dynamic complexities of South Asia as a location of feminist theory and praxis productively resists the reductive ways in which Western feminist frameworks incorporate their others. It is additionally our claim that such writing can also resist the parochialism of South Asian feminisms that function within nationalist frameworks.

The Western academy continues to offer spaces where feminists across national and regional divides can interact, spaces that are necessarily implicated in the geopolitical and institutional histories outlined above. Dialogues and collaborations between feminists from different South Asian nations—often made difficult by national hostilities, such as those between India and Pakistan—are also increasingly taking place in the region itself. In 1989 and 2006, South Asian Feminist Declarations were issued from Bangalore and Colombo, respectively. These declarations noted that various countries in the region are now polarized in terms of religion, with India becoming increasingly Hinduized, Pakistan and Bangladesh being Islamic states, and Sri Lanka virtually a Sinhala majority state. They noted "new configurations of power" at various levels: the rise of the United States and the "breakdown" of the United Nations, the escalation of global markets and economic neoliberalism leading to greater poverty and migration, greater repression of civil liberties at every level in the wake of the U.S.-led "War on Terror."[49] At these and other forums, feminists have been concerned about the growing disparities of wealth; the greater marginalization of poor, tribal, or minority women; and their growing vulnerability to violence.

Thus, the present volume's focus on "South Asian feminisms" is situ-

ANIA LOOMBA AND RITTY A. LUKOSE

ated at the intersection of two histories: first, an academic-political configuration in the West where "South Asia" and feminism have a particular valence and second, a more contemporary resurgence and revitalization of feminist thinking and organizing in the region. The essays themselves do not explicitly address what is gained or lost by a focus on South Asia, which may be a productive exercise in itself, and is in fact touched upon by some of the writers included. But the volume makes clear that as a "location" produced by the crisscrossing of geopolitics, history, and culture, South Asia is less a static place and more a dynamic crossroads of various regional, national, and global forces.

The interventions collected here from this dynamic space emphasize that feminism will be "post"-ed only when political life as we know it is over. This volume is assembled in the hope that it will enable meaningful and ongoing dialogues in several areas of study and activism, in South Asia as well as in places elsewhere. It is also assembled in the conviction that feminists who learn to speak of each other's specificities learn best to build solidarities.

NOTES

1. The conference "South Asian Feminisms: Gender, Culture, and Politics" was held at the University of Pennsylvania, March 28–29, 2008. Although the authors included here are not identical with the presenters at the conference, both groups included feminist academics, activists, and lawyers situated in South Asia and in the West.

2. There is, by now, a vast literature that tracks the effects of the mainstreaming of ideas about gender on feminist politics. See, for example, Mohanty, "On the Concept of 'Empowerment'"; and essays by Ratna Kapur, Malathi de Alwis, and Vasuki Nesiah in this volume. See also Sharma, *Logics of Empowerment*. For Bangladesh, see Karim, "Demystifying Micro-Credit."

3. Chaudhuri, *Feminism in India*, xi. Emphasis added.

4. Sangari and Vaid noted in their introduction to *Recasting Women* that "cultural history seems to be the richest, most integrated, and yet most difficult form available for feminist historiography" (3). Two literary critics also started *Manushi*, a pioneering feminist journal.

5. Nair, "The Troubled Relationship of Feminism and History," 57.

6. A very partial list of work published during the 1980s would include Agarwal, *Structures of Patriarchy*; Chatterji, *Woman, Image, Text*; Ardener, Dube, and Leacock, *Visibility and Power*; Joshi and Liddle, *Daughters of Independence*; Mies,

Women and Indian Patriarchy; Mukeherjee, *Realism and Reality*; Shiva, *Staying Alive*; Sangathana, *"We Were Making History"*; Kishwar, "Women in Gandhi"; and writings from the feminist journal *Manushi* of that period, which can be sampled in Kishwar and Vanita, *In Search of Answers*. Though published in 1992, K. Saradamoni's edited collection, *Finding the Household*, was part of a broad-based set of conferences and plenaries from throughout the 1980s that sought to bring feminist questions to sociological methodologies. It also interestingly takes as its framework "Asia" rather than India, and includes articles on the Philippines, Vietnam, and Korea. See also John, *Women's Studies in India*; Huq, Begum, Salahuddin, and Qadir, *Women in Bangladesh*; and Mumtaz and Shaheed, *Women of Pakistan*.

7. While history has continued to be an important arena for South Asian feminist engagements with postcolonial politics, since the 1980s other disciplines, such as political science, sociology, anthropology, media studies, and literary studies, have contributed as well. Samples of this work include Mukherjee, *Twice-Born Fiction*; Sunder Rajan, *The Lie of the Land*; Tharu and Lalita, *Women Writing in India*; Tharu, *Subject to Change*; Fernandes, *Producing Workers*; Menon, *Recovering Subversion*; Ray, *Fields of Protest*; Radhakrishnan, "Examining the Global Indian Middle Class"; Toor, "Moral Regulation in a Postcolonial Nation-State"; Mankekar, *Screening Culture, Viewing Politics*; Visweswaran, *Fictions of Feminist Ethnography*; John and Niranjana, "Mirror Politics"; Chatterjee, *Women, Labor and Post/Colonial Politics on an Indian Plantation*; Lukose, *Liberalization's Children*; Chaudhry, "Reconstituting Selves in the Karachi Conflict"; de Alwis, "Moral Mothers and Stalwart Sons"; Mukherjee, "Gendered Embodiments"; Siddiqi, "In the Name of Islam?"; Tamang, "Legalizing State Patriarchy in Nepal"; Sunder Rajan, *The Scandal of the State*; Oza, *The Making of Neoliberal India*; Sharma, *Logics of Empowerment*; John and Nair, *A Question of Silence?*; Rege, *The Sociology of Gender* and *Writing Caste/Writing Gender*; Rao, *Gender and Caste*.

8. Butalia, *The Other Side of Silence*, 4–5. See also Menon and Bhasin, *Borders and Boundaries*.

9. See, for example, the essays collected in Sarkar, *Hindu Wife, Hindu Nation*. See also Sarkar and Butalia, *Women and the Hindu Right*.

10. De Mel, *Women and the Nation's Narrative*, 21–22.

11. Mumtaz and Shaheed, *Women of Pakistan*, 2.

12. Mani, "Contentious Traditions."

13. See Sarkar, "Rhetoric against Age of Consent," 1869; and Loomba, "Dead Women Tell No Tales." Mani's own reflections on her work and its reception are important. See Mani, "Cultural Theory, Colonial Texts."

14. Najmabadi, "Beyond the Americas?"

15. See also Menon and Bhasin, *Borders and Boundaries*. Here Menon and Bhasin link their turn to oral histories to the exigencies of their specifically feminist questions, but also highlight how doing so challenged their feminism. Among the earliest uses of oral histories within feminist scholarship in India is the now classic *We Were Making History* by Stree Shakti Sanghatana. For critical reflections on the

ANIA LOOMBA AND RITTY A. LUKOSE

methodological, ethical, and political difficulties of collecting oral narratives in the context of ethnographic practice for the telling of nationalist histories by women, see Visweswaran, *Fictions of Feminist Ethnography*.

16. Such a dialogue is evident in books such as Ivekovic and Mostov, *From Gender to Nation*. See also Basu, *Women's Movements in Global Perspective*; Chaudhuri and Strobel, *Western Women and Imperialism*; Lewis, *Feminist Postcolonial Theory*; Mohanty, *Feminism without Borders*; Shohat, *Talking Visions*; Grewal and Kaplan, *Scattered Hegemonies*; Shohat, *Taboo Memories, Diasporic Voices*; Sarker and Niyogi De, *Trans-Status Subjects*; Arredonda, Hurtado, Klahn, Nájera-Ramírez, and Zavella, *Chicana Feminisms*; Oyeronke, *African Women and Feminism*; Mohanty and Alexander, *Feminist Genealogies, Colonial Legacies, Democratic Futures*; Mohanty, Russo, and Torres, *Third World Women and the Politics of Feminism*; Kaplan, Alarcon, and Moallem, *Between Women and Nation*.

17. See, for example, Sarkar and Butalia, *Women and the Hindu Right*; Oza, *The Making of Neoliberal India*; Bachetta, *Gender in the Hindu Nation*; Mumtaz and Shaheed, *Women of Pakistan*; Kabeer, "The Quest for National Identity"; Hassan, *Forging Identities*; Rouse, *Shifting Body Politics*; Jeffrey and Basu, *Appropriating Gender*.

18. Agnes, "Women's Movement in a Secular Framework," 1123.

19. The feminist movement in Pakistan originated within the Muslim league. See, among others, Rouse, "Gender, Nationalism(s) and Cultural Identity"; Ali, *The Emergence of Feminism among Indian Muslim Women*.

20. See, for example, the essays collected in Butalia and Sarkar, *Women and the Hindu Right*.

21. Butalia, *The Other Side of Silence*; Menon and Bhasin, *Borders and Boundaries*; Chakravarti and Haksar, *The Delhi Riots*.

22. De Mel, *Women and the Nation's Narrative*, 45.

23. For example, Sangari and Vaid, *Recasting Women*. Departures are increasingly evident, such as de Mel and Thiruchandran, *At the Cutting Edge*. Others include de Alwis and Jayawardena, *Embodied Violence*; Jeffrey and Basu, *Appropriating Gender*; Bhasin, Menon, and Khan, *Against All Odds*; Chatterjee, Desai, and Roy, *States of Trauma*; and "South Asian Feminisms: Negotiating New Terrains," the 2009 special issue of *Feminist Review*, edited by Firdous Azim, Nivedita Menon, and Dina Siddiqi. Quite apart from a South Asia framework, other attempts to create dialogues outside nation-state boundaries include conversations with French feminism (see Haase-Dubosc, John, Marini, Melkote, and Tharu, *French Feminism*) and more recent attempts to configure "Asian feminism" as a space of conversation, debate, and solidarity (see "Feminisms in Asia," the 2002 special issue of *Inter-Asia Cultural Studies*, edited by Tejaswini Niranjana and Mary E. John).

24. See, for example, Butalia, *The Other Side of Silence*; and Menon and Bhasin, *Borders and Boundaries*.

25. Menon, "Do Women Have a Country?" 57.

26. For Sri Lanka, see essays by de Alwis, Nesiah, and Perera in this volume. See

also de Mel, *Militarizing Sri Lanka*; Menon, Coomaraswamy, and Fonseka, *Peace Work*; Rajasingham-Senanayake, "Between Reality and Representation"; Perera-Rajasingham, Kois, and de Alwis, *Feminist Engagements with Violence*. For Bangladesh, see Mukherjee, "Remembering to Forget." For South Asia, see Manchanda, *Women, War, and Peace in South Asia*; Chenoy, *Militarism and Women in South Asia*; Coomaraswamy and Perera-Rajasingham, *Constellations of Violence*; Roy, "The Ethical Ambivalence of Resistant Violence."

27. Suleri, "Woman Skin Deep," 768. See also Khan, "Zina."

28. For example, there is no essay on militarization in Mary John's otherwise wide-ranging *Women's Studies in India*. But see Kazi, *Between Democracy and Nation*. There is a rich literature on the organic connections between Hindu nationalism, militancy, and women. See, for example, Sarkar and Butalia, *Women and the Hindu Right*; and Sen's essay in this volume. Of course, there is the classic work on women and armed struggle, namely Stree Shakti Sangathana, *"We Were Making History."* See also Barthakur and Goswami, "The Assam Movement."

29. See Shivali Tukdeo, "Indian Army and the Legacy of Rape in Manipur," *Counter Currents*, October 24, 2004, at countercurrents.org.

30. See Subhash Gatade, "Irom Sharmila: 'Iron Lady' of Manipur," *Counter Currents*, October 17, 2006, at countercurrents.org.

31. For Nepal, see Manchanda, "Maoist Insurgency in Nepal."

32. Sen, *A Space within the Struggle*; Kumar, *The History of Doing*; Kabeer, *The Power to Choose*; Gandhi and Shah, *The Issues at Stake*; Biyanwila, "Sri Lanka"; Rahman, "Bangladesh."

33. Mohanty and Alexander, *Feminist Genealogies, Colonial Legacies, Democratic Futures*, xix.

34. See note 15. In addition, for the specific case of India and the United States, see John, *Discrepant Dislocations*; as well as Spivak, *In Other Worlds*. Parallel explorations of such issues through other feminist locations abound; for example, see Barlow, "Globalization, China, and International Feminism."

35. In Britain, the essays that were central to the debate were Carby, "White Woman Listen!"; and Parmar and Amos, "Challenging Imperial Feminism." In the United States, they were Spivak, "Three Women's Texts and a Critique of Imperialism"; and Mohanty, "Under Western Eyes."

36. Chaudhuri, *Feminism in India*, xi. Chaudhuri also draws a distinction between Third World feminisms in the West and feminists located in the Third World, xlii, note 5.

37. Nair, "The Troubled Relationship of Feminism and History," 58.

38. For work on the family, scholarship on matriliny in Kerala has been especially powerful. See Saradamoni, *Matriliny Transformed*; and Arunima, *There Comes Papa*. See also Oldenburg, *Dowry Murder*.

39. See Janaki Nair's discussion of this issue, "The Troubled Relationship of Feminism and History." For an attempt to illustrate the importance of Indian feminist thought to Western feminism, see Gedalof, *Against Purity*.

40. See, for example, Tharu and Lalita, *Women Writing in India*, which also gives an extended critical bibliography on the subject.

41. See chap. 4, "Reservations for Women: 'Am I That Name?' " in Menon, *Recovering Subversion*, 106–203.

42. See, for example, Chandni Joshi, "Agendas for Gender: Follow-up on the Beijing Platform for Action from a UNIFEM Perspective"; and Preet Rastogi, "Dimensions of Gender Development in South Asia Based on Human Development Indicators," both in Bhatia, Bhano, and Samanta, *Gender Concerns in South Asia*, 77–122 and 301–31. See also Coomaraswamy, "Mission to Bangladesh, Nepal, and India."

43. The groups vary enormously in size, political affiliation, outlook, and reach—the India-based South Asia Women's Watch attends UNIFEM meetings, the Canada-based Sawnet is largely a resource for research, whereas a "South Asia Women's Fund" originates in Colombo but is organized on Facebook.

44. For a discussion of such attempts, see Shahnaz Khan, "Between Here and There: Feminist Solidarity and Afghan Women," *Genders* 33 (2001), at genders.org.

45. For a description of some of these efforts, see Adrienne McCormick, "The Women's Studies, Area, and International Studies Curriculum Integration Project at Thirteen Institutions," and the other essays in "Internationalizing the Curriculum," a special issue of *Women's Studies Quarterly* 26, nos. 3–4 (Fall–Winter 1998). See also "Curricular Crossings: Women's Studies and Area Studies," at http://www3 .amherst.edu.

46. There are terminological differences between these positions. For example, Grewal and Kaplan reject the formulation "international feminism" for what they see as its naturalization of the nation-state. They also reject "multicultural feminism" as a term rooted in liberal multiculturalism as opposed to what they see as the more progressive formulations of "transnational feminist cultural studies." See the introduction to *Scattered Hegemonies*, 1–33. At other times, these terms are used together, as in Mohanty's formulation of a "feminism without borders," in which the terms "transnational" and "international" are also deployed. See Mohanty, *Feminism without Borders*, 2. While these distinctions are important, for the purposes of our argument, what we would like to draw attention to is the larger critical labor of these different formulations—namely, the effort to decolonize Western feminism while creating new frameworks in and through which feminist praxis might be thought about in an increasingly globalized and transnational world.

47. Shohat, "Area Studies, Transnationalism, and the Feminist Production of Knowledge," 1269.

48. Ibid.

49. Siddiqi and de Alwis, *Feminist Activism in the 21st Century*.

I

FEMINISM, RELIGION, AND THE SECULAR

FLAVIA AGNES

From *Shah Bano* to *Kausar Bano*

Contextualizing the "Muslim Woman" within a Communalized Polity

THIS ESSAY EXPLORES the intersection of gender and identity and weaves together two significant, yet seemingly isolated incidents in Indian history—the verdict of the Supreme Court of India in the *Shah Bano* case in 1985, which upheld the right to maintenance of divorced Muslim women, and the controversy that followed, and the more recent communal carnage and the sexual violence that was unleashed on Muslim women in Gujarat in February and March, 2002.[1] Though apparently isolated, these two incidents bring to center stage subaltern Muslim women situated in a communally vitiated political arena, one that compels us to examine changing cultural and political figurations of "the Muslim woman" over the last several decades in dynamic relation with the lives of Muslim women. While marking the period of the rising wave of Hindu fundamentalism in the country, the two cases, and the two women they are named for, can be placed at opposite ends of the spectrum: Shah Bano at one end, and Kausar Bano, a victim of the Gujarat atrocities, at the other.

In this essay I want to examine the following questions: Within the confines of an identity that is both rigid and fluid, how does a Muslim woman negotiate the state structures and dictates of the community?[2] What are the contradictory pulls of culture, religion, law, and politics that play upon her life and how does she position herself within these contradictory pulls? Why does she always enter the political arena adorned with the mantle of victim-hood? Are there no moments of defiance and resistance, and why do these moments get overshadowed? Who are her allies and adversaries in her struggle for survival? What have been her gains and losses? How do the proponents of a uniform civil code view her? More important, how does she relate to the vocal, visible, and highly articulate women's movement, which brought gender concerns within the political arena with the slogan "The personal is political"? The women's movement has focused on the overarching hold of patriarchy on the lives of women and invoked state interventions through sustained campaigns to release women from its clutches. But how has this articulation addressed concerns of women who are at the margins of social boundaries, whose reality is marked not only by patriarchal dominations but also by racial, religious, and caste prejudices? These are important questions that have haunted some of us within the Indian feminist movement.

In any society, the way the question of gender is articulated depends on the hierarchy of social concerns in that society. A slogan coined by women of color in the United States succinctly captures this reality: "All the women are white, all the blacks are men, but some of us are brave." The slogan was coined to convey that when issues of women's rights are addressed, they are addressed in the context of white women, and when issues of race are addressed, they are in the context of black men.[3] Issues that specifically concern black women are addressed neither by the women's movement, which is predominantly white, nor by the predominantly male-dominated movements of people of color. Women of color had to carefully carve out their strategies by aligning with one or other of these movements. A similar dilemma faces women from minority communities in India. Even when gender concerns of minority women hit the headlines, they do so primarily to strengthen the prevailing stereotypical biases against the minority community at large. Rather than concern for Muslim women, it is antipathy to the Muslim community that gets foregrounded when mainstream media pays attention to the "plight" of Muslim women.

THE *SHAH BANO* JUDGMENT AND THE
CONTROVERSIAL MUSLIM WOMEN ACT

No example can better serve to explain the situation described above than the events that followed the Indian Supreme Court ruling in 1985, which upheld the right of a divorced Muslim woman for maintenance under Section 125 of the Criminal Procedure Code.[4] The adverse and derogatory comments in this ruling against the Prophet and Islam, and the call for a uniform civil code, resulted in a Muslim backlash and demand for a separate statute based on Islamic jurisprudence.[5] Bowing to the Muslim orthodoxy, the Congress government led by Rajiv Gandhi introduced a bill in Parliament, which sought to exclude divorced Muslim women from the purview of Section 125. This move came to be projected as the defeat of the principle of gender justice for Indian women, as well as the defeat of secular principles within the Indian polity. It was projected that the proposed act would deprive divorced Muslim women of the rights granted under a secular provision, that is, Section 125, on the basis of religion alone and violate the constitutional mandate of equality. The act would also be a clear departure from the directive principle enshrined in Article 44 of the Indian Constitution—"the state shall endeavor to enact a Uniform Civil Code."

Between the pronouncement of the judgment by a Constitutional Bench in April 1985 until the act was passed under a party whip in May 1986, Muslim women found themselves at the center of a controversy, with both sides justifying their respective positions. On one side were women's organizations and human rights and civil liberty groups, who shared an uneasy alliance with Hindu right-wing groups—such as the Bharatiya Janata Party and the Shiv Sena, who promote a vicious anti-Muslim propaganda—to whom they are usually opposed. On the other was the Muslim religious orthodoxy under the leadership of the Muslim Personal Law Board. The former grouping held that taking divorced Muslim women out of the purview of Section 125 would deprive them of their fundamental rights of equality. Instead, they demanded the enactment of a uniform civil code. Muslim religious leaders argued that the Supreme Court ruling was against the tenets of Islamic law, which views marriage as a contract: upon divorce the relationship of husband and wife is severed; hence it is un-Islamic (*haram*) for a divorced Muslim woman to claim maintenance from her former husband. They demanded a new act to reflect this. "The Muslim woman" was thus called upon to make a difficult choice between her claims for gender equality and equal protection of law, on the one hand, and her religious beliefs and community affiliations, on the other.

As the debate progressed, the media projected two insular and mutually exclusive positions. Those who opposed the bill and supported the demand for a uniform civil code were projected as modern, secular, and rational, and also nationalist. Those who opposed a uniform civil code were portrayed as fundamentalist, orthodox, male-chauvinist, communal and obscurantist, and antinational. This whipped up anti-Muslim sentiments in the country, and Muslims were increasingly defined as the "other," both of the nation and of the Hindus. They, in turn, could be mobilized to view this as yet another threat to their tenuous identity and violation of their constitutional guarantee of freedom of religion. Huge mobs of Muslims, including women, walked the streets to denounce the judgment and to demand the enactment of a new statute that would deprive Muslim women of the right of maintenance under Section 125. The controversy obscured the fact that at its heart was a paltry sum of 179.20 rupees per month, far too little to save the middle-aged, middle-class former wife of a successful Kanpur-based lawyer from vagrancy and destitution. This finally led Shah Bano herself to make a public declaration renouncing her claim—if it was against her religion, she declared, she would rather be a devout Muslim than claim maintenance from her former husband.

The hurriedly drafted new statute—the Muslim Women Act—was full of loopholes. Despite its limitations, it was of immense historical significance as the first attempt of independent India to codify a segment of the Muslim Personal Law and bring it within the purview of the constitutional framework of justiceable fundamental rights.[6] But the positions across the divide were so rigid that they left no space to contemplate the significance of this milestone.

THE UNFOLDING OF THE MUSLIM WOMEN ACT

The contentious litigation terrain of this act can be divided into two core components. The first is the challenge to the constitutionality of the act by social organizations, women's groups, and statutory bodies by way of writ petitions in the Supreme Court.[7] The second consists of the appeals filed by individual husbands in the Supreme Court against the judgments of various high courts that had awarded Muslim women lump sum settlements. While the writ petitions lay dormant in the Supreme Court over the next fifteen years, the act gradually unfolded itself in the lower courts.

Despite the act, which barred them from claiming maintenance, numerous deserted Muslim women filed applications for relief at the level of the lowly magistrates' courts.[8] In most cases, the husbands pronounced *talaq* (divorce) as a retaliatory measure to defeat the women's claims.[9] Thereafter, the maintenance rights of Muslim women had to be decided according to the provisions of the Muslim Women Act.[10] In appeals filed either by the divorced wife or by the husband, various high courts in the country awarded lump sum settlements to divorced Muslim women according to the provisions of the act. The husbands challenged the high court rulings by way of appeals to the Supreme Court. These appeals gradually started accumulating, along with the original writ petitions challenging the constitutionality of this act, which were filed by women's organizations and civil liberty groups.

What was intriguing for me, as a women's rights lawyer and legal scholar, was the question, if indeed the act was depriving women of their rights and was enabling husbands to wriggle out of their economic liability, why were the husbands finding themselves *aggrieved* by the orders passed under a blatantly antiwomen statute? This aroused a faint suspicion in me that perhaps the manner in which the act was unfolding itself in the lower courts was indicative of a different legal reality, defying the premonitions expressed by women's organizations that the act would deprive Muslim women of their basic rights of survival. This phenomenon provided the first indication that perhaps the ill-famed act could be invoked to secure the rights of divorced Muslim women.

It was clear to me that binaries that emerged in the uniform civil code debate ignored the fact that beneath the highly visible terrain of statutes lies a mundane yet dynamic subterrain: the contested terrain of litigation. Here rights are constantly negotiated, interpreted, and evolved. A silent revolution takes place when an aggrieved Muslim woman, a victim of patriarchal prejudices, initiates a process of litigation to claim maintenance in a magistrate's court. This is where the agency of an ordinary Muslim woman can be most vibrantly felt, where an aggrieved Muslim woman can negotiate the realm of law at her own instance, just the way Shah Bano had done before her claim became entangled within a political controversy. Such struggles rarely emerge as case law, and very few reach the higher courts or are discussed in law journals. Yet they are important markers of social reality and of emerging legal trends that require our critical scrutiny.

After an analysis of some of the reported judgments, it became evident that a seemingly innocuous clause, which had missed the attention of protesters and defenders alike, was being invoked by a section of the lower judiciary to support judgments that provided greater scope for protection against destitution than the earlier provisions under Section 125, where the maximum amount that could be claimed was only 500 rupees per month. Section 3 (1)(a) of the Muslim Women Act stipulated that a divorced Muslim woman is entitled to a "reasonable and fair provision and maintenance to be made and paid to her within the *iddat* period by her former husband."[11] This clause, along with the preamble, "An Act to protect the rights of Muslim women who have been divorced by, or have obtained divorce from their husbands," had been invoked by the judiciary in defense of Muslim women's rights.

The judgments were an indication of the possibility of widespread change. The high courts of Gujarat and Kerala were among the first to affirm that the new act was to *protect* the rights of divorced Muslim women and not to *deprive* them of their rights. They further stressed that any ambiguity within its clauses must be interpreted in such a manner as to reconcile it with the preamble. They declared that condemning divorced women to a life of destitution would not amount to protecting their rights as stipulated by the statute. The first significant judgment on this issue was pronounced by the Gujarat high court on February 18, 1988, within a year and a half of the enactment. But even before this, on January 6, 1988, the die had been cast in women's favor by a woman judicial magistrate in Lucknow, who awarded the applicant Fathima Sardar 85,000 rupees as fair and reasonable provision and maintenance during the iddat period. Justice M. B. Shah, while presiding over the Gujarat high court, explained: "The determination of fair and reasonable provision and maintenance would depend upon the needs of the divorced woman, standard of life enjoyed by her during her marriage and the means of her former Husband. The amount must include provision for her future residence, clothes, food and other articles for her livelihood."[12] In July and August of the same year, the

Kerala high court reaffirmed this position in *Ali v. Sufaira* and *Aliyar v. Pathu* and again, in 1990, in *Ahmed v. Aysha*.[13] In 1995, a division bench of the Kerala high court explained:

> The clause, *"reasonable and fair provision and maintenance to be made and paid to her within the iddat period"* is as follows: Provision is to be made and maintenance is to be paid. The provision has to be made to secure livelihood of the wife. This need not be in monetary terms; it could be by grant of immovable property or other valuable assets or other income yielding property. Provision must be made within the *iddat* period and it has to be fair and reasonable. . . . The revolt against the Shah Bano judgment by a section of Muslims was only in respect of a continued liability. There was no dispute regarding the liability of the husband to pay. The Act was passed to contain the revolt and protect the rights of divorced Muslim women. It is difficult to think that Parliament has, by enacting the Act, completely taken away the right of divorced Muslim women under Section 125, Cr.PC without making any provision as a compensatory measure.[14]

Later this trend was followed by the Madras and the Bombay high courts. A full bench of the Bombay high court further explained that the provision and maintenance is an amount designed to meet a future and continuing liability, and cannot be confused with *mehr* (in Muslim law, a sum of money assured at the time of marriage as a mark of respect to the wife and as her future security).[15] A full bench ruling of the high court of Punjab and Haryana in 1998 in *Kaka v. Hassan Bano* and division bench ruling of the Bombay high court in 1999 in *Jaitunbi Shaikh v. Mubarak Shaikh* also endorsed this view.[16]

THE LAW IS WHAT THE LAW DOES

The wording of a statute or dictate comes to life when it is contested in courtrooms and interpreted through judicial pronouncements. Hence the legal maxim "The law is what the law does." In a significant number of cases, a concerned and sensitive judiciary carved out a space for the protection of women's rights from what appeared to be an erroneously conceived, badly formulated, and blatantly discriminatory statute. For example, the lump sum provisions for future security, which the courts so carefully crafted out of the controversial legislation, in fact seemed to provide a better safeguard against destitution than the meager doles that women were entitled to under the earlier antivagrancy provision under Section 125.

The statute, enacted in haste at the insistence of the conservative leadership, seemed to have boomeranged. A reading of the judgments indicates that the act had rid itself of the agenda of alleviating vagrancy and destitution among divorced women (the defining feature of Section 125) and had extended itself to the claims of women from higher social strata, who could now claim larger amounts as "lump sum settlements" from their wealthy husbands. By endorsing the spirit of Islam and the Shariat and drawing upon the Islamic concept of *mataaoon bil ma'aroofe* (fair and reasonable provision), the courts opened a new portal for the protection of all divorced Muslim women. They read into the act precisely what the act in its title proclaimed—protection of the rights of divorced Muslim women. The ruling of the five-judge Constitutional Bench of the Supreme Court in the *Danial Latifi* case, pronounced on September 28, 2001, finally put its seal of approval on these positive interpretations.[17] In this way, and without invoking a political backlash, the judiciary ushered in a silent revolution in the realm of Muslim women's rights.

For the women, the crucial right of survival hinged upon interpretations and explanations of such words as "within" or "for," "and" or "or," "maintenance" or "provision." The spirit of the entire judgment hinged on the interpretation of these simple terms. Section 3 (1)(a) of the Muslim Women Act specifies "a reasonable and fair provision and maintenance *to be made and paid to her within the iddat period by her former husband.*" Consider "within," as opposed to "for." The latter would indicate that payment would be only *for* three months; the former requires that payment must be speedy. Or take the two words "made" and "paid"—have they been used to reflect two different rights or have they merely been repeated without any specific purpose? Can made *and* paid be interpreted as "made *or* paid"? Likewise, do "provision" and "maintenance" imply the same right or two distinct rights—one for future needs (provision) and the other for the immediate period of three months of *iddat* period (maintenance)? Through a laborious process each of these issues, along with many others, had to be ironed out and fought for.

In matrimonial litigation, the story of personal struggles of individual women within the dynamic terrain of courtrooms lies hidden beneath each

FLAVIA AGNES

citation. These struggles are rarely highlighted when landmark rulings or legal precedents are discussed. In this context, the claims of individual Muslim women who defied the dictates of patriarchy in defense of their rights have to be acknowledged as acts of assertion. The Supreme Court ruling in the *Danial Latifi* case was a great victory for many individual Muslim women, who had to fight every inch of the way due to the ambiguities caused by careless drafting. The act provided ample scope to husbands to exploit the situation, which led to protracted litigation beneficial to husbands and a nightmare to women. But women withstood the ordeal with courage and determination, with patience and perseverance. After a decade and a half, the end results of this contention were clearly visible. Individual Muslim women secured for themselves economic rights at the time of divorce, including the right to receive a lump sum settlement, a right that is currently lacking in matrimonial laws of other communities in India.

COMMUNALIZED MEDIA CAMPAIGN

Within the communally vitiated atmosphere that prevailed in India, the advances made by divorced Muslim women under the Muslim Women Act did not attract media attention. It became evident that the gains made by Muslim women had no news value. In order to fit the media formula, Muslim women had to be portrayed as victims of sexist and obscurantist biases within the community. Even after the path-breaking *Danial Latifi* ruling, the media continued to feature stories of Muslim women as victims of patriarchal biases and community prejudices. Take the case of Imrana, a Muslim woman from Muzaffar Nagar in Uttar Pradesh, who was raped by her father-in-law in July 2005. After a complaint was filed, a journalist approached a *maulana* of the Deoband school with the facts of this case and asked for a *fatwa*, or informed verdict based on Islamic jurisprudential principles. The facts were narrated as a hypothetical situation by the journalist and the opinion of the maulana was sought in general terms and not specifically in the context of the incident that had occurred. The maulana issued a fatwa that after a wife is raped by another man, her husband can no longer live with her. He should divorce her and then her father-in-law may marry her. This was projected as the dictate of sharia rather than the opinion of a particular maulana expressed in general terms.

The judgment led to a high-pitched debate in the media, where it was suggested that in order to counter these archaic antiwomen practices, sharia law should be abolished and a uniform civil code should be enacted. Incidents of a Hindu father-in-law raping his daughter-in-law do not get this type of fever-pitch publicity, suggesting that an incident of this sort could occur only among the Muslim community and that too with the sanction of sharia. Rather than deal with it as a case of rape and violence, the media addressed it as a "Muslim" issue. The entire debate revolved around the Islamic norm of fatwa and there was a general demand that "fatwas" should be banned. Imrana was placed in the center of the controversy despite Supreme Court guidelines that the identity of a rape victim not be revealed in press reports. For the media, Imrana was not just a woman, but a "Muslim," and thus was transformed into a victim of Islamic orthodoxy.[18]

Najma Bibi's case is yet another example of this trend. The incident occurred in 2004 in a small village in Badrak, Orissa. After a domestic quarrel, the husband pronounced talaq in an inebriated state. He later repented and obtained a fatwa from a local maulavi declaring that it was not a valid talaq and the couple could live together. Later, yet another fatwa was obtained by a rival group that declared it haram (un-Islamic) for a husband to live with his wife after he had earlier pronounced talaq. In order to cohabit, she would have to undergo the practice of *halala*, that is, marry and have intercourse with another man, and divorce him, before remarrying her first husband.[19] The media highlighted halala as yet another undesirable Islamic practice, and demanded the enactment of a uniform civil code. The Orissa State Women's Commission and the National Women's Commission had to intervene; the woman had to be given police protection and was compelled to seek shelter in a government rescue home. What did not receive media attention is the fact that the woman had approached the local family court for her right to cohabit with her husband and obtained a decree in her favor. When she was obstructed from cohabiting with her husband, the couple approached the Supreme Court, which gave a ruling in their favor and held that if two people wish to live together the community cannot interfere in the matter, thereby nullifying the doctrine of halala.[20]

Gudiya's case is the most tragic of them all. Her husband, Arif, who was serving in the Indian army in Kashmir, became a prisoner of war and was not heard of for five years. Subsequently she married Taufiq and became pregnant. Then the first husband returned and expressed his desire to re-unite with her. When this case was reported in the press, television channels jumped into the fray, harping on the anguish of a young girl. One channel went to the extent of holding a live *panchayat*, or informal community council used for deciding disputes. The distraught girl, eight months pregnant, was put on public display, and the panchayat gave its verdict in full public view that according to Islamic law, Gudiya should return to her first husband and that it was his prerogative to accept her child or discard it. All the channels had a field day with this story, broadcasting interviews with various relatives of the three persons concerned as well as the Muslim maulavis. Early in the proceedings it was projected that according to the rules of Islam, she would have to give up her child. Later, it was reported that since her husband had agreed to accept the child, Gudiya was happy to return to him. In her earlier interviews Gudiya had categorically stated that she did not wish to return to her husband, caustically commenting: "Yeh koi khel thody hai, aaj iske saath kal uske saath" ("This is not some sort of game that I am ordered to live with one person today and another person tomorrow"). Subsequently, it was reported that she appeared calm and had accepted the decision to return to her husband as her destiny.[21] The personal dilemma of an individual woman would not have been depicted in such voyeuristic detail by the media if she had not been Muslim and if the issue had not revolved around the Muslim personal law. A few months later a brief news item appeared in the press that Gudiya had died. There was no public attention or debate on how this happened.

In a communalized climate, Muslim women have become a way for the media to increase their ratings. One result of this heightened media attention to the "problems" of Muslim women has been defamation of the entire community. Isolated instances of non-Islamic and archaic practices are constantly projected as the norm of the community. Pitted against each other are local *qazis* or maulanas, who may or may not have the authority to give fatwas, and secular/women's rights activists. In order to make a sensational story, the media projects the most polarized opinions of these two segments. There is no space for shades of gray to emerge, or for moderate opinions within Muslim leadership, as they do not make a "good story."

The excessive publicity given to the victims of antiwomen practices, coupled with the lack of reporting of the gains made by Muslim women under the provisions of the Muslim Women Act, has harmed their cause. Individual stories of resistance and victories in court battles are rendered invisible. Even lawyers and women's rights activists continue to harbor the misconception that the rights of a divorced Muslim woman are extinguished at the expiry of the iddat period. The regressive views of a particular maulana are often engraved in the public mind as the norm of the community or, even more dangerously, as Quranic dictate. There seems to be an acceptance, both within the Muslim community and among social activists and scholars, of the positions that are projected as "Islamic principles." These polarized views then become the basis for discourse on community-based interventions for reform.

There is a communal agenda for making invisible any gains made by individual Muslim women. The image of the "victim" Muslim woman who is subjugated by personal laws can be sustained only by denying the fact that the Muslim Women Act provided for an alternate remedy far superior to the one that had been denied to Muslim women under Section 125. Interestingly, the Islamic premise of "no-fault divorce" and economic settlement at the time of divorce rather than the recurring liability of monthly maintenance have now become the accepted principles of family law in many Western countries, including the United States, United Kingdom, Canada, Australia, and New Zealand. Under this notion marriage is viewed as a contract rather than a lifelong "dependency."

INTERROGATING THE DEMAND
FOR A UNIFORM CIVIL CODE

One must examine the demand for a uniform civil code within a communalized polity. The myriad opinions expressed in support of the code are governed by three distinct presuppositions: those of gender equality, national integration, and modernity based on the European norm of Christian monogamy. Those concerned with gender equality project an all-encompassing and uniform code as a magic wand that will ameliorate the woes and sufferings of Indian women, especially Muslim women. Such a position places gender as a neutral terrain, distanced from contemporary political processes. Any possibility of change from within religious or other communities is seen as highly suspect, since women from these communities are understood as lacking a voice and an agency, both within their own community structures as well as within the existing court structures. It projects state intervention in the form of an enactment of a uniform code as the only way to bestow justice upon them.

For the liberal, modern, English-educated middle classes, the demand for a uniform civil code is laden with a moral agenda—that of abolishing polygamy and other "barbaric" customs of the minorities and extending to them the egalitarian code of the "enlightened majority." This position relies upon the Western model of family, nation, and liberal democracy. In the name of modernity it scorns the multiple sexual relationships that exist within polygamous marriages, all the while endorsing the sequential plurality of sexual relationships (through frequent divorces) and the more recent trend of informal cohabitations, which have gained legitimacy in the West. Within a communally vitiated political climate, the demand for a uniform civil code also implies the need for "national integration" and "communal harmony." At times the distinction between these two terms collapses and they become interchangeable. In this context, Muslims appear as the "other" of Hindus as well as of the Indian nation.

At the core of communal propaganda is the image of the polygamous Muslim, and the notion that the Muslim population is growing uncontrollably. Monogamy is understood as the need of the hour, not because it benefits women but because it will supposedly contain the growth of the Muslim population. Muslim scholars have focused upon poor socioeconomic conditions and low levels of education among Muslims as the root causes of a slight increase in the Muslim population, and insisted that a uniform civil code enforcing monogamy will not resolve this problem.[22] But monogamy also draws the unquestioning support of liberals whose sensibilities are influenced by Western notions of the normative family. For them, bigamy reflects premodern barbarism and monogamy symbolizes civilization, enlightenment, modernity, and progress.

It is of grave concern that these positions, advocated by the Hindu Right, are reinforced by the judgments of the Supreme Court of a self-proclaimed secular and pluralistic state.[23] It is worth noting that no matter what the core issue before it, the comments of the highest court regarding the enactment of a uniform civil code are always made in reference to "national integration" and contain either a veiled or direct insinuation against Muslim law, thus creating a fiction that Hindus are governed by a secular, egalitarian, and gender-sensitive family code that needs to be extended to Muslims to usher in modernity and gender equality among them. For instance, in 1984, when the Delhi high court upheld the archaic provision of restitution of conjugal rights under the Hindu Marriage Act, · which had been challenged on the basis that it violates freedom and equality, not only was there no mention of a uniform civil code and "national integration," but the court actually ruled: "Introduction of constitutional law in the home is most inappropriate. It is like pushing a bull into a china shop. It will prove to be a ruthless destroyer of the marriage institution and all that it stands for. In the privacy of the home and married life, neither Article 21 nor Article 14 have any place."[24] The Supreme Court later affirmed this decision.[25]

Frequently, comments on a uniform civil code are made and reported by blotting out the real issue at hand. Take the judgment pronounced by Chief Justice V. N. Khare in *John Vallamattom v. Union of India*, a 2003 case concerning a Christian priest's personal freedom to make a charitable bequest.[26] The petitioners had argued that it is an integral part of the Christian faith to contribute to religious and charitable purposes. The court did not agree, and in his judgment the Chief Justice commented that "there is no necessary connection between religious and personal law in a civilized society. . . . Parliament is still to take steps for framing a common civil code in the country. A common civil code will help the cause of national integration by removing the contradictions based on ideologies." The link between the Christian priest's personal freedom to make a religious-charitable bequest and the issue of national integration through the enactment of a uniform civil code was not explained, and this comment provided fuel for the media to interpret the judgment as against a minority and in favor of the code. In the weeks that followed, the newspapers were flooded with reports and editorials on the code, with quotes from the Muslim religious leadership and Muslim intelligentsia, on the one side, and from women's rights activists, on the other, while the judgment itself was relevant to neither Muslim identity nor women's rights. Similarly, in the *Sarla Mudgal* case of 1995, the core issue before the court was

FLAVIA AGNES

conversion and bigamy by Hindu men.[27] The court was examining the rights of two Hindu wives and the validity of the two marriages entered into by a bigamous Hindu husband. The first marriage was contracted under Hindu law and the second after a fraudulent conversion to Islam. Even though all parties to the litigation were Hindus, the judgment and the media publicity that followed focused primarily on the uniform civil code in the context of national integration and minority identity.

Out of the three major Supreme Court rulings on the issue of a uniform civil code—*Shah Bano, Sarla Mudgal,* and *John Vallamattom*—the *Shah Bano* case alone had an aggrieved Muslim woman at its center. The code question continued to be framed within the polarized positions put into place by the *Shah Bano* judgment, with a progressive-modernist section in support of a uniform civil code and a fundamentalist-obscurantist section in opposition to it, even though the lines between the two sections have become blurred in the two decades since that ruling.

The rise of the Hindu Right and its aggressively anti-Muslim agenda, the demolition of the Babri Masjid in 1992, the burning of Christian missionaries in Orissa in 1998, the demolition of churches in tribal areas of Gujarat in 1995, and the gruesome sexual violence inflicted upon Muslim women during communal violence in Gujarat in 2002—all these have necessitated a reexamination of the earlier call for a uniform civil code. Even as homes of poor Muslim women were looted, gutted, and razed to the ground in various communal riots, as teenage sons of Muslim women were killed at point-blank ranges in police firings, and as Muslim women were raped under floodlights in the riots following the destruction of the Babri Masjid, mainstream media and opinion continued to lament the "appeasement of Muslims" and the supposed denial of maintenance to "poor Muslim women/the Shah Banos." While the *Shah Bano* case symbolized the denial of Muslim women's economic rights within their own community, the communal riots brought into focus another kind of victimhood, this one based on religious identity and at the hands of the majority community. While both equally violated their dignity, the media continued to harp on the former. It conveniently overlooked the fact that abandonment and destitution of wives is as rampant among Hindus as among Muslims, that the matrimonial faults of adultery and bigamy are evenly distributed across communities, and that approximately 80 percent of all women burnt to death in their matrimonial homes as "punishment" for bringing insufficient dowry are urban, middle-class Hindus. Not just Muslim men, but Hindus, Christians, and Parsees (as well as men from communities governed by customary laws) guard patriarchal prerogatives within their respective personal or customary laws with equal zeal.

REFRAMING THE COVENANTS OF EQUALITY AND EQUAL PROTECTION

Continuing media sympathy for a Muslim woman oppressed by personal laws only serves to highlight the gruesome sexual violations of women during the communal violence of Gujarat in 2002.[28] Social activists have commented on the widespread and particularly intense use of sexual subjugation of women as an instrument of violence in the riots.[29] The woman's body was a site of almost inexhaustible violence, with infinitely plural and innovative forms of torture. Sexual and reproductive organs were attacked with a special savagery. Children, born and unborn, shared the attacks and were killed before their mothers' eyes.[30] To gauge the extent of horror one must see an affidavit filed by Firozbhai Khajamonuddin Sheikh, from Naroda Patia in Ahmedabad, regarding the murder of his wife, Kausar Bano, before the Commission of Enquiry (Shah and Nanavati Commission) in Ahmedabad:

> On 28th February, 2002, at about 10.30 A.M., a mob of about 3000 men surrounded our Chali. They were shouting slogans . . . "Jai Shri Ram." They were carrying swords, lathis, chains, pipes and some were carrying cans of what looked like petrol. They were wearing shorts and had "pattis" on their head. They had come running from the direction of Noorani Masjid. People started running for their lives. My wife was pregnant. She could not run so I carried her in my arms and was running through a lane going towards the Teesra Kuwa. Behind me the mob was setting the houses on fire, killing people, setting them ablaze. Near the Teesra Kuwa, I put my wife down and we were both running when about 20 to 25 persons caught up with us. They pulled my wife out of my arms. . . . Then they slit her stomach with a sword, pulled out our child from her stomach and paraded the baby on the tip of a sword. I think I heard my child

cry. Then they poured petrol on both of them and lit them. I hid behind a five feet wall, which is the boundary wall of a maidan [open ground] and witnessed what happened to my wife and child. Then I ran for fear of my life.[31]

Kausar Bano later became the symbol of the extent of debasement and sexual violence unleashed upon Muslim women during the communal carnage in Gujarat in 2002. This caused a major embarrassment to the ruling party (Bharatiya Janata Party), which tried to deny the incident, with a woman minister, Uma Bharati, commenting: "Who is she whose stomach was slit and fetus taken out? No one has heard of this woman. She is a fiction created by the media."[32]

When violence of this scale and intensity supersedes the confines of criminal jurisprudence—which is bound by conventions of proof and evidence, medical examinations, and forensic reports—and when criminal prosecution itself is a closed-end process in the hands of the state machinery, what legal measures can be invoked to bring justice to the dead and the surviving? On the other hand, the danger is that if these violations do not form part of "official records" they can be conveniently negated as "baseless allegations" or normalized as routine occurrences.[33] As one hears the narratives of young women, running helter-skelter, slipping, falling, and becoming prey to the marauding mobs, their violated and mutilated bodies being thrown into open fires, the question keeps recurring: where and how does one pin the culpability? How should concerned groups within civil society respond to this social and political reality? What are the myriad ways in which the seemingly innocuous laws get unfolded within the complex terrain of social hierarchies? When the moral basis for the rights itself shifts, where can one start the process of renegotiating and reframing the covenants of equality and equal protection? While exploring possible legal avenues to address these blood-curdling barbarities, one hits a dead end at each turn. It is then that these covenants mock you in the face.

The genocide in Gujarat, as well as the earlier communal riots, has taught a painful lesson to Muslim women: when threatened with a life-and-death situation, and in the face of bloodthirsty mobs, places like mosques, dargahs, and madrassas are transformed into oases of security and solace.[34] Women in relief camps have narrated incidents of camp organizers helping out with arrangements of food and first aid, and with cleansing bleeding wounds, extracting wooden splinters buried into the deepest crevices. While women gave birth in the open in those traumatic days, the men had no choice but to help in the birthing process. Before the meager aid declared by the government could be accessed, hungry children were fed only through hurriedly put-together community resources. Women partook in the marriage celebrations of young orphaned girls, arranged by camp leaders, which brought a semblance of normalcy to their shattered lives. They cried out when the men were picked up in combing operations and bore the brunt of police brutalities. The bonding between people under siege is cemented through shared grief and suffering. In the struggle for day-to-day survival, gender concerns and patriarchal oppressions seem remote. It is here that community and patriarchal identities get forged. The secular and women's rights voices are too distant from their harrowing realities.

In all this, the motif of the vigorously self-multiplying Muslim that had been effectively used to whip up Hindu sentiments in support of the uniform civil code was invoked again. The rhetoric among the Hindu middle class used in defense of the carnage included such lines as: "They had it coming. . . . [T]hey have been 'appeased' beyond tolerance. Why should they demand a separate law in a secular country? Why should they be allowed to marry four times? Why are Hindus alone bound by an obligation of maintenance?" These are mouthed not only by Hindu extremists but also by centrists, the liberals, the people who inhabit my social space, the urban, cosmopolitan, and middle class. Within the cultural ethos of the mainstream, an injustice to a Muslim wife gets magically transformed into a Hindu injury, which could be invoked to justify communal carnage. Without this tacit approval by the middle class, the violence in Gujarat could never have spread so wide or so deep.

As the gruesome sexual crimes continue to haunt us, I turn back to the questions that I started with. How do we, concerned citizens, human rights activists, and women's organizations, view the violations of Muslim women? Will these narratives of victimhood of Muslim women, borrowing a phrase from the black women's movement, be a "raceless tale of gender subordination" for feminists and a genderless narrative of minority victimization for the Muslim community?[35] Just as the stories of black women, caught up in the whirlwind of lynchings and the gendered genealogy of racist violence, had been hidden from history, will Muslim women, caught in the whirlwind of communal violence and having paid the price with their and their children's blood, get erased? To avoid this eventuality, Indian feminism will have to address questions of gender and community simultaneously rather than in isolation from each other, whereby the Shah Bano controversy and the demand for a uniform civil code is examined within the framework of gender justice, but the Gujarat carnage and the barbaric incident of Kausar Bano is examined through the rubric of communal conflicts and human rights violations. A similar challenge also confronts the women's movement when addressing the concerns of Dalit women, some of whom have highlighted the inadequacies of both the Dalit movement and the high-caste women's movement.[36]

Kimberlé Crenshaw, a feminist legal scholar and a critical race theorist, coined the word "intersectionality" in the 1980s to address issues of gender and race within a composite framework. She writes:

> If we aren't intersectional, some of us, the most vulnerable, are going to fall through the cracks. When we don't pay attention to the margins, when we don't acknowledge the intersection, where the places of power overlap, we not only fail to see the women who fall between our movements, sometimes we pit our movements against each other. The average sentence for someone convicted of raping a black woman is two years, and the sentence for raping a white woman is ten. This is what happens when our movements are pitted against each other. Women lose, people of color lose, we all lose. Women come from a whole range of backgrounds. If our visions of peace don't include these differences then our peace will be partial.[37]

Several African American feminist legal scholars have challenged the theories advocated by the predominantly white women's movement and have attempted to rewrite them within the "alchemy of race and rights."[38] As I have shown in this essay, covenants of equality and equal protection may unfold in diagonally opposite trajectories for the mainstream and the marginalized. We cannot even see these trajectories, let alone chart the best way forward, unless we bring questions of gender and community into not just simultaneous but *intersectional* focus. Otherwise our analysis will be fragmented and inadequate to the task of addressing the concerns of minority women in India.

NOTES

1. In a case that is now famous, Shah Bano, a poor Muslim woman, approached the courts for alimony. Kausar Bano, the pregnant woman who was killed along with her unborn child, symbolizes the extreme barbarity unleashed upon Muslims by Hindu right-wing organizations in Gujarat in 2002. Both incidents, and the controversies that followed, are detailed in this essay.

2. While I use the singular "Muslim woman" in what follows, I do not mean to suggest that all Muslim women are identical. But there are similarities in the way they are positioned in legal and popular discourse.

3. This was also the title of a book on black women's studies: Hull, Scott, and Smith, *But Some of Us Are Brave*.

4. *Mohd Ahmed Khan v. Shah Bano Begam*, AIR 1985 SC 945.

5. For example, paragraph 3 of the ruling states: "The Muslim husband enjoys the privilege of being able to discard his wife whenever he chooses to do so, for reasons good, bad or indifferent. Indeed for no reason at all." Paragraph 32 states: "A common civil code will help the cause of national integration by removing disparate loyalties to laws which have conflicting ideologies. . . . It is beyond the endurance of sensitive minds to allow injustice to be suffered when it is so palpable."

6. There had been a similar move during the preindependence period, which resulted in the enactment of the Dissolution of Muslim Marriages Act in 1939, which gave Muslim women a statutory right of divorce.

7. The National Commission for Women and the Centre for Women's Development Studies were two of the organizations involved.

8. These courts are of the lowest denominations, the first rung of the judicial hierarchy. The Supreme Court is at the top end with two other tiers below it—the sessions courts and the high courts.

9. Manipulations by lawyers (most often Hindu) play an important role here.

10. The Muslim Women (Protection of Rights on Divorce) Act, 1986.

11. Emphasis added. Iddat is the mandatory period of three months after the talaq is pronounced when the divorced woman is forbidden to remarry. According to the provisions of traditional (uncodified) Muslim law, the divorced woman is entitled to receive maintenance during this period from her ex-husband.

12. *Arab Ahemadhia Abdulla v. Arab Bail Mohmuna Saiyadbhai*, AIR 1988 Guj. 141.

13. 1988 (2) KLT 172 (single judgment for both *Ali v. Sufaira* and *Aliyar v. Pathu*); II (1990) DMC 110.

14. "*K. Kunhammed Haji v. K. Amina*," *Criminal Law Journal* (1995): 3371.

15. "*Karim Abdul Shaikh v. Shehnaz Karim Shaikh*," *Criminal Law Journal* (2000): 3560.

16. II (1998) DMC 85; and *Criminal Law Journal* (1999): 3846.

17. *Danial Latifi v. Union of India*, 2001 (7) SCC 740; *Criminal Law Journal* (2001): 4660. The *Danial Latifi* case gathered together all the writ petitions filed by secular

and women's groups as well as the appeals filed by husbands. Latifi, the lawyer who defended Shah Bano in the Supreme Court, was the first to file the writ petition challenging the validity of the act.

18. See, for example, "Imrana Fatwa Ties Secular Tongues," *Indian Express*, June 2005, at indianexpress.com; "BJP to Put Cong in Dock over Imrana Fatwa," *Rediff News*, June 2005, at rediffnews.com; and "Imrana Fatwa Violates Right of Equality: Jaitley," *Express India*, July 2005, at expressindia.com. Arun Jaitley is a prominent leader of the Bharatiya Janata Party and was law minister of the National Democratic Alliance coalition government during the 2002 Gujarat riots.

19. This Islamic practice was stipulated by the Prophet in order to curb the practice of arbitrary and hasty divorce. Although not in vogue, halala is often projected by right-wing Hindu organizations as one of the banes of Muslim law.

20. *Times of India*, April 14, 2006.

21. *Indian Express*, September 28, 2004.

22. H. Badshah, "Uniform Civil Code—Chasing a Mirage," *The Hindu*, December 24, 1995.

23. In India "secular" is interpreted to mean at an equal distance from all religions.

24. *Harvinder Kaur v. Harminder Singh*, AIR 1984 Del 66.

25. *Saroj Rani v. Sudarshan*, AIR 1984 SC 1562.

26. *John Vallamattom v. Union of India*, AIR 2003 SC 2902.

27. *Sarla Mudgal v. Union of India*, 1995 (3) SCC 635.

28. See Engineer, *The Gujarat Carnage*.

29. "Cry My Beloved Country," *Times of India*, March 20, 2002.

30. Sarkar, "Semiotics of Terror."

31. See Agnes, "Of Lofty Claims and Muffled Voices," booklet informally published by Majlis, Mumbai, 2002.

32. Uma Bharati was a minister in the National Democratic Alliance government and later the chief minister of Madhya Pradesh.

33. The defense minister in the right-wing National Democratic Alliance government, George Fernandes, commented in Parliament that rape of women is normal during communal riots. See Baxi, "The Second Gujarat Catastrophe."

34. Dargahs are tombs of Muslim saints; madrassas are Urdu-language religious schools for Muslim children.

35. The phrase is from Crenshaw, "Whose Story Is It, Anyway?," 434–35.

36. See Pawar, *The Weave of My Life*; Pawar and Moon, *We Also Made History*; and Rege, *Writing Caste/Writing Gender*.

37. This quote is from feminist.com. For a fuller development of the idea of intersectionality, see Crenshaw, "Mapping the Margins."

38. The phrase is from Williams, *The Alchemy of Race and Rights*.

AMINA JAMAL

Global Discourses, Situated Traditions, and Muslim Women's Agency in Pakistan

MUSLIM WOMEN'S MOVEMENTS face intense pressure to defend their struggles for women's rights while skepticism about universalized human rights discourses increases in Muslim communities, due to the stresses of the War on Terror and Islamophobia worldwide. Muslim feminist groups and activists must also confront the increasing activism of women who identify as Islamic and are opposed to feminism. At the present historical moment in South Asia, seemingly irreconcilable differences between feminism and Islam overwhelm national assembly debates, street protests, and media programs. Among Muslims in Pakistan, many of these confrontations are reflected in political struggles related to Islamization or the moral transformation of citizens through wide-reaching legal and political changes.[1] As a result, Pakistani women's politics and cultural activism diverge into exclusionary secular and politicoreligious forms.

The constructed opposition of secular and religious is particularly problematic for postcolonial feminist scholars of gender, Islam, and modernity, especially those in Muslim minority communities. These scholars perceive a contradiction between the imperative to question the hegemonic underpinnings of Western secularism and Muslim feminists' tendencies to struggle for avowedly secular projects of women's rights and freedoms.[2] Arguing that secular modernist ideas functioned historically to establish the superiority of Western culture in colonized Muslim societies, these scholars suspect that such ideas continue to influence feminist projects that pit secular ideas against Islam in Western and non-Western contexts. Even mainstream "secular" feminist movements in Muslim societies such as Pakistan are split between feminists who invoke Islamic scriptures in support of women's rights and those who advocate the traditional "Muslim secular" position of insisting on the separation of religion and politics.[3]

These controversies, while new for feminism, reflect long-standing cultural and historical debates in Muslim societies that are related to questions about the interrelationship of the pious subject, religious community, and modern nation-state.

Many contemporary Islamic reform and renewal movements derive legitimacy for their community-building projects from the Quranic injunction "amr bil maruf wa nahin anil munkir" ("to enjoin or promote good and forbid or restrain wrong").[4] The relationship between the individual and community at the heart of this injunction is also central to the debates about the individual versus the state that have emerged in many Muslim societies, including Pakistan, since the establishment of modern nation-states. Islamic thinkers from a variety of positions, including those deemed to be Islamist, have contemplated whether moral regulation of individuals is incumbent primarily on the individual believer or on the Muslim political collectivity as crystallized in the postcolonial state.[5] Indeed, it is to offset the impact of Islamist pressures on the nation-state that Muslim feminists in many Muslim societies (including mainstream feminists in Pakistan) uphold secular ideas of social integration. However, publicly contentious representations of religious-versus-secular obscure the common tendency of both Islamist and secular women's groups to mobilize a diversity of discourses that are neither strictly "Islamic" nor "secular." Islamist movements freely draw upon universalist notions of rights, the rule of law, and democracy, in addition to Islamic texts and traditions. Secular-progressive proponents of liberal rights and freedoms frequently invoke Islamic traditions, especially the more flexible ones that have been historically salient in South Asia.

In this essay, I discuss some of the conundrums related to constructing women's struggles as secular and religious, and the related issue of defining women's agency along these lines. In particular, I problematize some recent attempts by postcolonial scholars to disrupt the secular-religious divide by examining theories of religious agency that validate the activism of women who define themselves in religious terms. Since the opposition between religious and secular in Muslim societies also undermines mainstream *feminist* positions as un-Islamic, I emphasize the importance of contextually specific and historically nuanced accounts of feminism and Islamism as forms of women's struggles.

To understand debates among feminists and Islamist women in contemporary Pakistan, it is important to link gendered secular and religious politics to historical transformations in how Muslims came to see each other as religious and secular. One may begin by examining how Islamic discourses and traditions, such as *amr bil maruf*, were translocated by Islamist modernists from early exegetical contexts in the Hanbali communities of Iraq and Syria to a present-day Hanafi-majority society in Pakistan.[6] It is important to trace the various ways in which traditions of self and collectivity, public and private, have been theorized and invoked by Islamic movements at other moments in South Asia and elsewhere, and, in doing so, to address the implications of normalizing a transcendent Islamic subjectivity and agency, which these movements seek to accomplish. Such a genealogy may be helpful in explicating how women in Islamist movements in Pakistan have invoked certain historically specific understandings of religious subjectivity and agentive action as modes of self formation and community construction. To this end, I explicate some important ways in which the unique development of the Islamic modernist project in South Asia and the historical emergence of the nation-state in Pakistan have shaped contemporary Islamist women's activism. I map how Islamist women's appropriation of aspects of Islamic tradition shapes their imagining of the Muslim community in the form of the nation-state and also sustains differences between Muslim women's "religious" and "secular" agencies.

My discussion of this subject is based on interviews I conducted in Karachi and Lahore with some of the women leaders of the Jamaat-e-Islami, a transnational movement for Islamic renewal and reform that was founded in India in 1942 amid the waning of British colonial rule and widespread Muslim fears of ascendant Hindu nationalism.[7] My work corroborates contemporary scholarship on "political Islam" that suggests Islamist movements in Muslim societies, through their attempts to realize a modern Islamic state, are disseminating modes of being, knowing, and acting associated with modern citizenship and democracy, and so facilitating the processes of modernization.[8] In our conversations, Jamaat women repeatedly described their successful attempts at balancing religious obligations with modern subjectivity. Many linked their modern identities and modes of existence with the fulfillment of both citizenship rights and obligations they believed were enjoined upon (middle-class) Muslim women by the Quran and the "hadith" (recorded traditions and instructions) of the Prophet. At the same time, they refused to recognize similar attempts by Pakistani Muslim feminists to integrate their religious and worldly identities, preferring to see the latter as less authentic Muslims.[9] Jamaat women draw overwhelmingly on Maulana Maududi's 1968 elaboration of "amr bil maruf." Their support may be seen as an instantiation of the ways in which Maulana Maududi's intervention changed the orientation of modern Islamic reformism in twentieth-century South Asia.[10] Maududi, like other Islamists, deprived his followers of Islam's rich and wide-ranging discourses, by providing an ahistorical, decontextualized reading of the Quran—a reading that conflicted especially with Islamic practices developed in South Asia.

POSTCOLONIAL FEMINISM, SECULAR
AND RELIGIOUS AGENCY

Of particular significance for postcolonial scholars of Islam, gender, and modernity is Saba Mahmood's provocative exploration of the Eurocentric underpinnings of the key feminist notion of agency, defined as resistence to dominant norms. She argues that this definition holds limited explanatory power for understanding religious agency within the women's piety movement she studied in Egypt.[11] Mahmood further argues that to understand women's agency, we should not look primarily for evidence of resistance to patriarchal (religious) norms, but investigate how women inhabit norms within plural projects of self making. Furthermore, we should understand this as a type of agentive action—one that feminists should respect.

Also important for postcolonial and poststructuralist theories, and feminist politics anywhere, is Talal Asad's notion of an "Islamic discursive tradition," which is central to several arguments about Muslim women's religious agency, including Mahmood's.[12] While Foucauldian poststructuralists emphasize the discursive practices of power that pervade subject formation and shape human action in modern society, Asad has suggested that religious or pious agents are exceptional since their subjectivities are primarily shaped by the authority of the past or tradition, rather than the disciplinary practices of modern power.[13] Applying this to modern-day Islamists in Western societies, Asad says the selfhood and practices of religious agents must be understood in their own specificity, through their continuing engagements with an "Islamic discursive tradition," rather than the secular structures in which they live and act.

For many feminists in both Muslim majority and Muslim minority contexts, Asad's conceptualization of Islamist politics as validated by an Islamic discursive tradition has important implications, since he argues that the body of the (ungendered) Muslim is "not owned solely by the individual but [is] subject to a variety of obligations held by others as fellow Muslims."[14] This is significant because it is precisely the question of bodily integrity that tends to pit Muslim feminist projects against Islamist men and women in societies as far removed as North America and South Asia. By problematizing the individual subject of freedom and resistance at the heart of most contemporary political struggles, including those waged by Muslim feminists, these arguments legitimize other struggles that may appear oppressive to feminists. Indeed, for many Muslim feminists in both majority and minority contexts, the relationship between Islamism and secularism cannot be understood in the terms constructed by Asad, Mahmood, and many postcolonial feminists—that is, as primarily a counterhegemonic cultural and political challenge to the secular frameworks of the nation-state.[15] Furthermore, Asad's construction of the religious (Islamist) agent as outside the discursive hegemony of the modern state's secular power may encourage the construction of Muslim women as caught between the promises of Western secularism and Islamist assertions of religious citizenship. Certainly, many feminist scholars reject the conceptualization of feminism and Islamism as internally homogeneous discourses and recognize them as practices that need to be understood within the processes of modern nation-state formation.[16] While I am impressed by Asad's theoretical insights about the global dominance of Western secularism, I hesitate to extend his idea of an Islamic discursive tradition to Pakistan.

In Pakistan, where some of the fiercest battles between Islamism and ("secular" Muslim) feminism are being waged, Asad's understanding of

Islamists—as subject-interlocutors of an internally coherent Islamic tradition—obscures the profound influence of geography and historical context on both "modern" and "pious" Muslims. A genealogical study of what is deemed Islamic discursive tradition is needed in order to understand, within this specific context, the violent ruptures and continuities of cultural-social formation. It is important to demonstrate that many contemporary Islamists are arguably not linked in any seamless way to Islamic tradition or an Islamic past, but are (as Aamir Mufti insists) part of another modern formation: Islamism, or political Islam.[17] This is not to suggest that religious objectives may sometimes conceal political aims or that Islam as religion cannot be a catalyst for liberatory and pluralistic political struggles. Indeed, there have been moments in South Asian history when the reverse was evident, for example, during the Khilafat movement of the twentieth century.[18] Instead, I wish to highlight a particular coming together of a mode of being religious with national politics that, I would argue, reduces rather than expands the inclusionary principles of political-spiritual struggle.

In the following section I trace how the universalist and inclusive Quranic injunction of voluntarily "enjoining good" ("amr bil maruf") became linked with modern subjectivities and modes of disciplining citizens such that the imperative of violently "forbidding wrong" ("nahi anil munkir") has become the dominant framework for Islamization in Pakistan. The discursive complexities of Islamic and modern—or secular and religious—imperatives that underlie these constructions of gendered selves and national collectivity have implications for understanding the gendered political projects of both feminism and Islamism in Pakistan.

THE (GENDERED) GEOGRAPHIES
OF A HISTORICAL TRADITION

The vast literature on Islamic traditions in South Asia indicates that historically situated modes of participation, distinctive inflections of meaning, and locally constructed judgments may qualitatively alter the nature of belonging and traditions. Indeed, scholars such as Barbara Metcalf have proposed that the investigation of Islam as history and religion in South Asia calls for a distinct analytical task apart from global studies of Islam and Muslims.[19] In problematizing what she sees as unnecessary reliance on the concept of syncretism to explain the development of Islam in South Asia, Metcalf has opened the way for approaching the fundamentally opposing currents of puritanical and humanist reformism in South Asian Islam as more than either syncretic adaptation or purification. The uniquely South Asian theologies of Muslim scholars—their jurisprudential theses, the practices they have endorsed, and the translation of both into enactments of religion in the lives of Muslims—should not be read simply as overtures toward intercommunal harmony but as concerted attempts to construct a broader community while remaining faithful to the fundamental textual sources and sensibilities of Islam.[20] Thus in the context of South Asia, accounts of Islamic subject formation tend to read Islamic discourses in relation not only to Western secularism, but also the multiple modes of interpretation and authority construction in the region. Such analyses emphasize the innovative character of Islamic revivalism, explicate its role in shaping gendered and classed subjectivities among Indian Muslims, and point to the manifestation of moral discrimination and virtuous discipline as cultural nationalism in the communal politics of colonial India.[21] Such scholarship invariably links Islamic revivalism with attempts by nineteenth-century Muslim reformers to reconceptualize Islam in South Asia in a manner that would eventually enable the systematization of Islam as a modernist reform movement by Maulana Maududi in the twentieth century.[22]

South Asian scholarship brings to light a set of discriminatory tendencies—mostly directed at non-Muslims, but also used to mark off categories within the Indian Muslim community—encouraged by some Islamic revivalists in their efforts to construct subjects who could survive colonial cultural reforms while participating in the emerging discourses of Indian nationalism.[23] These reconceptualizations of religion have historically mediated local understandings of piety and community that are articulated through class, gender, and religion.

Ayesha Jalal has pointed to the tendency of Muslim reformist projects in the subcontinent to rework Islamic discourses for the purpose of constructing social and political difference. Discussing the renowned twentieth-century Indian Muslim leader and the Sufi scholar Maulana Abul Kalam Azad, Jalal notes the anticolonial meaning Azad gives to the Quranic injunction of "amr bil maruf."[24] Jalal contrasts Azad's reading of "jihad" and "amr bil maruf" with that of other twentieth-century Islamists, such as Rashid Ridha and Mohammed Abduh of Egypt, and accounts for their different interpretations by pointing to their commitments to differing traditions in Islam. Furthermore, Jalal emphasizes the implications for Muslim political subjectivity and religious agency as the Sufism-inspired Islam became undermined by the combination of the colonial categorization of communities in India and the rise of Islamic modernism. Cautioning that Muslim social identities were not simply a colonial artifact, Jalal emphasizes the link between the emergence of these identities and the constitutional politics of British rule in India, which in the twentieth century led to the rise, first, of religiously informed communalism and, then, eventually Muslim separatism.

Thus in response to the overwhelming force of colonial modernity imposed on South Asian society through the modernizing projects by the British, many Muslim reformers attempted to revive religious and cultural consciousness by tightening the boundaries of community against foreign encroachment. In the process, Islamist modernists, such as Maulana Maududi, began to envision "Muslim" as a social-political category rather than a religious identity, and severely constrained the boundaries of Muslim identity.

In a study of the role of traditional *ulema* (authoritative Islamic scholars), Muhammad Qasim Zaman underlines "the enormous rupture posed by the challenge of Western modernity" to traditional authority and individual agency, which makes it necessary to speak about a variety of discursive traditions within Islam.[25] Without constructing relativist notions of multiple Islams, Zaman distinguishes between Islam's traditional discourses and the formulations of Islamic modernizers/revivalists. Thus, as Zaman has observed, and as I try to argue here, the encounter with modernity ruptured Islam's history in South Asia in a manner that allowed modernists to regard Islam in a fundamentally different way than did the traditional ulema.

By severing ties with classical Islam in South Asia, modernist Muslims constructed community in ways that could strengthen their challenge to Western colonialism and Hindu nationalism. This entanglement of modernity and religion has been noted in the emergence of the Jamaat-e-Islami and theorized as a discriminatory impetus toward non-Muslims.[26] Seyyed Vali Reza Nasr argues that unlike some other twentieth-century Muslim reformers, Maulana Maududi was not concerned with soothing Muslim anxieties about modernity but with pressing them on toward the adoption of modern thought and abandonment of the past. His development of Islam as a system and emphasis on the harnessing of religious energy to politics was a deviation from traditional Islam, especially devotional forms derived from Persian and Turkish traditions that have flourished in South Asia from at least the thirteenth century.[27] Indeed, in the course of upholding Islam as primarily a social demarcator rather than a faith, Maududi compromised the Quran's inclusionary and humanist principles.[28] The gendered manifestations of some of the changes wrought by Islamic modernism in South Asia may be evinced from Jamaat women's position toward the Hisba Bill passed by the provincial government in Khyber-Pakhtoonkhwa in 2005.[29] The government argued that the bill would facilitate enforcement of measures mandated by the Shariah Act it had passed in 2003 but never implemented.[30] Among these was the establishment of a new provincial government institution responsible for building a moral community by promoting good and preventing evil among the province's Pakistani citizens.

I propose that we understand the political strategies of Islamist women —such as the women leaders of the Jamaat-e-Islami—as attempts to reverse sensibilities established over centuries of Islamic practices in South Asia rather than merely as attempts to challenge the dominance of liberal social and political groups. While their contestations of feminism, and feminist discourses of women's human rights, recalling Asad, may be seen as part of the ongoing construction of Islamic discursive tradition, it is important to note that this tradition both speaks to the Western secular tradition and is constituted by it in important ways. Furthermore, Jamaat women were also strongly influenced by political processes of nation-state formation in Pakistan. It was during the formative phase of the Pakistani state in the 1950s that Maulana Maududi developed the Jamaat-e-Islami from a religious movement into a political party. I contend that in the course of this development, which included short periods of the Jamaat's incorporation into government, the movement as a politicoreligious party appropriated many of the discursive practices of modern power to construct religious subjects as rights-bearing citizens.[31]

AMINA JAMAL

THE HISBA BILL: FEMINISM VERSUS
FUNDAMENTALISM?

Amr bil maruf wa nahi anil munkir: To enjoin what is good and forbid what is evil.
Implementation of Islamic way of life revolves around Amr-Bil-Maruf and Nahi-Anil-
Munkir and to achieve this objective it is necessary, apart from other steps, to establish an institution of accountability, which could keep a watch on securing legitimate
rights of various classes of the society, including females, minorities and children
and to protect them from emerging evils and injustices in the society.

FROM THE PREAMBLE TO THE HISBA BILL

In July 2005, the government of Pakistan's Khyber-Pakhtoonkhwa Province
—at that time led by the Muttahida Majlis Amal, a coalition of religiously
defined parties including the Jamaat-e-Islami—passed the Hisba Bill.[32] The
bill was seen as part of the coalition's mandate to implement the provisions
of the provincial Shariah Act of 2003 and promote Islamization.[33] Among
the act's provisions was the appointment of a religious ombudsman and
police force to promote morality among citizens and enforce Islamic duties
upon Muslims. A fervent national debate ensued over the relationship
between personal and public religious duties versus the fundamental rights
of citizens, and between traditional backwardness versus modern development. The Joint Action Committee, a forum of civil society groups, led the
political campaign against the bill on the grounds that it reflected the
Muttahida Majlis Amal government's "fascist desires to forcefully impose
its own nefarious wishes on people in the name of Islam."[34] Among the
most vocal members of the committee was the Human Rights Commission
of Pakistan.

In response to the widespread objections by human rights activists,
religious minority groups, and feminists, the Pakistani president Pervez
Musharraf—a staunch ally of the U.S. "War on Terror," and author of
a project to introduce "enlightened moderation" among Muslims internationally—prevented the bill from being signed by the governor of the
province (formerly the North-West Frontier Province). He sought the advice of the Supreme Court of Pakistan, which ruled several clauses of the
Hisba Bill, especially the clause relating to the powers of an ombudsman,
unconstitutional. The court advised the governor not to sign the law, thus
defeating the Hisba Bill.[35] Protests by politicoreligious groups, including
the Jamaat-e-Islami, ensued.

This was not the first time in Pakistan's recent history that an attempt to constitutionalize "amr bil maruf" was rejected by Pakistan's lawmaking bodies. The wide-ranging Islamization measures proposed by the provincial government in Khyber-Pakhtoonkhwa built on at least two failed attempts at the federal level during the 1990s to legally enforce the moral guidance of citizens.[36] Opposition to enforcing shariah measures was led by the Human Rights Commission of Pakistan, which publicized its long-standing reservations about the entire project, in particular the issue of hisba, in the Pakistani English-language daily, *Dawn*.[37] The organization's objections to hisba were explained by the commission chairperson, I. A. Rehman, in three ways. First, he questioned the motives of those proposing the bill, which he believed were not made explicit in its stated objectives. Next, he questioned whether there was any authoritative tradition according to which Islamic injunctions could be enforced by the state. Finally, he argued that areas included in the bill's statement of objectives would impinge on the state's jurisdiction, writing that "an unavoidable question is whether the proposed legislation is a bid to supplant the Constitution."[38]

A reading of the Rights Commission's trepidations as simply "secular" or "Western" would be disingenuous and limited, since Rehman, along with other secular-progressives in Pakistan, invoked not only liberal discourses, but also Islam's humanist tradition. In rejecting an Islamic basis for the state's ability to enforce Islamic code on the faithful, Rehman emphasized South Asian Islamic tradition. He said that official attempts to enforce morality among Muslims would not only be a disservice to Islam, but would also be short-sighted on the part of Pakistan's leaders. He urged them to seek guidance from the South Asian Islamic philosopher Mohammad Iqbal, the intellectual father of Pakistan, who emphasized the reconstruction of religious thought as a means of reconciling Islamic tradition with modern life.[39]

Shortly after the Hisba Bill's defeat, I discussed it with two Jamaat-e-Islami women: Atiya Nisar, convener of the Women's Commission of the Jamaat-e-Islami in Karachi, and Kausar Masood, deputy to Dr. Kauser Firdaus, then head of the Jamaat-e-Islami Women's Commission. In our discussion, I focused on the constitutional objections to "hisba" as presented by the Human Rights Commission, and on Rehman's explicit references to Islamic scriptures in his rejection of the act. The questions raised by Rehman and the answers given by Nisar and Masood both illustrate the intransigent constructions of "private" and "public" that are sustained by juxtapositions of secular and religious in the modern temporal space of the nation-state, even in its Islamic form in Pakistan. Since I understood the underlying issue as concerning the relationship between individual and collectivity, and the problems of defining the individual citizen's constitutional rights and freedoms versus the public space of an Islamic national community, I asked Nisar and Masood about the knotty question of defining private space and public space. In her response, Masood repeated an oft-cited Islamic parable:

> Let me recall for you the incident relating to Hazrath Usman, the third caliph, who once heard loud music and dancing coming from a house. He climbed the wall and seeing that there were dancing girls, alcohol, and music, Hazrath Usman arrested the home owner.[40] The home owner challenged Hazrath Usman, saying: "While it is true that I have committed one offence, you have committed three un-Islamic acts—you have spied on me, you trespassed, and invaded my privacy. These are all sins in Islam." The caliph asked for forgiveness and set him free. So if a person does any sin in their home, then they will not be caught by spying on them. This is a part of our history— and we respect it.[41]

I interpreted this as Nisar and Masood's way of soothing my feminist anxieties about Islamist ambitions for tighter regulation of the private and public lives of citizens—especially women—that we had witnessed in neighboring Afghanistan. Definitions of public and private, also contested and complex in the Western liberal traditions, become even more convoluted when transported from Western legal forms by secular modernizers, or when ahistorically applied by Islamists in matters of religious guidance. Secular-progressive demands in Pakistan, as articulated by anticolonial leftists, antiestablishment feminists, or individual/collective modernists keen to preserve the status quo, range from the individual's right to protection from sexual and bodily violence to more social-status-related demands for the "right" to organize balls and fashion shows, or to celebrate Valentine's Day and New Year's Eve.[42] Some groups acting in the name of Islam, including youth groups associated with Jamaat-e-Islami, have sought to disrupt New Year's Eve celebrations and threatened violence against women's groups for holding a walkathon in Lahore.

It is important to point out that rather than simple, spatialized demarcations, the Islamic tradition of "private" and "public" refers to more contingent form. "Private" may not be inherently so, but only as far as it is unknown or hidden from the public/community.[43] This led Rehman to ask: "What is meant by 'enforcement of Islamic values at public places'? What is the definition of a public place? Will it not cover the bazaar, debating halls, theatres, clubs and cinema halls?"[44] Here Rehman drew attention to the larger implications of the bill, which would not simply censor individual acts in government-owned sites, but also apply in privately owned establishments. This is because the Jamaat's conception of public includes all that comes into public view. Jamaat women, who concede that wrongdoing in private should be an issue between the believer and Allah, argue that what is "private" can easily be made the business of other members of the community, as when it becomes public knowledge or affects sensibilities through television, billboards, markets, or malls. Thus "hisba" could apply to the publicly visible acts of private citizens, such as a Muslim male seen not praying after the *azaan* (public call for prayers), or a woman dressed in a manner deemed un-Islamic.

Since my interlocutors insisted that "there is no compulsion in *din* [faith]," I urged them to explain their demand for the appointment of a *mohtasib* (ombudsman) to ensure that all Muslim men respond to azaan. They constructed a complex private-public relationship that brings together social, commercial, and religious realms. Although the mohtasib would not dragoon citizens for prayers, he would ensure that shops and markets close. These collective social and moral obligations would construct an Islamic society. As Masood explained:

> KM: This should not be seen as force—the obligation to pray is an unchallenged matter for Muslims. It is not compulsion to enforce it in our own country, an Islamic country, and it applies only to those who identify as Muslims.
>
> [AJ: Is it not compulsion to enforce prayers on Muslims?]
>
> KM: Let us be clear, there is no compulsion to enter the din—but once you enter the din, then it becomes an obligation to obey all its rules, just like any organization. You are not compelled to join, but once you do you have to obey its rules. Implementation of the obligation to perform prayers is a responsibility of the state—"amr bil

maruf wa nahi anil munkir." Prayer is a duty that must be enjoined on Muslims. It will not be forced on non-Muslims, of course.[45]

I asked Nisar and Masood to comment on the fears of feminist and human rights groups that the bill would "Talibanize" Pakistani society by extending the state's jurisdiction over the daily minutiae of individual lives and the performance of faith among Muslims. I also referred to Rehman's argument that the need for an intermediary to oblige the Muslim believer to obey the Quranic duties "has never been satisfactorily established" in Islamic tradition. It is noteworthy that Nisar framed her response not in the context of Islamic discursive tradition but within the milieu of the modern nation-state. She said: "Everywhere, in every state, all citizens are subject to a set of laws. Laws begin where the rights of the individual end. And individual freedom ends when it begins to affect the freedom of another individual. We all obey this, especially those of us who live in a state which also names itself an Islamic state."[46]

Islamists subscribe to a set of divinely obligated responsibilities aimed at the salvation of the individual and the group. Nisar's statement indicates that they also see themselves as belonging to a public realm that deems them individuals contractually related to other individuals through the laws enshrined in the modern nation-state. As self-described "religious" subjects, Jamaat women's moral agency emphasizes not individual fulfillment, but the promotion of obedience and the cultivation of patience. However, their notion of ethics and preservation of community is meaningful only if they understand themselves as sovereign citizens within the public realm of the nation-state constituted by representative democracy, citizenship, law and order, and civil liberties. As political activists, Jamaat women use their "modern" agency (never entirely severable from their religious identities) to make claims on the nation-state even as they destabilize liberal conceptions of sovereign personal ethics and aesthetics. Jamaat women fuse religious and secular agency in a productive manner to advance their political and cultural activism. Thus they can affirm that "there is no compulsion in din," while also asserting that the "injunctions of Islam are obligatory," and that an ideal polity must include "duties that are not a matter of choice" for the individual.[47] To my suggestion that their politics envisioned a singular understanding of Muslim identity that would be oppressive to Pakistani citizens, Nisar and Masood cited their own antipathy to the universalist strategies for Muslim women's empowerment promoted by the United Nations. To do so, they used a tautology that makes it impossible to differentiate between secular and religious intentions or arguments:

AJ: So only one point of view, only one interpretation of Islam, will prevail?

AN: I ask you, how come it never occurs to you that we too are imposed upon? Is it not an imposition that 33 percent of all local bodies' representatives must be women? Did it not compel us [Jamaat women] to compete for these seats instead of choosing whether we should be represented by males or females of our party?[48]

Together, Nisar and Masood outlined the series of measures designed to increase women's political and economic representation, introduced by the Pakistani government in compliance with the U.N. Convention on the Elimination of All Forms of Discrimination against Women. The measures brought hundreds of women, including large numbers of Jamaat women, into political bodies in the local and national elections of 2002. Nisar argued that in politicoreligious parties, such as the Jamaat-e-Islami and the Jamiat-e-Ulema-e-Islam, many women—including even those who had been elected—would have been happier if they had been allowed to nominate men to represent their interests. Jamaat women oppose setting quotas for women in political bodies and workplaces since, in Maududi's view, Islam commands men to be the providers for women and discourages women from venturing out of the home except in cases of necessity. It is important to note that Nisar was not lamenting the absence of a mechanism for women to opt out of public participation, since many middle-class women in Pakistan tend not to engage in political, cultural, or economic activities that require them to venture outside their family or community. Her concern was about the development of the kind of society where women would be encouraged, or even compelled, to become autonomous political and legal entities. Jamaat women strongly uphold the notion of male guardianship for Muslim women in political and legal matters. Thus Nisar said that by ignoring Jamaat women's opposition to the quotas, the state was ignoring their citizenship rights: "Are we not, too, citizens of Pakistan, who live here and want our voices to be heard?" For her, the reservation of seats for women amounted to secularizing power determined to impose its own ideas about self-representation and autonomy on women. Nisar appears to consider the ability to reject rights as a prerequisite of citizenship rights. Furthermore, in this situation, the condition of equality was to eliminate the imbalance that was likely to be created if one group of women was accorded the rights that were unacceptable to others. For her, the interest of the collectivity, if it were to live up to the Islamic ideals proposed by the Jamaat, should be to safeguard the rights of the most morally authentic Muslim women at the cost of denying them to those judged less religious.

The difference between obligations and rights, and between religious observation and retributive justice, is unclear in the above argument. Jamaat women must claim the space of the individual citizen-subject of modernity in order to demand their rights and freedom to live in an "Islamic" society. I propose that Jamaat women's attempts to achieve the Islamization of women's status through the state are a historically specific mode of engagement with modernist discourses of individual rights and national community. In the seemingly opposed projects of secular modernizers and religious reformers, we can identify overlapping processes of constructing subjects aimed at the middle class in Pakistan. These imbricated projects—one deemed "religious" and represented through discourses of Islamic modernism, and the other "secular" and embodied in ideas of national progress and neoliberal development—have become codes through which Muslim citizen-subjects differentiate between secular-modern and religious-traditional in their personal and political lives. As Asad emphasizes, this may obfuscate the many ways in which the religious and the secular always implicate each other. Even as Jamaat women speak from a position that may be defined as "religious," their concerns reflect their deep involvement with the more worldly relationship of state and citizen. While secular-progressives in Pakistan tend to view the Jamaat women's objectives for women as out of harmony with the goals of the modern nation-state, Jamaat women blame the successive leaders of Pakistan for having failed to harmonize modern democracy with the principles of Islam. They believe that such a project could be accomplished if the government were controlled by politicoreligious groups such as the Jamaat, which historically have failed to make much headway in electoral politics. Like "secular" feminists in Pakistan, Jamaat women cannot produce the conditions of living for their self-fulfillment without imagining a particular society—in this case, a community of believers that will facilitate the processes of becoming good and moral Muslims. Their desired community must be built from the same materials and in the same time-space of the nation-state.

CONCLUSION: PARADOX OF PIETY?

aashiq ham az islam kharab ast o ham az kufr
The Lover cares not for Islam or Kufr
parwana chirage haram o dayr na danad
Like the moth uncaring of the flame in temple or mosque.

MAULANA ABUL KALAM AZAD

In its South Asian formation, the relationship between Islamic agents is more agonistic and complex than the categories of "pious" and "non-pious" Muslims or "practicing" and "nonpracticing" Muslims suggest.[49] Rather than being considered oppositional, the discourses of history and eschatology, tradition and genealogy, piety and politics may be seen as mutually sustaining, in that the voluntaristic impetus of promoting good was overwhelmed by the coercive practices of forbidding wrong. This does not necessarily contradict the possibility, as Asad and Mahmood have suggested, that communities may be voluntarily created through the practices of Islamic moral discrimination and virtue acquisition. However, it underscores the likelihood that such practices, when fused with the power of the modern state, may retrospectively promote (and make hegemonic) particularistic concepts of community. This in turn may fashion new forms of the individual-community relationship, which may appear oppressive for feminists, other women, non-Muslim citizens, minority sects, gays, and the rural and urban poor.

Since Pakistani feminists cannot accept the Jamaat's version of Islam and Muslim women's rights, they identify themselves as "secular"—meaning they advocate the separation of religion from politics. Indeed, in its more recent invocations, secularism has been appropriated to counter the force of Islamist statist discourses. In this process, however, South Asian Muslim feminists surrender to politicoreligious groups their shared claims to the vast cultural-religious traditions of Muslims in the region. Identification with an unexamined secularism may flatten a variety of modes of relating to

Muslim identity and obfuscate our understanding of the complex experiences of the majority of Muslim women, who are unlikely to describe themselves either as Islamist or secular. Simply reframing Muslim feminist projects in religious terms, as some Pakistani feminists propose, is not enough, since it is important for many Muslims, like the Pakistani feminist Afiya Zia, to differentiate themselves from oppressive agendas framed as "Islamic."[50]

That does not excuse Muslim feminists from the imperative to acknowledge the validity of Muslims' engagements with Islam's textual and interpretive theological traditions. Indeed, Muslim feminists everywhere must vigorously debate the multiple meanings of both secularism and Islamism, and their complex relationships with Western modernity and Islam's traditions. Such discussions, through recovering and appropriating a variety of Muslim intellectual traditions, may help us apprehend the meaning of the South Asian Muslim secular beyond its dichotomous linkage with the religious, and draw attention to its interlocking with gender, class, caste, and community.[51] By situating secularism, modernity, and Islamism within Islam's polyvalent discourses and multiply constructed traditions, Muslim feminists may disrupt the Eurocentric conflation of Muslim, Islamism, and fundamentalism. They may open space for conversations, and perhaps limited collaborations, with modernist Islamist women in Pakistan.

NOTES

1. Jamal, "Transnational Feminism as Critical Practice"; Mumtaz and Shaheed, *Women of Pakistan*; and Weiss, "Implications of the Islamization Program for Women.

2. Abu-Lughod, "Introduction"; Baykan, "Politics, Women and Postmodernity"; Grewal and Kaplan, "Postcolonial Studies and Transnational Feminist Practices"; Mahmood, *Politics of Piety*; Najmabadi, "Feminism in an Islamic Republic"; and Razack, "The 'Sharia Law Debate' in Ontario."

3. Jamal, "Gendered Islam and Modernity in the Nation-Space"; and Zia, "The Reinvention of Feminism in Pakistan."

4. Quran, Sura Al Imran, ch. 3.110.

5. Following John L. Esposito and François Burgat, I use the term "Islamist" to refer to individuals and movements that seek the complete integration of shariah in society.

6. The four schools of Sunni Islamic jurisprudence—Hanafi, Shafai, Hanbali, and Maliki—are each named after a jurist. The majority of South Asian Muslims who are Sunnis follow the Hanafi school.

7. For a history of the Jamaat-e-Islami, see Nasr, *Mawdudi and the Making of Islamic Revivalism.*

8. See Esposito, "Introduction"; and Utvik, "The Modernizing Force of Islam."

9. Cf. Jamal, "Feminist 'Selves' and Feminism's 'Others'" and "Transnational Feminism as Critical Practice."

10. A'la Maududi, "Al Amr bil Marouf wa Nahin An al Munkir."

11. Mahmood, *Politics of Piety.*

12. Asad, *Formations of the Secular.*

13. For a discussion of Foucault's theory of power in the modern state, see Foucault, "Politics and the Study of Discourse."

14. Asad, *Formations of the Secular,* 91.

15. Ibid. For postcolonial accounts of Islamist women's agency, see Deeb, *An Enchanted Modern;* Gole, *The Forbidden Modern;* Mahmood, *Politics of Piety;* and Torab, *Performing Islam.*

16. Abu-Lughod, "Introduction"; and Najmabadi, "Feminism in an Islamic Republic."

17. See Mufti, "The Aura of Authenticity."

18. See Minault, *The Khilafat Movement;* and Tejani, *Indian Secularism.*

19. Barbara D. Metcalf, "The Study of Muslims in South Asia," lecture delivered at the University of California, Santa Barbara, December 2, 2005.

20. Ibid.

21. Ibid.; Nasr, *Mawdudi and the Making of Islamic Revivalism;* Robinson, *Islam and Muslim History;* and Smith, *Islam in Modern History.*

22. Robinson, *Islam and Muslim History.*

23. Alam, *The Languages of Political Islam;* and Ayesha Jalal, "The Religious and the Secular in Pre-colonial South Asia," *Daily Times,* April 21, 2002.

24. Jalal, "The Religious and the Secular in Pre-colonial South Asia."

25. Zaman, *The Ulama in Contemporary Islam,* 6.

26. A'la Maududi, *Purdah and the Status of Women in Islam;* Nasr, *Mawdudi and the Making of Islamic Revivalism;* and Robinson, *Islam and Muslim History.*

27. Nasr, *Mawdudi and the Making of Islamic Revivalism,* 63–66.

28. Jalal, "The Religious and the Secular in Pre-colonial South Asia."

29. Khyber-Pakhtoonkhwa is the name given to Pakistan's northwestern province by a parliamentary bill in March 2010. It was previously known as the North-West Frontier Province, the name given by British colonizers.

30. Soon after their election (2002) to power in Khyber-Pakhtoonkhwa province, the leaders of an Islamist alliance Muttahida Majlis-e-Amal passed the Shariah Act of 2003 that aimed to "Islamize" society by banning music and ensuring strict gender segregation. The same provincial government in 2005 passed the Hisba Bill to set up the legal and administrative structures needed for implementation of the Shariah measures. The term "hisba" is derived from "hisb" and "hisab," Arabic terms related to accounting; these are interchangeably referred to as "hisba" and "hasba" in Pakistan. I use hisba throughout.

31. See also Jamal, "Gendered Islam and Modernity in the Nation-Space."

32. For the full text of the Hisba Bill, see Dawn, July 16, 2005, at http://archives .dawn.com/2005/07/16/nat18.htm.

33. The Muttahida Majlis Amal, which came to power in Khyber-Pakhtoonkhwa (at the time still North-West Frontier Province), was voted out in February 2008.

34. Dawn Bureau Report, "Peshawar: Civil Society Groups Reject Proposed Shariah, Hasba Acts," Dawn, June 1, 2003, at http://archives.dawn.com/2003/06/01/ local18.htm.

35. Nasir Iqbal, "Hasba Clauses Ruled Contrary to Constitution: NWFP Governor May Not Assent to Law," Dawn, August 5, 2005, at http://dawn.com.

36. The most recent move at the national level, the Shariah Bill, or the 15th constitutional amendment (1985), sought to empower the government of then Prime Minister Nawaz Sharif to enforce shariah.

37. I. A. Rehman, chairperson of the Human Rights Commission of Pakistan, expressed the commission's concerns in an op-ed piece in Dawn. Rehman, "Look at the Hisba Bill Now," Dawn, July 25, 2003, at http://dawn.com.

38. Ibid.

39. Ibid. Muhammed Iqbal (1877–1938), a poet and philosopher of South Asia, is known throughout the Muslim world for his attempts to construct an Islamic response to Western modernity. Many of his writings, including his book in English, "The Reconstruction of Religious Thought in Islam," can be accessed at http://allamaiqbal.com/works/prose/english/reconstruction.

40. Usman was the third of four caliphs (khalifa in Arabic) who led the Muslim community after the death of the Prophet Muhammed, from 632 to 661 C.E. Muslims believe that these four men were true followers of the example of Prophet Muhammed and refer to them as the rightly guided caliphs (khulafa-e-rahideen).

41. Atiya Nisar and Kausar Masood, team interview with the author, Karachi, July 12, 2005. These women are associated with the Women's Commission, a nationwide organization set up by the Jamaat-e-Islami in 1998 to research women's issues and develop policy. The objective was to offset the gains of the Pakistan feminist women by proposing alternative strategies, deemed to be more Islamic, for addressing the social, political, and economic issues of Pakistan women.

42. Demands for the right to celebrate New Year's and Valentine's Day are frequently expressed through op-ed opinion pieces or letters to the editor of English-language dailies catering to the English-speaking middle class. For a Pakistan feminist analysis of such discussions, see Zia, "The Reinvention of Feminism in Pakistan."

43. For a good discussion of "private" and "public" in Islam as related to hisba, see Cook, Commanding Right and Forbidding Wrong in Islamic Thought.

44. Rehman, "Look at the Hisba Bill Now."

45. Atiya Nisar and Kausar Masood interview.

46. Ibid.

47. Ibid.

48. Ibid.

49. Quoted in Mahmood Jamal, *The Maulana and the Mahatma: Gandhi's Urdu Letters* (2008), at http://www.ideaindia.com.

50. For a good discussion of these debates in Pakistan, see Zia, "The Reinvention of Feminism in Pakistan."

51. See, for example, Chatterjee, *The Politics of the Governed*; Needham and Sunder Rajan, *The Crisis of Secularism in India*; and Tejani, *Indian Secularism*.

ATREYEE SEN

Martial Tales, Right-Wing Hindu Women, and "History Telling" in the Bombay Slums

Tanaji (one of Shivaji's aides) to Jijabai: O mother, we have lost Kondana fort. I have brought no prestige to your son Shivaji. He trusted me, and I have failed.

Jijabai: Don't lose heart. If you are a true Maratha lion, you will fight again and win back the fort. I will then declare you as a younger brother to Shivaji.

Tanaji: You are a symbol of courage and hope. I will return to war and ensure that the saffron flag flies high over the fort.

(Tanaji and Shivaji win back Kondana, but Tanaji is killed during the battle.)

Shivaji: Mother, I bring sad news. We have won the fort but lost our lion.

Jijabai (wailing, drawing out her sword and waving it in the air): I have given birth to another brave martyr, not from my womb, but from a woman's power and pride.

SUGRIBAI, A STORYTELLER IN BOMBAY'S NIRMAL NAGAR SLUM

IN THIS ESSAY I discuss the creative endeavors of women soldiers within the Shiv Sena movement in India to "invent traditions" of female martiality.[1] These women, often described by academics, activists, and journalists as "riot makers" from the slums of Bombay, have acquired combative identities through their long affiliation with the violent Hindu nationalist political party in western India. Women's aggression came to occupy a controversial position within the dominantly patriarchal structures of the slums and the movement. Over time, the young cadres developed strategies to contest a backlash against what slum men and male party leaders saw as "unnatural female ferociousness."[2] Summoning a history of women's militancy became one important ploy to prolong and legitimize women's contemporary religious activism. I use the lens of anthropology to explore how these Hindu nationalist women used oral traditions to return women to a martial, masculinist Hindu history. By creating a common "respectable past" for themselves, women leaders and cadres produced solidarity among rough, aggressive, and marginalized slum women, all within shifting climates of communal hate and hostility.

In accounting for the collective, prowomen actions of nationalist women, many feminists have sketched and obscured boundaries between women's agency and right-wing activism.[3] Kathleen Blee showed how U.S. women in the Ku Klux Klan developed a strategy of "selective adoption," following only those racial ideologies that sustained their gendered self-interests, while ignoring agendas forged by male white-supremacist leaders.[4] In India, feminist writers have long condemned right-wing women for blatantly hijacking the symbols of the secular women's movement. Bombay-based activists were particularly outraged when slogans such as "Hum Bharat ki nari hain, phool nahi angarey hain" (We are the women of India, not flowers but burning embers), used by them to protest violation of equal rights for women, were used by rioting Sena women during outbreaks of communal violence in the city. At the same time, they expressed concern over the rise of women's support for antifeminist, antiminority, and anti-Semitic movements, especially at a point in history when emancipatory opportunities were readily available to women from a range of socio-economic backgrounds.[5]

The question remains: why does feminism as an analytical and political project remain isolating and incomprehensible to some groups of women who are keen to pursue goals similar to that of feminism, but not within the progressive model of activism designed by the feminist movement? The Shiv Sena women (who became formally organized into a women's wing, the Mahila Aghadi, in the 1980s) appropriated feminist slogans, but they were careful *not* to develop the image of an elitist "NGO-type" organization where, in the words of a Mahila Aghadi member, "the women sitting on soft sofas in air-conditioned offices think troubled women from slums would come to them for help." Instead, Sena women visited households in

ATREYEE SEN

their constituencies to keep them informed about the Aghadi's gender-specific activities. Such active social networking not only built bonhomie among women in the slums, it also allowed the Aghadi members to devise and implement women-oriented policies. In this drive to distance themselves from forms of overt "feminist resistance," the Sena women were keen to create a more intimate and accommodating moral universe for slum women. While several feminist activists categorized and subsequently marginalized religiopolitical, nonliberal women as detrimental to their cause, the Aghadi allowed slum women to find a degree of delight and dignity as women, wives, workers, and warriors through a noncoercive approach of telling tales of martial queens who took pride in being soldierly women.

Madhusree Datta, a feminist filmmaker in Bombay, insightfully commented on the Sena women: "Our [feminists'] weakness is we did not realize this desire to belong. We thought of need, of rights, but not the desire to belong. Rebellion does not make a movement, does not make a craze. Rebellion remains an alienating, isolating factor."[6] As I show in what follows, Sena's women have aspired to a cohesive identity and political community neither in isolation from men nor as open rebels. Storytelling sessions were geared toward achieving multiple ends for various groups of slum women. They addressed concerns for creating an oral history for illiterate women; inculcated a sense of pride in poor women branded as petty gangsters; mobilized and retained slum women within a martial movement; identified storytelling and writing skits as an important political responsibility for women uninvolved in direct violence; created a culturally accepted space for women and children to meet and celebrate their history; attempted to legitimize women's autonomy in familial and public spheres; and strengthened the role of women and children as carriers of culture. Stories and storytelling sessions were also an effort to seek acceptance, if not salutation, of martial women by Hindu men. The internal rationale of these narratives and practices, which excluded Muslim men and women, challenged the feminist movement in Bombay, the latter being demoralized by its failure to collectivize slum women on an egalitarian, rights-based platform.

In this essay I examine how the Shiv Sena women's front used tactical storytelling to popularize a self-styled brand of "slum women's nationalism." In the following sections, I have tried to grasp a "women's logic" for making members of the Mahila Aghadi familiar with their martial past, and how these practices upheld the superiority of poor women in a militaristic social setting, in which their actual desires of marriage, motherhood, *and* martiality could be fulfilled. The multiple notions of agency and women's solidarity that emerged out of this cause perplexed feminist activists and also distanced Shiv Sena women cadres from orthodox nationalist women's fronts in India, especially the Rashtriya Swayamsevak Sangh.

Before proceeding with this analysis, however, I would like to underline the methodological and political difficulties of accurately speaking for "ugly women," a term used by Andrea Peto to describe fascist women and the theoretical challenge these "reactionary" female activists pose to feminist historians in contrast to the "worthy women" of liberal, left-wing women's movements.[7] Faye Ginsburg similarly describes the struggle resulting from the ideological gap between herself as a feminist researcher and the antiabortion informants/activists who are her subjects. Yet she advocates the importance of representing violent activists as an opportunity for alliance between women from both sides of a debate.[8] Instead of only posing as a critical counternarrative to feminist theory and practice, the ethnographic perspective in this essay also tries to enable feminist scholars to grasp how a localized politics of womanhood and belonging, embedded in different material conditions and political realities, produced varying forms of women's resistance.

THE MAHILA AGHADI: "BRUTE" POLITICS AND RITUALIZED STORYTELLING

The rise of Hindu nationalism and its violent manifestations in communal rioting have been an integral part of postcolonial politics in India. Hindu fundamentalism gave birth to a cluster of organizations that fostered national and local political, social, and religious insecurities. One such organization was the Shiv Sena (Shivaji's Army), a regional political party that has been led for several decades by the charismatic and controversial Balasaheb Thackeray. The Shiv Sena maintains the cultural supremacy of Hindus in Maharashtra and demands economic and political privileges for them.[9] In the late 1980s, the Shiv Sena developed nationalistic aspirations and decided to move "from region to religion." The party turned toward Hindutva, a pan-Indian movement that upholds the religious and historical superiority of Hindus.[10] After riding the communal wave for more than a decade, the Shiv Sena captured state power in Maharashtra in 1995.

Through the early 1990s the Mahila Aghadi played a vital role in sustaining communal tensions in Bombay, the capital of Maharashtra. Even though the wing was developed as a support network within a manifestly "male" movement, the Aghadi emerged as an autonomous task force with its own agenda of delivering "social justice." The participation of Sena women in orchestrating the 1992–93 Hindu-Muslim riots in Bombay brought the Aghadi into the political limelight.[11] Since then, the Aghadi women have represented themselves as champions of communal war, openly patrolling the streets of Bombay, and nurturing an infamous image as women vigilantes.

My earlier research has indicated ways in which the Mahila Aghadi manipulated the Hindutva discourse to address more localized gender interests.[12] The women's wing, which drew its primary membership from the expansive slums of Bombay, emerged as a "subgroup" through ideological and political patronage, but it gained local popularity by contesting restrictive decrees on poor women. The Sena women loyalists were first- or second-generation migrants from rural Maharashtra, and became engaged in a variety of legal and illegal economic activities to sustain their families in the slums. Almost all slum women experienced extreme poverty, displacement, class discrimination, evictions, familial alienation, domestic neglect, and sexual and financial vulnerability as workers in the informal/unskilled labor economy. The cadres used their reputation within the politics of urban fear to violently wrest temporary social and economic benefits for slum women. These "benefits" ranged from securing illegal taps, electricity, and cable connections (by threatening local suppliers), to organizing health care camps for women and children, to more intangible advantages such as ensuring women's safety and mobility by beating up male "predators."

These activities by armed women became a spectacle in the slums of Bombay, even though they did not *always* require the use of force. While several men in Sena-dominated constituencies remained ambivalent about female militancy, most male guardians within slum families became concerned about women's violence in public. Male brutality was easily naturalized, but women's martiality threatened to overturn gender hierarchies deeply entrenched in the slum areas. The women resented ostracization for their commitment to the Aghadi's martial rhetoric. Several slum women came together to discuss how male aggression remained unchallenged in the slums, deciding it was because men could draw from a repertoire of heroic tales about kings from the past. Thus female soldiering, whether it involved running a system of brute justice to favor poor women or attacking Muslim ghettos, also needed a gloss of religiohistorical legitimacy.

I conducted research in the Nirmal Nagar slum area in Bombay, a Sena stronghold, from 1999 to 2003. The Nirmal Nigar women displayed a unique collective aggression in regulating social, economic, and political activities. The party men in general, but the women in particular, were tactically obsessed with medieval mytho-histories about Shivaji's challenging of Muslim rulers. Aghadi members from a number of slums in Bombay (beyond Nirmal Nagar) felt that if women were to be involved in the conception and sustenance of contemporary Hindu militarism, it was imperative to recover women's agency in the martial society in Shivaji's times. Groups of slum women collectively decided to construct and celebrate a prestigious martial tradition for women in order to raise the self-esteem of Hindu women cadres in peripheral urban slums. I use the term "mytho-histories" because the stories collapsed time and space, past myth and contemporary reality, truth and fiction, stillness and change. The "formlessless" in the narratives could be molded strategically to contest present inequalities, and also to seek out a feminine voice in a political community's conception of its own past.[13] For all the Sena women, forms of narratives—whether "real," constructed, or modified—could gain authenticity through reiteration and repetition. Sena women with oratory skills circulated stories throughout the slum about Shivaji and his relationships with various women, constituting a myth-making apparatus. Some of these women were former stage actresses, some were Aghadi leaders, but most were housewives who had time to "tell stories." Slum women would collectively or individually narrate tales to men, women, children, and the odd anthropologist. Stories were told in children's parks, shakhas (local party offices), and temple complexes where the women met regularly to sing devotional songs. Slums even swapped storytellers to avoid boredom. The scattered stories, most of them lost in the mists of time, were collected, coordinated, and made conspicuous by the Sena women. Storytellers could embellish their stories since women's histories were not part of any fixed or

ATREYEE SEN

written texts. Most of the sessions were interactive, which allowed the storyteller to gauge what kinds of stories interested a particular audience.

THE PAST IN THE PRESENT: SHIVAJI AND HIS SOLDIERLY WOMEN

Shivaji (1630–80), a controversial figure in Maharashtrian history, has been attributed several identities ranging from "the liberator of the Marathi nation" to "a common bandit."[14] According to historians, he was born to a petty landlord (*jagirdar*) Shahaji Bhonsle and his wife Jijabai and grew up to be a self-proclaimed king, Chhatrapati. He annexed the regions of several neighboring Muslim and Hindu rulers to his own *jagir*, but since he carried on a prolonged struggle against the former, he was glorified as a Marathi "Hindu" hero.[15] He emerged as a national hero in the latter half of the nineteenth century after Tilak, leader of the anticolonial movement in Maharashtra, revived the Chhatrapati's "tales of gallantry" through the Shivaji festival, which celebrated heroism, masculinity, and the success of a local leader in overthrowing a powerful "foreign" empire.[16] The Shiv Sena was also inspired by this medieval ruler, their primary focus being Shivaji's attempts to carve a strong Hindu nation out of a Muslim empire. Within this primarily masculinist discourse on a hero and his heroism, the Aghadi tried to give significance to a few scattered tales where women played an influential role in Shivaji's designs to create a Hindu *padpadshahi*, or political and social empire.

The narrators tried to characterize Shivaji as sensitive to women and gave recognition to women's "special" contribution to society. Shivaji's father abandoned Jijabai after his second marriage.[17] The Sena women explained that the proximate relationship between Shivaji and his mother, and the absence of a strong male presence, allowed him to respect the ideals of womanhood. In this context, the Sena women storytellers narrowed down and highlighted those "true tales" (*sacchi kahania*) in which their icon was honorable to women from various social and political backgrounds.

The Aghadi drew careful attention to stories of Shivaji's protective attitude toward women. According to one mytho-history Shivaji withdrew an honor from one of his men when he discovered that he lusted after a soldier's widow. Another tale is about "the brave Rani Savitribai," queen of

Bellary, who was produced in Shivaji's court in chains after her kingdom was raided by an arrogant general, Sakuji, in an act of vengeance. Shivaji apologized to the queen, chided his general for ill-treating a woman, and returned the kingdom to her. Yet another story is about a beautiful Muslim girl who was captured and presented to Shivaji by one of his generals. Shivaji addressed the girl as his sister and kept her in safe custody until she was sent back to her family. The last story always ended with a prolonged phase of lamentation by the Sena women that similar treatment was not meted out to Hindu women captured by Muslim soldiers. In all these stories, the Sena women portrayed Shivaji as a leader with "the strength of a man, and the heart of a woman."

During Aghadi meetings, these tales were retold in the form of questions and answers, which gave the narration clarity and a feeling of immediacy. Their wild gesticulations, voice modulations, and rolling of their eyes allowed the past to filter into the present so that history was not "a history of long ago, but a history of just yesterday."[18] For example, in the case of Rani Savitribai, the story goes (with the words *phir boley*, "then it was said," used as interjections):

COURTIER 1: "Who is that woman covered in blood and bound in chains?"

"That is Rani Savitribai, the glorious queen of Bellary," whispered the second courtier. "She fought a great battle to free her small kingdom. I heard that she charged ahead on her horse, roaring like a wounded lioness, swinging her sword in the air, her hair flying in the wind. She was a leader of her troops, stronger than many kings, braver than many generals. But she was finally defeated by General Sakuji."

COURTIER 1: "Hush, here comes our king."

A courtroom of noblemen, aristocrats and generals took their seats. The women shivered in sympathy for the wounded Hindu queen and sat huddled together behind the partition screens. The courtroom guards fell into muted silence. They all wondered, they all looked towards the throne.

SHIVAJI (IN ANGER): "Sakuji, you whipped the queen? If you have insulted a woman, you have insulted my mother. You are dismissed in shame."

TURNING TO SAVITRIBAI: "Mother, will you not pardon your own son?"

Savitribai, with tears in her eyes: "Son, I am glad that you showed respect for me. It has turned me into your compatriot. I will now fight with you for the Hindu Swaraj."

And so she took her place beside Shivaji. Everyone in the court cheered.

The Shiv Sena women also clapped loudly.

The narrators depicted the events as a series of images that the women had viewed, as if they had been present during the exchange. Most women were celebratory that a martial queen had been given equal status as an independent Hindu ruler. By meting out justice to Rani Savistribai, the king had "freed" all Hindu women throughout the generations. The public cheering of Shivaji's support for women became the wing's strategy for recovering agency for women in history. The front tried to show that women, like the queen of Bellary, once unchained, were promising warriors in the struggle to carve out a martial Hindu society. The Sena women asserted that if they received similar treatment, then they had the capacity to mold a militaristic, Hindu-dominated society. Hence these stories claiming that women had a place in history and were linked to a rich tradition of Hindu martiality enhanced the self-respect of ordinary women cadres.

MARSHALLING A MILITANT FUTURE:
SLUM CHILDREN, SKITS, AND STORIES

Most Aghadi members, being armed and aggressive women, shared a difficult yet proximate relationship with their children, especially their boys. Even though several boys became confused about notions of masculinity and martiality in their everyday slum life (where men are often unemployed and/or alcoholics, and women have assertive public personas), they remained supportive of their prominent and influential mothers, elder sisters, and aunts.[19] During the storytelling sessions, children were especially drawn to another tale of Shivaji outwitting a Muslim general, Afzal Khan. The khan had invited Shivaji to come in peace to his tent to reach an amicable settlement. The general, however, had conspired to throttle the Marathi leader. Shivaji came unarmed but stuck the claws of a tiger to his fingers; when the khan jumped on Shivaji and grabbed his throat, Shivaji tore the general's guts out. This story was narrated repeatedly during various Shivaji festivals held in the preindependence period, when the enemy was the British.[20] The story was later changed to promote Hindu militancy against a Muslim enemy.[21] In the Sena shakhas (party offices), the story was enacted in children's dramas, most of which were directed by women. Several children knew this tale by heart, and had learned from it the value of remaining in a state of preparedness for counterattacks and upholding a legacy of "bravery."

Shivaji Jayanti (a festival to mark the birthday of Shivaji) generated enormous festivities in the slums, coordinated by the shakhas. Besides food and finery, the occasion was celebrated with parades and the performance of Shivaji plays. During the only Shivaji Jayanti that I witnessed in Bombay, children practiced for their upcoming performance on the shakha premises. When they rehearsed without parental inspection, they would intersperse their usual Marathi dialogues with Mumbaiya colloquial Hindi abuses (often using the body language of film stars) that degraded the Muslim community. This made the other children roll in laughter. For example, a child enacting the character of Shivaji would say:

Shivaji: "Abey chutia Afzal, tu mereku marega? Mereku? Rand ki aulad, tu us din mar gaya tha jis din tu landya ban gaya."
(You fucker Afzal, you will kill me? Kill me? Son of a whore, you died that day when you were circumcised.)

"That means he died as a child," one of the children explained to me, rubbing the tears of laughter from his eyes. While the performance of violence sustained the larger Hindu nationalist understanding of history, women's and children's dialogues with their past were easily negotiated through what Pradeep Jeganathan describes as "violence in performance."[22]

Over time, keeping alive the Marathi plays on Shivaji had turned into a crusade among some of the older members of the Aghadi. Shobha, a retired stage actress, said: "My drive is to keep alive the Shivaji performances through the children. It should not be a dying art. But the children, after watching too many films, try and act out the role of Shivaji as Amitabh Bacchan [a megastar in Bombay]." While some defended the "authentic" folk versions, other women reformulated the plays on modern lines to make these adaptations popular among children. Shobha said sarcastically: "Since the next generation should not forget the Shivaji tradition, let's repackage it: that was the motivation." On one occasion, when the army of Shivaji was dressed in modern paramilitary (green and brown patched) combat outfits with automatic toy weapons, the children were relieved that the army appeared better prepared for modern warfare. But they were not totally averse to traditional performances "as long as Shivaji got to beat the shit out of the Mughals and prove we won."

Another episode that women enjoyed narrating was a directive from Jijabai (Shivaji's mother) to her son to recapture Kondana Fort (later renamed Singhad, after Tanaji), where Jijabai had been imprisoned. Capturing the fort from the Mughals was of strategic importance to the Marathi leader.[23] For the Sena women, however, the directive was the proof of overt militancy in a wronged Hindu mother, who could boldly send her son to a "just" war. The more contemporary celebration of Jijabai's orders seemed to highlight the contribution of right-wing women in creating martial sons, well trained for combat situations.

> JIJABAI: "My son, I have trained you to become the best warrior in the country. You have the blood of a proud Hindu mother running through your veins. You have been nurtured on my milk, the milk of purity and courage. I have unflinchingly put a sword in your hand. Will you not free the fort where your mother remained captive for long and take revenge for her humiliation?"
>
> SHIVAJI: "O Mother, your valor runs in my blood. Your wish is my command."
>
> And the mighty king bowed his head before his gallant mother. Her spirit rode out with her son as his horse galloped toward Kondana.

This tale held up an ideal relationship between a Hindu mother and a good, fearless Hindu son. After one of these interactive storytelling sessions, several women claimed to have shared a womb with Jijabai ("still giving birth to many Shivajis"), another strategy to emphasize women's position in a continuing tradition of martial motherhood.

Most of these women-centric mytho-histories became increasingly popular as nascent rebellions against Sena men, young and old, who still remained skeptical of women's strength. The tales appealed for sanctioning of women's "warrior" status. "If Shivaji, the great Maratha ruler, had allowed a woman to be his compatriot, what can our men say to oppose his ruling?" asked Nandini, who always played a primary role in the narration of these tales. I often spoke to the Sena men about these mytho-histories and women's desire to gain visibility within the movement, and reached two conclusions. First, the men played a very nominal role in developing and narrating mytho-histories. Second, most men preferred titillating tales about Muslim women, who were objects of Shivaji's generosity, even though the king had "the right" to abuse them to avenge himself against the Mughals. They seemed curious about the Aghadi's effort to revive tales of Shivaji's "respect" for martial Hindu women. Chandan, a Sena aide, said: "These stories are quite sensational. I had never heard some of them in my life. I do wonder whether these women can really re-create a martial society." "At least he is beginning to wonder," his wife, an active Aghadi member, murmured to me. Most men within the party referred to Meena Thackeray, the late wife of their party leader, Balasaheb Thackeray, as Matoshree, the name used by Shivaji to reverentially address his mother. She was idolized as the "good" wife and mother, who supported Thackeray through his political career but remained out of the public limelight. Aghadi leaders remained deferential in public; yet, they categorically refused to accept Meena Thackeray as their icon. "To be honest, she was just too passive," they would say. The image of an inspirational and militant mother was more appealing for the Sena women. The narratives developed by the storytellers attempted to change the orientation of slum men across generations, toward women's active involvement in social reconstruction.

OLD STORIES, NEW GARB: THE MUTABILITY OF WOMEN'S HISTORY

What we see here are pools of highly illustrative stories that were identified and narrated by women as their "history." Yet, it was striking that *all* the Sena women I met had never set foot on Singhad or Raighad (Shivaji's capital) or Shivneri (Shivaji's birthplace) to pay their tribute to their great leader. This evidenced a demarcation between heritage and the strategic use of history. Heritage was static, unchanging, and of no social value to the women. History, however, could be a collection of dramatic, spicy stories that could grab the attention of listeners. It was malleable enough to be transformed through embellishments. It had the potential to empower a group of marginalized right-wing women to develop a valorous identity.

According to Daniel, the concerns of academic historiography are oriented to the future even though they may be about the past. Thus, "history is not so much about *finding* truth as it is about *making* true."[24] Insofar as it is future-oriented, historiography nurtures the hope that when a line of inquiry is pursued long enough, then there will be a congregation of academics who will agree that a definite picture about the past has emerged. Mytho-histories, in contrast, insist that past "actualities" are contemporaneous, that what is now is what was then, and what was then is what is now.[25] "It is this collapse of time, where past becomes present enactment, that characterizes myths."[26] In a mythic world, the very same conditions and concerns that made past events possible still prevail. In the construction of mytho-histories by the Sena women, society in the past was marked by Muslim aggression, the Hindu effort to counter it, the aggressive role of women in public, and the subsequent creation of a martial society. The concerns at that time were to regain hegemony over the Muslims, and reclaim land and honor that had been taken away by them. The contingencies remained the same at present.

Pradeep Jeganathan points out that the history of the transformation of the Liberation Tigers of Tamil Eelam, a Tamil rebel group in Sri Lanka, was what we think of as an optic encounter for the Sinhala Buddhists.[27] Tamil terrorism and its performances of masculinity was a lived experience; the emergence of Tamil groups as militant organizations was a development the Sinhalese population could *see*. Hence the Sinhalese could easily identify all Tamils as their enemy. In the case of Maharashtra, there were no Islamic organizations that displayed militancy in their operations. The women were aware of Islamic fundamentalism in other parts of India, mainly through their association with the movement and through the media. In their everyday urban life, they encountered Muslims from neighboring slums (for example, Hoshairpur, a Muslim slum, was located at the edge of Nirmal Nagar); and despite petty business rivalries and occasional clashes with Muslims for seats during train journeys, the Aghadi women did not imagine poor Muslims as a real threat to their community. The viewing of Muslims as a dangerous, lustful enemy of Marathi Hindus, particularly women, had to be purely through the lens of the past. So the relation between the past and the present as viewed by the Sena women cannot be understood in temporal terms. Women did not imagine history as a written chronology or as a linear progression of episodes. Their narrations of history were performative, ritualistic, and flexible and had no relationship with unitary truths. Within the constraints of a masculinist discourse, these tales of valor and justice "restored women to history and history to women."

While recovering the idea of a female Hindu agency in the past, the Sena women inextricably linked it to their agency at present. If the past casts light on the present, current actions must also enrich their past. According to a leader, Neelamtai, "The Marathi women have always fought for their religion and honor. We are still fighting for our religion; it would make Shivaji really proud of us." So Shivaji was not a chapter that had been closed; he was still being written. Marathi women were continuing to satisfy his aspirations for Hindu supremacy. Neelamtai rounded off the discussion by saying: "Through our heroic actions, we will become the glorious past for the next generation of Marathi Hindu women." Sena women saw themselves as participants in the process of history. As "descendants" of newly constructed martial traditions, poor women wanted to accentuate their roles in carrying out social and historical responsibilities.

The Sena women, however, were often hesitant to be *too* radical in recovering women's agency. They preferred negotiation without any overt hostility to men and the movement. What surprised me was the definite unpopularity of Rani Laxmibai of Jhansi, the warrior queen in the revolt of 1857, among the Sena women. Laxmibai was the image of militant motherhood developed by the extremists during the anticolonial movement. In order to justify her role as head of state, the rani had led her troops as the regent of her infant son, adopted as the prospective male heir. At first the Sena women were dismissive about Laxmibai; then they claimed that they were not well aware of her history. In the course of time it became evident to me that the highly rebellious image of the rani was not acceptable to the Mahila Aghadi or to the male members of the organization. The Aghadi cadres could be "affiliated" with a masculine hero (like the queen of Bellary's comradeship with Shivaji), but the women could not be identified as completely independent actors. The Sena women carefully negotiated the language of "autonomy," articulating a desire for greater freedom in an urban context (*sheher mein azaadi*), but not declaring their complete independence from the community. They sought an advance toward *partial* autonomy from constant male supervision in the slums, and subservience before directives from party men.[28] Even though Rani Laxmibai acted on behalf of her son, she was a sovereign queen, independent of male aides. As part of Shivaji's Sena, men would like to believe that women were "granted" their freedom rather than asserting it. Women would like the men to believe so, as long as they occupied and enjoyed that small space of freedom.

FRACTURING SOLIDARITIES? SENA WOMEN VERSUS
WOMEN OF RASHTRIYA SWAYAMSEVAK SANGH

A strategic flexibility, especially in conjuring up iconic women from a foggy "past," separated the Aghadi from the women's wings of other fundamentalist groups in India. Many critics of right-wing Hindu fundamentalist parties felt the *similarities* between the women of Rashtriya Swayamsevak Sangh and the Shiv Sena were striking. While debating the influence of leadership in shaping a nationalist identity Paul Brass suggests that] "they shape group consciousness by manipulating symbols of group identity to achieve power for the group."[29] This is true for the women's wing of both parties, since they innovatively used a range of cultural symbols to promote their ideology among women. The women's wing (the Samiti) of the Rashtriya Swayamsevak Sangh, however, had a robust middle-class membership. The Samiti consisted primarily of educated women who underwent *formal* processes of ideological indoctrination (such as sessions for the reading and analysis of religious texts, exercise classes for carrying able-bodied Hindu sons, etc).[30] Female power, in the character of Laxmibai for example, was discussed, debated, and openly idealized among the Samiti women. Since most martial queens embodied a certain upper-class heritage, it was probably far easier for these elite women to identify with Laxmibai. According to Sikata Banerjee: "Women in visible Hindu nationalist groups . . . draw on images of women as heroic mother, chaste wives and celibate masculinized warrior to negotiate their way into this [nationalist] landscape."[31] In her research of women's political participation in India, she also tries to uncover the ways in which women's active roles within right-wing organizations create a tension between models of feminine and feminist activism; she argues that the latter construes the "gender and nation" imagery evoked by nationalist discourses as curtailment of women's choices and freedom. The Sena women were free to choose the "heroic mother" and "chaste wife" model to interpret and articulate their martial history, but the celibate warrior/female monk was not a potent metaphor for addressing the concerns of militant, married Aghadi women in the slums. It was viewed with suspicion, and eventually discarded.

CONCLUSION

The Aghadi women were trying to rediscover a past (through tales of Shivaji) where they were participants in the creation of social honor and martiality in a Hindu society. They wanted to assert that the martialization of women's identities was not in disjunction with the past because the social and political concerns remained the same. They were making women prominent in a martial past, so that their conspicuous militant roles within the contemporary Sena movement would not be seen as female deviancy. The Aghadi manipulated the past in shaping the present and creating a favorable position for Marathi Hindu women in society.

Several scholars offer compelling analyses of gender in conflict situations and uncover the links between gender relations and militarized violence that occur in the course of and, significantly, in the absence of direct conflict. Among them, Sara Ruddick comments that women need men to protect them and men need war to protect women and children: "The culture of militarisation—coercive power structures and practices, hierarchies and discipline—relies on patriarchal patterns and patriarchy in turn relies on militarization. . . . War magnifies the already existing inequalities of peacetime."[32] When a community feels under siege, women are pressured to embrace identity constructs that undermine their authority and autonomy. To reverse that trend and manage their survival, the Sena women were trying to place themselves in a long history of women's militancy. They were trying to construct a critical consciousness, typically using the politics of self-defense in a conflict situation, by developing gendered insights into a social framework that acknowledges the necessity of militarism, not just to protect women but also to ensure the survival of the Hindu society and religion. The Aghadi cadres can be seen as agents of social transformation, with the *potential* to upturn gross power imbalances within a social system that remains openly prejudicial against women. Women's experiences of everyday and extraordinary violence (extending from home to the street to "battlefield" riot situations) are not homogeneous, and thus their coping mechanisms are also diverse. The Sena women's visions were structured by the fact that women's expressions of support and resistance flow from their own cultural experiences of being discriminated against and disempowered. If women felt that their recourse to organized violence offered them relief from quotidian moral restrictions, it was linked to their own immediate, maybe narrow, construction of women's visibility, everyday empowerment, and social worth.

Hayden White, who comments on the representation of reality in legends, fables, and folk tales, argues that public telling of biographical narratives in any society is determined by cultural contexts and local "sense-making" mechanisms.[33] He maintains that members of a community with a strong tradition in telling tales can emphasize the dominance of one perspective over another, and reflect their own life experiences in narrating myths and legends. That is, stories have the potential to become community "histories." Stuart Blackburn reinterprets White's perspective in the context of Tamil prophecies, songs, and religious texts, opening up an analytical space for narratives and "truth-telling."[34] He argues that narrating life histories of popular mythical characters can serve as a vehicle for "revealing historical wrongs, naming the guilty," and in due course, setting the record straight.[35] Unlike Blackburn's rural informants, most Sena women did not have any real experience of traditional storytelling. Large sections of poor women had been distanced from their village pasts, while some of the younger women cadres had been born and/or raised in the slums of Bombay. The practice of public and interactive storytelling developed by Aghadi members may have been rooted in traditions of narrating myths and legends in the remote past that survived within a cluster of households (for example, grandmothers who tell night-time stories about ghosts and demons to children). But collective forms of storytelling were absent within the rush and squalor of the Bombay ghettoes. In this essay I have highlighted the strategic creativity among slum women to pursue the power of public storytelling, develop a common interpretative schema, publicize it successfully as women's history, and turn the practice into a tool for binding the interests of poor women from scattered urban slums. Women strategically adopt the softer approach of storytelling (as against public political activism) to avoid direct confrontation with a male-dominated nationalist movement. With the limited social, material, and ideological capital accessible to slum women, they seek to contest the marginalization of women's historical traditions.

My arguments deviate from the wider literature on storytelling events within communities characterized by prolonged conflict. For example, Sasanka Perera's account of ghost stories and demon possession in Sri Lanka and Michael Jackson's research on public storytelling in Sierra Leone understand the act of telling lives as a coping mechanism for communities that builds a peaceful community life in the context of war.[36] My research on the Shiv Sena women shows how storytelling becomes a mechanism for *prolonging* conflict and celebrating violence. While telling themselves into a history of Hindu women's martiality, the Aghadi members also identified Muslims as their historical enemies, *precluding* the possibility of negotiation with them.

To configure a female-friendly Hindu nationalism, even the conservative Samiti reproduced Rashtriya Swayamsevak Sangh representations, but interpreted them differently. According to Bacchetta, sometimes the Samiti ideologues drew from sources the Sangh ignored to construct feminine identities beyond their imagination (such as iconicizing Rani Laxmibai to mobilize segregated women beyond their homes): "As a result, different aspects of the Samiti discourse are coherent with, or asymmetrically 'complementary' to, or even antagonistic to, the RSS discourse."[37] Marking a significant deviation from the pan-Indian Hindu nationalist movement and its models for the ideal social order, the Sena women's stories did not invoke "the mythic, Hindu past of Lord Ram" envisioned in the Hindutva discourse. "Ramrajya nahi chahiye" (we don't want Ram's kingdom), they said. During the peaceful and patriarchal reign of Lord Ram, the absence of crises put women "safely" in their homes. Instead, the women's mythonarratives focused on a medieval, "historical Hindu past" (Shivaji's *Hindu padpadshahi*), where women had achieved a degree of autonomy. The Aghadi consciously countered nostalgia for a serene Ramrajya, and promoted an image of a society that was perpetually threatened by enemies. The latter society "required" men *and* women to organize themselves as an army, and women would have to carry out militaristic activities for the security of the Hindu community.

ATREYEE SEN

With regard to the wider debate on women, urban activism, and violence, I have identified a number of vexed socio-political realities that determine the dynamism of right-wing movements in non-Western societies (especially among the more subaltern sections). Women usually support a nationalist movement from the periphery, but at crucial points of communal tension, they can actively participate in violence to assert their presence within a struggle. I have shown how poor women observe and experience the social and emotional value of working collectively, even if within the context of a violent struggle. Women's attempts to construct and restructure their "history" underline the experience of collective action as the most potent lever to reorganize male discursive practices. Instead of only critiquing women's involvement in violence from a secular or feminist perspective, I have preferred to look at the Sena women's unique perception of the course of the Hindu fundamentalist rhetoric, and discussed one of their strategies for making their violent public role indispensable within the movement.

NOTES

I would like to thank Filippo Osella, Chris Fuller, Stef Jansen, Carolyn Nordstrom, and Nilanjan Sarkar for their comments on this essay.

1. Hobsbawm, "Introduction," 1.

2. For a detailed analysis of these strategies, see Sen, *Shiv Sena Women*.

3. Chakravarti and Haksar, *The Delhi Riots*; Dietrich, "Women and Religious Identities in India after Ayodya"; Gedalof, *Against Purity*; Sarkar and Butalia, *Women and Right-wing Movements*; Bacchetta, "Women in the Hindu Nationalist Discourse"; and Kovacs, "You Don't Understand, We Are at War!"

4. Blee, "Becoming a Racist."

5. Agnes, Agarkar, and Dutta, *The Nation, the State and the Indian Identity*; Setalvad, "The Woman Shiv Sainik and Her Sister Swayamsevika"; and Banerjee, *Warriors in Politics*.

6. Quoted in Banerjee, *Warriors in Politics*, 228.

7. See Peto, "Who Is Afraid of the 'Ugly Women'?," 147–51.

8. Ginsberg, *Contested Lives*.

9. See Gupta, *Nativism in a Metropolis*; and Katzenstein, *Ethnicity and Equality*.

10. The Shiv Sena's political ambitions and perception of "the other" has varied over time. Katzenstein, Mehta, and Thakkar, "The Rebirth of the Shiv Sena in Maharashtra."

11. In December 1992 Hindu nationalists destroyed the Babri Masjid, a controversial mosque located in a temple town in north India, and demanded that a temple dedicated to the Hindu god Ram be built in its place. This sparked communal riots across India, which in some cases persisted for months.

12. Sen, "Reflecting on Resistance."

13. Doniger, *The Implied Spider*; and Tambiah, *Leveling Crowds*.

14. Duff, *History of the Marathas*; Laine, *Shivaji*; Sarkar, *Shivaji and His Times*; Sen, *Foreign Biographies of Shivaji*; Takakhav, *Life of Shivaji*; and Lane-Poole, *Aurangzeb*.

15. Bhave, *From the Death of Shivaji to the Death of Aurangzeb*; Bakshi and Sharma, *The Great Marathas*.

16. Bakshi and Sharma, *The Great Marathas*.

17. Sarkar, *Shivaji and His Times*.

18. Daniel, *Charred Lullabies*, 27.

19. Sen, *Shiv Sena Women*.

20. Ahluwalia, *Shivaji and Indian Nationalism*; and Samarath, *Shivaji and the Indian Movement*.

21. Sarkar and Butalia, *Women and Right-wing Movements*.

22. Jeganathan, "A Space for Violence," 52.

23. Bhave, *From the Death of Shivaji to the Death of Aurangzeb*.

24. Daniel, *Charred Lullabies*, 70.

25. Tambiah, *Leveling Crowds*.

26. Daniel, *Charred Lullabies*, 52.

27. Jeganathan, "A Space for Violence."

28. Sen, "Reflecting on Resistance."

29. Brass, *Language, Religion and Politics in India*, 45.

30. Bacchetta, "Women in the Hindu Nationalist Discourse"; and Sarkar, "The Woman as Communal Subject."

31. Banerjee, *Warriors in Politics*, 63.

32. Ruddick, "Women of Peace," 212.

33. White, *The Content of the Form*, 172.

34. Blackburn, "Life Histories as Narrative Strategy."

35. Ibid., 205.

36. Jackson, *The Politics of Story-telling*; and Perera, "Spirit Possessions and Avenging Ghosts."

37. Bacchetta, "Hindu Nationalist Women Imagine Spatialities/Imagine Themselves," 47.

II

FEMINISM, LABOR, AND GLOBALIZATION

SONALI PERERA

Of Moments, Not Monuments
Feminism and Labor Activism
in Postnational Sri Lanka

Trade Unions are certainly not encouraged within the Free Trade Zone
but it is not solely for this reason that there has [sic] been no trade
unions within the zone. In fact, there is no significant growth of trade
unions in this sector of the industry even outside the zone. Not only is
employment security in this sector low but also the future of each garment manufacturing enterprise is itself so insecure that the workers
involved, the bulk of whom are young females, do not wish to jeopardize
their jobs through agitation for better wages and living conditions.

BATTY R. WEERAKOON, *THE EVOLUTION OF LABOR LAW IN SRI LANKA*

You can get more work out of them . . . they are disciplined . . . obedient. . . . Ideas like these proliferate because the majority of workers in
free trade zone factories happen to be women. The only way we can
change these mythologies is through our own unbiased efforts.

STRI NIRMANA

INTRODUCTION: NGOIZATION AND THE UNMAKING
OF THE SRI LANKAN WORKING CLASS

As a historical object for Sri Lankan feminism and class politics, the garment factory worker presents an interesting and
instructive paradox. In terms of political meaning making,
the sentimentalized figure—simultaneously invisible and hy-
pervisible, absent and ubiquitous, local and global—is used to
different ends. She is summoned up to give credence to ideologically diverse, sometimes competing, (global) feminist and

(local) working-class interests. This essay, however, will focus on the ethi-copolitical use to which she is put in the writings of Sri Lankan NGO activists as well as garment factory workers themselves. I consider how the iconic figure is constituted, deauthorized, and reimagined in the garment factory workers' creative production, and how nationalist anxieties and global perspectives are shaped, framed, and interrupted in working-class literature. Specifically, I read a selection of poems, political commentary, and short fiction—some anonymous, some collaborative—produced by the worker-writers of the Dabindu collective from the Katunayake free trade zone regions in Sri Lanka. The period under consideration is 1984–2001, which covers the passage of Dabindu's transformation from a work-ers' collective organized loosely around the production and distribution of a free trade zone periodical and other forms of alternative organizing into an internationally funded development NGO.

Some might argue that in the contemporary historical moment, the "new proletariat" is best represented by the figure of the woman worker in the global South.[1] Distinct from organized labor in industrialized countries of the North, the occluded agent of production in this "postindustrial" age is the heavily exploited worker in postcolonial, "developing" countries with extraverted, rather than autocentric, economies.[2] In government-issued business brochures, targeted at foreign direct investment, she is sold as "cheap," "docile," "famous for her manual dexterity." Nationalist historians and trade unionists do not identify her with revolutionary possibilities. For U.S. feminism, she cannot be easily written into labor history because she represents, disturbingly, the containment of the wage bargaining power of struggling women workers closer to home.[3]

Terese Agnew's artwork *Portrait of a Textile Worker* (2005) is a 98-by-110-inch monument to this figure—the unseen, anonymous agent of economic globalization.[4] Making use of the rhetoric and sentiment of the global antisweatshop movement, the artist plays with perspective to "fa-miliarize" the Northern consumer with the unthinkable abstraction of the international division of labor. From a distance, we get a view, from the waist up, of a woman clothed in a sari. Prominent in the foreground is the ubiquitous Juki-brand sewing machine. The woman's face with down-cast eyes appears completely absorbed in the task at hand. There she is—performing her signature docility and dexterity. Up close, the image disin-tegrates into a cacophony of proper names. Made up of 30,000 brand name

SONALI PERERA

labels, as Agnew explains on her personal website, "from 20 feet away, the composition is a representational image of a remote place. As you move closer, the illusionistic devices dissolve into labels as intimately familiar as your own clothes . . . the repetition of thousands of other people cutting their labels is retained in the piece. It amplifies the presence of the woman we finally see."[5] The artist envisions her collaborative composition as an experiment in socialized labor. Although it runs counter to the divisive rhetoric of outsourcing, and is offered up as representational reparation to the undervalued labor of the South Asian garment factory worker, Agnew's explanation, nevertheless, comes off as a paradoxical gesture. Making visible the unseen garment factory worker is predicated on substituting and overwriting her labor with the "labor" of socially conscious consumers. Ultimately artistic labor is substituted as a proxy for the labor of factory workers. "It amplifies the presence of the woman we finally see" is the artist's statement. Her ethical objective—circumscribed within metropolitan feminism—is to call attention to a secret history of commodity fetishism. The use of the word "amplify" reveals the desire to restore voice agency to the Third World worker in this "postindustrial" age. We are familiar with the arguments that caution against confusing the two different senses—aesthetic and political—of representation. But we also recognize this as a principled intervention—an effort to reveal the hidden global assembly line.[6]

From a different vantage point from across the international division of labor, the same archetypal and pathetic figure of the factory worker is immediately recognizable within the texts of Sri Lanka's development NGOS:

This is the story of an unfolding tragedy—that of garment factory workers in Sri Lanka. These case studies portray the plight of thousands of young women. They highlight, with the [sic] unobtrusive realism, the social background, and appalling working conditions of garment factory workers. . . . The best years of their lives are spent slaving for establishments that have the least amount of concern imaginable for their welfare. They are living examples of history being repeated—in this case, that of capitalism's crudest incipient stages that third world countries like Sri Lanka are forced to undergo due to a lack of viable choices.[7]

The garment factory worker's narrative-image resurfaces to different effect in the writings of Sri Lankan trade unionist socialism. In a slim pamphlet titled *The Evolution of Labor Law in Sri Lanka*, Batty Weerakoon, a left party activist and trade unionist (turned parliamentarian) seems to suggest that in a country formerly noted for a history of trade unionism there is currently no organized protest in free trade zone factories perhaps (at least partly) because of the docile nature of "young, female" workers.[8] An entire setup of historical events—the dissolution of the early anticolonial Trotskyite labor parties, the increasing marginalization of the electoral "Left," the United National Party's economic policy shift from welfarism to development in 1977—are all elided in such simplistic and gendered formulations of global capitalism. For a more complex, textured view, we must turn to such historians as Kumari Jayawardena, telling the story of the rise of the labor movement in Ceylon in the wake of the emergence of Sinhala chauvinism.[9] Weerakoon, for his part, in *The Evolution of Labor Law in Sri Lanka*, recounts the unmaking of the Sri Lankan working class. Writing close upon the heels of the brutal breakup of the 1980s general strike, Weerakoon retroactively constitutes the decline of the labor movement mainly as a consequence of privatization and deregulation: gender operates as a hidden seam of meaning: "Not only is employment security in this sector low but also the future of each garment manufacturing enterprise is itself so insecure that the workers involved, the bulk of whom are young females, do not wish to jeopardize their jobs through agitation for better wages and living conditions."[10] An interesting slippage happens here. The fact that "the bulk of them are young females" is stated parenthetically but serves as corollary historical and sociological evidence. It is a foregone conclusion that in an industry dominated by young females, a climate of compliance and complaisance instead of unionized resistance will prevail. In terms of periodization, the endpoints of "plantation" and "free trade zone" are not simply arbitrary division markers along the timeline of labor law, they also invoke —although Weerakoon leaves the overdeterminations largely unexamined —the racialized social divide between (upcountry Tamil) women agricultural workers and (Sinhala) women industrial workers. According to such theses, the present period of labor history corresponds to the end of national working-class history even as it coincides with the rise of development NGOs and a new direction for social redistribution agendas.[11]

SONALI PERERA

In Sri Lanka, the timeline of organized military campaigns between the government of Sri Lanka and the Liberation Tigers of Tamil Eelam (LTTE) (1983–2009) intersects with economic liberalization (1977 to the present), a period that has produced a set of diversely disabling political and historical effects. Newton Gunasinghe plots a structural, not aberrational, connection between ethnic conflict and economic globalization. He argues that a rise in ethnic hostilities can be traced to the opening up of the economy as Tamil-minority entrepreneurs finally acquire access to a field of competition, up to this point restricted by state patronage trade permits to the majority Sinhalese. In this twisted history, the new ruling party's embrace of free market ideals and the decimation of the labor movement occur in tandem with a gradual rise of prosperity and hard-won gains for a new Tamil entrepreneurial class.[12] In the neoliberal era of disaster capitalism and postconflict reconstruction, the Sri Lankan Textile and Garment Conglomerate comes forward to ventriloquize the desire of garment workers. "We want trade, not aid" is their collective pronouncement.[13] Meanwhile, the European Union's decision to withdraw Sri Lanka's preferential trade access is premised on the state's failure to improve its human rights record.

Indeed, Sri Lanka, today, presents us with a pressing quandary, caught as it is between two very different ideologically invested senses of temporality—"development" and "crisis." Feminists and activists rightfully elaborate a trenchant critique of the ideology of development NGOs (versus human rights NGOs) operating in places of protracted struggles, exposing the limitations of the very mind-set of "crisis management." Such work calls our attention to the creation of a new sector called "conflicts" for funding purposes. As Vasuki Nesiah argues in this volume, the linkage of a neoliberal economic agenda to feminist peace building generates the conditions and constraints of a new mode of discourse—"international conflict feminism." Women-as-victims and hence as objects of protection (of distant donor communities) are the axioms on which this strand of Sri Lankan feminism is founded. When we speak of NGOization of feminism, or as Malathi de Alwis discusses it following Nivedita Menon, the "professionalization of feminism" (in Sri Lanka), we must consider how the improvisational ad hoc strategies of earlier feminist class struggles have been "dispersed, diluted, and fragmented today into projects and programs focused on 'women's empowerment,' 'gender sensitization,' 'mainstreaming gender' . . . 'conflict resolution,' and 'conflict transformation.' "[14]

The criticism of the NGOization of feminism and its foreign donor-driven political agendas is now widespread—and it is directed by many of us who benefited from the proliferation of feminist institutions. And yet, we must continue to explore the productive, creative possibilities for local and international NGOs, especially in the context of war-torn Sri Lanka, where it remains important to question the sovereignty of the nation-state from within, even as neoliberal globalization breaks down the boundaries of a fragile national economy toward very different ends. A more nuanced way of understanding the pressures of nongovernmental and transnational advocacy groups is called for alongside the implementation of postwar devolution plans and power-sharing initiatives. To this end, it is important to recall the history, ideology, and ethics of voluntary associations and other collectivities long before they were institutionally validated as NGOs. What brought these groups together before they were designated NGOS? What existing structures were they built upon? What political practices continue to overreach the limits of institutions?

In the case of the Dabindu periodicals brought out by free trade zone workers in Sri Lanka, for example, it is a matter of record that some of the group's worker education projects were funded by the Canadian International Development Agency. Recent scholarship on garment factory workers identifies Dabindu as either an NGO or—when referring to the publications of the group—as "alternative media."[15] My work, instead, emphasizes its earlier history, beginning with the story of the free trade zone newspaper conceived as an expedient strategy for communication in a climate where trade unions were effectively prohibited.[16] As the following section of this essay attempts to show, to reduce the shifting dynamics of the Dabindu collective to the static, generic, descriptive "NGO" is to obscure vast domains of improvised political practice that exceed the parameters of donor agencies' set agendas.

Here I consider the improvisational strategies and formal experimentation of Dabindu texts as working-class writing. Some of the worker-writers and feminist activists writing therein embrace anonymity as a rhetorical and political strategy. Others attempt to ventriloquize the transnational corporation. Still others tell their stories in solidarity with the upcountry Tamil tea plantation worker. How is the garment factory worker's story told in postnational Sri Lanka?[17] What is the "structure of feeling"— if not clear-cut ideology—of feminist working-class consciousness that emerges here?

While much has been written about the internationalization of production and the feminization of labor by anthropologists and economists, there is hardly any consideration of what working-class writings can teach us about Sri Lankan feminism. The writings in the Dabindu periodicals reveal feminism as project and process, rather than perfected ideology. They allow us to examine a space that is constantly negotiated and inhabited with a range of emotions from defeatism to mourning to protest.

FROM WORKER-WRITERS' COLLECTIVE TO NGO: READING SRI LANKAN FREE TRADE ZONE PERIODICALS

The free trade zone paper *Dabindu* (Drops of sweat) traces its origins to September 1984, when a group of women workers, newly employed in the free trade zone regions, joined together with cultural workers and grassroots labor activists to devise an alternative means of communicating in a climate where trade unions were effectively prohibited and speech was censored. Sri Lanka's first free trade zone was created in 1978 under the guidance of the World Bank and International Monetary Fund as part of the conditions for global aid. These plans were implemented by the rightist United National Party government, whose national economic policies charted a shift from welfarism to development. Dismantling the infrastructure of labor laws that were the result of hard-won gains of the 1930s anticolonial working-class movement, the new free trade regime of the United National Party promised investment protection, tax holidays, and the availability of cheap labor to foreign capital. Seven years after the first factories were built and operational, the Dabindu collective first met to discuss the strange separate space that they inhabited. Here, by fiat of the Greater Colombo Economic Commission, their workplaces were declared exempt from the Trade Unions Ordinance and the Maternity Benefits Ordinance, as well as the Factories Ordinance, among other laws of the country.

In the beginning there were no resources for a printing press. The founding members of the group pieced together a first edition from photocopies of anonymous letters, protest poems, testimonials, and worker biographies. They distributed these copies free of charge among the cramped quarters of the boardinghouses where many of the garment factory workers lived. After the first installment, it was discovered that the paper would find its way down the assembly line to factory notice boards. In other instances, it would be smuggled into the premises slipped in between the sheets of the dailies that they used as wrapping paper for their meager lunches. Since the first meeting in September 1984, regular publication was discontinued just once, for a three-month period in 1989, coinciding with the second Janatha Vimukthi Peramuna uprising following the disappearances and murders of some of the worker-activists connected with the collective.[18] During that time *Dabindu* was proscribed as an antigovernment publication. Since the old days of forbidden pages smuggled into the factory, the periodical has received some measure of visibility with the Dabindu collective's transformation into a local NGO.

The newspaper was originally conceptualized as a medium for publishing workers' correspondences, factory reports, and news of struggles with management, and for bringing together national and international labor news. It was also, however, conceived as a means of publishing the preliminary "beginning/amateur" literary efforts of worker-writers. The preface to the 1988 International Women's Day commemorative booklet titled *Stri Nirmana* (Women's writing) addresses a general feminist readership and calls for a specific mode of reception: "Therefore, because [the writings] found here are only amateur creative efforts [*adhunika nirmana*, sometimes translated as 'modern'], we hope in the event of shortcomings and failures for your unbiased response."[19] In their creative writings, the garment workers drew a political picture of the organization of society counter to the new mythologies constructed by the state that extolled the virtues of their obedience and manual dexterity. For example, in poems such as "Apatada Nidahasak Natha" (For us, there is no freedom) they write themselves as set apart from the declarations of independence sounded by political parties in postcolonial Sri Lanka.[20] The unsigned poem, appearing on the cover of the February 1998 edition, published to coincide with postcolonial celebrations of fifty years of freedom, is a critique of the nationalist rhetoric of independence as well as an exposition of the terms of economic imperialism. The first two stanzas read:

SONALI PERERA

Although fifty years ago today
This land received its freedom
Oh, for the sisters of the zone
There is still no freedom from enslavement

Today, as then, under foreign rule
They are
Like prisoners
Oh, when do they become free?

The writing is a mix of colloquial and literary Sinhala. Each stanza registers a different meter. On some occasions we find words shortened with a literary license according to some metrical scheme that is impossible to discern, or erratic variations indicating collaboration between different writers.

While the text of the free trade zone periodical is produced by a "collective," it does not offer us a model for a "synchronic" subject in the readily available sense; that is to say, it does not represent some seamless cultural unity of contemporary women's working-class struggles. Rather, the subject of *Dabindu* figures a "unity-in-dispersal"—heterogeneity and contradictions gathered under a collective signature.[21] Writings are contributed by named and unnamed garment factory workers and mediated by the interventions of volunteer editors. The very concept of (private) authorship becomes unstable in the context of such publication history and material production, recalling Terry Eagleton's insight that "community and cooperative publishing enterprises are associated projects, concerned not simply with a literature wedded to alternative social values, *but with one which challenges and changes the existing social relations between writers, publishers, readers and other literary workers.*"[22]

Eagleton goes on to describe a concept of (British) working-class writing that portends the interrogation of unitary authorship and, indeed, "ruling *definitions* of literature." The point resonates with the example of the free trade zone worker-writers collective also. If we consider the form of the free trade zone newspapers, we see that the text itself is a creative mishmash of genres—bits and pieces of political analysis and cultural critique interspersed with romantic melodrama, nationalist poetry, letters, didactic leftist literature, reportage on local strikes, and international labor news. It is important to note that while the periodical is composed of writing contributed by garment factory workers, pieces are sometimes edited and selected by feminist activists. While these two constituencies (of feminism and the working class) are not always mutually exclusive, as Kumudini Samuel points out, the periodical's editors belong to different formations within organized feminism in Sri Lanka, reflecting *Dabindu's* shifting political tenor over the span of different editions.[23] Kumudhini Rosa, one of the conveners of the collective and the founding editor of the periodical, explains *Dabindu's* historical conjuncture in these terms: "In Sri Lanka, the new wave of the women's movement arose in the late 1970s, at the same time as the FTZ (Free Trade Zone)."[24] Along these lines—and also in its current incarnation as an internationally (and locally) funded NGO—it goes without saying that the Dabindu collective categorically cannot lay claim to some ideologically uncontaminated space outside relations of capital and class within globalization.[25]

Cultural anthropology studies of the *Dabindu* periodicals have focused mainly on the segments of prose writings as sociological evidence of working-class consciousness among the women of the Sri Lankan garment industry. There are, for example, wonderful texts such as grotesque cartoons personifying the World Bank, comparative studies of the exploited garment industry workers in Bangladesh, and opinionated discussion pieces on the international implications of U.S. child labor legislation.[26] In an otherwise close reading of the vocabulary of "class" in the free trade zone factories of Katunayake, the anthropologists Sandya Hewamanne and James Brow briefly dismiss the fiction pages with a general remark: "In their fiction writings . . . the heroines unfailingly overcome the pressures of outside forces to uphold moral values. . . . It could be that some of the writings are addressed to a general readership in an attempt to convey the message that there are 'moral heroines' within the FTZ."[27]

But in addition to tales of moral heroines, the *Dabindu* periodicals encompass a vast heterogeneity of other narrative forms, including worker biographies, realist reportage, short stories about recanting JVP insurgents, romantic melodramas with the interethnic civil war as their backdrop, didactic stories critical of Sinhala ethnonationalism, poems dedicated to soldiers on the front lines, poems addressing the Tamil tea plantation workers, free verse (*nisandas*) poetry addressing that abstract entity named the MNC (multinational corporation, *bahujathika samagama*), socialist fiction celebrating great Russian and Latin American Marxist leaders, love

SONALI PERERA

stories and other elliptical utterances—and perhaps most poignantly, stories and poems mourning lost opportunities for higher education in the university system.[28]

In the poem "Apatada Nidahasak Natha" (For us, there is no freedom), we discerned the traces of a nonindividual subject in the irregular lines and erratic rhythms of an unsigned poem. On the other hand, in "Padada Pathum" (Vagabond wishes) by A. C. Perera in the June 1994 issue of *Dabindu*, we see the abstract entity of the multinational corporation as a speaking subject whose sovereign speech act brings into being the terrible order of things. The poem is written in colloquial Sinhala:

Garment for girls
Army for boys
Heavenly comforts for us . . .
Say the multinationals
Together with those-who-lay-waste-to-the-country . . .[29]

The poem illustrates a brief anatomy of the national sexual division of labor in terms of the militarization of the state. Its form is quite simply a short list of actors in a staging of post-independence Sri Lankan history. The list includes working-class women of the export-oriented garment industry, men of the Sri Lankan armed forces fighting a savage war to maintain a unitary state, as well as multinational corporations and a set of unnamed agents: those who ruin or lay waste to the country. The English translation fails to capture the stark brevity of that final line as well as the planned slippage between the words for those who "rule" (*deshapalana or deshpalaka*) and those who "ruin" (*deshapaluvan*). In the context of contemporary historiography, the poem is crucially significant in that it shifts the focus of dominant narratives of the Tamil-Sinhala interethnic conflict, placing the blame not on Tamil separatist nationalism but on the governing elite, who collude with global capital to perpetuate the war industry. Perera's poem uncovers a hidden complicity between "free trade," the slogan of the multinational corporation, and "freedom," the patriotic rhetoric of the postcolonial Sinhala-Buddhist government. (Less "literary" techniques mediate the language of the antiwar statement of the Committee for Democracy and Justice in Sri Lanka published in the 1995 September–October edition of *Dabindu*.)[30]

"Padada Pathum," written in the short, staccato language of the pamphleteering traditions represents the macropolitics of nationalism-as-an-alibi-for-global capitalism in terms of a compact, accessible, gendered logic. Deepika Thrima Vitana's "Chintanaya Nidahas Nam" (Thinking freedom [1984]), on the other hand, dramatizes the micropolitics of internalized gendering in a modernist short story that stages the interior monologue of a former "Marxist" insurgent. The time frame is shortly after the abortive Janatha Vimukthi Peramuna (JVP) insurgency of 1989 in the southern part of Sri Lanka.[31] The protagonist, Sahra, is the only one in a group of operatives who manages to escape her captor, and only after an army officer brands her face with his cigarette, leaving her permanently disfigured. The narrative of this scarring, however, is withheld in the order of narrative sequencing. Starting with the opening scene in which we see Sahra walking out on her lover, the story moves backward and forward as bits and pieces of the heroine's life story are given as a series of retroversions through reported speech, but without quotation marks. The title, which I translate as "Thinking Freedom," also underscores a movement in the text where the former JVP recruit gives up the phraseology of mechanical Marxism—the *harabara vachana, tharaka vada* (heavy-duty words and logical arguments)—of "the organization" to discover her "self" through a process of uncollected thoughts, disconnected sentences—a collection of textual interferences, rather than the speech of the autonomous, intending subject.

Sahra remembers episodes of university life, leaving the university to work full time for "the organization," a failed love affair, the scarring of her face. Rooted to the spot by the river where the primary action of the story takes place, she also inhabits the present. She overhears village women discussing the marks on her face: "One of those 'Che Guevara' types; when these words beat against Sahra's ears she feels incredible pain. That she had committed herself on behalf of their children no one seemed to acknowledge." In the final turn of the story, Sahra contemplates her reflection in the water and resolves to no longer ask for validation from disaffected party ideologues or grieving family members. "If she died in that jungle—that would have been something. Now how do you keep an unmarriageable woman in the house?" The comment of the village women is a statement, rather than a question. In the closing scene, the protagonist counters with her own philosophy of Marxism, feminism, and history as she reconstructs her image in the water: "She began to feel the strong need for

SONALI PERERA

independence of thought. There is no possibility of returning to university to continue studies. Well, whatever happens, tomorrow, by first light [I] must go to the fair and find some greens, potatoes, yams. Life is beautiful but there must also be independence of thought. She saw in her face a strange beauty from under the water."

WOMEN'S WORKING-CLASS WRITING
AND THE POLITICAL IMAGINATION

Ultimately, Vitana's short story connects the narrative of the gendered revolutionary working-class subject to a different duration from either "crisis" or "development" (the proletarian female bildungsroman). Rather, "Chintanaya Nidahas Nam" (like S. Udyalata Menike's "Mai Dinaya" [May Day]) is an autocritical text of nonrevolutionary socialism. The protagonist's final thoughts register as a hymn to ordinariness—a rededication to inglorious, mundane affairs. Ultimately "Chintanaya Nidahas Nam" strains to connect the rhythms of the daily task to the historic event of the revolutionary conjuncture. Vitana's protagonist measures "history" not in terms of the logic of revolutions, but in the unceasing back-and-forth movements of daily life that construct and erase the present.

It is particularly telling that the best-known *Dabindu* poem, originally published in the 1987 July–August edition of the periodical and since reproduced in local and foreign development NGO and human rights publications, is K. G. Jayasundera Menike's realist testimonial, which describes with play-by-play precision the factory scene at Star Garments.[32] In this, stanzas are organized by segments of clock time as Menike's poem faithfully replicates the mind-numbing mechanical rhythm of the working day at a garment factory. Caught within this exacting tempo, our thoughts bind to the factory floors and here we cannot begin to imagine different times and other measures for thinking collectivities beyond trade unionist socialism and class politics as usual. Still, despite the unresolved critical debate on Marxist aesthetics, the relationship between working-class writing and literary realism continues to be taken as dogma. Tony Davies writes, "That relationship, in one strong tradition, is simply taken for granted. According to this view, working-class writing is realistic in the most unpremeditated and unselfconscious fashion: autobiographical, documentary, or commemorative, rooted in the experience of family, community, locality, it 'tells it as it is' (or, more often was) in plain words, valued for their sincerity and simple truth."[33] Still, beyond realism and the genre of testimonial writing, then, how are the truth claims of working-class literature constructed—and according to what terms?

These working-class women have been dubbed by some as "the good girls of Sri Lankan modernity."[34] But from the writings published in this single periodical it is clear that they actively write against such crisis management myths of the state. We might ask how, in fact, do they themselves define the interruption that is the "modern" (*adhunika*)—that is, the new? Theirs, as we see, are collaborative writings, not self-writing in any smooth, seamless way. They are not necessarily rooted in family or locality. Strategic achrony, not clock time or nation-building projects, constitute their measure. In the *Dabindu* periodicals, I believe that perhaps the most politically imaginative (but at the same time tenuously situated) writings are a group of Sinhala poems, stories, and letters addressing and identifying with the stateless Tamil women workers of the upcountry tea plantations/estates.

Some pieces haphazardly blur the lines between collective identity and class interest. For example, in one segment of a long-running, anonymous epistolary novel, one protagonist (a free trade zone factory worker) compares her marginalization with the disenfranchisement of Indian-origin "recent" Tamils: "Just like those plantation workers . . . They, too, were brought over from India . . . got their work done by them . . . After that they were discarded like dirt . . . Did anyone think about what happens to these people? . . . No . . . How many years has this been going on? Still these people don't have citizenship . . . That's how we are."[35] The historical analogy is forced. Despite numerous palliative reform measures, ever since 1948 (the year of Ceylon's independence from Britain), countless numbers of Indian-origin Tamils by birth and descent have been denied national citizenship. Here, the narrator reaches for a comparison, invoking a national scandal to give meaning to her own sense of social betrayal. Other texts approach the plantation workers' struggles more cautiously, acknowledging limitations and marking communication failings. "Kalapayen Vathukarayata" (From zone to plantation), for example, resists the ethically compromised stance of recognition through assimilation.[36] The exergue preceding the heading identifies this writing as the second part of a serialized letter, but there is no specific addressee. "Put together," not "written by," as the credits disclose, it disclaims unitary authorship and, as such, metonymically mirrors the bricolage aesthetic of the *Dabindu* page. Part reportage, part analysis, part journal entry, embedded speeches (translated, we are told, into Tamil by Sinhala-speaking Tamil activists) take onboard the challenge of opening a collective dialogue in the face of race war (*jathi vadaya*). As one labor activist who is quoted puts it, calling for solidarity in alienation: "I too am a garment factory worker. I don't own what I produce. Plantation workers are the same. Production has no caste, race, or religion. And yet we remain divided in that way" (9). From the margins, though, a personal observation (submitted by "the compiler") provides a quiet counterpoint to slogans. Upon entering the linerooms, she notes: "they welcomed us with love. But how do we inquire about their day-to-day lives? We don't understand Tamil. But this doesn't pose a problem for us because Arumugam speaks Sinhalese. The other brothers and sisters that accompanied us could also speak both Sinhala and Tamil. I felt a sense of shame because the only language I know is Sinhalese."[37] Counter to the communalizing ploys of the Sinhala Commission, texts such as these, as well as others like "Vathu Kamkaru Striya" (Plantation worker woman) and "Kandurelle Kandulu Binduva" (Teardrops from the hills) (both written in the voice consciousness of the plantation worker), imagine cartographies of labor that attempt to displace competing nationalist imaginaries.[38]

CONCLUSION: THE AESTHETICS OF UNITY-IN-DISPERSAL AND THE WORKING-CLASS SUBJECT

While historians of the Sri Lankan trade union movement and ideologues of left party politics cannot imagine a connection, the *Dabindu* writers attempt to articulate the historical and ideological gap between the separate social enclaves of the plantation and free trade zone. In contrast to narratives of trade unionist history, the collective's efforts might be understood, instead, in light of feminist NGOs' ongoing efforts at organizing disparate but related sectors of unorganized labor. A Women's Political Forum pamphlet takes onboard the question of the feminization of the proletariat as a question of national economy: "Women form an important part of the labor force, and their struggles have ended discrimination in pay, compared with men, in many sectors. But especially in rural, unregulated or non-unionized sectors, women receive very low wages and are considered less skilled. Cheap female labor in plantations and factories, foreign employment accounts for the bulk of the country's foreign exchange earnings."[39]

Against the backdrop of trade union history, accounts of transformations in national economy and the changing landscape of feminist organizing, I hope to have demonstrated in this essay how neither the tempo of factory discipline nor the temporality of nationalist development narratives dictates the breaks and resumptions of the *Dabindu* texts. In their stories, poems, and polemical essays *Dabindu* writers imagine labor history as logically prior to national history, but the meaning of history that emerges in these pages is also shaped by conditions and constraints of form. Serial form lends itself to figuring history not as a fait accompli, but as an unfinished process. Against the efforts of metropolitan feminism to bring her into view, no distinctive, *individual* portrait of a textile worker comes into focus. Rather, the political and textual effects of *Dabindu* writings model a unity-in-dispersal. An aesthetic of elliptical marks, interruptions, and speech interferences takes the measure of moments, not monuments, in working-class history and feminist labor struggles.

NOTES

This essay follows the arc of a broader argument developed in my book *All That Is Present and Moving: Working-Class Writing in the Age of Globalization* (Columbia University Press, forthcoming). An earlier, longer version of the essay was published in *differences* (see Perera, "Rethinking Working-Class Literature"). I am grateful to Ritty Lukose and Ania Loomba for their insightful comments and suggestions on previous drafts.

The second epigraph in the introduction, from the periodical *Stri Nirmana*, is taken from "Dear Sisters," a letter signed Kumudini, reprinted in *Stri Nirmana* 42. The direct translation of the title *Stri Nirmana* is "Women's Creative Production/ Making."

All translations from the Sinhala are my own, but I am extremely grateful to Professor Victor Hapuarachchi, formerly of Colombo and Kelaniya Universities, for taking the time to review my work.

1. This is Swasti Mitter's term. Mitter, *Common Fate Common Bond*, 1–24.

2. See Amin, *Unequal Development*, 203–14, on the origins of extraversion. Some might say that globalization has made Amin's and Mitter's observations outdated and only of historical value. But the structures of the international division of labor that they describe persist today, in the interstices of global finance capital.

SONALI PERERA

3. See Olsen, "I Want You Women Up North to Know," 179–81, for an interesting exception.

4. Agnew, "Portrait of a Textile Worker." Clothing labels, thread, fabric backing, 98 x 110 in., at http://tardart.com/html/ptw.php. The representation of the iconic South Asian figure is based on a photograph of a Bangladeshi garment factory worker taken by Charles Kernaghan, the director of the National Labor Committee, on an undercover visit to a factory in Bangladesh.

5. Ibid.

6. The aesthetic effort needs to be supplemented with a commensurate effort at feminist labor internationalism. I call attention to Ananya Bhattarcharjee's work on this score. On November 30, 2004, Bhattacharjee, Ashim Roy, and V. Chandra, among others, presented "A New Path for Indian Labor? International Solidarity in the Age of Outsourcing?" at a forum on outsourcing and organizing convened by the Cornell Global Labor Institute at Ithaca, New York. The conference brought members of the New Trade Union Initiative in India together with a coalition of U.S. unionized workers (affiliated with Jobs for Justice) to discuss prospects for dialogue, solidarity, and effective compromises on a global scale.

7. So goes the preface to *Garment Factory Workers: A Few Selected Interviews by* PEFDA *(Peoples Forum for Development Alternatives)* (Colombo: Centre for Society and Religion, 1998), i.

8. Weerakoon, *The Evolution of Labor Law in Sri Lanka*, 58.

9. Jayawardena, *The Rise of the Labor Movement in Ceylon.*

10. Weerakoon, *The Evolution of Labor Law in Sri Lanka*, 58.

11. A school of cultural anthropological feminism arrives at the same point, through a different historical explanation: Caitrin Lynch offers a painstaking analysis of the language of presidential speeches, reports, and interviews with factory bosses, and finds free trade zone women workers to be unwittingly complicit with a Sinhala nationalist development agenda. See Lynch, "The 'Good Girls' of Sri Lankan Modernity."

12. See Gunasinghe, "Politics of Ethnicity and Religion." Sunil Bastian's ongoing research into the ideological and racialized divide separating the operations of development NGOs and human rights NGOs might be seen as an extension but also redirection of this line of thinking. Such work has implications for how we parse the present history of the NGOization of feminism. See, for example, Bastian, *The Politics of Foreign Aid in Sri Lanka.*

13. This rallying cry, a common slogan of textile industrialists, was taken up in the aftermath of the December 2004 tsunami.

14. See de Alwis, "Feminist Politics and Maternalist Agonism" in the present volume. Her critique of the "professionalization of feminism" builds on Menon, *Recovering Subversion*, 219–20.

15. See Hewamanne, *Stitching Identities in a Free Trade Zone*, 40–43.

16. See Perera, "Rethinking Working-Class Literature," 10–18 and 22–23.

17. I use "postnational" as a postwar term—one that indexes anticipation that the effort at power sharing and openness will be commensurate to a multiethnic polity premised in the devolution of state power.

18. The Janatha Vimukthi Peramuna (in English, People's Liberation Front), or JVP, needs to be distinguished from the Trotskyite old left parties in Sri Lanka. The JVP, it has been argued, once was the voice of the Sinhala-educated unemployed. It is now, since the 1970s insurgency, perhaps better defined as a pseudo-Marxist party in the service of Sinhala nationalism. It continues to be routinely and *incorrectly* described as "Marxist" in newspapers. For a more nuanced reading of this complex phenomenon (which cannot possibly be contained within a footnote), see "The JVP and the Ethnic Question," Jayawardena, *Ethnic and Class Conflict in Sri Lanka*, 95–102. For a general historical overview of Sri Lankan Marxist parties, see also Kearney, "The Marxist Parties of Ceylon."

19. Organizing Committee, preface, *Stri Nirmana*, n.p. The *Stri Nirmana* booklet is the collaborative effort of some *Dabindu* writers and feminist activists of the Women's Education and Research Center in Kandana.

20. Anonymous, "Apatada Nidahasak Natha," *Dabindu* 13, no. 6 (February 1998), 1.

21. Certainly the framing of such questions of subjectivity and representation are not without complications. Perhaps it also remains to be asked whose "interest" does staking a claim for such a subject—one that figures "unity-in-dispersal"— serve? If Spivak's admonition in "Can the Subaltern Speak" (addressed to French poststructuralist thinkers) was not to assume the working class was monolithic, even in the avowed interest of theorizing a coalitional politics, it is an admonition to be heeded also by Marxist-feminist literary critics, even as they reach to articulate the terms of a feminist class politics across the new international division of labor, in the shadow of economisms like comparative advantage—or what has been called the NGOization of feminism.

22. Eagleton, *Literary Theory*, 216. Emphasis mine.

23. Kumudini Samuel, personal communication, Colombo, Sri Lanka, June 16, 2005. This again underscores the fact that Dabindu represents a heterogeneous, dynamic collectivity, rather than a synchronous collective class subject. I am indebted to Kumudini Samuel for drawing my attention to the point that the changing volunteer editors of the periodical (who are not identified or credited in later editions) are affiliated with a range of different feminist and human rights groups in Sri Lanka. There is also an unwritten history of ideological battles and left party politics (such as those of the Revolutionary Marxist Party) associated with the convening of the initial organizational group.

24. Rosa, "The Conditions and Organisational Activities of Women in Free Trade Zones," 75. See also Rosa, "Strategies of Organisation and Resistance."

25. Some of Dabindu's worker education projects were funded by the Canadian International Development Agency during the period 1998–2000. However, the commemorative histories and "self-representations" of Dabindu tend to omit the

specific details of the group's transformation into an NGO. See, for example, H. I. Samanmalie, "The Birth of Dabindu," *Dabindu* 16, no. 1 (September 2000): 2–3.

26. See the cartoon "Mulu Bara Janathava Matha" (The entire weight lies upon the people): a pinstripe-suited, seven-headed G7 monster rides upon the shoulders of the World Bank, personified as riding the "common man"—while sticking a sharp stick (labeled, in English, "condition-alities") into his rear end. The man is shown sweating in his attempt to grab the money bag (labeled $) which the World Bank figure dangles just out of his reach. (It seems particularly interesting that here *Dabindu* represents "the people" in the neocolonialism terms of a sarong-clad man. *Dabindu* 13, no. 3 (November 1997): 1. See also "Bangladesheye Lama Kamkaru Sevaka Prashna" (The question of child-workers in Bangladesh), *Dabindu* 13, no. 3 (November 1997): 2, 8; and "Bangladeheye Kanthavange Aithivasikam" (Bangladeshi women's rights), *Dabindu* 12, no. 10 (July 1997): 2.

27. Hewamanne and Brow, "If They Allow Us We Will Fight," 22.

28. See Deepika Thrima Vitana, "Chintanaya Nidahas Nam" (Thinking freedom), *Dabindu* (June 1994): 4; Charuni Gamage, "Nonimi Ginna" (The unstoppable fire), *Dabindu* 10, no. 12 (March 1994): 6; Deniyaye Arosha, "Mavu Kusin Nova Mihi Kusin SiriLaka Upan Viru Daruvane . . ." (O heroic children born not of mother's womb, but of the earth of mother Lanka . . ."), *Dabindu* (April–May 1998): 6; D. W. Vijayalatha, "Vathu Kamkaru Striya" (The tea plantation worker woman); Swarna P. Galappaththi, "Vathu Kamkaru Striya" (The tea plantation worker woman), *Stri Nirmana* 27, 37; A. C. Perera, "Padada Pathum" (Vagabond wishes), *Dabindu* (June 1994): 5; S. Udayalata Menike, "Mai Dinaya" (May Day), *Dabindu* (April 2000): 6.

29. These ellipses occur in the poem. The word "garment," here, is shorthand for "garment industry," *aghalum karmanthaya*, properly, but here the colloquial term is rendered from English into phonetic Sinhala. It is important to consider the "universality" of this lexicalization across the South, and Southeast Asia, where "garment" always "means" garment industry or garment factory, lexicalized into the mother tongue.

30. See the proposal advocating decentralization and devolution: Sri Lankan Branch, Committee for Democracy and Justice in Sri Lanka, "Yudha Umathuva Parajaya Kara Deshapalana Visaduma Perata Gena Emu" (Let's defeat the call for war and push for a parliamentary solution), *Dabindu* (September–October 1995): 3.

31. Deepika Thrima Vitana, "Chintanaya Nidahas Nam" (Thinking freedom), *Dabindu* (June 1994): 4. The direct translation of the title would actually involve the subjunctive mood construction: "if . . . were": "If there were freedom of the act-of-thinking."

32. K. G. Jayasundera Manike's "Jivithaya" (Life) is quoted in its entirety in Rosa, "The Conditions and Organisational Activities of Women in Free Trade Zones" and in Gunaratna, *A Review of Free Trade Zones in Sri Lanka*.

33. Tony Davies, "Unfinished Business," 125.

34. It is over and against the ideological construction of "woman" in these official texts of historiography that I read the literature of these factory workers in an attempt to approach how woman as subject for history is imagined. See Lynch, "The 'Good Girls' of Sri Lankan Modernity."

35. "Hasuna" (Letter), *Dabindu* 15, no. 12 (August 2000), 7.

36. Somalatha, "Kalapayen Vathukarayata" (From zone to plantation), *Dabindu* 13, no. 1 (September 1997), 8–9.

37. Ibid., 8.

38. In August 2001, a militant nationalist organization calling itself the Sinhala Commission recommended to the ruling government that, as a means of righting British colonial wrongs, it take measures to retroactively deny citizenship to the descendents of Indian-origin Tamil workers, imported as indentured labor to serve on the coffee and tea plantations of the colonial period. The recommendation constitutes a scandalous use of the epistemology of postcolonialism in the service of Sinhala nationalism. In a Sri Lanka still riven in the aftermath of an inter-ethnic war, working-class history is daily being erased and reconstructed by political institutions such as the Sinhala Commission. To this end, I do not construe the (Sinhala) *Dabindu* periodicals as *the* representative example of Sri Lankan working-class creative production, but rather as one formation among many underresearched examples within the literature of labor and feminism.

39. The statement continues with recommendations addressed to politicians and employees: "While particular attention has to be paid to working women's wages, hours of work, and work and living conditions—their right to organize, their right to health facilities and crèches and other benefits—must also be addressed by politicians and employers." Women's Political Forum, *Women's Manifesto 2001* (Colombo, n.d.), 9.

ANANNYA BHATTACHARJEE

Feminism, Migration, and Labor
Movement Building in a Globalized World

PROLOGUE

My political engagements have been shaped by my migration
and journeys within and between India and the United States,
against the backdrop of unprecedented globalization and migration. The United States is a country shaped by both immigration from all parts of the world and by global domination. In
India, international and interstate migration in search of employment are growing exponentially and changing the urban
landscape. Migration gives every context shifting complexities,
making them dynamic and ever changing. Migration not only
changes the home but also the destination, not just external
objective conditions but also internal subjectivities.

My own political engagements moved between, and were
anchored by, struggles against U.S. imperialism, women's oppression, and the subjugation of the global working class. In
my attempts to use immigration/emigration policies as tools to
further these struggles, I discovered bourgeois feminisms, radical feminisms, revolutionary politics, antiracist politics, Marx-
isms, communism, socialism, and struggles for democracy. As a
woman, as a feminist of color, as a Third World feminist, I have
found that whether my work is within or peripheral to the
women's movement, I am nonetheless influenced by feminism's
potential for combining objective and subjective politics.

In this essay, I explore political trajectories that are perforce intertwined with personal journeys. I relate my own personal narrative in order to demonstrate how objective and subjective experiences anchored in migration give rise to a certain set of politics. In the contemporary world, migration—much like industrialization or colonization at other historical junctures—shapes our politics. Yet it is greatly underestimated by the Left as a political phenomenon precisely because it must be understood not just objectively but also subjectively, a type of understanding that is undervalued by exclusively orthodox, class-centered left politics.

Feminism, which is very useful in unraveling subjectivities, helps us understand conditions that create and are shaped by migration. However, the practice of unraveling subjectivities without due attention to objective conditions has been a continual source of danger in bourgeois feminisms practiced by dominant women's movements. Such feminisms end up becoming what they began fighting—from the frying pan of patriarchal universalities to the fire of bourgeois feminist universalities. Even in radical feminisms, which have been redefined over the years by women of color and Third World women, the issue of class is often the "elephant in the room." These questions, shortcomings, and potentials are long-standing ones, and important reminders for us to think without complacency of our engagements with feminism as part of a freshly critical process.

As a theorist, one can embrace a dynamic process that challenges universal definitions and essentialisms and allows for a state of answers-in-the-making. But as an activist, one has to strive toward comprehensive resolutions that clinch matters. After all, one would like to move from a revolution that is always in the making to a revolution that is more or less made. This complex state of affairs—balancing the continual unraveling of shifting subjectivities in the context of objective conditions, while at the same time capturing political moments and implementing conclusive strategies—is where the rubber of feminist theories hits the road of radical and revolutionary practice.

THE FRAME OF MY JOURNEY

During my journey of political development in the context of migration, feminisms have been a constant, but often publicly unacknowledged, companion. My journey to the United States was triggered by oppressive shackles that I struggled against as a girl growing up in a traditional lower-middle-class family in urban India. With financial assistance, I arrived in the United States as an undergraduate student. To my surprise, I found my new environs to be at once empty and dislocating yet thick and hard to maneuver within. It would take enormous effort just to get up in the morning, and each morning that I did get up seemed like a personal victory.

The public university I attended drew students like a beacon from all over the U.S. South. It had poor and working-class students, mainly white but with a small black and growing Chicano population, as well as very rich students. The majority of the South Asian students came from wealthy families and sought upward mobility. I found this Indian community to be quite foreign to me. Had we been in India, our paths would have been unlikely to cross. But here I suddenly found myself in social gatherings with them, thrown into their mix by the dynamics of immigration. The cooperative I stayed in mainly attracted white low-income students. I was the only South Asian in the co-ops. It was easier, I found, to connect across racial gaps with white women and women of color than it was to connect across class gaps with other South Asians.

I remember the first of the numerous political meetings that I attended on that campus. It was a meeting of students who were engaged in solidarity work broadly defined as peace and justice work. Although South Asians were not entirely invisible, they were absent in such settings, especially in the southern United States. At this innocuous enough political meeting, called to support political prisoners, I had my first encounter with the struggles of the legendary imprisoned Native American revolutionary Leonard Peltier, who opened a window in my heart.[1] I had found my place at last and took a whole-hearted plunge into campus politics in the following years. I felt a spark light up inside me that drew me out of the nameless depression that had haunted me in India and that had beset me after my arrival in this foreign country. Although I did not realize it at the time, I had begun my search for "community" as a new immigrant in the United States.

I became deeply involved in the opposition to the U.S. invasion of Central America and in the antiapartheid movement. I primarily identified with left student movements, even though I was the sole Indian presence in such organizations. These spaces allowed me to connect my subjectivity with different political traditions. During the years that I—a woman in a lower-middle-class family from West Bengal—was growing up, Naxalbari became synonymous in the world's eyes with revolutionary politics. At the same time, my family raged with a violence that penetrated the most intimate sphere. Although I engaged with anti-imperialism struggles in the public sphere, I engaged with feminism in the private sphere as I struggled to shed the shackles of my upbringing.

I was initially surprised to find that involving Central American foreign students in anti-imperialist movements in the United States was next to impossible. Then I realized that these students were from wealthy, anti-revolutionary families. Political and economic refugees and underground workers, fleeing from the U.S.-backed military violence in Central America, were struggling just to remain alive in the United States. The disconnect between anti-imperialist struggles and the communities that are products of such imperialism convinced me of the need to rethink my own engagements.

By the time I left college—forced out prematurely by the administration in retaliation for my campus activities—I had come to believe that U.S.-based anti-imperialist struggles are crucial but cannot sustain a deep popular support until they are integrated with domestic struggles. Important as they are, such struggles do not facilitate solidarity based on political equality and reciprocity across the poles of imperialist relationships. Without this solidarity, imperialism cannot be comprehensively confronted. Anti-imperialist struggles need to be built from the inside out in order to make politically equal and reciprocal relationships possible. It is important to work for change from within the United States because anti-imperialist solidarity with people from other nations can only take place after local solidarity has been formed among people within one nation. It is harder and takes longer, but it is necessary.

Domestic economic struggles within the United States are not conventionally analyzed within the framework of global imperialism. This means that antiwar and anti-imperialist movements are usually not associated with movements for economic justice. This distinction is maintained by spurious analytical disjunctures between the state and the market: the state controls the military while the market is "free," the state grants public benefits while the market does not, the state is democratic while the market is capitalist, the state is patriotic while the market has borderless loyalties that must be brought into line by the patriotic state. These disjunctures are

ANANNYA BHATTACHARJEE

further solidified when conflicts between capital and labor within national borders are seen as wholly unrelated from the nation-state's attempt to militarily tame inter(national) capital. Ultimately, this leads to an analytical and operational disconnect between those involved in domestic, corporate-focused economic justice movements and those involved in international, nation-state-focused antiwar movements. The dialectical relationships between market and nation-state, between inter(national) capital and "foreign" (often used as a euphemism for "military") policy, are lost. This gap between social justice and anti-imperialist movements needs to be urgently addressed, especially at a time when the migration of working people, mobility of capital across borders, and geopolitical power struggles are integrally linked across a world drawn increasingly closer through technology and communication.

Moving to New York City, I joined the ranks of the new immigrants in one of the fastest-growing new immigrant communities in the country. I began to feel the personal and political importance of linking with local communities and people with whom I could share my immigration history. For the most part, the South Asian community had a limited history of civic engagement. Given my belief in the importance of enlisting local communities within the United States in antiwar and anti-imperialist movements, and given that social justice work had not yet taken hold in the South Asian community, I decided that this was an important place for me to start both types of organizing. However, anti-imperialist and social justice work require very different types of knowledge and skill sets. I knew little about immigration history in the United States, and could only sense that I was experiencing a time of massive changes in the South Asian immigrant community, without being able to grasp the historical significance of these changes.

I organized in the South Asian community as an Indian immigrant woman, the subjectivity immediately available to me. I began by helping to establish a women's organization. Violence against women had silently shaped my politics and pulled me into the world of feminism. Gradually I became more deeply engaged with the problems of state violence against immigrants and U.S.-born people of color. Around the time of the historic protests against the World Trade Organization in Seattle in the year 2000, I was drawn into the movement against the imperialist globalization policies of the U.S. government. However, once again, I found externally oriented anti-imperialist globalization activism functioning without links to local communities within the United States. Like many other colleagues who worked in immigrant communities and communities of color, I began to believe even more strongly that antiglobalization movements must be linked to immigrant communities adversely affected by globalization within the United States in conjunction with the home countries of these communities.

When organization for the World Social Forum in Brazil began, I hoped to find room to develop grassroots links between communities of color in the United States and movements in the global South. When it was decided that the World Social Forum was going to be held in India, I returned to India to organize and try to build the North-South linkages that seemed so politically urgent. Since that time, a binational, biregional, or North-South framework has remained an important part of my work. However, my firm belief that such work would have to be located in the grass roots of both countries or regions continues to define my own practice. My belief has been strengthened by a realization that new paths for social transformation have to be created in this fast changing world. The only way to chart freshly conceived left politics in the rapidly globalizing world is from the bottom up. Only through such a process can one arrive at a sturdy theoretical base.

Today, migration is a defining feature of local communities all over the world. Such communities are shaped by the multiple interactions within various contexts that migrants carry with them. Contemporary social movements cannot ultimately succeed without absorbing the implications of this dynamic, along with its multidimensional context, which has been formed by the unprecedented scale of domestic and international migration in search of jobs, the emergence of new structures of work and labor, and shifting loyalties of nationality, region, race, and caste. Efforts for social transformation cannot succeed unless they pay attention to the intersecting economic, social, and political dimensions of communities in an increasingly mobile world. Attempts to simplify or gloss over complexities only fracture social movement building along already existing fault lines. Yet, in practice, it is sometimes necessary to gloss over complexities. Either too much or too little glossing can make or break a movement. The task is theoretically and operationally challenging, yet it is critical to building robust contemporary movements. How, then, does one build feminist global movements against capitalist exploitation in the global North and

South, while paying due attention to the regional imperatives of developing economies? How does one build solidarity in an unequal world? Finally, what is a responsible and expansive feminism?

SOUTH TO NORTH: POLITICS OF MIGRATION AND
VIOLENCE AGAINST WOMEN

Indian immigration to the United States has, since the early twentieth
century, ebbed and flowed according to changes in the political impetus
and labor needs of the United States. Pravin Sheth writes about a community of about five thousand Sikhs who worked in fig orchards, vineyards,
and rice lands in California.[2] He distinguishes between these early immigrants, who struggled against anti-immigrant sentiments in California and
at the same time "actively took up the cause of nationalism by helping
India's struggle for freedom from the British," and the post-1965 immigrants who, "free from psycho-political environment, were more involved
in their individual economic and professional pursuits."[3] In the last two decades, immigration has swelled the Asian population in the United States to
at least 10.2 million. The largest increase during this period was in the
number of immigrants coming from India.[4] This second wave of South
Asians followed a trend of migration from the Third World and postcolonial countries during the postindustrial period in the United States. Juan
Gonsalez notes that unlike earlier European immigrants who arrived at the
turn of the twentieth century, postindustrial immigrants to the United
States could no longer use unskilled factory jobs as a path to middle-class
life.[5] This was also a period of increasing American dominance against the
backdrop of the rise of postcolonial independent nation-states.

Following earlier decades that witnessed independence movements
worldwide, civil rights struggles, women's movements, and identity-based
rights movements, the 1980s saw the Reagan era and the rise of the Right.
The proliferation of nonprofits and the privatization of social struggles
began to smooth out the edges of radical politics, so that protest began to
seem like a well-behaved routine. The organized union movement was
decaying in anti-immigrant and racist politics. Feminist practices had
moved far from earlier revolutionary goals to focus on individualistic
change and careerist feminism. Professional notions of service provision
had ossified to become the dominant strand. Meanwhile, other forms of

more radical feminist analysis rooted in colonialism and racism, and responsive to African American, Latina, and other marginalized communities were not immediately visible. The practice of organizing labor outside organized unions in immigrant communities and communities of color was in its infancy.

In the 1980s, the South Asian immigrant community was beginning to be recognized as a growing and significant immigrant community. A group of women, including myself, began to come together and respond to the widespread domestic violence faced by South Asian women in the New York metropolitan area. We saw this issue as a window through which we could find, serve, and therefore engage with South Asians. In the process, we established the second South Asian women's organization in the country and the first one in a region that was the largest home to South Asians.[6] The organization developed crisis response tools for handling calls for help from women facing family violence. It was conceived as a means of locating and serving an already existing community. However, as it became clear to us, a view of community as static and only to be located is historically inaccurate; it is often adopted by new immigrants such as myself who perceive themselves to be entering into preexisting communities. A new immigrant may assume communities-in-existence, unaware of his or her role in fashioning communities-in-formation. Responding to a crisis is also an intervention in the latent process of a community-in-formation. Intervening in violence against women as a defensive act modeled around social work and management, as opposed to social transformation or constructive community-building, risks becoming self-referential and limiting. Such efforts are ultimately unable to leverage the power of community-based work for social transformation, as they continue to relegate the domain of the social and the ideological to regressive or value-neutral forces.[7]

Intervening in minority community formation through a defensive crisis mechanism reinforces a sense of marginalization and victimhood. When disconnected from a broader framework for radical transformation, this can ultimately drain constructive energy and promote a nontransformative, paternalistic feminism. In this context, women's organizations grappled with questions of the ethnic identity of the person who answers the survivor's call for assistance, the kind of food served in shelters and at meetings, culturally sensitive counseling, cultural training for law enforcement, etc. All these issues are important; but rather than being means to

ANANNYA BHATTACHARJEE

an end, they became ends in themselves. The more feminist practices remained trapped within parameters of ethnic difference, the more the discourse of the homogeneity of oppression and victimhood flourished. As Chandra Mohanty puts it, "the *discursively consensual homogeneity* of women as a group is mistaken for the historically specific material reality of groups of women."[8]

SOUTH TO NORTH: POLITICS OF MIGRATION AND LABOR

At a later stage, South Asian domestic workers began to approach our organization because they faced terrible exploitation from their employers. During the process of working with them, several new contradictions developed.[9] Whereas earlier they could come together as women, the question of labor practices now ruptured any unity assumed on the basis of gender. Their employers might also be South Asian survivors of domestic violence. Whereas these survivors could claim a feminist space within the discourse of family, the issues raised by domestic workers marked the limits of such feminist spaces. Organizational commitment to gender violence did not easily stretch to issues of class exploitation.[10] The organization's inability to take on board class oppression had a cascading effect on its understanding of race and ethnicity. A women's movement responsive to class analysis could have accommodated these new working-class identity formations; but such a movement was absent in the United States. Working with these women, I learned that gender violence among the working class could not be isolated from issues of class and labor. The domestic workers came from classes in their home countries that ranged from lower middle to middle class. Some were working for wages for the first time, and class conflict was new to many of them. They spiraled down in class and status, which had previously been guaranteed only through marriage or positions within a family structure that was now lost to them. It was only a matter of time before the class consciousness would seep into a previously presumed gender unity. Exchanges and meetings with organized workers greatly helped politicize their identities as workers.

I continued organizing domestic workers and later worked with efforts to organize workers in small-scale retail shops, restaurants, and taxi companies. Collective organizing among domestic workers was more conceivable than among survivors of domestic violence because the labor movement has a collective organizing and bargaining orientation. In a political space where unions were not immediately visible or accessible, we were attracted to the emerging form of community-based worker organizing under the banner of worker centers. Community organizations *were* both visible and accessible, and originated from within ethnically defined organizations designed to attend to workers ignored by mainstream unions. I joined with others who were organizing among immigrant workers through such centers, which existed outside mainstream unions until the U.S. union movement made explicit its commitment to immigrant workers in 2000. I learned the fallacy of looking at workers as disembodied workplace units shorn of political and social history, and that organizing workers means taking on the intersections of many isms and discovering new ones.

THE NORTHERN STATE'S LAW ENFORCEMENT
AND MILITARIZATION: TWO SIDES OF A BORDER

Organizing around gender violence and, later, around labor exploitation among immigrant communities and communities of color revealed the intimate role played by a nation-state's law enforcement machinery. It also showed me that such organizing could not long avoid taking on issues of state violence. Fear of police and immigration authorities was a paramount factor wherever I worked. This was even more the case after September 11, when "safety" and "security" became watchwords in the United States. The term "safety" was undoubtedly used to refer to freedom from *exclusively* warlike violence of the kind that 9/11 had come to represent in the popular imagination. The term "security" was in turn *narrowed* to exclusively refer to measures that provide safety from such warlike violence. This exclusivity allowed the U.S. administration to focus, within and outside its borders, on the virtues of a primarily militaristic government, embodied in the War on Terror.

Historically, in the United States the concept of civil citizenship—encompassing individual liberties and rights—was richly elaborated, while the concept of social citizenship—the idea that citizens are entitled to a modicum of security and a decent standard of living—was largely absent.[11] The state is primarily motivated by the logic of law and order. Social

ANANNYA BHATTACHARJEE

problems such as substance abuse, homelessness, poverty, secure housing, labor law violations, and the quality of public education are translated into law-and-order problems whose solution is more law enforcement. The critical discourse on law enforcement is insufficiently attentive to this logic. An individualistic, and one may add masculinist, rights framework erases any sense of community within which individual men and women live their lives. Law and order is viewed as a "hard sector"—characterized by weapons, uniformed officers, drugs, and violent crime—with no relevance for the "soft sector"—home life, children, job security, health, and safety. Unless we analyze and integrate into our work the implications of such a state, we will not be able to formulate comprehensive strategies within our movements.[12]

The insufficient integration of the issue of state violence into movements around economic justice or gender violence also affects the ability of U.S.-based movements to understand the place of the U.S. government's military deployments in furthering the corporate-led globalization policies of the U.S. government. Domestic law enforcement is directed primarily toward communities of color and immigrants, and the U.S. military actions are directed toward these communities' countries of origin. Angela Davis's statement is instructive: "Those of us who have been active in the anti-prison movement for the last decade or so have noticed a striking resemblance between the representation of the terrorist and the representation of the criminal. In many ways, the public was already prepared for the mobilization of nationalist emotions based on fear of a racialized enemy."[13]

In order to understand more fully the implications of a state devoted to a law-and-order framework, we need to understand the impact of law enforcement on issues of basic security—which have also been cornerstones of feminist movements—such as home life, care giving, reproduction, sexuality, and paid work. The U.S. government's global policing outside its borders and its criminalizing of social injustices within its borders must be politically connected. History shows that when movements fighting state violence domestically joined the fight against U.S. imperialism abroad, the result was a rapid internationalization of communities that were trapped in miseries within the borders of the United States. In fact I would go further to say that as long as U.S. anti-imperialist and antiglobalization movements are delinked from the role of the U.S. law enforcement and military within and outside the U.S. borders, they will not be able to connect on terms of equality and reciprocity with struggles in other nations.

TWO POLES OF NORTH AND SOUTH

Some years ago, I became engaged in binational work between India and the United States. At this time, I became determined to forge the missing links between left movements based in immigrant communities and communities of color in the United States and these communities' home countries. As the binational work grew, we were called upon to assist in the fierce struggles around H-2B, or guest worker, visas (for nonagricultural workers) among labor and immigrant rights activists in the United States, who claim that this visa is a modern-day form of indentured labor.[14] One scandal involved the U.S.-based company Signal International using Indian and American recruiters to bring hundreds of skilled manufacturing workers from India to the United States on H-2B visas only to subject them to fraud, terror, and exploitation. The nexus of trafficking in cheap labor, coercion, state-supported raids, detention, and criminalization has placed unsuspecting and vulnerable workers in the grip of unemployment, terror, and desperation. These workers have been fighting for justice against fraudulent recruiting by Indian and U.S. recruiters, and exploitation by Signal International. They have raised issues of labor rights, immigrant rights, fraudulence, and dignity.

In India, in the meantime, wives, children, and retired parents form the bulk of the H-2B workers' dependents. In India we initiated a parallel organizing effort to develop a network of the families of the workers. They have raised issues about India's emigration policy, the connections between human rights and labor rights, national sovereignty, and workers' remittances. This binational organizing effort continues to build a narrative and path of struggle spanning the two countries. Just as the issue of economic injustice is inextricably linked to state violence in the United States, the issue of development is connected to that of remittances and state negligence in India. The concepts of national sovereignty and jurisdiction are often deployed by the state to abdicate responsibility for workers and their families.

Both the United States and the Indian state claim an entitlement over workers and their families when it comes to sanctioning multinationals'

ANANNYA BHATTACHARJEE

need for their labor, facilitating recruiting agents' profits and access across borders, and adding revenue from workers' remittances to national coffers. Both states claim to lack jurisdictional power when it comes to protecting the legal rights of the workers, holding multinational companies and recruiting agents responsible for violations, and protecting workers' families who sink into poverty as a result of this transnational transaction. At the same time that the workers are denied legal status in the United States, the Indian government claims that they are outside the domain of Indian sovereignty. Thus they become subjects not recognized by either state. The binational campaign highlights such enforced statelessness and attempts to connect disrupted households across borders.

GLOBAL MARKET-LED DEVELOPMENT
IN THE SOUTH AND INTERSTATE MIGRATION

Binational work next led to my involvement in an industrial collective bargaining campaign, the Asia Floor Wage campaign, across the global supply chain of one of the world's oldest global industries, the garment industry.[15] My physical proximity to one of the largest urban industrial hubs in the world producing garments for the global market—the National Capital Region, which includes Delhi, Haryana, Uttar Pradesh—drew me to this vast pool of unorganized workers. Most of the workers are migrants, backward castes, Dalits, or Muslims from regions in India that have been devastated by wanton industrialization, landlessness, and unemployment.[16] Gurgaon's industrial area, one major site in the capital region, is a place of dislocation operating within newly developing capitalist regimes. Fairness and justice seem remote, while brute force and survival are the realities of the working class. Gurgaon thus mixes new capitalist structures with almost feudal powers and practices. Politically and culturally desolate, Gurgaon's single focus is on production and profit. Other places like Gurgaon are increasingly being developed around urban areas and along highway corridors.[17]

Gurgaon's development has drawn hundreds of thousands of migrant workers from poorer states in India such as Bihar, Orissa, Uttar Pradesh, Jharkhand, and West Bengal. According to official numbers from the Gurgaon district website the employment generated in the current industrial sector exceeds 200,000. The police commissioner in Gurgaon claims that there are 1,000,000 migrants.[18] Workers and local residents in these areas claim that there are over 2,500,000 migrant workers. These workers are nonentities as far as state-recognized subjects go. Although migrant workers have been staying in the area for many years, they do not have legal identification and are not counted by the census. Government data or any other research data are not available for this population, which remains neglected and hidden in the shadows of illegality. There is no indication that the government has any plans to satisfy the development needs of this huge workforce, which exists fewer than twenty kilometers away from the Parliament of India.

The migrant workers very rarely possess any kind of identification. The election officer at Gurgaon admits that migrant workers and their families are rarely on the voters list. This means that they lack voter IDs, which are critically important documents because they indicate legality. Without a voter ID, workers are considered vagrants, are unable to hold bank accounts, educate their children, or buy groceries through the public distribution system. They are essentially noncitizens. The wanton exploitation that workers suffer daily prevents them from getting voter IDs. Caught in a catch-22, they are unable to get necessary documents proving their residence and earnings precisely because they do not have voter IDs and so cannot open bank accounts and demand rent agreements. Working round the clock seven days a week, workers are unable to access services during government office hours. They also fear government authorities because of their experiences of discrimination and violence. Even if workers do manage to fill out forms correctly, when inspectors are sent to workers' residences for verification, the workers may be in the factory and local landlords deny that they live there.

While the condition of being a noncitizen is ubiquitous, the working class in Gurgaon is anything but monolithic. It is not possible to develop meaningful strategies without intentionally and systematically delving into the problems that obstruct community building and unity of purpose. We found that a workers' organization here needs to be woven out of various threads of organizing efforts that reflect the diversity of the workers themselves, situated within the context of production that is the central force bringing the diverse workers together at a given place and time. Workers' social relations are extremely complex and deeply rooted in layered identities—such as home village, home district, religion, caste, gender, class,

ANANNYA BHATTACHARJEE

language, and dialect. Unity can be transitory and circumstantial; it can also be deep and lasting. Workers may be longtime migrants who have not stabilized their living arrangements. In this scenario, if community formation is delayed indefinitely, migrants may sink into a stagnated state of noncommunity. Yet another danger is that migrants may find refuge in informal social groupings defined on parochial terms. These conditions can bring paralysis to organizing.

Community organizing is about overcoming this paralysis. For a worker to identify as a worker is not the same as identifying as a member of the working class. Without an analysis of economic and political systems of power, community formations based on social identities have no other result except to bring to the surface latent parochial identities or short-term opportunistic alliances. Such articulations, without the lens of contested powers, allow for immersion in feel-good familiarity, which is important but not sufficient to fight against exploitation and oppression. Moreover, the working class is not a monolithic identity. As Marx himself said, "The human essence is no abstraction inherent in each single individual. In its reality it is the ensemble of the social relations."[19] This is especially true today where migration and displacement are restructuring social relations rapidly and, for the working class, adding a new chaotic and exploitative dimension. Evelyn Nakano Glenn says in the context of the United States, "Race and gender are organizing principles of social institutions. Social arrangements, such as labor market segmentation, residential segregation, and stratification of government benefits along race and gender lines, produce and reproduce real-life difference."[20] To this I would add the issue of *migration* as it relates to social relations of production.

Gurgaon is an example of interstate migration in what is termed an emerging economy—in other words, a national economy that has decided to join the ranks of neoliberal economic policies, and whose priorities are to serve global market needs regardless of the needs of people within its borders. As I complete this essay, we are in the midst of two types of state-sponsored violence within India in the service of global capital. One is the Indian government's full-scale national-level military deployment to "wipe out" so-called Maoist guerrillas and Naxalites—oft-used euphemisms for the armed *and* nonviolent democratic struggles of India's most exploited people against multinational extractive industries. The other is state-sponsored violence in Gurgaon, where management, with the explicit and implicit support of the police force and the state government, murdered one and seriously injured forty workers at a lockout site outside a manufacturing company. Paramilitary forces were subsequently deployed on a peaceful assembly.

FEMINIST PRIORITIES AND RESPONSIBILITIES

I find it useful to break down the task of organizing migrant labor into two components: first, identity articulation and community assertion; second, organization and movement building. These are not discrete or sequential phases, but are rather in dialectic relation with one another. I find them to be helpful markers in the migrant circuits of organizing. Feminism's ability to combine subjective and objective politics in theory and in practice provides a valuable framework for understanding and harnessing identity articulation. Identity is both static and dynamic, grounded in instant reality, as well as in history. At any given time, a person may articulate different aspects of his or her identity. The choice of which aspect to articulate is not based on a singular internal authentic voice but rather out of a need or desire to establish one's relationship to the contemporary reality.

In my work, a curious situation has arisen repeatedly: while the articulation of identities is an important step toward unraveling the complexity of workers' conditions, not all identities are conducive to building class consciousness. As Ernesto Laclau and Chantal Mouffe have warned, "working class" may be the name of a specific position occupied by particular agents, but other positions occupied by these agents are not necessarily also working class.[21] However, to sidestep this process altogether threatens the building of lasting class consciousness and unity. The question then arises, how does one facilitate identity articulation for social transformation? Identity articulation can be a radicalizing process or a taming process, raising fundamental issues of transformation versus accommodation.

Another aspect of identity articulation is critical. The discourse on migrants' identity is central to defining citizenship in the broad sense of entitlements, or the "public" in both domestic and international contexts. This is the "public" that benefits from public assistance, state welfare, public schools, public hospitals, and public voting. It is the visible public that has access to law and order. An image that springs to mind is a negative of a photo: the lighter or highlighted portions of the picture are the immigrants or people of color or the nonpublic. But what they serve to define are outlying areas in dark shades that are the substance of citizenship or public. The discourse is not about who is an entitled member of the public, but rather about who is not. The "migrant" is a crucial category whose negated presence defines "local," "nonmigrant," and "static" publics.

In this dynamic situation, it becomes even more necessary for organizers to have clarity about the purpose of identity articulation. Is the purpose of identity articulation to stimulate critical participation, to ultimately develop class consciousness, to develop a democratic society, to facilitate public participation, or is it something else? As Bill Fletcher Jr. says, "Any illusion, accepted by workers, can become a material obstacle to the development of class consciousness and the blocking of forward motion."[22] Choice of identity can become such an obstacle.

Feminism has taught me the theory and practice of deconstruction and reconstruction of subjectivities on individual and collective levels. Earlier, I introduced the notion of communities-in-formation. And since "what has been exploded is the idea and the reality itself of a unique space of constitution of the political," the power lies in the strategic articulation of identities that simultaneously affirms differences and confirms common interests, leading to communities that have the potential for realizing liberation and transformation.[23] "Undoubtedly, there is no essential necessity for these demands to be articulated in this way. But nor is there an essential necessity for them to be articulated in any other way, given that the relation of articulation is not a relation of necessity. What the discourse of 'historical interests' does is to make hegemonic certain demands."[24] Organizing within a framework of migration requires paying close attention to identity articulation and community assertion that are building blocks for social transformation.

Organizations are vehicles through which collectives can act. Identity articulation and community assertion can result in action only through methodical organization building. However, like identity and community, organization building can also follow innumerable paths. The choice of path should be self-consciously guided toward the larger goal. Having experienced the wide spectrum of nonprofits as well as mainstream trade unions in the United States, I have learned that building efficient organizations does not necessarily lead to building transformative organizations, or politically effective organizations. At the same time, my experiences in India have taught me that politically articulate organizations do not necessarily deliver without efficiency in functioning. Comparing organization building in India and the United States has taught me the value of both types.

Movement building is essentially about building relationships that link unrelated organizations. Migrants carry the seeds for making spatial connections between the center and the periphery, slowly overturning those very definitions in the process. At the heart of movement building resides the desire to achieve a dream that is beyond the reach of any single organization or country. Identity articulation and community assertion, organization and movement building, require a dialectical process of breaking old molds and building new ones across new geographies. At the heart of this process is the desire for a just world for those who are oppressed and exploited, and a deep appreciation for the complexities of identities and communities that have been further complicated by migration and mobility. The laborious construction of the working class, globally—not in an essentialist manner, but qualified by the complexities analyzed above—is the task at hand. For practical organizers with operational obligations, it is important to understand multifarious struggles and at the same time be able to identify anchoring nodes that are historically informed. The working class continues to be a central anchor that has withstood the test of history.

I have tried to suggest in this essay that a political anchor need not be a rusted and rigid weight. An anchor must be positioned thoughtfully as it endures through the waves of migration. It must stand the test of an intersectional politics intensified by the contemporary phenomenon of migration that transposes center and periphery. Feminism has taught me the importance of discursive as well as material transformation. Feminism, by itself, is a subjective phenomenon with limited power. Feminism's strength and power comes from its thoughtful, care-giving, and militant interactions and intersections with objective conditions. It is transformed and becomes transformative.

NOTES

1. Leonard Peltier, a member of the American Indian Movement, was sentenced in 1977 to two consecutive terms of life imprisonment for the murder of two FBI agents during a 1975 shootout on the Pine Ridge Indian Reservation.

2. Sheth, *Indians in America*, 19.

3. Ibid., 39.

4. El Nasser and Overberg, "Census Shows Growth among Asians," *USA Today*, May 11, 2011.

5. Gonsalez, *Harvest of Empire*, xiv.

6. Bhattacharjee, "Habit of Ex-nomination."

7. Bhattacharjee, "Migration and Organising."

8. Mohanty, *Feminism without Borders*, 23.

9. Bhattacharjee, "Immigrant Dreams and Nightmares."

10. Bhattacharjee, "A Slippery Path."

11. Ibid., 31.

12. "Law enforcement" refers to police agencies, prison systems, the U.S. Border Patrol and interior immigration enforcement agents, U.S. Customs, and the rapidly expanding immigration detention system. Both activists and researchers have noted an increasing integration of seemingly disparate law-enforcement systems of immigration and criminal justice.

13. Davis, "Reflections on Post–September 11 America," 326.

14. H-2B workers are legally bound to particular employers.

15. See asiafloorwage.org.

16. The term "backward caste" is a commonly used term to refer to those castes that belong to what the state designates as "Other Backward Classes," caste groups understood to be historically discriminated against within the Hindu caste system. The term "backward" commonly refers to the status of these groups as economically and socially disadvantaged.

17. Bhattacharjee, "Migration and Organising," 149.

18. Society for Labour and Development and the Indian Social Institute, *Gurgaon: How the Other Half Lives* (New Delhi, November 2009).

19. Marx, "Theses on Feuerbach," 145.

20. Glenn, *Unequal Freedom*, 14.

21. Laclau and Mouffe, *Hegemony and Socialist Strategy*, 119.

22. Speech at Labor Notes Conference, *Labor Net*, September 2003, http://www.labornet.org/news/0903/fletch.htm.

23. Quotation from Laclau and Mouffe, *Hegemony and Socialist Strategy*, 184.

24. Ibid., 121.

III

FEMINISM, WAR, AND PEACE

VASUKI NESIAH

Uncomfortable Alliances
Women, Peace, and Security in Sri Lanka

SECURITY COUNCIL RESOLUTION 1325 AND FEMINIST ACTIVISM

Postindependence Sri Lanka has seen a decades-long struggle over the terms of pluralism and interethnic justice carried out by multiple actors on multiple terrains—from Parliament to the battlefield, from the realm of popular culture to the realm of law and constitutional rights. The peace process that stretched from 2000 to 2006 was a phase in this complex history, which evinced an unprecedented level of international engagement. Sandwiched by periods of high-intensity war, the 2002 ceasefire negotiated by the Norwegian government inaugurated a fraught peace process between the government of Sri Lanka armed forces and the Liberation Tigers of Tamil Eelam (LTTE). In October 2002, just as the peace process was gathering momentum, a network of multiethnic women's groups in Sri Lanka launched a fact-finding mission to assess and draw attention to women's experience of the war and priorities for peace.[1] Their report led to the formation of the all-woman Sub-Committee on Gender Issues, with five nominees each from the government and the LTTE, mandated to "explore the effective inclusion of gender concerns in the peace process."[2] The subcommittee "sought to identify issues of concern to women and bring those into the agenda of the peace process. This mechanism is possibly the first of its kind established within a formal peace process at a pre-substantive stage of negotiations."[3] The subcommittee was inserted into the framework of the official process so that it could report directly to the plenary sessions of talks between the government and the LTTE.[4]

The resulting report and the Sub-Committee on Gender Issues itself were heralded at the time as success stories for U.N. Security Council Resolution 1325, passed by the Security Council in 2000 to focus on the gendered impact of war and the potential contribution of women to peace building.[5] Its advocates celebrated the resolution as the first Security Council action focused exclusively on women.[6] The resolution urges member states, U.N. agencies, and other parties involved in conflict to take measures to prevent violence against women and incorporate "women's participation" and "gender perspectives" in domains such as conflict resolution and postconflict reconstruction.[7]

Resolution 1325 has many genealogies. Its more immediate predecessors include the global mobilization regarding comfort women in the 1980s and 1990s, the Beijing platform on women and conflict, and the prosecution of rape in the tribunals convened following the war in the former Yugoslavia and the genocide in Rwanda, all of which led to an unprecedented focus on women in the context of war on the global stage. The resolution highlighted violence against women and the marginalization of women in decision making as priorities in the international law and policy landscape. These issues began to define the international feminist agenda going forward. Other issues, such as economic inequities, had little uptake in the influential international feminist circles that mobilized for the resolution. Rather, the global law and policy agenda has, over the past decade, been dominated by what I term international conflict feminism, the holy grail of which remains Resolution 1325.[8]

Initiatives like the aforementioned fact-finding mission are not unique in the Lankan women's movement, which has long been active in analyzing the ethnic conflict.[9] However, after Resolution 1325 was passed, these initiatives were assimilated into a global narrative about women, peace, and security. The resolution was implemented in workshops and the dissemination of information, through which it began to frame national activities and render them audible in a language that travels from Colombo to Geneva to New York.[10] It became the framework through which U.N. agencies, international NGOs (INGOs), and other NGOs shape their work,[11] as well as a criterion for donor funding priorities and therefore a central factor in the political economy of conflict contexts. For example, it was adopted as the policy framework for all gender aid disbursed by the European Union in conflict zones. In effect, the world of international conflict feminism activated by Resolution 1325 provides a consolidated instance of what Sally Merry has described as a culture of "transnational modernity," whose practitioners subscribe to shared norms regarding "the importance of the international domain, universal standards, and procedures for decision making," and a shared lexicon with terms such as "gender mainstreaming" and "capacity building."[12]

This dynamic's impact, in the context of the internationalized peace process in Sri Lanka, is the central focus of this essay. In this sense, the essay is more about international conflict feminism in Sri Lanka than just Lankan feminism as such. It traces how a national-global feedback loop amplifies the impact of the assimilation of national feminist initiatives into the global framework of the resolution. The political economy and discursive capital of the feedback loop carry implications for national women's movements seeking international recognition, funding, and collaboration, especially in a context such as the Lankan peace process, where "national" politics were internationalized. While in an earlier period women's peace activism may have been read primarily as intervening in national politics, within the context of an internationalized peace process they are animated by a global template whose political vocabulary includes gender, failed states, and an international responsibility to intervene.[13] Resolution 1325 contributes to the broader interpolative work of "violence," "civil wars," and "internecine conflict," which situates countries such as Sri Lanka on a spectrum that stretches from states that have failed women to states that have simply failed.

In the following sections I first situate Sri Lanka within the discursive framework of the conflict and postconflict periods, anchored in the globally dominant institutions, practices, and political economies of the human rights and conflict resolution fields. From there, I explore one part of this field, international conflict feminism, in Sri Lanka.

PRODUCING A CONFLICT ZONE

The 2002–6 peace process emerged in the context of dominant depictions of Sri Lanka as a conflict zone that stretches indefinitely into a past and future of bombings and assassinations, terror and counterterror, without responsible international engagement. In this context ethnic violence is often seen to have dismantled political society and the apparatus of governance. The dominant conflict lexicon of international institutions script a country scarred by this kind of "unthinkable" violence as a failed state that has interrupted history's march, as a political *terra nullius* that requires external intervention to restore a model of governance that allows its people to march forward.[14] This depiction is both symptom and trigger of "hegemonic internationalism," which ranges from the overtly ideological neocon worldview represented by the Bush regime and Washington consensus to the more technocratic and multilateralist approaches to conflict or violence found in the United Nations, European Union, and human rights–focused INGOs.

The production of Sri Lanka as a conflict zone on the international radar screen has many different markers. In the global public sphere it appears in war reporting on suicide bombs and militant terrorists, academic explorations of the anthropology of violence, the political science of conflict resolution, and U.N. discussions of war crimes and the responsibility to protect.[15] Concomitantly, Sri Lanka emerges as a field operation for conflict resolution–focused NGOs and INGOs, and a recipient of international donor funds for peace- and nation-building activities.[16] Across these many spheres, "violence" translates Sri Lanka, rendering it recognizable in the "conflict" lexicon of the international law and policy world as an irrational, ahistorical arena saturated by violence and the failure of modern institutions, so that it now requires international intervention to restore order.

PEACE BUILDING AND NEOLIBERAL GOVERNANCE

In the wake of the wars in Iraq and Afghanistan, while military interventions have come under widespread critical scrutiny across the political spectrum, "peace-building" interventions are normalized and legitimated as the preferred mode of international engagement.[17] Yet peace-building interventions can share disturbing continuities with technologies of knowledge and governance that we associate with the politics of "empire." For example, the orientation of international interventions in conflict zones

VASUKI NESIAH

often reflect Michael Ignatieff's "free markets equal free people" equation in advancing neoliberal economic policy and liberal statecraft.[18] Thus Vance Culbert's study of "conflict-sensitive" aid in Sri Lanka notes that "donors see promotion of liberal governance as a long-term structural approach to ameliorating conflict," and Sunil Bastian's study notes that "free markets" were the companion economic policy of foreign aid to Sri Lanka.[19] This was especially true in the context of the peace process, during which donors advocated policy initiatives such as "rule of law" programs and privatization as core elements of a peace-building tool kit.[20] Because the international conflict industry is less likely to foreground an explicitly ideological vision for these interventions, they are framed in more subtle and "neutral" terms, described as "best practices" and "lessons learned" regarding good governance with a normative human rights foundation. The international conflict resolution industry is the most significant domain across which we can observe a shift in the focus of international human rights after 1989—from a focus on rights against the state to a focus on state-building. With the "zoning" of Sri Lanka as a "failed state," the political economy of foreign aid and the moral economy of human rights come together to redeem and normalize peace-building interventions.

FEMINISM IN A CONFLICT ZONE

For international conflict feminism, the scripted production of a "conflict zone" redeems and normalizes globally hegemonic political choices in the name of women affected by conflict. The framing of feminist agendas in Sri Lanka in terms of Resolution 1325 is one instance of this dynamic. Here, women's physical insecurity necessitates the promotion of liberal governance to restore security and order. The prominent NGO International Alert was exemplary in this regard when it convened consultations on Resolution 1325 in South Asia in 2003. Foregrounding women's experiences of violence in Sri Lanka, Nepal, and Kashmir, it advocated a turn to international laws, norms, and policies. In such discourse, international laws and norms promise to transport a country away from the gendered brutality of war into the folds of an international legal order that respects women's rights. Characterizing the region as the site of unending violence,

International Alert writes that "during the 20th century, the South Asia region has been plagued by a series of internal and internationally influenced conflicts [during which] women and girls suffer disproportionately. While experiencing the same trauma as men, women and girls are also targeted for specific forms of violence, including different types of sexual abuse, exploitation and extortion."[21] While international conflict feminism seeks to "represent" women in a context of conflict, by foregrounding women's insecurity it also presents that context as a conflict zone. This framing of women's insecurity underscores international conflict feminism's purpose and helps build the rationale for international intervention in the name of "peace building."

Even as Resolution 1325 becomes mainstreamed into international policy making, its advocates still perceive their work as fighting against a sexist mainstream, and policy decisions referring to the resolution are characterized as subverting established policy priorities.[22] Thus Resolution 1325 has become a central plank in what counts in the international law and policy world as "progressive" responses to conflict situations.

The preceding discussion has briefly laid out the background dynamic, but to better understand how this plays out in Sri Lanka, we should turn now to the specific initiatives advanced there in the name of international conflict feminism. I have grouped different international conflict feminism initiatives in two broad categories: initiatives aimed at promoting "good governance" and initiatives aimed at promoting reconciliation. Both are seen as important in advancing women's peace and security in Sri Lanka, and in implementing Resolution 1325.

The focus on good governance initiatives on the one hand, and reconciliation initiatives on the other, may have some resonances with liberal feminism and cultural feminism, respectively; but they also share a family resemblance with the justice and reconciliation strands of the transitional justice field. Within feminist circles, the justice and reconciliation strands often translate into pressure for the transitional justice agenda on two distinct fronts: reform-focused initiatives (for example, in prosecuting gender-based war crimes as diligently as other war crimes), and culture-focused initiatives (for example, in ensuring that a pacifist feminist culture of reconciliation is prioritized in conflict resolution efforts). It is unclear if such resonances reflect deeper ideological influences, but they do demonstrate some overlap in terms of priorities.

PROMOTING GOOD GOVERNANCE

Good governance has now come to mean a vast array of initiatives associated with the Washington consensus, from anticorruption efforts to structural adjustment. The discussion below highlights only three strands of this policy constellation that have been critical elements to international conflict feminism's invocation of Resolution 1325—rule-of-law advocacy, inclusion policies, and civil society promotion.

Advocacy of the rule of law has been an important priority for the United Nations, donor community, and INGOs in initiatives informed by this resolution. The rule-of-law agenda can run the gamut from formalizing legal property titles to domestic violence legislation. Any of these agendas can be given legal legs in ways that have widely varying political and socioeconomic implications. Yet contextual analysis of the pros and cons of these implications is often eschewed in favor of the promotion of liberal statecraft in abstract and transhistorical terms. For example, these initiatives are often promoted as efforts to move a country from the realm of violence and war to the realm of democracy and law. As Culbert notes, in Sri Lanka, too, "liberal governance institutions" and "neo-liberal economic policies" were advocated as essential to the shift from war to law.[23]

Resolution 1325–focused initiatives, such as the International Alert study and its report, depict an epic battle that pit the forces of violence and mayhem against those of law, good governance, and the rights and interests of conflict-affected women. Aligning with the forces of order makes available the prescription of the "rule of law" to salvage and sanitize domains that converge with donor agendas regarding political and legal reform. For example, one study of Resolution 1325 initiatives praises an international program for regularizing the legal regime for private property rights because it privileges titles for women. The report notes: "This Lankan project provides a good example for other countries."[24] Here we see once again that embedding Resolution 1325 in global progress narratives that seek to carry "conflict zones" on a path to liberalism is accompanied by the ahistorical valorization of the "rule of law" as universalizable in policy prescriptions.[25] Concomitantly, the domain of the political—and feminism's involvement in it—is narrowed to that of elections, constitutionalism, and the establishment of a regulatory order to guarantee security in property and contract.

However, analysis of rule-of-law initiatives suggests that the relationship between women, war, and law is much more complex than suggested by Resolution 1325–based advocacy of the rule of law as a feminist agenda. It is not that war has not been catastrophic for women, but that the distinction between violence and law reveals little about the sociopolitical meaning of violence or law in Sri Lanka. The argument advanced here is not against law as such. Rather, I argue that we can understand the stakes of law not in the contrast between law and war but only in the distributive and ideological implications of different legal architectures.

Analysis of Lankan legal history suggests that violence and militarism articulate *through* law, rather than *against* law. From the regulation of sex workers near military camps, to the censorship of films that seem to challenge the military, to the Prevention of Terrorism Act, law has legitimated state violence to persecute minorities by prosecuting them. Law invariably refracts social dynamics of prejudice, hierarchy, and exclusion into supportive legal technologies.[26] As a range of Lankan feminist scholars has shown, militarism saturates many areas of daily life outside of armed combat, military camps, and checkpoints.[27] For example, militarism has penetrated tsunami reconstruction, and militaristic attitudes inform World Bank poverty-reduction strategy papers (compilations that document a country's strategy for reducing poverty). Moreover, legalism has facilitated militarism in these domains rather than fortified against the reach of war and conflict. The war has been intricately tied to the rule of law on many fronts—from parliamentary modalities enacting emergency regulations to constitutional provisions entrenching discrimination. In many different areas, law and legality have shaped the terrains of political violence in Sri Lanka.

Resolution 1325–activated advocacy of the rule of law mythologizes the nexus between law and security in ways that obscure this mutually constitutive history of law and violence in Sri Lanka. An example of this is when conflict societies are depicted simply as places where the rule of law or democratic institutions have failed. The focus on violence rather than the social contestations that shape and are shaped by such institutions renders the resolution distant from any of the messy politics of these struggles. Rather, it occupies a higher ground of moral clarity that cleanly delineates good from bad, peace and security from war and insecurity.

Resolution 1325 promotes an arithmetical approach to gender distribution as the most germane interpretive lens in advancing an agenda for the inclusion of women. As Christy Fujio notes, "The first four numbered paragraphs of 1325 urge the Member States and the Secretary General to take steps to increase representation of women at all decision-making levels."[28] This translates into detailed policy prescriptions on how to incorporate a significant percentage of women in the peace-making process. While defining inclusion simply in terms of gender arithmetic does not automatically have a particular ideological tilt, this approach risks reducing inclusion to those women who are less likely to challenge the dominant political and economic order and its parameters on the policy conversation. The U.N. secretary general asserted his own commitment to this greater representation of women, urging, "We must do far more to involve women in conflict prevention, peace negotiations and recovery after the guns fall silent," and calling on member states to come forward with more women candidates.[29] Defined in this way, the specific political orientations or agendas of women slated for "inclusion" in the process are not part of the arithmetic of inclusion. The provisions of Resolution 1325 treat women as a homogeneous category, making it unsurprising that its implementation efforts do not attend to how ethnicity, class, or other social fissures shape women's realities. For instance, a workshop on the resolution at the Karuna Center focused on knowledge of its contents, skills for participation in public life, empowerment of women's groups for advocacy of a quota for women in office, and establishing women's networks to support women seeking public office.[30] Given the complex sociopolitical issues at stake, this is a narrow interpretation of women's agendas for peace, but one that is fairly typical for initiatives inspired by this resolution. The relationship to dominant framings, questions of interethnic justice, and questions of distribution are elided in this view of the political. Rather, changes in the number of women who participate in peace-building initiatives are itself conceived as meaningful political reform.

One of the most important consequences of a decontextualized focus on "number" in Sri Lanka is that a Resolution 1325–referenced gender politics has been happy to sanction hegemonic politics if the inclusion of women is on the agenda. The women's group Gender Action has applauded the World Bank's postconflict reconstruction (PCR) initiatives in Sri Lanka because these "consistently 'mainstreamed gender' into PCR projects."[31] Women's Campaign International's involvement in Sri Lanka on Resolution 1325 implementation is illustrative of a similar approach. One of the key thrusts of its activities has included collaboration with the Business for Peace Alliance, a local countrywide business network that promotes best practices and sustainable peace building. An illustrative initiative was an event entitled "Empowering Women Entrepreneurs through a North-East Exchange with the South," which brought together women from different communities to participate in a trade fair and build links that were to strengthen their market agendas while also advancing intercommunity reconciliation. It is unclear if these initiatives advance reconciliation, or if in empowering those actors best positioned to take advantage of the new markets opened by the peace process they reproduce majoritarian power relations.

What is clear is that the thrust of such peace-building initiatives are comfortably embedded in market logics and concomitant efforts to strengthen the business sector and empower women entrepreneurs. Resolution 1325–focused work has been happy to endorse a narrowed discussion of economic reform as long as it integrates women economic actors into the fabric of macropolitical economic policy advanced by the international financial institutions and donor governments more generally.[32] The World Bank itself has taken on board this approach to gender mainstreaming and placed significant priority on inclusion of women.[33] Reducing inclusion to the numbers of women participating at different levels of decision making is not in itself a "neoliberal" definition, but it is one that enables and normalizes the dominant order by narrowing the parameters of the economic policy conversation. Thus, Resolution 1325 implementation could be invoked to legitimate globally hegemonic economic choices by focusing on the inclusion of women as economic actors rather than the specific economic policies that will shape the script within which they act. Women's participation as fully empowered actors in neoliberal economic reforms becomes a strategy to bring together international conflict feminism with donor agendas. If the discussion above probed how law reform agendas embedded women's interests in liberal and often neoliberal statecraft, here we see a parallel and intersecting dynamic where a reform agenda premised on an arithmetic approach to the politics of inclusion tightens the nexus with hegemonic economic policies.

Civil society promotion is another domain of international conflict feminism peace-building initiatives that has important implications for national feminist politics. Seira Tamang's characterization of international postconflict initiatives in Nepal as seeking to "civilize" Nepali "civil society" has resonances in Sri Lanka and other postconflict environments.[34] As Tamang notes, the "donor liturgy" of "democracy, development, empowerment, gender" get advanced as "free-floating normative orders" with little attention to implications for local hierarchies and differences.

Dominant trends in civil-society funding over the past decade have not only reproduced existing social inequalities, but even amplified them.[35] They have done this by further empowering precisely those NGOs that are already privileged—privileged either because they are linked to national political power blocks or because they are urban, Westernized, and adroit in formulating their political interests in donor-friendly discourse.[36] Both these dynamics were present in Sri Lanka during the peace process. Funding was channeled to NGOs that were politically privileged because of their ties to powerful political actors, or because they were Colombo-based, English-speaking, professionalized, and better positioned to navigate internationalized political discourses, practices, and institutions.[37] These dynamics have had an adverse impact on more robust traditions of democratic participation and have stunted politically transformative solidarities and social movements in many countries. In Sri Lanka, one of the impacts of dependence on donor funding may have been to make the human rights and peace agenda of the period between 2002 and 2006 more alienated from social movements and more divorced from fighting the injustices underlying human rights violations.[38] Similarly, some feminists have argued that the NGOization of women's groups has come at the cost of a more critical, engaged women's movement that will risk alienating donors and push for more radical political transformation.[39] Thus in the civil society landscape of the peace process period, dissenting and subaltern political agendas were threatened by extremist politics, on the one hand, and marginalized by the corporatizing, mainstreaming push of NGOization, on the other.[40]

Civil society promotion efforts may also have an adverse impact because they enter the political landscape included in packages of structural adjustment policies aimed at reducing state services in favor of private actors.[41] Such clustered initiatives have a particularly harmful impact on socioeconomically marginalized groups. While some women's groups may have benefited from Resolution 1325's focus on civil society, those most vulnerable and most dependent on state services have been disempowered. The global phenomenon of NGO empowerment over the last two decades has a complex relationship with structural adjustment policies that have weakened the state, empowered the private sector, and increased dependence on and vulnerability to global economic and political hegemonies. Even initiatives—such as the compilation of International Monetary Fund and World Bank's poverty reduction strategy papers—ostensibly designed to empower national participation have often generated "a process to develop a *national* plan that implements *international* anti-poverty objectives."[42] Thus while Resolution 1325 advocates have often pushed for civil society promotion and the greater inclusion of women's groups in that process, there has been little attention to how that agenda could fit into and further entrench dominant political hegemonies. Historically, the global circulation of feminist solidarities and agendas has been enriching for many Lankan women's NGOs and contributed to critical, counterhegemonic interventions. Yet the interpenetration of new governance modalities into these transnational flows has had many contradictory implications for the trajectories of feminist initiatives.

PROMOTING RECONCILIATION: WOMEN AS AGENTS OF PEACE AND VICTIMS OF CONFLICT

The field of reconciliation is more internally diverse than good governance initiatives. The strands that have most relevance to this discussion of international conflict feminism in Sri Lanka are those that pertain specifically to women's dual role as agents of peace and victims of war.

Women's participation in peace-building processes is the signature call of Resolution 1325. The inclusion proposals discussed above are premised on a political ethic of "equality" as the rationale for women's role in conflict resolution. Another rationale for women's role in peace building is the notion that women bring to reconciliation efforts particular insights and skills indispensable for any sustainable peace-building process. Invoking what in other contexts has been described as "affirmative gender essentialism," these arguments sometimes involve naturalist theories about women's biological propensity to preserve life rather than destroy it.[43] They are also often predicated on an experiential theory that women's engagement with peace building is significantly informed by women's experience of conflict. Women develop insights regarding the costs of war because they suffer the consequences of war in different and disproportionate ways. Moreover, it is argued that women learn to negotiate life-sustaining space within conflicts through a political practice of empathy and reconciliation that contributes to peace making and long-term nation building. Thus the notion of women as victims of conflict informs the construction of women as agents of peace.

Reconciliation initiatives are often accompanied by a disavowal of any explicit political stake in the conflict. The eschewing of the official political platform may risk closing off women's potential influence in the formal political sphere, but that very disavowal is also a source of legitimation.[44] Elissa Helms argues that in a terrain discredited and corrupted by "politics," women free of the taint of politics are especially well situated to "achieve a significant measure of trust and cooperation" across ethnic lines.[45] Similarly, Lesley Abdela cites a recent conference participant's comment that "in current peace processes the peace is not for the people, it is for the male power groups."[46] Seconding the participant's comments, Abdela says that the analysis of formal peace processes as fundamentally patriarchal has wide relevance for countries such as Sri Lanka, where "women's groups lobbied both domestic political leaders and the Norwegians who were acting as peace-brokers but they made no progress, and the killing goes on. Indeed, the art of peace building is far more subtle than the practice of warfare (in which men in power have had centuries of experience). It requires almost opposite characteristics: among them patience, creative dialogue, imagination, empathy, attention to the critical minutiae, and avoidance of grandstanding."[47] For Abdela, the neglect of women's peace-making role in Sri Lanka reflects the dire need to act fast and implement Resolution 1325. Concomitantly, it has been urged by others that "the incorporation of gender studies into peace theories" will be pivotal to conflict resolution initiatives.[48]

This approach is not unique to Sri Lanka, but resonates with international conflict feminism in other conflict contexts. The Lankan case reflects a larger global trajectory of international conflict feminism and its nexus with a hegemonic internationalism. For example, Abdela's discussion of Nepal echoes her discussion of Sri Lanka. In Nepal issues such as land distribution, minority rights, and federalism were critical areas of difference between the Maoists and the seven-party alliance. However, these issues are not addressed in Abdela's analysis of Nepalese negotiations, in which she focuses on the "art" of peace building. In her discussion, the stakes of "official politics" emerges as the process itself rather than material issues such as land. Conventional discussions of the stakes of politics in terms of "distribution" and "recognition"—in other words, claims to power—have little purchase for Abdela.[49] Rather, what is at stake in peacebuilding processes is the ethics of political practice—more specifically, an ethics that revalues what in her gender taxonomy are identified as women's contributions and woman-identified values, such as patience and empathy, in political engagement.

A critique of this essentialist understanding of women and peace is not new. Yet, Resolution 1325 has nonetheless reempowered this equation. The essentialized construction of women's postconflict contribution is also trafficked in and by the donor community. Helms notes that "donors have especially targeted women for projects of ethnic reconciliation" and the European commissioner for humanitarian aid presses the notion that women can be the "driving forces towards reconciliation and rehabilitation."[50]

In addition to their "gender essentialism," these initiatives advance a discourse of communal harmony that sidesteps discussion of the nationalist pressures and interethnic injustices responsible for the conflict. The message endorsed by Resolution 1325, that feminist peace building will restore normality, clear misunderstandings, and bring about intercommunity reconciliation, is invested in a thin view of the sociopolitical structures and associative ties that engender solidarities and differences, political affinities, and social conflict. For instance, Malathi de Alwis has noted that much of the Resolution 1325–inspired peace activity by feminist groups in Sri Lanka has been focused on bringing together women from the North and South, much like the women entrepreneurs' meeting described earlier. In initiative after initiative, enabling interethnic interactions has been the primary model of women's peace work because these strategies are " 'hot' among the funders."[51] Such initiatives see the primary problem as one of understanding and intercommunity rapport, rather than larger structural issues. Peace building is about encouraging mutual understanding, rather than political and socioeconomic change. Strikingly then, although it deploys a different framework of inclusion from the gender equality argument of reform initiatives, the "feminized" conflict resolution discourse also gives international conflict feminism a depoliticizing thrust. Here too, work inspired by Resolution 1325 presents itself as innocent of power, just requesting a seat at the table for community reconciliation.

In addition to viewing women as agents of peace, Resolution 1325 initiatives highlight women as victims of conflict. This victim paradigm has been channeled into the focus on sexual violence, the production of women's subjectivity in conflict as bodies that have suffered injury, and the corresponding perception of men as the primary agents of war and conflict.[52] The focus on women as victims has been the dominant focus of international law and policy developments in relation to women and war since the early to mid-nineties, and was consolidated further by Resolution 1325 and its follow-up resolutions.[53]

The long history of impunity regarding sexual violence in the Lankan conflict needs attention. However, the exclusive focus on women's experience of armed conflict within the framework of victimhood raises several issues. First, from women cadres in the LTTE to female heads of state in the government of Sri Lanka, women have played a key role in the war.[54] Even though Lankan feminist scholarship has focused on this dimension of women's experience of conflict, it has not garnered similar attention in the victim paradigm of Resolution 1325 initiatives. Equally significant is the focus on sexual violence as the primary harm women experience in war. Feminist engagement with international courts addressing war crimes in the former Yugoslavia, Rwanda, and Sierra Leone, and now the International Criminal Court, have centered on the quest for recognition of the female subject so that she can be identified as the "victim" of bodily injuries that constitute international crimes.[55] Sexual violence, rather than more complex sociopolitical analysis of these conflicts, emerges as the privileged narrative for international law interventions. Sexual violence is undoubtedly a problem in the Lankan context. However, women's experience of conflict cannot be understood without attention to ethnicity, region, socioeconomic status, and party affiliation, all of which are lost in Resolution 1325's view of gender as a free-standing category. Thus, when Ban Ki-moon "announced plans to shortly appoint a Messenger of Peace tasked *entirely* with advocacy for ending violence against women," the "entirely" indexes the limit of victim politics rather than an expansive recognition of its significance.[56]

International conflict feminism and Lankan feminism are interrelated domains. The global structure of laws and norms, and the funding lines that emerge from the political economy of aid and conflict, have complex links with Lankan feminism. The array of approaches discussed above, from "good governance" advocacy to the focus on women as agents of peace and victims of conflict, have continuities with political-legal reform and reconciliation initiatives that were present in Lankan feminism for many decades. While reform and reconciliation are not new dimensions of Lankan feminist agendas, in the particular historical conjuncture of an internationalized peace process these agendas get framed under the rubric of Resolution 1325.

A contrast with an earlier moment may be helpful here in highlighting the new terrain marked by international conflict feminism. "Motherhood," which had been the touchstone for gender issues in the public sphere in the early 1990s, was replaced by "violence" during the rise of international conflict feminism.[57] The focus on motherhood is not politically "preferable" to the focus on women as "victims" of sexual violence, as both are problematic. However, these differences have import and we need to be alert to what doors we are closing and what doors we are opening in privileging different rubrics of political identity and interest. For example, during the 1990s the "Mother's Front" was a cross-class social movement that thousands of women identified with. No similar mass mobilization has been inspired by international instruments dealing with rape in contexts of armed conflict. Those who can speak the language of international conflict feminism and frame proposals that have resonance with Resolution 1325 priorities are more likely to get funding, visibility, and support. This is valuable currency in working the complex technologies through which feminist groups gain entry into global women's rights networks and "expert" knowledge of U.N. discourses and institutional practices.[58]

This reality has pressured national women's groups to negotiate their interventions in ways that "produce," enable, and constrain their own priorities, and concede to global agendas that determine which projects are viable. For example, Sally Merry notes that a women's group is more likely to get consultative status and a seat at the table in discussions regarding international documents if it can show that "it is promoting the goals of the UN." This, in turn, "improves their ability to fundraise" because "participating in these meetings" will "provide information on donor agendas."[59] Reflecting this dynamic, "the gender agenda has not distanced itself from the neoliberal state building policies of many peace building interventions," even though the fact that "deregulation, privatization and liberalization negatively affect women" could have provided the basis for a "powerful critique of the dominant peace building paradigm."[60] Diverse assessments of the impact of aid on the conflict have consistently shown that the focus on free markets and privatization has exacerbated the war, widened regional inequalities, and distorted political accountability in ways that have corroded democratic participation.[61] Yet these assessments have not prompted a rethinking of efforts to ensure market-friendly gender inclusion policies. Rather, the ease with which a market-friendly gender inclusion agenda could be incorporated into the peace-building framework has quelled those criticisms.[62] Among other things, the preceding discussion has shown that, rather than a neutral commitment to arithmetic equality or a benign vote for reconciliation over war, the quest inspired by Resolution 1325 for representation in peace building is often a Trojan horse for far-reaching commitments to globally hegemonic economic and political choices. While Resolution 1325 advocacy presents itself as a transformative expansion of the peace process and a challenge to inherited hierarchies, the resolution often works seamlessly with local and global processes that endorse and legitimize dominant ideologies.

In some instances of international conflict feminism's presence in Sri Lanka, decades-old social change agendas have been repackaged in terms that resonate with the resolution. In others, older reference points for reform (such as Marxist constructions of class exploitation) are overtaken by those of the international postconflict industry.[63] Sometimes focused on the realm of "official politics," sometimes on the realm of "culture," international conflict feminism, as the agent empowered by Resolution 1325 to fight violence and failed states, mobilizes a diverse array of techniques and ideologies to advance particular models of global, gendered subjectivity. This range of international interventions extends from funding streams generated by the resolution, to workshops on women and the "rule of law," to "gender sensitivity" training for military forces. By rendering an agenda of inclusion as the passport to being "audible" on national and international stages, the resolution has undoubtedly impacted the terrain of Lankan feminism. In Sri Lanka Resolution 1325 has occupied and constrained the landscape of peace and security in ways that have legitimated a politics of hegemonic internationalism in the name of women affected by conflict.

CONCLUSION: INTERNATIONAL CONFLICT FEMINISM AND GOVERNANCE

The power of international conflict feminism as evidenced in the mainstreaming of feminist initiatives (such as Resolution 1325) in such realms as donor conditions and criminal law codes is captured by what Janet Halley and colleagues describe as "governance feminisms."[64] The focus on "good governance" reforms on the one hand and reconciliation on the other could be seen as representing the "official politics" and the "informal (or 'cultural') politics" ends of feminism. In elaborating on "governance feminism," Halley has described feminism's will to power, and its infusion into statecraft, law, and culture. In particular, she notes that the "international legal order is increasingly receiving feminists into its power elites and that feminist law reform is emerging as a formidable new source of legal ideas."[65] I would argue that the passage of Resolution 1325 and its subsequent mainstreaming into the international policy-making apparatus described above is a profound instance of this dynamic.

This essay has explored how Resolution 1325 was "presented" in Sri Lanka by unpacking the structure of arguments it mobilized and the subject of global feminism that it deployed in the context of an internationalized peace process. The next step would require additional research on the global feminist subject activated by Resolution 1325 movements, and its implications for local and global struggles against systemic injustice and dominant ideologies. We may want to explore whether the emphasis on inclusion of women in peace processes deflects questions regarding the distributive and ideological dimensions of the hegemonic nation-building project. We might look at the quest for women's representation in that project, and scrutinize what is foregrounded and what obscured by it, which issues confronted and which deferred, which social forces empowered and which defeated.

The last decade has seen international conflict feminism pushed into an ambivalent relationship with global hegemonic, political, and military power.[66] On a global terrain, international conflict feminism has been invoked to seamlessly legitimize that power.[67] It is in this sense that I situate the different strands of feminism activated by Resolution 1325 within the framework of governance feminism, namely, the "installation of feminist ideas in actual legal institutional power" in ways that "piggyback on existing forms of power, intervening in them and participating in them."[68] The resolution does not necessarily carry a torch for liberal statecraft or free market economics. However, to the extent that these vehicles offer it wide scope for engagement with peace processes and nation-building efforts, international conflict feminism works with those ideologies and institutions and makes them its own. It is a dialectical process in which the international community's intervention processes have spurred the momentum for international conflict feminism's dominance.

Despite the value that Resolution 1325 may have in some contexts, we must remember that the terms "women," "peace," and "security" are not innocent of power. Rather, they are embedded in particular configurations of meaning and resources implicit in the dominant ideologies and political economies of international intervention in conflict and postconflict contexts.

NOTES

1. Richard Strickland, "Gender, Human Security, and Peacebuilding: Finding Links between Policy and Practice," United Nations Division for the Advancement of Women (DAW), EGM/PEACE/2003/EP.9, November 2003, 7. http://www.un.org/womenwatch/daw/egm/peace2003/reports/CASESTUDY.pdf.

2. Sitralega Maunaguru, Elizabeth Nissan, et al., *Findings and Recommendations of the Report of the International Women's Mission to the North East of Sri Lanka, 12– 17th October 2002.* For an announcement regarding the inaugural meeting of the Sub-Committee on Gender Issues (March 6, 2003), see http://peaceinsrilanka.org/negotiations/rng-051.

3. Kumi Samuel, "Women's Agency in Peace Making within the Context of Democracy and Citizenship—The Case of Sri Lanka," paper presented at a panel discussion (with the Philippines-based group Development Alternatives with Women for a New Era) on "Citizenship: Democracy, Retribution and Rights," at the World Social Forum meeting, Nairobi, Kenya, 2007.

4. Ibid.

5. Security Council Resolution 1325 (2000), s/res/1325 (2000) on Women, Peace and Security.

6. See Marcia Greenberg and Elaine Zuckerman, "The Gender Dimensions of Post-Conflict Reconstruction: The Challenges in Development Aid," paper presented at the Eighth International Women's Policy Research Conference, "When Women Gain, So Does the World," Washington, D.C., June 2005.

7. See "Landmark Resolution on Women, Peace and Security" (n.d.), at the website of the Office of the Special Adviser on Gender Issues and the Advancement of Women (OSAGI), http://un.org/womenwatch/osagi/wps.

8. Tellingly, the Security Council's follow-up action to Resolution 1325 was the passage of Resolution 1820 (in 2008) and of Resolutions 1888 and 1889 (in 2009). All of these focus on sexual violence against women and girls in conflict zones.

9. De Mel, *Militarizing Sri Lanka*; Nanthini Sornorajah, "The Experiences of Tamil Women," *lines*, February 2004, at lines-magazine.org; and Maunaguru, "Gendering Tamil Nationalism."

10. See, e.g., the report by the Karuna Center, "Team 1325 and Women in Sri Lanka: Building a Common Platform for Peace," Fall 2008, at the Karuna Center for Peacebuilding website, karunacenter.org. For the U.N. country team's report, see *UNnews*, the UN Sri Lanka Quarterly newsletter, April–June 2009, http://undg.org/docs/10212/UN-News-Sri-Lanka-2Q-2009.pdf. And for rural Resolution 1325 workshops, see "Our 1325 Rural Workshops in Sri Lanka," October 13, 2005, at open Democracy.net/blog.

11. Sri Lanka is not unique in this regard. For instance, one can tell a parallel story to the one told here about international conflict feminism, Resolution 1325, and women's activism in relation to peace building in Liberia.

12. Merry, *Human Rights and Gender Violence*, 31, 48.

13. For example, the mobilization of the Mothers' Front, historically the largest women's antiwar initiative in the country, was decisive in the 1994 elections and was read primarily in terms of its import for national politics.

14. Mamdani, "Making Sense of Political Violence in Postcolonial Africa." See also Nesiah, "The Specter of Violence That Haunts the UDHR." On the discourse of failed states, see Gordon, "Saving Failed States," 903.

15. See Jeganathan, " 'Violence' as an Analytical Problem."

16. Vance Culbert, "Business as Usual: Conflict Sensitive Aid in Sri Lanka," Master's thesis, Simon Fraser University, 2004, 56.

17. Nesiah, "From Berlin to Bonn."

18. Quoted in Tahira Gonsalves, "Gender and Peacebuilding: A Sri Lankan Case Study," International Development Research Centre, 2004, 3, at the International Development Research Centre Digital Library website, idl-bnc.idrc.ca. See also Michael Ignatieff, "The American Empire: The Burden," *New York Times Magazine*, January 5, 2003.

19. Culbert, "Business as Usual," 57. See also Bastian, "Foreign Aid, Globalisation and Conflict in Sri Lanka," 23.

20. Bastian, "Foreign Aid, Globalisation and Conflict in Sri Lanka," 97. See also Nesiah, "The Specter of Violence That Haunts the UDHR."

21. Nicola Johnston, "UNSC Resolution 1325: South Asian Women's Perspectives," *International Alert*, June 2003, 6.

22. This corresponds with the dynamic that Halley describes in saying that feminism denies its own power. See Halley, Kotiswaran, Shamir, and Thomas, "From the International to the Local in Feminist Legal Responses," 335.

23. Culbert, "Business as Usual," 29–30.

24. Greenberg and Zuckerman, "The Gender Dimensions of Post-Conflict Reconstruction."

25. The Convention on the Elimination of All Forms of Discrimination against Women (CEDAW) stresses the "rule of law" as a key policy prescription. See CEDAW, "Thematic Briefing on 'Women and Armed Conflict,'" May 3, 2009, at peace women.org. See also Patricia Viseur-Sellers, "The Rule of Law Applies to Women," *DHA News* (online publication of United Nations Department of Humanitarian Affairs, Office for the Coordination of Humanitarian Affairs), April–May 1997, at reliefweb.int/OCHA_ol.

26. The constitutional history of Sri Lanka suggests that, rather than preventing abuse, liberal constitutionalism conferred political legitimacy on specific zones of abuse. See Nesiah, "The Princely Imposter."

27. De Mel, *Militarizing Sri Lanka*.

28. Fujio, "From Soft to Hard Law," 221.

29. Press release of Security Council, United Nations, 2008.

30. Karuna Center, "Team 1325 and Women in Sri Lanka." Note the workshop objectives listed on page 3 of the report.

31. Greenberg and Zuckerman, "The Gender Dimensions of Post-Conflict Reconstruction," 7.

32. Culbert, "Business as Usual," 57. Culbert notes that "together with Japanese foreign assistance, IFIS [international financial institutions] account for eight-five percent of all development funding in Sri Lanka"; but, given the role of the World Bank in coordinating aid, shaping the PRSP, and the Sri Lanka government's economic and policy agenda more generally, "their influence is even greater than this proportion would suggest."

33. World Bank, "Integrating Gender into the World Bank's Work: A Strategy for Action" (Washington, D.C.: World Bank, 2002).

34. Tamang, "Civilising Civil Society."

35. For example, Tamang argues that in Nepal it has "reinforced the structural inequalities of caste, ethnicity, gender, and religious belief. Ibid., 6.

36. Merry, *Human Rights and Gender Violence*, 53.

37. Goodhand, *Aid, Conflict, and Peacebuilding in Sri Lanka*, 40; and Culbert, "Business as Usual."

38. Nesiah and Keenan, "Human Rights and Sacred Cows."

39. See Malathi de Alwis, "Feminist Peace Activism in Sri Lanka," lecture at the

Boston Consortium on Gender, Security, and Human Rights, John F. Kennedy School, Harvard University, February 23, 2004, at genderandsecurity.umb.edu.

40. One of the most striking elements of the last peace process was that many internationals made alliances with the LTTE. See Culbert, "Business as Usual," 63–79.

41. For example, microfinance projects that provide poor women access to capital have this dual thrust. See Rankin, "Governing Development." Thanks to S. Nanthikesan for this insight.

42. The International Monetary Fund describes the poverty reduction strategy paper as developed through "a participatory process involving domestic stakeholders as well as external development partners." See International Monetary Fund, "Poverty Reduction Strategy Papers (PRSP)" fact sheet, updated April 8, 2011, http://imf.org/external/NP/prsp/prsp.asp.

43. Helms, "Women as Agents of Ethnic Reconciliation?," 1.

44. Ibid.

45. Ibid., 11.

46. Lesley Abdela, "When Will They Ever Learn? Women, Men and Peace-Building," *Open Democracy*, March 6, 2008, at http://open democracy.net.

47. Ibid.

48. Catia Confortini, "Galtung, Violence, and Gender: The Case for a Peace Studies/Feminism Alliance," paper presented at the annual meeting of the International Studies Association, Montreal, Canada, March 17, 2004.

49. For the classic elaboration of the distribution and recognition paradigm, see Fraser and Honneth, *Redistribution or Recognition*. I invoke this classical left-liberal understanding of "the political" not to advance or naturalize it, but to illustrate how Abdela's understanding deviates from it.

50. Helms, "Women as Agents of Ethnic Reconciliation?," 5, 7.

51. De Alwis, "Feminist Peace Activism," 3.

52. In the genocide trials in Rwanda, the classification of rape in the same category as murder may have accentuated women's experience of rape as equivalent to death.

53. Follow-up resolutions include those numbered 1820, 1888, and 1889. See Merry, *Human Rights and Gender Violence*, 21–22; and Franke, "Gendered Subjects of Transitional Justice."

54. Sornorajah, "The Experiences of Tamil Women"; Maunaguru, "Gendering Tamil Nationalism."

55. Mackinnon, "Rape, Genocide and Women's Human Rights." For a critical perspective, see Engle, "Feminism and Its (Dis)contents." Also see Vasuki Nesiah, "Missionary Zeal for a Secular Mission," in *Feminist Perspectives on Contemporary International Law: Between Resistance and Compliance*, ed. Sari Kuovo and Zoe Peterson (London: Hart Publishing, forthcoming).

56. Ban Ki-moon, in "UN Security Council 5916th Meeting Minutes," June 19, 2008, at http://un.org/News/Press/docs/2008/sc9364.doc.htm.

57. De Alwis, "Motherhood as a Space of Protest."

58. Merry, *Human Rights and Gender Violence*, 53–54.

59. Ibid., 53.

60. Gonsalves, "Gender and Peace-building."

61. Dunham and Jayasuriya, "Equity, Growth, and Insurrection." See also Goodhand, *Aid, Conflict, and Peacebuilding in Sri Lanka*; Bastian, "Foreign Aid, Globalisation, and Conflict in Sri Lanka"; and Culbert, "Business as Usual."

62. For example, Gonsalves, "Gender and Peace-building," 3.

63. Jayewardena, *Feminism and Nationalism in the Third World*.

64. Halley, Kotiswaran, Shamir, and Thomas, "From the International to the Local in Feminist Legal Responses."

65. Ibid., 419.

66. See Engle, "Calling in the Troops." See also Nesiah, "From Berlin to Bonn."

67. Ibid. President George W. Bush invoked gender equality issues in describing the impact of the intervention in Afghanistan; in his words, "The mothers and daughters of Afghanistan were captives in their own homes, forbidden from working or going to school. Today women are free, and are part of Afghanistan's new government." Transcript of President Bush's State of the Union Address to Congress and the Nation, *New York Times*, January 2002.

68. Halley, Kotiswaran, Shamir, and Thomas, "From the International to the Local in Feminist Legal Responses," 340–41.

MALATHI DE ALWIS

Feminist Politics and Maternalist Agonism

DURING AN INTERVIEW for a feature article on International Women's Day, in the latter half of February 2009, a young journalist at the *Sunday Times* sought my views on the latest configurations of the civil war in Sri Lanka.[1] "Some women I spoke with are angry and disappointed," she noted, "that not a single feminist group has issued a statement about the current situation." In this essay, I wish to contemplate how feminist politics in Sri Lanka seems to have become primarily equated with "issuing statements," as suggested in the above comment; I do this through a broader exploration of how "the political" has been constituted in Sri Lanka in conjunction with feminist peace activism. As a long-time feminist peace activist myself, I consider this exercise to be a crucial form of self-critique, despite Seyla Benhabib's observation that the "nostalgia for situated criticism" may be "a nostalgia for home," an issue I return to later on in this essay.[2]

Chantal Mouffe, who, along with Ernesto Laclau, significantly contributed toward a reconceptualization of radical democratic politics, subsequently provided a useful and precise distinction between "politics" and "the political."[3] Following Carl Schmitt, Mouffe defines "the political" as having to do with "the dimension of antagonism which is present in social relations, with the ever present possibility of a 'us'/'them' relation to be construed in terms of a 'friend'/'enemy.'"[4] "Politics," on the other hand, "refers to the ensemble of practices, discourses and institutions which seek to establish a certain order and to organize human coexistence in conditions which are always potentially conflictual because they are affected by the dimension of 'the political.' "[5] Derrida's notion of the "constitutive outside" is helpful to better understand "the political" as it reveals the impossibility of drawing an absolute distinction between interior and exterior, us and them; the "constitutive outside" is "present within the inside as its always real possibility."[6] Thus, political practice in a democratic society does not consist in defending the rights of preconstituted identities, but rather, in constituting those identities themselves "in a precarious and always vulnerable terrain."[7]

It is this processual and contingent nature of "the political" that Judith Butler also highlights by distinguishing between "the constitution of a political field that produces *and naturalizes* that constitutive outside and a political field that produces and *renders contingent* the specific parameters of that political field."[8] The latter formulation enables the conceptualization of political struggles that put the "parameters of the political itself into question." This is an important concern for feminists given the gendering of "the political," that is, its construction through unmarked racial and gender exclusions and the conflation of politics with masculinity and public life that, in turn, feminizes the private and renders it prepolitical.[9] This is a significant advance on prior feminist conceptualizations of "the political," which were unable to avoid resorting to preconstituted identities, a priori notions of agency, and the foreclosure of political boundaries.[10] In the following sections I discuss several key moments of feminist as well as maternalist peace activism in Sri Lanka through an engagement with this notion of "the political."

The past three decades in Sri Lanka were dominated by extraordinary unfoldings of violence—an anti-Tamil pogrom in 1983, a Sinhala youth (Janatha Vimukthi Peramuna, JVP) antistate uprising in the south from 1987 to 1990, and a protracted civil war in the north and east, fought between the Sri Lankan state and Tamil separatists (primarily the Liberation Tigers of Tamil Eelam, or LTTE, and its breakaway factions)—that limped from one failed ceasefire to another until the military defeat of the LTTE in May 2009. Women's lives today continue to be imbricated in the contours of civil war while they simultaneously bear the scars—both physical and psychic—from previous events and processes of violence. While war widows, now ubiquitous across the island, are grim reminders of one of the most destructive aspects of war, women soldiers and women/girl militants are equally troubling reminders of women's active participation in war. Nonetheless, it is also women, and particularly feminists, who have been at the vanguard of antiwar struggles, and have collectively and publicly agitated for peace by calling for a political resolution of the ethnic conflict in the north and east and the cessation of state and JVP-led atrocities in the south.[11]

One of the most significant political outcomes of the 1980s and 1990s in Sri Lanka was the collective mobilization of "motherhood" as a counter to violence, both in the context of the civil war in the north and east as well as in the JVP uprising in the south.[12] I define "motherhood" as "encompassing women's biological reproduction as well as women's signification as moral guardians, care givers and nurturers."[13] I gloss the political mobilization of "motherhood" as "maternalism," following Seth Koven and Sonya Michel's observation that maternalism always operates on two levels: "Extol[ling] the virtues of domesticity while simultaneously legitimating women's public relationships to politics and the state, to community, workplace and marketplace."[14] While evoking "traditional" images of womanliness, it also implicitly challenges the socially constructed boundaries between public and private, women and men, state and civil society.[15] Maternalism is not a new phenomenon. It has been mobilized in different parts of the globe at different moments in history. For example, in the 1960s, the U.S. organization Women Strike for Peace pushed babies in strollers into city halls and federal buildings to protest the proliferation of nuclear arms. Similarly, in the late 1970s, the Madres of Argentina silently and continuously circled the Plaza de Mayo wearing white headscarves evocative of diapers and holding photographs of their "disappeared" sons and daughters. In the 1980s, the Relatives' Action Committee in Northern Ireland observed fasting vigils, wrapped themselves in blankets, and chained themselves, all to call attention to the harsh prison conditions in which their sons were being kept.[16] In the early 1990s, the Committee of Soldiers' Mothers in Russia braved artillery fire in Grozny, Chechnya, to stop their sons from fighting what they perceived to be a pointless war.[17] Finally, within the last decade, members of the All-Manipur Social Reformation and Development Samaj responded to the rape of a young Manipuri girl at the hands of the Indian Army by publicly baring their aged bodies and demanding that they all be raped

MALATHI DE ALWIS

because they were all mothers of the raped girl.[18] Each reiteration of maternalism is an indication of the dynamism of what feminists have variously described as women's "female consciousness," "preservative love," "maternal thinking," and "moral motherhood," among others.[19]

In 1984, the Mothers' Front was formed in Jaffna to protest the mass arrest of Tamil youth by the Sri Lankan state. This organization was controlled by and consisted of Tamil women from all classes. The feminist Rajani Thiranagama, assassinated by the LTTE for her fearless, forthright, and critical voice, documented how these women "mobilized mass rallies, and picketed public officials demanding the removal of military occupation [by the Sri Lankan state]."[20] It was not only the spirit, observed Thiranagama, but also the enormous numbers that this group was able to mobilize which "spoke loudly of the high point to which such mass organizations, especially of women [could] rise."[21] Though the members of the Mothers' Front had spontaneously mobilized their maternal identity in the face of state repression, they were also quick to criticize the blatant manipulation of such an identity when Tamil militant groups put up posters inciting women to have more babies in order to further the cause of separatism.[22]

The northern Mothers' Front also inspired Tamil women in the Eastern Province to begin their own branch of this organization. In 1986, the eastern Mothers' Front took to the streets with rice pounders to prevent a massacre of members of the Tamil Eelam Liberation Organization by the LTTE.[23] In 1987, one of its members, Annai Pupathi, fasted to death to protest the presence of the Indian Peace Keeping Forces. She was subsequently immortalized by the LTTE (it was common knowledge that the LTTE had forced her to keep at her fast) through a public memorial and a scholarship offered in her memory.[24] It was finally the increasing hegemony of the LTTE and its suppression of all independent, democratic organizations that did not "toe the line" that pushed the Mothers' Front in the north and east into political conformism and reduced its wide appeal and militancy. Thiranagama mourns its metamorphosis into "another Y.W.C.A.," as its central core of primarily middle-class women began to confine their activities to works of charity.[25] Many members who refused to work under LTTE hegemony had to flee abroad or to Colombo.

In July 1990, a Mothers' Front of Sinhala women was formed in the south to protest the disappearance of their male kin during the JVP uprising of 1987–90.[26] These women's central demand was for "a climate where we can raise our sons to manhood, have our husbands with us and lead normal women's lives."[27] Their mass rallies and *deva kannalawwas* (beseeching of the gods) had a tremendous impact on Sinhala society during the two years in which this organization was especially active.[28] The seemingly unquestionable authenticity of these women's grief and espousal of "traditional" family values provided the southern Mothers' Front with an important space for protest at a time when feminist and human rights activists who were critical of either state or jvp violence were being killed with impunity.[29]

While many feminists in the south celebrated the successful campaign of the southern Mothers' Front and participated in their rallies, they were nevertheless divided on how best to respond to such a movement, for a variety of reasons: though the front identified itself as the largest grassroots women's movement in the country (with an estimated membership of 25,000 women), it was common knowledge that it was founded, funded, and coordinated by the main opposition party in the country—the Sri Lanka Freedom Party—whose politburo was predominantly middle-class and male. As members of autonomous women's groups, feminists felt very uncomfortable about working with a political party that not only did not espouse a particular feminist ideology but in fact was perceived to be using the Mothers' Front for its own political ends.[30] Feminists were also concerned about the limited agenda of the southern Mothers' Front, which excluded any attention to similar issues faced by Tamil and Muslim women in the northern and eastern regions of the island. Many feminists who had reservations about the front's mobilization of "motherhood" felt that they would have been more willing to compromise if it had been used as a space within which a mass movement of women from different ethnic groups could have united and launched a collective critique of the violence perpetrated by the state as well as militant groups.[31]

As I have argued elsewhere, despite the limited agenda, ethnic homogeneity, and nonfeminist standpoint of the southern Mothers' Front, this movement had continuously put the parameters of "the political" into question through a disavowal of the state's definition of them as "political."[32] They consistently declared that they were merely mothers seeking their children's return to the family fold so that they could lead "normal women's lives."[33] I would like to term this seemingly conservative, resistant,

MALATHI DE ALWIS

yet nonantagonistic reiteration of normative femininity as "maternalist agonism," following Mark Bahnische's broad definition of agonism as "a rhetorical process of constructing political identities and subjects" and Bonnie Honig's insistence that agonism can be detached from its masculinist, heroic, and violent associations.[34] That agonism shares a Greek word root (*agonia*: contest, anguish) with agony and agonize, I find poignantly apposite in this context.

I have sought to coin such a term as "maternalist agonism" in order to retain maternalism's resiliency and malleability, its complicated unfoldings, while disrupting the rather predictable feminist debates it has engendered regarding whether it essentializes or empowers, whether it produces victims or agents. Such dichotomous thinking has only debilitated political praxis; we have become so caught up in the binary logics of our arguments that we have failed to see beyond them or out of them. Similarly, our obsessive concern with assigning agency to women has ignored the crucial, prior move that must be made—the careful consideration of the constitution of the subject of agency, for "the constituted character of the subject is the very production of its agency."[35]

The maternalist agonism of the southern Mothers' Front was buttressed by street demonstrations, meetings, and religious rituals that powerfully encompassed both tears and curses, grief and anger.[36] Such rhetoric and practices posed a tremendous conundrum for the Sri Lankan state, which expended much energy and effort on refashioning its own rhetoric and practices to counter and delegitimize those mobilized by the Mothers' Front.[37] These contingent articulations of maternalism were epitomized in an editorial: "When mothers emerge as a political force it means that our political institutions and society as a whole have reached a critical moment."[38] They were particularly effective because it was Sinhala mothers and Sinhala families who were the "victims" of state atrocities and they thus appealed to a certain Sinhala nationalism hegemonic within the country.[39] This is particularly clear when one compares the very poor coverage that the English- and Sinhala-language media gave to the northern and eastern Mothers' Fronts, in the 1980s.[40]

Feminist peace activists in Sri Lanka have had to contend with this kind of insular, ethnonationalist valorization of Sinhala maternalism, on the one hand, and the vilification of any critique of militarism and ethnic chauvinism, and the advocacy of a political solution to the ethnic conflict as being pro-Tiger (the LTTE are commonly referred to as Tigers) and thus unpatriotic, on the other.[41] As a matter of fact, a significant and painful split within the feminist movement occurred between those who condemned the anti-Tamil riots of 1983 and those who condoned them. Women for Peace, an autonomous, Colombo-based, primarily middle-class, multiethnic, multilingual, and multireligious group, founded in 1984, and of which I was a member, was frequently censured by Sinhala nationalists who labeled us "Women for Pieces"—that is, women who seek to divide the country by advocating the devolution of state power. Despite having to constantly negotiate the minefield of antipatriotic accusations, the primary strength of Women for Peace lay in its heterogeneity and the willingness of its members to accommodate dissent and ideological differences; every plan of action was produced through negotiation and compromise. The organization's loss of direction and eventual disintegration in the 1990s were symptomatic of the gradual shift in feminist political practices, which I characterize as that from "refusal to request" and discuss at length below.

Many early feminist interventions against militarism and ethnic chauvinism that were launched as long-term, oppositional campaigns in the early 1980s have gradually become dispersed, diluted, and fragmented today into projects and programs focused on "women's empowerment," "gender sensitization," "mainstreaming gender," "violence against women," "good governance," "conflict resolution" and "conflict transformation," documenting human rights abuses, campaigns to change legislation on domestic violence and increase women's political participation, and more recently, tsunami relief and rehabilitation.[42] Today, there exists no autonomous feminist peace movement in the country, and the voices of feminist peace activists are rarely heard at the national level. This does not mean that feminists are not involved in antiwar activism but rather that it is no longer the primary and sole focus of feminist organizations, an extremely unfortunate outcome in a country that has been engulfed in civil war for the past thirty years.

One of the central reasons for this lack of visibility and voice, I would argue, is the complexity of the political and social situation within which feminists in Sri Lanka live and work. They are simultaneously pulled in many different directions, resulting in a general exhaustion within the movement: the same pool of feminists have marched on the streets calling for peace talks and protesting rapes at checkpoints, the conscription of child soldiers, and the proliferation of nuclear weapons in South Asia. They have also agitated for better legislation against domestic violence and the removal of punitive legislation against gays and lesbians, campaigned for women's political representation in Parliament, and, more recently, highlighted the harassment, marginalization, and exploitation of women survivors of the tsunami and lobbied for more equitable gender representation in state-supported tsunami relief and rehabilitation processes and mechanisms. Such "stretching" has led to the dissipation and nonsustenance of many protest campaigns over the long term.

Another reason, I suggest, is the institutionalization and professionalization of feminism; with the flooding of international humanitarian and development aid to Sri Lanka, one can now find employment as a full-time feminist. Obviously this has lent a certain stability to feminists' lives, made their work more efficient and enabled them to concentrate fully on their activist work. One could also argue that the institutionalization of feminism supported by a continuous source of funding has enabled the sustainability of feminist organizations.[43] However, it has also produced new "comfort zones" and sometimes the need to sustain such institutions has become the primary concern of feminist activists at the cost of the activism that they may have originally sustained. This was sadly the case with Women for Peace, which in its last few years struggled to maintain its small office and staff, with the international funds it received, to the detriment of its antimilitarist and antichauvinist campaigns. In such a context then, the very appellation of "activism"—actions produced within particular ideological framings, oppositional practices that place one "at risk"—to such practices becomes moot. Nivedita Menon, remarking on a similar trend that occurred in India during the 1990s, and after which very few of the autonomous women's groups of the 1980s remained unfunded, puts it even more starkly: "Feminism need not be a political practice any longer, it can be a profession."[44]

The most obvious fallout of the professionalization of feminism is the now well-known figure of the temporary, careerist, "nine-to-five feminist."[45] But as Menon warns us, the implications of such professionalization are far deeper than the production and promotion of activists who have no clear feminist perspective: "The compulsion of taking up and 'successfully' completing specific projects has meant that there is hardly any fresh thinking on what constitutes 'feminism.' . . . It is as if we know what 'feminism' is, and only need to apply it unproblematically to specific instances."[46] Such a "codification" of "feminism" has also circumscribed our ability to conceptualize and participate in political struggles that are constantly reflective of what constitutes "the political" and what is meant by "struggle." This is particularly clear when one reflects on the strategies of protest that feminist peace activists, myself included, have mobilized in Sri Lanka this past decade. I have sought to characterize this as a shift from strategies of "refusal" to strategies of "request."[47] Strategies of refusal would include forms of noncooperation that encompass the more risk-prone, vulnerable terrains of strikes, fasts, go-slows, and other forms of civil disobedience. Strategies of request would include making demands of the state through legal reforms, lobbying, signature campaigns, charters, or email petitions and other forms of "virtual resistance," to use a term coined by Arundhati Roy.[48] Such a formulation is underwritten by the distinction Etienne Balibar draws between "insurrectional politics" and "constitutional politics."[49] In other words, "a politics of permanent, unin-terrupted revolution," as opposed to "a politics of the state as institutional order" that is reformist, regulatory, or philanthropic, that is, indistinguish-able from projects of governance.[50] These two forms of politics are "ob-viously antinomical," notes Balibar, because they are encompassed by a "discursive matrix of political action" that is founded on the "constitutive instability of the equation man = citizen," given that the rights of the citizen will always circumscribe the equality and sovereignty of "man."[51] It is this irreducible contradiction of modern citizenship that leads to the irreducible contradiction of politics.

This formulation "from refuse to request" also takes into account that there have been many instances in the political history of Sri Lanka in which people who made requests to the state or militant groups (which operate as quasi-states) for the restitution of their/others' rights have been arrested, disappeared, or killed. However, I wish to highlight the crucial political distinction that should be made between, on the one hand, mak-ing requests of or demands of the state or militant groups, which ac-quiesces to a preexisting framing of the political and the defending of preconstituted identities, and, on the other, refusing to acknowledge the pregiven framings of the state or the militants—where in fact, the very parameters of the political are put into question and thus made contingent, where identities are constituted processually.[52]

MALATHI DE ALWIS

By increasingly mobilizing strategies of request, feminist peace activists in Sri Lanka have primarily shifted to appealing to and making requests or demands of the state. I do not wish to posit that there is only one way to agitate for one's rights or that one should not grab any space or platform that one can find, but what I am vehemently opposed to is the presentation of one set of practices as the norm or best solution to the problem so that radical, socialist, and liberal feminists start mobilizing the same strategies.[53] This coalescing of strategies—signature campaigns, petitions, charters, and so on—I suggest, is strongly influenced by a common funding source that supports most feminist organizations in Sri Lanka, be they radical, socialist, or liberal. International donors such as the Canadian International Development Agency and HIVOS (Humanistisch Instituut voor Ontwikkelingssamenwerking, or the Humanist Institute for Development Cooperation, Netherlands) are seen as "gender-sensitive" funders and thus their liberal agendas less questioned.[54]

It is also worth considering how influential the processes adopted by the United Nations have been in circumscribing feminist practices this way. Since 1975, since meetings in Mexico, Nairobi, and Beijing and those convened post-Beijing, a great deal of local feminists' energies has gone into disseminating information about these meetings nationally and petitioning governments and holding them accountable to international charters, plans of action, and so on, that are promulgated at these meetings. Here, I wish to distinguish the political efficacy of internationalizing issues—for which the United Nations is undoubtedly a crucial and powerful platform—from what happens after that within the United Nations framework; the bureaucratization of initiatives and the frequent disjunctures that arise between international and national agendas.[55]

Not surprisingly, this kind of critique, albeit a self-critique, of feminist peace activism is rarely appreciated as it is often perceived as a form of disloyalty and breaking of ranks, especially in today's context, both nationally and globally, of knee-jerk NGO bashing, the discrediting of such organizations merely on the grounds of their being foreign-funded and thus presumed to be antinational and pushing "Western" agendas. However, my central concern is that we are losing our critical—or if one wishes, radical—edge in this shift to professionalization and to political initiatives that are driven by compulsions of funding.[56]

One could also argue that my definition of "the political," which is primarily formulated in oppositional or antagonistic terms, as taking risks, as seeking to put into question the very parameters of the political, is too narrow or too radical or too utopian. But is it so? Constantly questioning what is political about our practices, consistently seeking to push those boundaries, seems particularly imperative in an era where the "field of emancipatory possibility," to use David Kennedy's apt phrase, is dominated by human rights discourses: "Alternatives can now only be thought, perhaps unhelpfully, as negations of what human rights asserts—passion to its reason, local to its global, etc."[57]

Such a critique is particularly ironic given the "battle" "won" by liberal feminists in the early 1990s to link women's rights with human rights. The paradoxical unfolding of rights discourses—the recognition of rights on the one hand and the infringement of freedoms on the other—has been a topic of debate among feminists for quite some time.[58] However, it is Indian feminists such as Menon and Nandita Haksar who have come out most forcefully to argue that human rights discourses may have reached their limits at this historical juncture. Recourse to the law, while offering temporary and short-term redress, should not be considered a "subversive site," notes Menon, while Haksar foregrounds the contradictory relationship between law and feminist politics by positing that feminists' or human rights activists' continuous wrangling with the law is "a substitute for the other harder option of building a movement for an alternative vision."[59]

This search for an alternative vision or, more precisely, new forms of political engagement in realms not previously considered leads Menon to engage with the now well-known distinction that Partha Chatterjee draws between "civil society" and "political society" within a postcolonial context.[60] Chatterjee returns to the old idea (i.e., of Hegel and Marx) of civil society as bourgeois society to nevertheless address its working out within a different form of modernity, modernity encountered through colonialism. In postcolonial situations, a civil society of citizens shaped by the normative ideals of Western modernity is only a small, elite group that assumes a "pedagogical mission" of enlightenment toward the vast, excluded mass of the population, which Chatterjee places within "political society."[61] When Menon speaks of "the political" it is primarily in reference to the potential of feminists "to subvert, to destabilize, not just dominant values and structures, but ourselves"; it is a "realm of struggles" to produce an alternative to

MALATHI DE ALWIS

the "common sense of civil society."[62] Indeed, it is because we are primarily caught up with the "common sense of civil society" (steeped in constitutionalism and marked by modernity), notes Menon, that we are unable to conceptualize or recognize emancipatory alternatives within political society whose democratic aspirations often violate institutional norms of liberal civil society.[63] Such initiatives, Menon further argues, may not necessarily conform to our understanding of what is "progressive" or "emancipatory"—they could be struggles of squatters on government land seeking to claim residence rights or the decision of a village *panchayat* to kill a woman accused of adultery.[64] However, what is important here is that "any project of radical democratic transformation would have to engage and collide with the ideas, beliefs and practices in *this* sphere. . . . Feminist politics then, will have to surrender its reliance on the certainties offered by civil society, and acknowledge the uncertainties and unpredictability of attempts to wage a struggle in political society."[65] This is a very provocative and radical rendering of "the political" and opens up an entirely new terrain for discussion. However, I am concerned that this challenge posed for us by both Chatterjee and Menon is nevertheless dependent upon a sociological category—an entity called "political society"—constituted, for example, by a group of squatters tapping electricity or a religious sect preserving its leader's corpse. But what are the political consequences of seeking the constitution of political subjectivities through political practices, not social groups? Such a formulation, I suggest, falls back on a priori notions of social identity that exclude and rule out contingent articulations of group identity that have the potential to be more inclusive and nonhierarchical. Butler's call for a constant destabilizing and contesting of "the political," as delineated at the beginning of this essay and also discussed vis-à-vis the Mothers' Fronts, I find, offers a more radical alternative. Is this not where the emancipatory potential of any society lies?

Yet, why have we in Sri Lanka been unable to sustain such a destabilizing and contesting of "the political"? Have we, as political activists, been unable to address a far deeper malaise that is afflicting our compatriots? A malaise akin to that of "psychic numbing" after several decades of living with unrelenting violence and atrocity upon this "lacerated terrain," to borrow a phrase from the poet Jean Arasanayagam?[66] Perhaps the need of the hour rather is to interrogate "the political" *via* more affectual categories such as grief, injury, and suffering.

Judith Butler's more recent writings seek to push us in such a direction through her formulation that grief is a tie that binds. It is "the thrall in which our relations with others hold us" in ways that we may not be able to account; it challenges the notion of ourselves as autonomous and in control: "I am gripped and undone by these very relations."[67] Discounting arguments that it is intellectually unproductive and psychically debilitating to be interminably caught up in the thrall of our grief, Butler revels instead in this relational undoing and insists that to grieve is not to be resigned to inaction. For it is in this undoing, this submitting to a transformation due to loss, that a space for politics unfolds.[68]

This undoing, for Butler, is both psychical and physical: "One is undone, in the face of the other, by the touch, by the scent, by the feel, by the prospect of the touch, by the memory of the feel."[69] Thus, at the same time as we struggle for autonomy over our bodies, we are also confronted by the fact that we carry the "enigmatic traces of others" that we are interdependent and physically vulnerable to each other.[70] This unboundedness of flesh and fluids, this corporeal vulnerability, argues Butler, must surely engender an imagining of another kind of political community that implicates us in "lives that are not our own," and develops "a point of identification with suffering itself."[71]

It is clear that Butler's envisioned audience here is primarily those in the United States or First World who, having been made vulnerable through extraordinary acts of violence (such as 9/11), have resorted to war, to defining who is human and deciding whose deaths are grievable and whose not. But there is nothing to preclude such a standpoint being adopted by any dominant group, be they Americans vis-à-vis Iraqis and Afghans or Sinhalese vis-à-vis Tamils and Muslims: "To be injured means that one has the chance to reflect upon injury, to find out the mechanisms of its distribution, to find out who else suffers from permeable borders, unexpected violence, dispossession, and fear, and in what ways. . . . [It] offers a chance to start to imagine a world in which that violence might be minimised, in which an inevitable interdependency becomes acknowledged as the basis for global political community."[72] Butler's formulation here recalls prior conceptualizations of the political purchase of compassion, sympathy, and empathy but also significantly extends them: while prior conceptualizations have focused on how literary representations of the sufferings of the

MALATHI DE ALWIS

marginalized and exploited are used to produce a moral community of abolitionists of slavery, or how shared narratives of suffering help sustain resistance movements, Butler appeals to the very persons who have been injured and made vulnerable to recognize the injury of others, rather than only dwelling upon their own suffering and hurt.[73] This "recognition" is not merely driven by compassion or empathy but warrants a more open and daring mind-set, one that acknowledges leakages, undoings, and interdependencies which remind us in turn that we carry the "enigmatic traces of others."[74] While Butler acknowledges the fact that she does not yet know how to theorize this interdependency, I find her resolve to rethink international political coalitions, in light of this and previous feminist critiques, and her stress on requiring "new modes of cultural translation," particularly productive.[75] What such translations would exactly entail Butler is unclear on but nevertheless sure that it would differ from "appreciating this or that position or asking for recognition in ways that assume that we are all fixed and frozen in our various locations and 'subject positions.' "[76]

Butler's innovative formulation of injury and interdependency pushes me to rethink my previous arguments, which I set out above, regarding political communities in Sri Lanka in the wake of atrocity. While criticizing the ethnically majoritarian Sinhala community for translating their perception of vulnerability to that of further discriminating and waging war against the Tamil minority, I, along with many other feminist peace activists, was willing to settle for Sinhala and Tamil women to be politically allied under the aegis of "motherhood"—using such a subject position contingently of course. But our conceptualization of such an alliance failed to adequately plumb the depths of this maternalist agonism—rather than turning outward, across communalized boundaries, to acknowledge a common experience of motherhood as well as of shared vulnerability and injury, these women's grief was turned inward, individualized and Sinhalized. It is clear then that the formation of alliances under the mark of grief also requires the reconceptualization of not only "the political" but also injury and grief. Indeed, political communities of the sorrowing do not and cannot spring forth spontaneously and "naturally"; they must be made. One could argue that this is too utopian a proposition, but for those of us who have tried all else and failed it is such utopian reconceptualizations and reformulations that sustain an optimism of the will.

NOTES

Earlier versions of this essay appeared in *Economic and Political Weekly of India* 10 (March 7–13, 2009): 51–54, and in *Feminist Review* 91 (2009): 81–93. I am indebted to Ritty Lukose and Ania Loomba for their thoughtful questions and suggestions.

1. She was referring to the increasing number of civilian casualties in the northeast of Sri Lanka due to government forces gradually and steadily cornering the Liberation Tigers of Tamil Eelam on a narrow spit of land, along with around 200,000 Tamil civilians, the majority of whom were being held hostage by the LTTE. Civilians who did manage to escape were reporting that the LTTE was shooting those who were trying to flee, conscripting their children, and shooting at government troops from within the "no fire zone" designated for civilians—which in turn led to retaliatory fire by government troops, causing many civilian deaths and grievous injuries. In addition, around 60,000 civilians who had managed to flee the LTTE were being incarcerated in militarized displacement camps, where they were frequently separated from family members and where their movement and communication with the outside world were restricted due to security measures aimed at weeding out LTTE cadres among them. I have addressed the issue of the silence of peace activists in Colombo elsewhere; see Malathi de Alwis, "Sri Lanka's Divided Demonstrators," *Guardian*, April 15, 2009, at http://guardian.co.uk/; and Malathi de Alwis, "The Silence in the South," *Lines*, April 8, 2009, at http://lines-magazine.org.

2. Benhabib, "Feminism and Postmodernism," 28.

3. Laclau and Mouffe, *Hegemony and Socialist Strategy*; and Mouffe, "For a Politics of Democratic Identity."

4. Mouffe, "For a Politics of Democratic Identity." See also Schmitt, *The Concept of the Political*.

5. Mouffe, "For a Politics of Democratic Identity."

6. Ibid.

7. Ibid.

8. Butler, "Contingent Foundations," 20.

9. Butler arrives at this formulation through an engagement with the work of Laclau and Mouffe, *Hegemony and Socialist Strategy*; and Connelly, *Political Theory and Modernity*. For a fascinating debate between Judith Butler and Seyla Benhabib regarding political effects and the importance or unimportance of normative foundations for emancipatory politics, see Benhabib, Butler, Cornell, and Fraser, *Feminist Contentions*.

10. See Butler, "Contingent Foundations," for a thoughtful engagement with some of these positions and Benhabib, Butler, Cornell, and Fraser, *Feminist Contentions*, for a critique of some of her arguments.

11. For a location of these struggles within the broader context of women's/feminist interventions in pre- and postindependence Sri Lanka, see Jayawardena and de Alwis, "The Contingent Politics of the Women's Movement."

12. De Alwis, "Millennial Musings on Maternalism."

13. De Alwis, "Motherhood as a Space of Protest," 186.

14. Koven and Michel, *Mothers of a New World*, 6.

15. Ibid.

16. For the American example, see Swerdlow, "Female Culture, Pacifism, and Feminism." See also Steinson, "Mother Half of Humanity," and Strange, "Mothers on the March." For the Argentinean case, see Simpson and Bennett, *The Disappeared and Mothers of the Plaza*; Navarro, "The Personal Is Political"; Fisher, *Mothers of the Disappeared*; and Taylor, *Disappearing Acts*. For the Irish case, see Aretxaga, *Shattering Silence*, and McAuley, *Women in a War Zone*.

17. Zawilski, "Saving Russia's Sons," and "Soldiers Mothers on the Move: The Case of Women in Chechnya," paper presented at the Workshop on Women in Conflict Zones, York University, Canada, May 31–June 1, 1997.

18. Das, "Ethnicity and Democracy Meet When Mothers Protest."

19. Kaplan, "Female Consciousness and Collective Action"; Ruddick, "Maternal Thinking" and *Maternal Thinking*. See also Key, *The Century of the Child*; Schreiner, *Women and Labour*; Elshtain, "On Beautiful Souls"; Elshtain, *Women and War*; and di Leonardo, "Morals, Mothers and Militarism."

20. Hoole et al., *The Broken Palmyrah*, 303.

21. Ibid.

22. *Saturday Review*, April 1985, quoted in Jayawardena, "Time to Mobilise for Women's Liberation," 17.

23. Hensman, "Feminism and Ethnic Nationalism in Sri Lanka," 503.

24. De Alwis, "Motherhood as a Space of Protest."

25. Hoole et al., *The Broken Palmyrah*.

26. Women also joined the Organization of Parents and Family Members of the Disappeared, which was formed on May 20, 1990. This group was closely aligned with Vasudeva Nanayakkara, opposition member of Parliament and member of the left-wing Nava Sama Samaja Pakshaya politburo. Members of this group often attended the rallies of the Mothers' Front, whose members often attended the group's rallies, though the group pursued a much more radical agenda. While this group did not mobilize around "motherhood," they nevertheless valorized (non-gendered) familial identities. De Alwis, "Motherhood as a Space of Protest," 37.

27. "Sri Lankan Mothers' Front Plans to Hold Mass Rally," *Island*, February 9, 1991.

28. See de Alwis, "Motherhood as a Space of Protest" and "Ambivalent Maternalisms."

29. The southern Mothers' Front as well as the northern and eastern Mothers' Fronts share certain similarities (but many more differences) with various maternalist movements that arose in Latin America, such as the Madres of Plaza de Mayo in Argentina, CONAVIGUA (the National Coordinator of Widows in Guatemala) and GAM (Mutual Support Group for the Reappearance of Our Sons, Fathers, Husbands and Brothers) in Guatemala, the CoMadres in El Salvador, and AFDD (Asso-

ciation of Relatives of the Disappeared) in Chile. For a discussion of some of these similarities, see de Alwis, "Motherhood as a Space of Protest" and "The 'Language of the Organs.'"

30. De Alwis, "Millennial Musings on Maternalism."

31. Ibid.

32. De Alwis, "Feminism."

33. "Sri Lankan Mothers' Front Plans to Hold Mass Rally," *Island*, February 9, 1991.

34. Mark Bahnische, "Derrida, Schmitt, and the Essence of the Political," paper presented at the Jubilee Conference of the Australasian Political Studies Association, Canberra, October 2002; Honig, "Toward an Antagonistic Feminism"; and Mouffe, "Antagonisms."

35. Butler, "Contingent Foundations," 12.

36. De Alwis, "Motherhood as a Space of Protest" and "The 'Language of the Organs.'" See de Alwis, "Ambivalent Maternalisms," for how these mothers' angry curses and calls for divine vengeance on perpetrators of "disappearances" were nevertheless incorporated within a broader sentimentalization of maternalized suffering by the Sinhala media.

37. De Alwis, "The 'Language of the Organs'" and "Motherhood as a Space of Protest." Similarities between the rhetoric of the southern Mothers' Front and those mobilized by maternalist groups in Latin America, vis-à-vis the state, have been further discussed in de Alwis, "Motherhood as a Space of Protest" and "Feminism." This discussion is primarily an engagement with the thoughtful analyses of Schirmer, "Those Who Die for Life Cannot Be Called Dead" and "The Seeking of Truth and the Gendering of Consciousness."

38. De Alwis, "The 'Language of the Organs,'" 205.

39. De Alwis, "The 'Language of the Organs.'"

40. De Alwis, "Motherhood as a Space of Protest."

41. De Alwis, "Critical Costs."

42. For an analysis of some of these early interventions, see Jayawardena, "The Women's Movement in Sri Lanka"; and Jayawardena and de Alwis, "The Contingent Politics of the Women's Movement."

43. The institutionalization and professionalization of feminism is an issue that has begun to be much debated among feminists, in different parts of the world. For example, see Alvarez, "Advocating Feminism"; John, *Discrepant Dislocations*; Lang, "The NGOization of Feminism"; and Menon, *Recovering Subversion*. My grateful thanks also to the members of many women's organizations in Pakistan, India, Bangladesh, and Sri Lanka who shared their disillusionment and frustration regarding this new "turn" with much wit and honesty, during the time I was researching this topic in 1999–2000. I am indebted to Mahnaz Ispahani and the Ford Foundation, New York, for supporting this research study.

44. Menon, *Recovering Subversion*, 219–20.

45. This very apt term was used to describe professional feminists by a "women's movement veteran" in a personal communication to Nivedita Menon. Ibid., 242.

46. Ibid., 220.

47. I am grateful to Pradeep Jeganathan for providing me with this useful shorthand.

48. Quoted in Shoma Chaudhuri, "India Is Colonising Itself: Interview with Arundhati Roy," *Daily Mirror*, April 4, 2007. The two extremes of these two axes, of course, are participating in armed struggle and joining the government bureaucracy, of which feminists in Sri Lanka have done both.

49. Balibar, *Masses, Classes, Ideas*, 51.

50. Ibid.

51. Ibid.

52. Butler, "Contingent Foundations," 3; and Mouffe, "Antagonisms."

53. A rights-based approach of course has its own limits, which I briefly address below, but for a complicated and nuanced critique of such an approach, see Brown, *States of Injury*.

54. The limited, social reformist agenda is exemplified in the catchwords that I listed above: "good governance," "mainstreaming gender," etc. Even the term "civil society" thus takes on a particular valence in such a context. See below for a brief discussion of this in terms of the work of Partha Chatterjee. Chatterjee, "Beyond the Nation?," "On Civil and Political Society in Post-colonial Democracies," and *The Politics of the Governed*; and Menon, *Recovering Subversion*. Arundhati Roy extends this critique with a comment that even mass demonstrations are now funded: "Meetings against SEZs [special economic zones] [are] sponsored by the biggest promoters of SEZs. Awards and grants for environmental activism and community action [are] given by corporations responsible for devastating whole eco systems." Quoted in Chaudhuri, "India Is Colonising Itself."

55. For an innovative argument regarding the production of "subalterns" within the U.N. system, see Spivak, "Righting Wrongs."

56. A much more productive and substantial critique has been offered by Srila Roy. See Roy, "Melancholic Politics and the Politics of Melancholia." She argues that the bemoaning of a lost "golden age" of feminist radicalism is a form of feminist melancholia and seeks to contain feminism in a once loved but now lost "home."

57. Kennedy, "The International Human Rights Movement," 112.

58. See, for example, Petchesky, *Abortion and Women's Choice*; and Brown, *States of Injury*.

59. Menon, *Recovering Subversion*; Haksar, "Human Rights Layering," 76.

60. Chatterjee, "Beyond the Nation?," "On Civil and Political Society in Post-colonial Democracies," and *Politics of the Governed*.

61. Chatterjee, "Beyond the Nation?"

62. Menon, *Recovering Subversion*, 219, 217.

63. Ibid., 217.

64. Ibid., 218.

65. Ibid., 218–19.

66. Lifton, *Death in Life*; Arasanayagam, "Numerals."

67. Butler, *Precarious Life*, 23.

68. In this regard, Butler differs significantly from political theorists such as Hannah Arendt who advocated the separation of emotional life from political life and insisted that there was nothing to be gained and, in fact, much to be lost, through public discussions about suffering on the grounds that this would lead to the political abuse of suffering. See Arendt, *On Revolution*, 75, 119. I have benefited from Spelman's discussion of Arendt's arguments regarding pain and compassion in Spelman, *Fruits of Sorrow*.

69. Butler, *Precarious Life*, 24.

70. Ibid., 46.

71. Ibid., 28, 30.

72. Ibid., xiii.

73. For example, Bosco, "The Madres of Plaza de Mayo"; Morris, "About Suffering"; and Spelman, *Fruits of Sorrow*.

74. Butler, *Precarious Life*, 46.

75. Ibid., 47.

76. Ibid.

ANGANA P. CHATTERJI

Witnessing as Feminist Intervention
in India-Administered Kashmir

The blood in my veins is still. Sleep is haunted with dreams of the earth, thick soil separated into graves, pressed with bodies dead from fake encounters. The soldiers' boot tramples Kashmir. Barbed wire strangulates our land. The dust of this occupation chokes the lung.

GRAVEDIGGER, BARAMULLA DISTRICT[1]

ON THE NIGHT OF April 29, 2010, the Indian Armed Forces executed Shahzad Ahmad, Riyaz Ahmad, and Mohammad Shafi, three Muslim youth, in a fake "encounter" in Kupwara district, in India-administered Kashmir,[2] claiming them to be "foreign militants" from Pakistan.[3] Between June 11 and August 8, Indian military, paramilitary, and police forces killed fifty-one civilians. In late June 2010, Srinagar was under curfew: "security forces" open fire on protesters, turning political grievances into military matters. My colleague Khurram Parvez says that we cannot visit family members of three youth who had been executed by Indian forces this week. "S" says that surveillance on us has intensified. "If you are indoors, writing, they feel it is dangerous. If you are outside, they think they can control you in their prison."

The dominion of Kashmir, of Kashmiri peoples, has been a prerequisite for the consolidation of the Indian nation-state. Engaging the effects of India's rule in Kashmir thus demands an acknowledgment of India's neoimperial configuration as "nation" and a recognition of the nation as a compulsorily violent and heteronormative entity. In Kashmir, violence is anticipated, experienced, and proximate to everyday lives. There are those that are its direct targets and others that are concomitantly affected.

This essay speaks to diverse contexts of militarization and violence in Kashmir as mediated by gender dynamics. In the first section, I elaborate on military governance in Kashmir and the shaping of a people's tribunal as a way of soliciting countermemory. The second segment, "States of Exception," speaks to a specific case where rape and murder were used to enforce political subjugation. The essay as a whole explores ways in which the work of "writing Kashmir" (through documenting everyday lives and experiences of sustained violence) may constitute a feminist praxis, one that integrates critiques of gendered violence and attention to the complex labor of witnessing as intervention, as instantiated by a people's tribunal.

Kashmir retains its iconic status in the Indian imaginary as a symbol of statist unification. In the Hindu majoritarian sacralization of "official" history, Kashmir is habitually evoked as "integral" to India.[4] India's integrity in fact hinges on its militaristic and discursive ability to possess Kashmir, and on its refusal of Kashmir's claim to self-determination.[5] An extraordinary militarization, consolidated through a xenophobic authoritarianism, and put into practice by violence, suffuses all public and domestic life in Kashmir. Institutions of democracy—the judiciary, educational institutions, media—are neutralized by the government of Kashmir and the Indian Armed Forces, as they function in tandem, continuing what in effect constitutes "military governance."

In Kashmir, state nationalism merges forms of democracy with practices of authoritarianism.[6] Along with the violence of Indian cultural nationalism this normalizes what Giorgio Agamben calls a "state of exception" in law and polity.[7] The Indian military and paramilitary have been aligned predominantly with Hindu majoritarian ideological interests with regard to the state of Jammu and Kashmir.[8] Indian Armed Forces collaborate with Hindu nationalist or militant groups in development enterprises such as Operation Sadhbhavana, a campaign started in the late 1990s that enabled military encroachment into development activities calculated to control and appease civil society. One such activity is the formation of village defense committees, which have been constituted in Jammu as civilian "self-defense" militias against increased infiltration, made opera-

ANGANA P. CHATTERJI

tional by security forces and supported by the state. Defense committee members are predominantly men, of Hindu and Sikh descent, with some "trustworthy" Muslims recruited by Hindu nationalist groups. Sometimes, campaigns are organized as retribution for "antinational" activities. This presents militarization as a necessity to securing the rights of local non-Muslim minorities, while obscuring the relations of the Indian state to militarized Hindu nationalism.

The disputed region of Jammu and Kashmir has been a flashpoint in relations between India and Pakistan since their inception. The current conflict in (and about) Jammu and Kashmir began in October 1947 and spans issues of history, identity, territory, and resources. India, Pakistan, and China have all fought wars over Jammu and Kashmir, as a result of which the area has been divided and subdivided while still being contested.[9] The territory comprises India-held Jammu and Kashmir, Pakistan-held Azad Jammu and Kashmir, and a fragment controlled by China.[10] The Pakistan state has used militant groups to infiltrate Kashmir and, at present, it struggles to control misogynist and violent groups in the region. The Indian state, meanwhile, deems the "dispute" over Jammu and Kashmir an "internal matter," and therefore refuses to admit any international scrutiny or mediation.[11] The Indian state and certain media institutions continue to link cross-border militancy (acts by the state of Pakistan or Pakistani groups acting independently or with the state) with struggles by Kashmiri civil society groups (seeking to build a collective consensus toward defining self-determination), branding both as "terrorist activity," even though, in the present, by far the larger part of Kashmiri civil society dissent is nonviolent and locally conceptualized. The reality and reasons behind Kashmiri civil society's political and ideological disassociation from violent and misogynist groups across the border zones of Pakistan and Afghanistan are not acknowledged. These groups, such as the Taliban and Lashkar-e-Toiba, have been emboldened by the breakdowns of order in Afghanistan and the military and political stratagems of the United States in the region, as well as the inability of international institutions to support Pakistan's security. Pakistan's security issues are, moreover, compounded by the actions of its ruling elite.

India justifies its militarization of India-held Kashmir as necessary to securing the India-Pakistan border. Infiltrations and movements across the Line of Control (the name given to the contested border between these regions of India and Pakistan) into India-administered Kashmir are real and significant. But the Indian state exaggerates these realities, and its linking of "foreign terror" to local Kashmiri civilians and their protests enables the state administration and troops to proceed against them with impunity. India refuses to admit that such militarization is primarily targeted at Kashmiri society and to acknowledge that it radically affects civil, political, cultural, and economic life.

The period 1947–87 witnessed people's struggles through nonviolent militant action for the right of self-determination in India-held Kashmir.[12] The armed militancy of the 1990s, prompted by civil discontent with Indian rule, was widely understood as a freedom struggle by Kashmiris but labeled "separatism" by India. The people's armed resistance began in 1988, but between 2004 and 2007, the movement turned to nonviolent dissent. In India-held Kashmir, local resistance groups distinguish themselves as "armed militants" or "nonviolent militants," but all see themselves as "freedom fighters." Struggle, whether armed or nonviolent, is constructed by India as "terrorism" and "antinationalism."[13] The divergent positions on self-determination and civil society held by the various profreedom leaders in Kashmir are conflated.

Reacting to Kashmir's strong profreedom stance, the Indian state, civil society, and media are complicit in imagining the Kashmiri Muslim both as an *enemy* and as a *potential convert*.[14] Kashmiri Muslims are execrated as "violent" and as an "enemy," with allegiance to an entity other than India. Kashmiri Muslims are the intimate and viral "other" who can never be fully trusted and must be assimilated into the norm to become obedient national-subjects.

India's governance of Kashmir requires the use of disciplinary practices and massacre as techniques of social control. Discipline is effected through a military presence that practices surveillance, punishment, and exacts fear; it rewards forgetting, isolation, and depoliticization. Death is inflicted through "extrajudicial" means and by measures authorized by law. Psychosocial control is exercised through the use of killing and deception. To administer such repression in India-held Kashmir requires approximately 671,000 troops, while official figures record the presence of approximately 1,000 militants. It also requires the isolation of Kashmir: international organizations and institutions that have access to other places have not

ANGANA P. CHATTERJI

been allowed to visit Kashmir, and human rights defenders and journalists have been denied passports.

Following the killings at the Gawakadal bridge in Srinagar in January 1990, a state of emergency was imposed and then became the norm. The militarization of Kashmir resulted in a huge wave of crimes against humanity, leaving more than 70,000 people dead between 1989 and 2009, including deaths by extrajudicial executions (often labeled as occurring during an "encounter"), custodial brutality, and other means, and over 8,000 enforced disappearances.[15] Landmines are used as weapons. Illegal and long detentions, and torture in detention and interrogation centers, such as the Special Operations Group camps in Haft Chinar and Humhama, have become routine. Approximately 250,000 people have been displaced, including minority Kashmiri Pandits of Hindu descent, and between 209 and 765 Kashmiri Pandits have been killed.[16] The Indian state has meanwhile attempted to "nationalize" Kashmiri Pandits in its effort to create opposition to Kashmiri demands for self-determination, an attempt consistent with its strategy to religionize the issue.

The context of killings in Kashmir has engendered a landscape where the deaths of men (it is largely men who have died) have rendered women and children vulnerable. Violence against civilian men has opened further spaces for enacting violence against women. Women have been forced to assume, disproportionately, the task of caregiving to disintegrated families and to undertake the work of seeking justice following disappearances and deaths. A 2002 study noted deterioration in health care, evidenced in a rise in stillbirths.[17] Conflict-induced social conservatism has placed taboos on contraception, increasing the number of unsanitary abortions. More than 60,000 people have been tortured, many children orphaned, and the population suffers a very high rate of suicidal behaviors. In 2009, more than 100,000 persons visited Kashmir's sole psychiatric hospital, risking social stigma, to receive outpatient care.

The saturation of Kashmiri society, polity, economy, environment, and psyche with the corporeality of militarized governance profoundly affects and shapes the "everyday." Life under militarization undermines people's capacity to intervene in regularized and intimate impairments. Subjugation, however, also requires the complicity of Kashmiris, and forms a collaborator class whose actions and allegiances are complex. Moreover, approach to governance gives rise to an increasingly privatized domestic realm, and alienated subjects. In such a landscape, countermemory is camouflaged and harsh.[18] "Every other home in Kashmir has a history of suffering, every other square is witness to sacrifice, rape, torture, deaths, forced disappearances, and suppression as weapons of war," says Khurram Parvez, a human rights advocate of unusual courage, an amputee whose leg was severed by a landmine during a citizen's election monitoring effort in 2004.[19]

A PEOPLE'S TRIBUNAL AS COUNTERMEMORY

My work in India-administered Kashmir included fourteen trips between July 2006 and July 2010, and involved collecting oral histories, conducting interviews, undertaking archival and legal research, organizing research trainings, compiling testimonials on militarization and human rights violations, and alliance building and advocacy work with civil society coalitions. It has necessitated the construction of an archive in countermemory to interrogate hegemonic constitutions of present-day Kashmir.

In July 2006, Parvez Imroz invited me to collaborate in imagining and instituting the International People's Tribunal on Human Rights and Justice in India-administered Kashmir.[20] A defiant and formidable figure, Imroz has been repeatedly targeted for principled advocacy for justice.[21] He is a human rights lawyer and founding member of the Jammu Kashmir Coalition of Civil Society and the Association of Parents of Disappeared Persons. We determined to constitute the tribunal as an alliance between scholars and activists of Kashmir and India, to intercede on perceptions that such an alliance is "antinational" and impossible.[22] I am the sole woman convener of the tribunal. We considered inviting other women from Kashmir to the tribunal's convening body. Those we approached were few in number and in danger of being unable to retain their employment. Allies suggested that we should be content with trying to include women's lives and experience in various ways and investigating the gendered dynamic of violence in Kashmir.

A people's tribunal in what has repeatedly been termed "the most dangerous place on earth" is difficult to institute and sustain.[23] If organized through local consent and collectives, it can engage people's daily struggles that are both difficult and exhausting. In our context, sustained alliances

ANGANA P. CHATTERJI

between local communities and the tribunal have been enabled for the excavation of the living conditions induced by militarized governance, allowing us to move between "fact finding," bearing witness, and creating methodical contexts for understanding the psychosocial dimensions of oppression.

Our workplace is in Lal Chowk, the battered and resilient nucleus of Srinagar; it is marked by barbed wire, abandoned buildings, bullet holes, insistent street life, protests, and demonstrations, amid vacuous modernization and ubiquitous surveillance posts. Lal Chowk evidences how the Indian state's militarist presence penetrates every facet of life in Kashmir. Lal Chowk, a crucial economic and civic pulse of the city, is seething with paramilitary deployments: bunkers and watchtowers, checkpoints, detour signs, security personnel, counterinsurgents, and vehicular and electronic espionage. Close by are detention and interrogation centers, and the army cantonment, recalling Michel Foucault's description of the Panopticon "as a mechanism to carry out experiments, to alter behavior, to train or correct individuals," to "try out different punishments."[24] Lal Chowk is organized to enforce a continuous surveillance, whose violence and warning reverberate across Srinagar city and beyond, and is, in turn, internalized by the citizenry. Kashmiris regularly live in conditions of social and collectivized "internment." Acts of civilian dissent (everyday pacifist refusals) are classified as testaments of "rage," as "agitational terrorism," upon which institutions of state expend public and sequestered punishment. Armed control and disciplining of collective and individual "disobedience" function to regulate and govern people's very bodies. To legitimate the discursive and physical violence of the military, which is presented as "necessary" protection for the maintenance of the Indian (read: majoritarian Hindu or Hindu-secular) nation, the state has invented pathologies of "violent Muslims."[25]

Between January 2007 and March 2008, we charted the purpose and course of the tribunal. Stakeholders in civil society across rural and urban spaces were keen that this process be instituted. We met with a spectrum of people, including women who struggle for *recognition* as "half-widows"(women whose husbands have disappeared), mothers of disappeared sons, former militants now peace activists, diggers of mass graves, feminists in hijab struggling against the confines of militarization, union workers, daily wage laborers, college professors, lawyers, journalists, observant Muslims, the irreligious, socialists, Hindu Pandit activists, Gujjars subjected to internal displacement, Dogra civilians, psychiatrists, state employees in resistance to state institutions.[26] Segments of civil society across Kashmir stated that local, regional, and international political processes bypassed them, withholding their right to participation and decision making. They asked that the "international community" engage their experience of protracted isolation and the diminishing of cultural and public life.[27] We listened to a woman who was pursuing a triple murder case; a male youth who had contemplated suicide; the brother of a businessman killed in a fake encounter and portrayed by the security forces as a "terrorist from Pakistan"; the friend of a self-identified gay male youth seeking to define "liberation"; and the sister of a woman survivor of rape. These myriad voices shaped the tribunal's mandate.

The tribunal convened on April 5, 2008.[28] In June, we undertook investigations into hidden, unmarked, and mass graves in India-held Kashmir. These graves, placed next to homes, fields, and schools, and in rubble, thick grass, hillside, and flatland, produce daunting effects on women and children. By November 2009, we identified 2,700 such graves, containing over 2,943 bodies, mostly of men, across fifty-five villages in Bandipora, Baramulla, and Kupwara districts of Kashmir.[29] The graves were dug by locals on village land at the coercion of the armed forces and police. Circulating state mythology claims that these graves uniformly house "foreign militants," and that the demand for self-determination is predominantly external. In fact, the graves indicate massacre by institutions of state: the bodies they conceal bear markings of torture, burns, and desecration. Exhumation and identification have not occurred in most cases. Where they have, they indicate the dead to be local people, ordinary citizens, killed in fake encounters. We examined fifty alleged "encounter" killings by Indian military and paramilitary forces in numerous districts in Kashmir. Of these, thirty-nine persons were of Muslim descent; four were of Hindu descent; seven were not determined. Of these cases, forty-nine had been labeled militants or foreign insurgents by security forces, and one body was drowned. After investigations, forty-seven persons were found killed in fake encounters and only one person was identifiable as a local militant.

Between July 2008 and June 2010, the tribunal documented fake-encounter deaths, extrajudicial killings, and torture testimonies; it worked with legal cases, families of disappeared persons, and half-widows. We

ANGANA P. CHATTERJI

authored reports and briefs, filed an allegation with the United Nations, and wrote to Omar Abdullah, chief minister of Jammu and Kashmir. We conducted workshops with former militants who were now peace activists, some among them making reparations with women that the militancy had violated. We conducted trainings with youth and hosted solidarity visits. Our ability to work became contingent on events and circumstances. What we had assumed would be a one-year process, by necessity has now stretched beyond that envisioned limit.

What does it mean to have a people's tribunal adjudicate on the failures of a powerful state? What narration is possible? What rigor and solidarity must it empower? Feminist commitments to witnessing as intervention render official and dominant knowledges unstable, making vulnerable those that participate in its formation. Witnessing requires that we disrupt sanctioned truth and power relations as a precondition to cultivating accountability.[30] Witnessing shapes countermemory, as historiographic and provisional intervention. Its production is "inconvenient" and contingent on deconstructions of official "truth."[31] Countermemory, as knowledge of resistance and as resistance itself, takes an advocacy position that risks reprisal. Speech is performative dissent that pushes against the confines that organize dynamics of "fear" and "reprisal." Such counterhegemonic endeavors struggle with the boundless (im)possibility of "voicing."[32]

Narrating a genealogy of Kashmir's present locates discourses and events in relations and corollaries of power.[33] These relations of power are attached to institutions and cultural practices, and elucidate "truth effects." To discern the effects of "truth" is to contend with violence as a category of analysis. Violence, as a category of analysis, makes present the ways in which violence drives decision and response, and constitutes lives, community, place, politics, and gender.[34] As some of us had written earlier, "The study of gendered violence . . . should operate not just as shorthand for understanding violence on and against women, but also as an analytical category that is equally attentive to the ways in which normative ideas of masculinity and heterosexuality are disseminated amidst a pervasive context of militarism."[35] Violence, as a category of analysis, reveals the distance and continuity between routine and spectacular violences. A project in countermemory, in Kashmir, requires scrutiny of the "networks of violence that constitute the state and nation."[36]

For me as a feminist, the work of the tribunal is rife with contradictions.

Those I encounter struggle within militarization, patriarchy, and the neo-colonial polity. The efficacy of our work hinges on people's ability to speak, even as soliciting speech risks reproducing individual and collective trauma. We are forced to continually rethink our practices in order to create spaces where subordinated subjects can speak as acts of resistance.

STATES OF EXCEPTION

Death is very familiar. Every day brings the expectation of horror.
WOMAN ACTIVIST, KASHMIR

On May 29, 2009, Asiya Jan and Neelofar Jan were raped, reportedly by more than one person, and murdered. This incident, and what followed, exemplify the gendered nature of state violence in Kashmir. Asiya and Neelofar, Muslim women residents of Shopian town, in Shopian district of India-administered Kashmir, were seventeen and twenty-two years of age respectively.[37] On May 29, at approximately 4:30 P.M., Asiya and Neelofar left their home and traveled together to the family apple orchard nearby for the upkeep work usually undertaken by women in an area with numerous plantations.[38] To travel there they had to pass the limits of Shopian town, across the *nullah* (tributary) of the Rambi-Ara. That evening they were reported missing by Shakeel Ahmad Ahanger. Neelofar was married to Ahanger, who operates a small business in Central Market in Shopian; Ahanger is also Asiya's brother.

On the morning of May 30, the bodies of Asiya Jan and Neelofar Jan were located by the police and family members. Their bodies were found 1.5 kilometers apart, near the paramilitary Central Reserve Police Force (CRPF) and police camps bordering Shopian town. Neelofar Jan's body was laid, face down, head resting on a stone in the nullah. Her *phiran* (long tunic) had been lifted to reveal the upper part of her body. Scuffmarks were imprinted on her face, chest, and buttocks. Her gold jewelry had not been removed. Neelofar, her family stated, was two or three months pregnant. Asiya Jan's body had been placed on two boulders on the eastern bank of the nullah. Her forehead was fractured, clothes torn and bloodstained.

The bodies were found in a high-security "Red Zone," where, after daylight hours, civic activity is disallowed. Approximately 3,000 police, the CRPF, Rashtriya Rifles, and Special Operations Group personnel monitor

ANGANA P. CHATTERJI

the area.[39] The transportation of the bodies to the stony ground of the nullah would have been visible to security forces. The District Hospital cited drowning as the cause of death, even though the water level in the nullah is between ankle-deep and knee-high, with various dry areas, making death by drowning of two adults in full possession of their faculties unlikely. It was later disclosed that "the nails were clean of any dust, clay, or any other substance," indicating that there had been no struggle against drowning.[40] A Gujjar community that resided in temporary shelters near the police camp, and whom Ahanger had met on May 29, was no longer there the next morning, leading to speculation that they had witnessed some part of the events, and were thus forced to relocate. Two eyewitnesses, Ghulam Mohiuddin Lone and Abdul Rashid Pampuri, saw a Tata 407 police van parked at the end of the bridge on the nullah between 7:30 and 8:15 P.M. on May 29. They heard more than one woman's voice: "Mauji Bachao. Bhai bachao" (Save me. Brother, save me.).

This event staggered Kashmir, impelling women and men to the streets, chanting against the impunity of militarization and for *azaadi* (freedom). In response, security personnel stoned homes and businesses. Civilians, in retaliation, engaged in intermittent stone pelting. Security forces countered with armed violence. Rumors, reportedly circulated by security personnel, denigrated Asiya Jan and Neelofar Jan, presenting the rape as a "sexual encounter" (thereby also legitimating the abuse of those who are characterized as "immoral," such as sex workers). A week later, on June 7, police filed a "first information report" (no. 112/2009), under Section 376 (rape) of the Ranbir Penal Code. On June 10, charges of murder were added, under Section 302. On June 12, a forensics report confirmed the presence of multiple spermatozoa on the women, establishing that they were the victims of "gang rapes."

On July 4, the Jammu and Kashmir High Court ordered that the bodies of Asiya Jan and Neelofar Jan be exhumed in order to gather DNA evidence. On July 8, an inquiry commission appointed by Chief Minister Abdullah and headed by a retired justice, Muzaffar Jan, submitted its report. On July 10, demonstrations across Kashmir protested its content. On July 12, it became known that the police had doctored the commission's findings. The police were partners in Justice Jan's investigations, even as the police were themselves being investigated for their involvement in the Shopian case. The commission's findings noted that Asiya Jan and Neelofar Jan had been raped, and that their murder had been committed to conceal the rapes, but it did not investigate the probability of collective or custodial rape, or the use of rape as an act of torture.[41] And while the report speculated about Shakeel Ahmad's involvement in the case, noting that "the involvement of some agency of J&K police, in the present incident, cannot be completely ruled out," it did not pursue that line of inquiry.[42] The commission did not identify the perpetrators or investigate the chain of command by which the investigative process was subverted and evidence and testimony falsified. Only police, and not CRPF personnel, were placed under scrutiny. The police, reportedly 81,370 strong in Kashmir, are understood to be "locals" (read: Muslims); the CRPF, meanwhile, with 75,000 personnel in Kashmir, is recognized as an "Indian" force, trained increasingly to function in a capacity corresponding to the military.

Asserting civil disobedience as the sole mechanism available in seeking justice, for forty-seven consecutive days, beginning May 30, public protests continued in Shopian, led by the Majlis-e-Mushawarat and allied groups, joined in solidarity by others across India-held Kashmir. Economic and social life remained disrupted. Finally, on July 15, the Jammu and Kashmir High Court ordered the arrest of four police officers for destruction of evidence. The court also ordered that the officers be subject to DNA profiling and narco analysis, which requires the administration of drugs without consent and is banned in several countries as a form of torture; narco analysis was declared illegal by the Supreme Court of India in May 2010. Chief Justice Barin Ghosh asked the people of Shopian to call off their civil disobedience action; nothing was stated about how justice would be delivered and what the next steps would be. On July 17, two of the arrested police officers, Javed Iqbal Mattoo and Rohit Baskotra, petitioned the Supreme Court of India, "seeking stay of the Jammu and Kashmir High Court order."

What does it signify when the investigations of a judicial inquiry commission set up by the ruling government are vitiated? The complicity of security forces and impassivity of institutions of state pointed to the obstruction of justice at the highest levels. The Shopian investigations focused on locating "collaborators" and manufacturing scapegoats to subdue public outcry, on "control" rather than "justice." How might allocating feminist attention to the writing of this event restructure witnessing as intervention? If "writing Kashmir" is an excavation into techniques of

ANGANA P. CHATTERJI

government as they organize domination, systems of knowledge, and subject formations, how might "witnessing" enable the politicization of community and help empower new forms of resistance?

THE WAR "WITHIN"

Sexualized violence, as acts of power, as torture, and as weapons in war, has a long and complex history, across colonialism and in postcoloniality. A large body of literature has analyzed the deployment of sexualized violence on women of the "other" as vindication by members of a dominant culture.[43] The body is signified as cultural property, and rape as a deliverance of "justice" enacted to punish the woman. Through targeting the individual, militarization by dominant nationalist forces deploys sexualized violence to undermine if not destroy the political and cultural identity of subjugated groups. The violence employed by nationalistic factions combines both militarization and patriarchy, as has been noted in literature on Israel's subjugation of Palestine, the Srebrenica genocide, and the troubles of Northern Ireland.[44]

Gendered and sexualized subjection inevitably marks militarized nationalism in Kashmir.[45] The discourse of "nation building" in this region equates hypermasculinization with decolonization; India's military prowess requires the subjugation of Muslim women in Kashmir.[46] But these women reject that ploy, their resistance profoundly shaped by the Indian state's targeting of Kashmiri Muslim men. Meanwhile, the women's participation in cultural and economic life and their refusal to be made docile anger those who seek their submission, such as Indian soldiers, themselves "patriotic" bodies configured as artillery made to inflict terror on Muslim women. Thus the care, dissent, and solidarity of Kashmiri women are predicated on conventions of gender *and* their disruption.[47]

The relations between a Hindu-dominant Indian state and its governance of Muslim-prevalent Kashmir are shaped by gendered hierarchies of power. India's production of the Kashmiri Muslim as a distinct and monolithic subjective identity, in which religion is the essential marker, portrays the conflict as essentially religious in character, and assumes that the political sensibilities of all Kashmiris correlate with their religious identities. Islam, Muslims, and violence are interpreted as coextensive with one another, and "democracy" is dissociated from Islam.[48] Public discourse is suppressed in order to make invisible the infliction of violence on Muslim women's bodies by the state. Instead, Muslim men, racialized as hypersexual, are held responsible for the violation of their women.[49] Muslim male violence is understood as representative of the culture. Military and political discourse posits Kashmiris as "dangerous," and India's military is signified as the protector of Kashmiri women against ravaging Muslim men, and the protector of Muslim men from themselves.[50] India's security forces occupy 1,054,721 kanals (about 52,736 hectares) of land in Jammu and Kashmir, on which, in Kashmir, 671 security camps are located.[51] The structure of militarization ensures a gendered logic to the violence, as the placement of the camps regularize forced encounters between local women and security forces. Males, young and old, who refuse to participate in the sexual exploitation of women have been sodomized. Women whose male partners are missing, "half-widows," and widows have been maltreated. Former militants have been forcibly engaged in counterterrorism operations, commandeered by approximately 32,000 security personnel, requiring the use of fraudulent and unlawful measures in outreaching to suspected militants. Security personnel have searched, detained, leered at, propositioned, extorted, initiated unsolicited physical contact, psychologically tortured, and sexually assaulted girls/minors and women. Women who do not wear the hijab or burkha have been compelled to use them to shield themselves from the advances of soldiers. Victimization and fear have led to social and physical displacements, as in certain villages where parents have arranged marriages for girl children, who are forced to relocate to the village of their male partners to escape being targeted. In 1991, between twenty-three and one hundred women, including minors and the elderly, those pregnant, and those with disabilities, were allegedly raped by the 4th Rajputana Rifles Unit in Kunan Poshpora.[52] In 1997, in Wavoosa, seven women were reportedly raped during a "routine" cordon-and-search operation.[53] Further, the psychological health of the Indian armed forces remains in question. Thirty-four soldiers committed suicide in Kashmir in 2008, and 52 fratricidal killings were reported between January 21, 2004 and July 14, 2009.

These abuses take place in a larger context of violence sheltered by Indian law. Human Rights Watch has noted that "army and paramilitary forces deployed in the state by the federal government are protected by the immunity provisions of the Criminal Procedure Code of 1973."[54] The Kash-

ANGANA P. CHATTERJI

miri authorities are aware of this fact. On February 26, 2009, Chief Minister Abdullah stated that the Armed Forces Special Powers Act of 1958 (AFSPA), used with sadistic effect on civilian populations, should be revoked. The armed forces challenged his authority, stating "any move to revoke AFSPA in Jammu and Kashmir would be detrimental to the security of the Valley and would provide a boost to the terrorists."[55] Committees on demilitarization have repeatedly deferred troop reduction and the repeal of draconian laws. In pursuing these courses, the Indian state ignores the real possibility that, if the situation continues, it would likely induce Kashmiri civilians to take up armed militancy once again, continuing the cycles of violence. As Amnesty International has stated: "Until the Indian government provides accountability for the conduct of the armed forces in Kashmir, it will continue to face discontent from the residents."[56]

CONTINUITIES

In June 2008, peaceful demonstrations had protested Hindu nationalist demands for control of 800 kanals (40 hectares) of pilgrimage land linked to the Amarnath shrine. Such demands, designed to further render the Kashmir conflict as religious in nature, were supported by the Hindu nationalist Bharatiya Janata Party and Hindu militant Shiv Sena. Soon thereafter, between May and July 2009, Kashmir witnessed an uprising, as millions of people, in nonviolent protest, demanded azaadi.[57] Reminiscent of the early 1990s, curfews, accompanied by shoot-on-sight orders, were imposed to stop civilian dissent, resulting in sixty deaths and two thousand civilian injuries.[58] Amid surveillance, tight security, and disquiet that encapsulated localities, tourist and Hindu pilgrimage routes remained open.

Later that year, on September 8, 2009, Mohammad Hussain Zargar, a local leader working with the Majlis-e-Mushawarat in Shopian, was found dead. In mid-September, the investigations into the death of Asiya Jan and Neelofar Jan of Shopian were transferred to the Central Bureau of Investigation.[59] On September 28, the bodies of Asiya Jan and Neelofar Jan were exhumed. Rumors circulated that the doctors had testified under coercion by local people, and that the determination of rape and murder may be rendered inconclusive. Citizens' bodies and the Srinagar High Court Bar Association held that the state government was using the Central Bureau of Investigation to stage a cover-up. In January 2010, the Majlis-e-Mushawarat asked the People's Tribunal to probe into the inconstancies and violations of state investigations, to deliver an accurate understanding of the matter and define a mechanism for justice.

MARGINALIA

On June 20, 2008, Parvez Imroz and I were detained by state forces while investigating unmarked and mass graves in Kupwara district. On June 30, 2008, Imroz and his family were targeted, reportedly by security personnel, and a grenade hurled at their home. I was stopped at Delhi airport, without explanation, while returning to San Francisco. My mother, residing alone in Calcutta, received visits from intelligence officials, and colleagues in Kashmir and Orissa were questioned about my work. In late July 2008, I wrote an article for the English edition of *Etalaat*, a daily newspaper from Srinagar, on those unmarked graves, and in the same month the European Parliament Subcommittee passed a resolution (RC B6–0349/2008) calling for an investigation into the graves, and I offered testimony to the European Parliament's Subcommittee on Human Rights in Brussels on the investigations of the International People's Tribunal into the graves. In July, a first information report was filed by the police under Section 505 of the Ranbir Penal Code. The report (no. 54 of 2008), without a statute of limitation, charged the tribunal's coconvener and the editor of *Etalaat*, Zahir-Ud-Din, and me with intent to cause "fear and alarm among a particular section of the public" to "induce them to commit an offense against the state." We were charged with failing to appear in court, while, in actuality, we had not been summoned.[60]

The tribunal is witness to India's grip in sign and performance on Kashmir's hypermilitarized body. In domesticating Muslim subjects to Hindu majoritarian rule, the sustained militarization in Kashmir portrays the reach of the security apparatus under what is *not* termed "military rule" in the context of an ongoing conflict, suppressing civil society demands for territorial and political self-determination.[61] Article 42 of the Hague Convention, which characterizes conditions of "occupation," may be used in referring to the sanction and jurisdiction of the military and paramilitary in Kashmir, as its people remain "under the authority of the hostile army," whose reach and power "has been established and can be exercised."[62]

ANGANA P. CHATTERJI

Thinking of the tribunal's work as that of a "truth commission" is an invitation to inquire into spaces that are perverted via the maneuverings of "truth." Foucault tells us that "one 'fictions' history on the basis of a political reality that makes it true, one 'fictions' a politics not yet in existence on the basis of a historical truth."[63] "Truth" and "history" are both volatile topographies in Kashmir. The amassing and circulation of discourse by the state seek to normalize civic and legal states of exception. In the official nationalism of the state and the cultural nationalism of majoritarian Hindus, "truth" functions to obfuscate, to rewrite history.[64] In the postcolony, official "truth" overwrites memory.[65] Within the battlefields of knowledge/power, official "truth" becomes the contagion sustaining cultures of grief and it intrudes on grieving.

Khurram Parvez asks me: "What would make you not return to Kashmir? How do we know you will keep coming back?"[66] I am reminded of my father's world in Narkeldanga and Rajabazar, Calcutta, 1971. I was four years old, returning home with my mother, the writing in red paint across the side of a railway over-bridge: "Bhola Chatterji's head for 10,000 Rupees." My father was a socialist, of incendiary intellect, combatant against British rule, of Hindu descent, an advocate against dominant Hindu societal oppression of subaltern "others." I learned from him, from my grandmothers, mother, aunts, an extended circle of women who grew me, that returns to things that matter are fraught, uneasy. We attempt them, nonetheless, in literal and figurative capacity.

In Shopian, Shakeel Ahmad grieves the death of Asiya and Neelofar. His son, S. Shakeel, is two years of age. "He does not stop crying. He keeps asking for his mother. I do not know what to tell him. I do not know what to tell myself. Each night is a nightmare as life goes on." As we return to Srinagar on the evening of June 13, 2009, the roads are dusty. Pointed rifles, shattered economies, the ominous barking of street dogs. Fatigued-yet-resilient civil disobedience. Persistent militarization storied through every home, each life. The aporias of history. Across the beautiful and decimated Dal Lake the evening *azaan* (call to prayer) rises in lament.

NOTES

My deep appreciation to Ania Loomba and Ritty Lukose for their generosity of care in helping me define the logics of this essay. I acknowledge my debt to colleagues in Kashmir, especially Parvez Imroz, Khurram Parvez, and Zahir-Ud-Din, and to Richard Shapiro. My affectionate thanks to Christina Mansfield, Heidi Andréa Restrepo Rhodes, Alejandro Urruzmendi, and Pei-hsuan Wu for their comments.

1. Name and specific location withheld for reasons of confidentiality and security. Personal communication, June 2008.

2. Unless otherwise specified, "Kashmir" refers to India-held Kashmir.

3. Encounter killing: Extrajudicial killing of civilians, under the pretext that the killing took place in the context of an attack or encounter; in fact, the killings occur most often while the civilians are in the custody of state forces.

4. Ministry of Home Affairs, Government of India, at the ministry's website, http://mha.nic.in.

5. Such understanding prevails amid a large section of the Muslim population and segments of the small remaining Pandit Hindu population in Kashmir. The population of India-held Kashmir was recorded at approximately 6,900,000 in 2008, of which Muslims were approximately 95 percent. Eighty percent of those were of Sufi heritage. Hindu Pandits, Dogra Hindus, Buddhists, Sikhs, Christians, indigenous groups, and others also inhabit Jammu and Kashmir. Government of India, Office of the Registrar General and Census Commissioner, *Census 2001: State-wise Population by Religion* (New Delhi: Government of India, 2001).

6. Jalal, *Democracy and Authoritarianism in South Asia*; and Navlakha, "India in Kashmir."

7. Agamben, *State of Exception*.

8. Together these two regions form one of India's constituent states—the state of Jammu and Kashmir. See note 10 for the territorial dispute over the state.

9. The "First Kashmir War" between India and Pakistan was in 1947–48, followed by wars in 1965, 1971, and 1999.

10. India currently controls the largest portion of disputed Jammu and Kashmir, including the Kashmir Valley, Jammu, Ladakh, and much of the Siachen glacier. Pakistan controls Azad Kashmir and northern areas of Gilgit and Baltistan. China controls Aksai Chin and the Shaksgam Valley. Access to Azad (Free) Kashmir remains restricted, and human rights violations are mostly not reported. Human Rights Watch, "With Friends Like These."

11. Article 370, First Schedule, Constitution of India, recognizes the special status and autonomy of the state of Jammu and Kashmir. Indian nationalists refute its provisions as well as the United Nations Resolution 47 of 1948, which requires a plebiscite to determine Kashmir's future. Lamb, *Incomplete Partition*.

12. Article 15 of the United Nations Universal Declaration of Human Rights endorses the right of individuals to a nationality and the right to change one's nationality. Buchanan, *Justice, Legitimacy, and Self-Determination*, 243–52, 301–14.

13. Robert Wirsing states that after 2001 "the Kashmiri freedom struggle was being increasingly conflated with . . . terrorism." Wirsing, *Kashmir in the Shadow of Rivalries in a Nuclear Age*, 118.

ANGANA P. CHATTERJI

14. Richard Shapiro, "A Just Peace in Kashmir? Reflections on Dynamics of Change," *Rising Kashmir*, August 13, 2009; and "Notes on Christian Cultural Dominance in the Secular West" (2010).

15. Human Rights Watch, "India's Secret Army in Kashmir"; and Michael Kolodner, "Violence as Policy in the Occupations of Palestine, Kashmir, and Northern Ireland," master's thesis, Amherst College, 1996.

16. Muzamil Jaleel, "209 Kashmiri Pandits Killed since 1989, Say J-K Cops in First Report," *Indian Express*, May 4, 2008.

17. Women's Initiative, "Women's Testimonies from Kashmir," 94.

18. Foucault, "The Statement and the Archive."

19. Personal communication, July 2006. This mine had been placed by militants. In 2009, Parvez participated in a campaign securing a commitment from militants to abjure the use of mines. The government of India is not a signatory to the Convention on the Prohibition of the Use, Stockpiling, Production and Transfer of Anti-Personnel Mines and on Their Destruction.

20. We constituted the Kashmir process as an "international" rather than an "Indian" people's tribunal, as most "Kashmir" processes have been coopted by New Delhi and Islamabad. We limited our investigations to Kashmir, and selectively to Jammu and Ladakh, as, given the politics of borders, we are able to access only India-administered areas defined by the 700-kilometer Line of Control established at the end of the 1947–48 war between India and Pakistan. "Tribunal" and "IPTK," at kashmirprocess.org.

21. Two attempts have been made on his life by militants and security forces, and he continues to be denied a passport since 2005.

22. Tribunal conveners are Angana Chatterji, Parvez Imroz, Gautam Navlakha (a journalist from Delhi), Zahir-Ud-Din (also a journalist); its legal counsel is Mihir Desai (lawyer, Mumbai High Court and Supreme Court of India); the liaison is Khurram Parvez (civil rights activist). We determined to finance the tribunal from our personal incomes.

23. William J. Clinton. See Peter Popham, " 'The World's Most Dangerous Place' Is Already at War," *Independent*, March 18, 2000.

24. Foucault, *Discipline and Punish*, 203–4.

25. See Kleinman, "The Violences of Everyday Life."

26. Gujjar: tribal group, here usually identified as Muslims.

27. An "international community" is an intentional constitution. Kashmiris note the problem of engaging state institutions, for example, the United States with its flagrant record of violations in Afghanistan and Iraq. Political pressure from the Indian government and hypernationalist advocacy groups in the diaspora has resulted in the marginalization of the Kashmir issue in U.S. foreign policy as integral to determining "peace" and "security" in South Asia.

28. For context, see Sarkaria, "On Trial."

29. Among the graves, 154 contained two bodies each and 23 contained between three and seventeen bodies. Angana P. Chatterji, Parvez Imroz, et al., "Buried

Evidence: Unknown, Unmarked, and Mass Graves in Indian-Administered Kashmir, a Preliminary Report" (Srinagar: IPTK, 2009).

30. Agamben, *Remnants of Auschwitz*.

31. Foucault, "Nietzsche, Genealogy, History," 154.

32. I am thankful to Ania Loomba and Ritty Lukose for helping me think this through. My account of feminist witnessing, within the context of the International People's Tribunal on Human Rights and Justice, draws on a broad-based task of feminist advocacy and scholarship that seeks to bring to voice what is silenced, that seeks to make visible the invisible. In particular, the framing of oral narratives as countermemory and counterhistory provides a rich tradition for contextualizing the notion of feminist witnessing that I am developing here. Within the South Asian context, examples occur in works such as Sangathana, "*We Were Making History*"; Menon and Bhasin, *Borders and Boundaries*; and Butalia, *The Other Side of Silence*.

33. Genealogy, as a practice of thinking the present. See Chatterji, *Violent Gods*, 20; Foucault, "Nietzsche, Genealogy, History," 160, and *Discipline and Punish*, 161.

34. Enloe, *Does Khaki Become You?*

35. Banerjee, Chatterji, Chaudry, Desai, Toor, and Visweswaran, *Engendering Violence*, 132–33.

36. Ibid., 128.

37. Sources used in this section are documented in Chatterji, Imroz, et al., *Militarization with Impunity*. Also see kashmirprocess.org/shopian. On June 13, I traveled to Shopian with IPTK colleagues.

38. Shopian town has approximately 60,000–70,000 residents.

39. Additionally, over 20,000 security personnel are deployed across Shopian district.

40. Justice Muzaffar Jan Inquiry Commission, *Jan Enquiry Commission Report*, Greater Kashmir, July 11, 2009.

41. The International Criminal Court identifies rape as prosecutable as both a crime against humanity and a war crime. The European Court on Human Rights and the Inter-American Commission on Human Rights recognize rape as a form of torture.

42. Ibid.

43. For example, Sa'di and Abu-Lughod, *Nakba*; and Spivak, "Can the Subaltern Speak?," 296.

44. Butler, *Undoing Gender*; Feldman, *Formations of Violence*; Hinton, *Annihilating Difference*; and Weizman, *Hollow Land*.

45. Asia Watch and Physicians for Human Rights, "The Human Rights Crisis in Kashmir." Asia Watch is a division of Human Rights Watch.

46. *Jashn-e-Azadi* (How we celebrate freedom); Khan, *Islam, Women, and Violence in Kashmir*; and Moser and Clark, *Victims, Perpetrators, or Actors?*

47. Kazi, *Between Democracy and Nation*.

48. Asad, *On Suicide Bombing*; and Roy, *Globalized Islam*, 1–6, 97–99, 232–89.

49. Said, *Orientalism*.

50. Foucault, *The Birth of Biopolitics*.

51. Eight kanals = 0.4 hectare or 1 acre. Figures have been assembled from various archival materials on file with IPTK.

52. Human Rights Watch, "Abdication of Responsibility," 14.

53. Radhika Coomaraswamy, "Violence against Women Perpetrated and/or Condoned by the State During Times of Armed Conflict (1997–2000)," U.N. Commission on Human Rights E/CN.4/2001/73 (2001).

54. Human Rights Watch, " 'Everyone Lives in Fear.' "

55. "Army Opposes Omar's Plans to Revoke AFSPA," *Times of India*, February 26, 2009.

56. Amnesty International, "One Killed, 150 Injured as Protests Continue in Jammu & Kashmir Following Rape and Murder of Two Young Women," press statement, June 10, 2009.

57. Roy, *Field Notes to Democracy*.

58. Doctors, ambulances, and journalists were targeted by India's security forces. In some instances, as men left to bury the dead, security personnel returned to threaten and attack women.

59. India's investigative agency in charge of national security issues and the acquisition of criminal intelligence.

60. The Human Rights Council of the United Nations sent a letter of allegations on July 8, 2008, inquiring into the intimidation and harassment of tribunal conveners. The government of India responded on March 19, 2009, denying the allegations. U.N. General Assembly, A/HRC/11/4/Add.1, May 27, 2009, "Promotion and Protection of All Human Rights, Civil, Political, Economic, Social, and Cultural Rights, Including the Right to Development; Summary of Cases Transmitted to Governments and Replies Received," U.N. Human Rights Council, Eleventh Session, Agenda Item 3, 2009, 192–93.

61. Rai, *Hindu Rulers, Muslim Subjects*.

62. Hague Convention, "Laws and Customs of War on Land," Article 42, Hague IV, 1907.

63. Foucault, *Power/Knowledge*, 193.

64. Navlakha, "Invoking Union."

65. Loomba, Kaul, Bunzl, Burton, and Esty, *Postcolonial Studies and Beyond*; and Mbembe, *On the Postcolony*.

66. Personal communication, February 2009.

IV

FEMINISM, FIGURATION, AND THE POLITICS OF READING AND WRITING

LAMIA KARIM

Transnational Politics of Reading and the (Un)Making of Taslima Nasreen

What do you think of Madam Taslima? Has she not said the "truth" about Muslims? . . . Muslim men have ten wives and thirty-five male children. . . . Madam Taslima has revealed the "truth" about the "dirty" things that happen in Muslim culture.

YOUNG MAN TO AUTHOR, KOLKATA, 2007

Taslima is a nonissue. By writing about her, you raise the specter of communal violence and play into Hindutva politics.

A BANGLADESHI SCHOLAR TO AUTHOR, 2007

THIS ESSAY IS AN ANALYSIS of how the feminist author Taslima Nasreen has been appropriated alternately as a symbol of feminist consciousness and as a blasphemer by vested groups in South Asia. Taslima Nasreen is a Bangladeshi feminist writer who has lived in exile since 1994.[1] In telling the Taslima story, I am struck by the absence of feminist sympathy for her and her literary works in Bangladesh, and by the adulation for Taslima as a writer and feminist among Indians whom I encountered. In this essay, I want to reflect upon this difference: why do Indians and Bangladeshis view the same female author in such contradictory ways? How do we make sense of this paradox?

In order to comprehend the divergent responses to Taslima's literary credentials and feminist consciousness, I have employed two categories of analysis. The first relates to bourgeois notions of "decorum, propriety and decency" that shape the norm of conduct for Bangladeshi women.[2] Whereas Taslima is a flagrant trespasser of social conventions and boundaries, the majority of Bangladeshi women regulate social trespasses within a moral order that reconstructs them as good women. The terms "obscene," "blasphemous," and "pornographic" have been used to describe her work. As I show, the ways in which these terms are instantiated are subject to the political mood and the transnational locations of the reading public.

The second category of analysis relates to the suspicion of domination that characterizes South Asian transnational relations. As the epigraphs to this essay indicate, Bangladeshi-Indian and larger Muslim-Hindu social relations in South Asia are characterized by suspicion and fear on the part of subjects who perceive themselves to be under threat. Such suspicion originates from the colonial period when Muslim rulers lost power to the British, a transition that was accompanied by the rise of new mercantile and landed Hindu classes. The 1905 partition of Bengal further pitted Muslims and Hindus against each other, an antagonism that was entrenched by the 1947 partition of India. In 1971, when the Indian army assisted Bangladeshi freedom fighters in the breakup of Pakistan and the creation of Bangladesh, many Bangladeshis began to view India as the new "colonial" master. Bangladeshis now speak of their government as under siege by India, with the economy dominated by Indian businesses and their country infiltrated by Indian secret service agents.[3] In recent years, the demand by the Indian government for transit through Bangladesh to India's northeastern states has become a thorny issue of mutual distrust.[4] For Indians, the fear of Muslims also stems from the influx of undocumented Bangladeshi migrant workers into India since the 1970s.

My interest in Taslima began in 1993 when I first read about events surrounding the publication of her banned book *Lajja*.[5] At that time, I began to interview Bangladeshi and Indian women living in the United States about their views on her feminism.[6] On subsequent visits to Bangladesh and India, I had occasion to discuss Taslima with women, scholars, and feminists. The following discussion is made up of fragments from an ethnography that has unfolded over more than a decade. It is organized around three sets of publics—middle-class Bangladeshi women and feminists, the clergy, and the Bengali male literati.

How did Taslima, a relatively unknown writer in her native country, become an iconic crusader against Islamic intolerance and a champion of
free speech in the early 1990s? Taslima catapulted to global fame with the
publication of her novella *Lajja,* for which she received death threats from
Islamic groups in Bangladesh. It was published just two months after more
than two thousand Muslims in India had been killed during communal
riots following the destruction of the Babri Masjid in Ayodhya, India. In
Bangladesh, the reaction to this violence was swift, with Hindu homes
targeted and torched. (However, the killing was minor compared to the
violence against Muslims in India.) *Lajja* is a poorly constructed seventy-
page novella that chronicles the life of a Hindu family—the parents, Sud-
hamoi and Kironmoye, and their son and daughter, Suranjon and Maya—
that suffered brutalization at the hands of Muslims in Bangladesh as revenge for the destruction of the Babri Masjid and the killings of Muslims in
India. The story ends with the abduction and rape of Maya by Muslim
youths. Among Hindutva followers, the novel took on the status of an
eyewitness account. *Lajja* was a godsend for the Hindu-nationalist Bharatiya Janata Party (BJP). BJP cadres made unauthorized translations of the
book into several vernacular languages, and distributed it for free to their
followers as evidence of the violence committed against Hindus in neighboring Bangladesh. In Bangladesh, Muslim militants attacked Taslima for
promoting anti-Islamic views in *Lajja.* Anticipating political unrest, the
Bangladeshi government banned her book, and later forced her into exile.[7]

Taslima grew up in a provincial town in modest circumstances. Although trained as a physician, she began to publish poetry and novels in
her early twenties. By 1993, she had published fifteen novels and collections
of poetry. Her limited fame came from polemical writings published in
a vernacular weekly called *Jai Jai Din.* She had gained notoriety within
Dhaka's literati because of her advocacy of a radical female sexual politics,
her public display of her private life (two divorces and open cohabitation
with a third partner), her advocacy of a woman's right to premarital sex
and sexual satisfaction, and her smoking and drinking. All this was in a
conservative Muslim society. Her writing was considered unremarkable,
but the fact that a woman was writing about sexuality made it titillating for

her male audience. Within certain literary circles, she was disliked "for launching direct attacks in her newspaper columns against named, or easily recognizable, individuals—especially men whose acts she viewed as chauvinistic or misogynistic."[8]

While feminists in Bangladesh formed a united front against the clergy for the latter's attacks on Taslima, their solidarity did not extend to her brand of feminism, which they viewed as crude and lacking in a rigorous analysis of patriarchy. The leading feminists in Dhaka are drawn from its upper classes, and the women's movement is NGO-based with close ties to donors and international agencies. Its focus is along the programmatic lines laid down by the Convention for the Elimination for All Forms of Discrimination against Women, which emphasizes a rural development model based on legal and economic rights for women. The goal is to lift women from poverty and offer them tools with which to fight social discrimination. Taslima, the provincial doctor turned writer, thus existed at the margins of the feminist movement in Bangladesh.

With the publication of *Lajja*, Taslima faced attacks from a coalition of Islamic groups that had been agitating for political power since the country's transition to democracy in the 1990s. Prior to the publication of *Lajja*, the clergy had termed her writing "obscene" and requested the government to ban her books, but they had not taken to the streets to protest it.[9] The center-right Bangladesh Nationalist Party (BNP) came to power with a near majority in parliament in 1991. The leading opposition party, the Awami League, along with several Islamic political parties—including Ja'maat-i-Islami, the seven-party alliance Islamic Oikye Jote, and a number of other fringe parties—sought to take advantage of this situation by weakening the BNP-led government, and forcing a midterm election. Capitalizing on *Lajja* as an issue, the Islamic political parties demanded the imposition of sharia, or Islamic law, and the introduction of blasphemy laws at the national level. It is at this critical juncture that Taslima's speech was recast from obscene to "blasphemous," a charge punishable by death under sharia, which, however, is not in force in Bangladesh. These Islamic groups intended to increase their power through the Islamization of the state. By leveling the charge of blasphemy against Taslima, they could demonstrate to their followers—largely madrassa students—the absolute moral corruption of the state where a woman could dare to critique the Quran. By accusing Taslima of blasphemy, these groups hoped to provoke the ma-drassa students to agitate against Taslima and use the resulting crisis to weaken the government.[10]

Remarkably, these attacks from Islamic groups provoked Taslima instead of silencing her. In 1993, she appeared in a BBC interview where she was shown smoking and casually holding the Quran.[11] Then in May 1993, she was quoted in an interview with the *Statesman* newspaper of Kolkata as saying, "The Quran should be revised thoroughly."[12] Although the following morning she clarified that she had referred to the sharia and not the Quran, news of her interview had spread like wildfire in Bangladesh. A little-known group called the Council of Soldiers of Islam placed a fatwa on Taslima's head for five thousand U.S. dollars, claiming that she had besmirched Islam.[13] On the streets of Dhaka, thousands of Islamic militants demanded her death as an apostate.[14]

At this point, the demonstrations against Taslima expanded to become a critique of Westernization in general, and spread from Dhaka out into the rural areas of Bangladesh. The publication of *Lajja* fed into a simmering discontent with the work of NGOs in rural areas. NGOs had begun to displace the existing rural power structures by introducing social programs to poor villagers and recruiting rural women into the market economy. The NGOs were accused of proselytizing, teaching children Christianity in their schools, bringing rural women into contact with nonkin men—all of which threaten to weaken existing rural power structures and displace clerical authority.[15] In addition to burning NGO offices and schools and attacking women beneficiaries of NGOs, the clergy and rural elites accused several young women of adultery, and punished them by stoning in extrajudicial sharia courts. In the face of such attacks, feminist NGOs faced great difficulty in reestablishing their work.

Facing increased pressure from the Islamic political parties to bring Taslima to trial, the Bangladeshi government charged her under the Bangladesh Penal Code Section 295A for "hurting religious sentiment by allegedly calling for a revision of the Qur'an to ensure women's rights."[16] Finally, under pressure from Western diplomats and the International Writers Association, the government exiled Taslima to Sweden on December 10, 1994.

In 1992, the Western media discovered in Taslima a young Muslim woman who had fearlessly spoken against Islam.[17] Her global reception is intimately connected to the 1989 fatwa on Salman Rushdie for his book *Satanic Verses*. In both instances, the Western media showed young Muslim men burning books to demonstrate against speech critical of Islam or its practices.[18] The Western media appropriated Taslima as the victim of Islamic oppression and "identified her with reason, enlightenment, and secularism, not to mention individual freedom of expression, and by doing so they defined her opponents as embodying the opposite values."[19] While these demonstrations were primarily spurred by the political ambitions of parties within the country, they became part of a larger transnational discourse about the place of Muslims in the contemporary world.

In India, the media and the Hindu-right political party Bharatiya Janata Party constructed Taslima as a leading spokesperson for the oppression of the minority Hindu population in Bangladesh. Many Indian secularists became instant fans of her work. While these secularists rejected the communalism of the BJP, they saw in Taslima a champion of free speech and secularism that was at grave risk in Muslim-dominated Bangladesh.[20] In these circles, the fact that she was female and Muslim from Bangladesh enhanced the credibility of her speech.

In contrast to these circulating discourses, the popular discourse in Bangladesh viewed these events as purposefully orchestrated by the usual suspects—the U.S. Central Intelligence Agency and India's secret service, the Research and Analysis Wing—in order to cast Bangladesh in a negative light, and to undermine Muslims in general. The BJP's endorsement of Taslima gave rise to the speculation in Bangladesh that the BJP had paid her to write *Lajja* in order to destabilize communal relations between the two countries. While there was no evidence in support of this assertion, it did feed into local suspicions of India's desire to politically dominate Bangladesh.[21]

Taslima's critics alleged that she was hungry for recognition, and would speak "untruths" to gain international acclaim. They found the prose of *Lajja* uninspiring, its storyline flat, suggesting that it read more like a newspaper report than a carefully crafted novel with characters and depth. They questioned how was it that a novel lacking any serious literary merit could gain so much popularity in India, with its long tradition of great literature. They pointed out that Taslima won the highest literary award in

Kolkata—the Ananda Puroshkar in 1992—for her book *Selected Writings*, in which she had plagiarized the work of the eminent Sanskrit scholar Dr. Shukumari Bhattacharya on the Hindu scriptures.[22] Many of them wondered how the judges of the news magazine *Ananda Bazaar Patrika*, which awarded this prize, were not aware of this plagiarism. Many Bangladeshis saw the literary award as a deliberate attempt by West Bengal's elite Hindus, many of whom were refugees from East Bengal after 1947, to besmirch Bangladeshi Muslim society. Consequently, her credibility as a legitimate critic of communalism or patriarchy was overridden by South Asian Muslim-Hindu dynamics that framed this debate.

TASLIMA AND BANGLADESHI WOMEN

In the early 1990s, Taslima expressed a sharp critique of patriarchal control of female sexuality in her *Selected Writings* (1991), *Tell Him the Secret* (1994), *Revenge* (1992).[23] Taslima critiqued the Bangladeshi woman as one who exchanged marriage for financial security and surrendered her body to a "polygynous" man. In her controversial poem "Happy Marriage," Taslima criticized Islam and (Muslim) male sexuality through oblique references to verse 4:34 of the Quran, writing, "If he wishes, he can, with no qualms whatsoever, use a whip on me" and "if he wishes he can chop off my hands, my finger." In *Selected Writings*, Taslima wrote that as a physician she was made brutally aware of venereal diseases in the married women she treated, many of whom failed to realize that their husbands had infected them. She writes:

When a dog is following you, beware.
The dog has rabies.
If a man is chasing you, beware.
That man has syphilis.[24]

In her novel *Revenge*, the husband suspects that his wife has slept with another man before their marriage because she does not bleed on their wedding night. When the wife becomes pregnant six weeks later, he believes that the child is not his. He forces his wife to have an abortion. Following the abortion, she decides to take revenge. She finds a secret lover and becomes pregnant, and passes the child off as her husband's. In the absence of paternity tests in Bangladesh, Taslima's text revealed the hidden powers of female reproductive agency that were deeply disturbing to bourgeois codes of sexual morality.

In *Tell Him the Secret*, Taslima narrates the story of a woman who discovers after her marriage that her husband is impotent. Night after night she lies next to him unfulfilled. When she asks her husband to seek help, he not only refuses but also becomes violent toward her. When the woman leaves her husband, her family accepts his explanation that she is in love with another man. She begins to live independently, finds a job, enrolls in college, and finally meets a man with whom she has an orgasm.

Despite the fact that Taslima wrote about women's issues such as domestic violence, marital rape, and female sexual autonomy, she had few female allies in Bangladesh. Her fans were primarily young college women, many from provincial towns like her. Their move to the city had freed these women from the patriarchal control of their families. They had fewer restrictions placed on their movements, and could meet and date men. Taslima's writings offered them a way of imagining their own agency. In a discussion I had organized with several students from Dhaka University, a young woman said to the group, "I like Taslima. I have every right to live with a man without getting married." In the context of Dhaka culture, where a woman is expected to behave with sexual restraint in public, this was a bold statement in front of her peers and teachers.

Taslima attempted to make female sexual politics visible in middle-class Bangladeshi society, but failed to garner the empathy of the women who were her reading public. Given the restrictions on female conduct, the majority of women who found themselves in unfulfilled marital relations could not openly endorse her position on female sexual agency. In other cases, they did not accept her ideas. In interviews with me, an older generation of Bangladeshi women in both Bangladesh and the United States repeatedly said that what they found most offensive about Taslima's speech was her advocacy of free love. In contrast, the younger generation of women, both in Bangladesh and the United States, accepted Taslima's sexual politics. They pointed to discrimination on the part of parents and society between daughters and sons. For these women, especially diasporic ones, Taslima had adopted Western and Indian attitudes against Muslims. Below is an excerpt from an interview with a woman in her mid-forties who is married and employed as an engineer in Dhaka. She expressed sentiments that were held by many similarly situated women in Bangladesh and the United States.

> She is supposed to have said that women should be able to sleep with anyone they choose, bear the child of anyone they want. This is totally her opinion. Did she take a poll to find out how women feel about these issues? Bangladeshi women do not want to bear the child of any man or sleep with any man. There are more pressing issues facing our women. She talked about issues that affect women *like her* and not the majority of women. (Emphasis added)

Several women (and men) pointed out to me that Taslima had made outrageous comments that defied Bengali female behavior. For example, Taslima wrote that since men rape women, women too should rape men, and that Muslim women should be allowed to marry four times like Muslim men.[25] These women said that desire for sexual violence was not a model to which Bengali women aspired. These women failed to read Taslima's critique as a rhetorical device to create a new vocabulary of female rage toward society. Instead, it was read literally, and silenced as the unruly speech of a bad woman. A young married woman offered a perceptive critique of such attitudes.

> What women do not like about her writings is her advocacy of marital infidelity. Infidelity goes on in Bangladeshi society all the time . . . in the poorer classes as well as in the middle classes . . . but you do not talk about it openly. . . . As long as you do not flaunt it, society accepts these trespasses. But Taslima went further, she not only flaunted it, she advocated the right of women to take lovers, live singly, divorce their partners, and so on. I find that it is this marital infidelity issue that antagonized more women and men than her religious views.

Middle-class morality is organized around familial duties such as marriage, family, bearing male children, a woman's duty to her husband and in-laws, all of which form the bedrock principles regulating social life. There is a ditty in Bengali that goes "Sangsar shukher hoi rominer gune" (the family is made happy by a virtuous woman). The illicit relationships through which she shows an alternative female sexual agency occur routinely, but behind closed doors. The wife who figuratively embodies family honor was rendered as the potential agent of family dishonor. It should not be surprising, then, that middle-class women rejected Taslima and distanced themselves from her views.

In contrast, the five middle-aged Indian women I interviewed had all read Talisma's novels and liked her. One of them, a college professor, had translated her poetry. Each one of them remarked to me that they did not expect such a liberated woman to come from Bangladesh. In the words of one, she was a "revolutionary." Another, a homemaker, said to me: "I love Taslima's writings. When I read her, tears fill my eyes. How many women can talk about marital rape? When my husband commands, 'Open your legs,' I have to lie down, and let him do it." Perhaps what explains the divergent responses of Bangladeshi and Indian women is that, for Bangladeshi women, Taslima had entangled the politics of the female body with the politics of the nation. Thus, for them to concur with Taslima's notions would mean playing into Hindu right-wing politics and diminishing one's husband, religion, and nation. For Indian women, the script was different. They had a more developed discourse of female desire and sexuality, perhaps because since the 1980s there has been a growing openness to sex among Indian feminists in Kolkata. The films of Aparna Sen, and books such as *Nahonnate*, the autobiography of Maitrayee Debi, and the erotic writings of Sangeeta Bandopahya, have all helped shape this relative openness to female sexuality.[26] In spite of this, one wonders whether their response would be the same if their religion was under attack and subject to global scrutiny.

Taslima also alienated feminists in Bangladesh, another group that should have been her natural ally. She often denigrated the work of other Bengali poets and activists.[27] In interviews with the Western press, Taslima alleged that Bangladeshi feminists were happy to be housewives.[28] In an interview with the *New York Times*, she added, "Other women write love stories, I write about sexual oppression. . . . I have no shyness in describing anything about a woman's body or a man's body because I am a doctor. . . . [Feminists] have decided that women should not talk about sex, that it is a man's place."[29] In a conservative Muslim society, Bangladeshi feminists have to be strategic in their advocacy of women's rights and, especially, sexuality. They focus on alleviating rural poverty and in creating legal and economic safeguards for women, and avoid discussions around sexuality unless it deals with sexual violence, sex workers, or health issues. For example, lesbianism is often dismissed by them as a Western concept, not critical for women's rights in Bangladesh.[30] Feminist organizations such as Ain-o-Salish Kendro, Nijera Kori, Nari Pokko, and Sammilito Nari Samaj all focus on providing an effective advocacy network at the rural and urban levels. Feminists have pointed out that Taslima has not worked with rural women, nor does her writing reflect the concerns of poor women. They suggest that her feminist concern about sexual rights is not high on the agenda of poor and illiterate women. These feminists are constrained and circumscribed by cultural notions of "decorum, decency, and propriety," which shape their response to Taslima's polemical writings on female sexuality and emancipation.[31]

TASLIMA AND THE CLERGY

In 1998, the government of Bangladesh allowed Taslima into the country to visit her mother, who was dying of cancer.[32] The newspapers carried the news of her arrival in the country, and although there were some sporadic demands for her death from Islamic groups, there was no organized Islamic political backlash against her. After her departure from Bangladesh, Taslima published a poem about her mother, entitled "My Mother's Story," in the foremost literary journal in Kolkata, *Desh Patrika*. While that particular issue of *Desh* was banned in Bangladesh, the poem was reprinted in a local tabloid, *Manab Zamin*, with the name of the Prophet blacked out. The paper was widely available. In the poem, Taslima critiques the promises of sexual gratification granted to Muslim men in heaven.

Still, I want to believe in Heaven
over the seventh sky, or somewhere,
a fabulous, magnificent heaven
where my mother reached
crossing the impossible bridge, the Pulsirat, with ease.
And a very handsome man, the prophet Muhammed,
has welcomed her, embraced her, felt her melt on his hairy chest.

. . . .

Allah Himself will come by foot into the garden to meet her,
put a red flower into her hair, kiss her passionately.[33]

This poem would be considered extremely distasteful by many in Bangladesh, and even heresy in some quarters. But the reaction to its publication was relatively tame. Muslim leaders welcomed the government's decision to seize copies of, and ban, that particular issue of *Desh* magazine. They claimed that they did not know the contents of the poem and would consider action after reading it.[34] A few demonstrations were organized against Taslima, but these soon petered out. What had occurred between 1993 and 1998 that had tamed clerical attitudes toward Taslima? By 1998, she had been exhausted as a political sign in Bangladesh, and no longer had the power to provoke the people. The Islamists had turned to other minority groups, such as the Ahmadiyya Muslim Ja'maat, to foment unrest. But most important, the Islamists had arrived at a consensus with the government to accomplish some of their goals. Since the early 1990s, the government allowed Islamic NGOs and madrassas to grow unregulated and receive funds from overseas. These are the two sources of recruitment for the Islamic movement in Bangladesh, and as long as the pipeline was left undisturbed, the Islamic parties would not react against the state.

Middle-class Bangladeshis were weary of Taslima, and saw this as yet another attempt by her for media attention and as Indian machinations to create trouble. According to some people, the poem showed her lack of morality and taste. As some concluded, why would *Desh Patrika* print such smut as poetry unless it was meant to create disturbances within Bangladesh? And would they print such filth against Hindu gods? In these circulating suspicions of the other, her feminist critique of how Islam grants men special privileges, even in death, was displaced within a familial structure of kin obligations. She was recast within a moral code as the "bad daughter" for violating the mother-daughter bond by sexualizing her mother in death.

TASLIMA AND MALE LITERATI

In my conversations with Bangladeshi male literati, they pointed out that male writers also make satirical comments about the Prophet Muhammad. For example, the preeminent male novelist Humayun Ahmed, had written in his novel *Srabon Diner Megh* (Cloudy days of monsoon) that "Our Allah was not terribly good at math. The Koran got it all wrong when it came to the division of parental property between men and women."[35] While the Islamic militants had demanded Ahmed's death as an apostate, they did not mobilize against him. Similarly, they brought the charge of apostate (*murtad*) against another writer, Humayun Azad, for his novel *Nari* (Woman) because it contained "many objectionable and anti-Islamic comments."[36] Citing these examples of tolerance, her critics argued that religious dissent was possible in Bangladesh. They further alleged that Taslima had deliberately tried to provoke the wrath of the clergy to get Western and Indian media attention. In this masculinist discourse, the way in which the speaker's gender determined authority remained unacknowledged. Instead, Taslima was discredited as an agent of Indian communalism and Western imperialism.

Commenting on Taslima and *Lajja*, the Bangladeshi poet Ahmed Sofa wrote:

[If] she had written the book with the desire to change communalism among Bangladeshis, then the book would have to be written differently. If she had taken the time to express how humanity is cultivated despite the kinds of violence she represented, then she would have earned the respect of this nation. . . . She fed the communalism in Bangladesh as fodder to Indian communalists. . . . Imperial India and BJP cadres used her book as a shield to deflect attention from their communal activities.[37]

Sofa went on to note that activists had condemned the inactions of the government, and while curfew was in place for three days in Bangladesh, it was in place for three weeks in neighboring Kolkata. He added, "When Taslima blamed the whole country for communal attacks on Hindus, how much truth was there in her words?"

In contrast, Swati Ghosh's review of *Lajja* displays what Bangladeshis term as the prevailing anti-Muslim attitude in India toward their society.

From the passionate point of view of a screaming protester, Taslima probes deep into the spring of thoughtless hatred that burst into a flood after December 6, 1992. On that day a dilapidated structure in Ayodhya . . . was destroyed. The crumbling stones came down in a roar that reverberated in Bangladesh too. Taslima then describes how the world fell apart for Suranjan and his family till they decided to leave for India.[38]

Ghosh amplified the rape of the Hindu daughter: "Maya's hands were still soiled with the rice and curry she had been mixing for her father. Her clothes were in disarray as wild-eyed she screamed to her mother for help."[39] Gupta's review would have been less biased had she also commented on Suranjan's rape of the Muslim sex worker as vengeance for his sister, and shown how violence destroyed both the perpetrator and the victim.

A turning point in Taslima's writing occurred in 1999. She published the first part of her four-part autobiography entitled *Amar Meyebela* (My girlhood). Turning to the confessional mode, Taslima found a new tool with which to push the boundaries of acceptable speech. In an otherwise tedious rendition of her early childhood, she brings up the controversial issue of child molestation and incest that she elaborates through her rape as a child. While some sections of the book are highly critical of Islamic practice in Bangladesh, the discussion of incest received the most attention in middle-class society.

Instead of acknowledging the prevalence of incest and sexual abuse of children in families, often at the hands of older male relatives, Taslima's confession became evidence of her "deranged" status. It was generally believed that a woman who was sexually molested as a child could not have a healthy attitude toward men or sexuality. The autobiography also generated a peculiar kind of sympathy from women who had once rejected her. As some women remarked to me, "I can now understand why this *poor* woman hates men so much." Thus, instead of addressing the critical issue of sexual violence against children, her words lost their power of social critique and she became pathologized as a victim of sexual abuse, a condition that "explained" the content of her writings.

The incest incident generated some peculiar responses among some of my West Bengal colleagues. I have been asked by friends, "Have you heard that she talks about *incest* in her latest book?" The sexual violence against Taslima the child was rewritten under an Orientalist notion of a hyper-Muslim male sexuality. Incest became equated with Islam and Bangladeshi male sexuality, and Taslima was read as someone offering "dirty" secrets about Bangladeshi society, as if incest occurred only in Muslim societies. Let me offer two anecdotes to illustrate this point.

The young Hindu taxi driver who drove me to Dum Dum airport in 2007 commenced a monologue about "Madam Taslima" when he heard that I was traveling to Bangladesh. The young man, who had dropped out of school after class ten, was smart and articulate. Turning to me, he said, "What do you think of Madam Taslima? Has she not said the 'truth' about

Muslims?" When I asked him what the "truth" was, he laughed and said: "Sister, Muslim men have ten wives and thirty-five male children. Madam Taslima has revealed the 'truth' about the obscene things that happen in Muslim culture. Everyone knows this."

I let him talk while I wondered what provoked him to speak in these terms about Muslims. Was he not aware that I was probably Muslim since I was traveling to Bangladesh? Did he speak in this manner precisely because he knew I was Muslim? Or had the anti-Muslim rhetoric become so naturalized that civility could be easily abandoned? As I listened to him speak, I wondered why Taslima had not penned a single book on the dire living conditions of India's Muslims? If seeking the truth was the passion of her pen, why not use the same pen to talk about the conditions of Muslims in democratic India similar to what she said about the conditions facing Hindus in Bangladesh in *Lajja*?

At the International Ethnological Society meeting in Kolkata in 2004, I presented a paper on the persecution of minorities in Bangladesh. Afterward, a Kolkata-based Bengali professor came up to me. He said that he liked what I had to say, and asked me where I taught. When he heard that I lived in the United States, he remarked, "I see, another Taslima Nasreen." How does one make sense of this remark, "another Taslima Nasreen," made in Kolkata, a city that has sent hundreds of its best and brightest women to teach at American universities? Linking my critique of the persecution of minorities with his construction of me as a secular person, he assumes that, like Taslima, I could not live in Bangladesh, the den of intolerance and darkness. The Indian professor's comment, and I have heard many such, feeds into a dominant discourse, according to which Bangladesh fell victim to Islamization and backwardness with the departure from East Bengal in 1947 of high-caste Bengali Hindus, the custodians of Bengali culture.[40] Hence, it could no longer be a place where secular values could be cultivated.

With the publication of the third volume of her autobiography, *Dwikhondito* (Split in two), in 2003, Taslima returns to the question of male privilege with a vengeance.[41] In it, she questions the sexual hypocrisy of the male public intellectual and reveals the sexual dalliances of Bangladesh's and Kolkata's male literary giants. The Bangladeshi novelist Shamsul Haq brought a defamation suit against Taslima and sought to ban her book for depicting him as a philanderer, and for writing that he had an extramarital relationship with his sister-in-law. Several Kolkata male intellectuals spoke out against the book. The writer Sunil Gangopadhya said that he found the sexual content of the book "distasteful." He went on to add: "Everybody knows that adults enter a sexual relationship on the basis of an unwritten pact. . . . If someone breaks that trust, it is a breach of contract and confidentiality which is not only distasteful but also an offence."[42]

Kolkata's Left Front government, which had previously protected Taslima's free speech, now banned the book. A government spokesman claimed that her speech had to be censored because her book "slanders the Prophet Muhammad and Islam," and delves into the "sexual lives" of eminent literary figures in both India and Bangladesh.[43] Charges of slandering Islam had never led the West Bengal government to proscribe the anti-Muslim hate literature that is circulated by the Hindu Right in the name of freedom of speech.[44] But even the male secularists in West Bengal who had defended her right to free speech in the past now collectively defended the censorship of *Dwikhondito* on the grounds that the book was injurious to "eminent personalities." Eventually, in May 2004, the highest court in Kolkata ordered the state to remove the ban on her book.

In these bourgeois evaluations of obscenity and freedom of speech, the male elite defined the boundaries between acceptable and offensive speech. Acceptable speech protected upper-class male privilege. The West Bengal state, which is made up from this social stratum, was complicit in protecting this privilege. It should be noted that this same public would have been unwilling to protect the sentiments of Muslims who are offended by Taslima's criticisms of Islam and the Prophet Muhammad. However, the threatened exposure of the secret lives of "eminent personalities" trumped the mutual suspicions on the part of Muslim and Hindu male literary figures in Bangladesh and Kolkata and forged an alliance between them.

I have shown that Taslima's story reveals the mutual suspicions harbored by both Bangladeshis and Indians. By tracking the politics of Taslima's reception we can see how Taslima has functioned as a "banner for diverse and contradictory political projects."[45] As such, she brings different groups together to garner support for shared political ends. Furthermore, "cultural notions of decency, decorum, and propriety" have shaped the debate over her work to a larger extent than have discourses of obscenity or blasphemy. Such middle-class notions of propriety are, as Priya Kumar puts it, deeply "imbricated with religious and nationalist agendas and often serve as their

LAMIA KARIM

alibis."[46] They threaten to subsume Taslima's radical critique of Islam, patriarchy, and sexuality in a landscape that is uniquely South Asian.

NOTES

1. This essay is based on interviews conducted in Bangladesh, the United States, and India between 1994 and 2007. I thank Bishnupriya Ghosh for sharing her unpublished manuscript with me. A shorter version of this essay was presented at "Obscenity: An Obermann Center Humanities Symposium" at the University of Iowa, March 1–4, 2007. I thank Loren Glass and Priya Kumar for their comments on an earlier draft. Thanks to Ritty Lukose, Ania Loomba, and an anonymous reviewer for their helpful comments.

Taslima and Nasreen (also spelled Nasrin) are first names and not indicators of her familial descent. By choosing her own last name, Taslima has crafted an autonomous identity separate from kinship descent.

Like the riots in Bangladesh in 1993–94, riots led by the All India Minority Forum and Jamiat-e-Ulema-e-Hind broke out in Kolkata in 2007 over the expulsion of Taslima from India. See Riaz, "Constructing Outraged Communities and State Responses."

2. Priya Kumar, commentator at the symposium on obscenity (see note 1).

3. See Baxter, *Bangladesh*.

4. See, for example, Abid Bahar, "Seven Reasons Why Bangladesh Should Never Allow Transit to India," Isha Khan's weblog, July 18, 2008.

5. *Lajja* (Shame) was published in February 1993 by Pearl Publications, Dhaka. It has been reprinted multiple times and translated into several European and South Asian languages.

6. I interviewed a total of twenty women. The Bangladeshi women were all Muslim, middle class, and college educated. Some of them were employed, and others were homemakers. In the United States, the women I interviewed were recent immigrants. I interviewed five Indian women, who were Hindu, middle class, and college educated.

7. See Riaz, "Taslima Nasrin."

8. Carolyn Wright, "Taslima Nasreen's Campaign Endangers Other Women," *Christian Science Monitor*, August 10, 1994, 19.

9. Obscene is *osleel* in Bengali, and refers to immodesty in thought and behavior.

10. John Anderson, "Dispute Goes beyond Religion, *International Herald Tribune*, August 5, 1994.

11. Wright, "Taslima Nasreen's Campaign Endangers Other Women."

12. Sujata Sen, "I Write Because I Want to Change Society," *Statesman* (Kolkata), May 10, 1993.

13. Sue Leeman, "Feminist Author 'Sacrificed Normal Life' for Free Speech," *American Statesman*, February 18, 1995.

14. The clergy I refer to belong to the leading madrassas in the country. The madrassa graduates run the various mosques in the country. Many of them are members of the Islamic political parties. It should be noted that within the clergy there are many who eschew violence and have often protected minorities.

15. See Siddiqi, "Taslima Nasreen and Others."

16. Hossain, " 'Apostates,' Ahmadis, and Advocates," 85–86.

17. The Western media have lost interest in Taslima with the emergence of Westernized critics such as Irshad Manji and Ayaan Hirsi Ali.

18. See Mary Ann Weaver, "A Fugitive from Justice," *New Yorker*, September 12, 1994, 48–60.

19. Riaz, "Taslima Nasrin," 22.

20. See Ananya J. Kabir, "Figurehead or Spearhead?," *Statesman*, September 4, 1994.

21. "A Lightning Conductor for the Islamic Town," *Sunday Times* (London), August 14, 1994.

22. When I met Dr. Shukumari Bhattachary in Dhaka in 1999 and asked her to comment on Taslima's plagiarism of her work, she answered that while she did not approve of what Taslima had done, she did not think her plagiarism should negate the importance of her work. See Taslima's essay on the status of Hindu women in *Nirbachita Kolam* (1993): 20–23.

23. The Bengali titles are *Nirbachito Kolam, Bromer Koyeia Jai, Shudh.*

24. "Woman under a Death Sentence," *Sunday Times* (London), September 7, 1994.

25. Sanjoy Hazarika, "Bangladesh Seeks Writer, Charging She Insults Islam," *New York Times*, June 8, 1994.

26. My thanks to Sangita Gopal for sharing this with me.

27. Wright, "Taslima Nasreen's Campaign Endangers Other Women."

28. See also Sen, "I Write Because I Want to Change Society."

29. Deborah Baker, "Fundamentalists, Feminists in Bangladesh," *New York Times*, September 4, 1994.

30. In 1999, when I raised the topic of lesbian rights in a feminist gathering in Dhaka, my remarks were not well received. Later some of the older feminists told me not to confuse Western ideas with local feminist struggles. Nari Pokkho is the only feminist organization that allows lesbians to gather on its premises.

31. In 1995, I attended a meeting of Indian feminists organized by Ain-o-Salish Kendro, a feminist NGO in Bangladesh. The discussion, often argumentative, was over the use of communal language by the Indian media and feminists to debate the events that unfolded in Bangladesh in 1993–94.

32. Barry Bearak, "Defiant Author, Dying Mother, and Wrath of Islam," *New York Times*, October 28, 1998.

33. English translations of Taslima's poems are online at her personal website, http://taslimanasrin.com.

34. Bearak, "Defiant Author, Dying Mother and Wrath of Islam." I was in Dhaka during this time as well.

35. United Press International, "Islamic Groups Target Novelist," December 10, 1994.

36. British Broadcasting Service, "Writers under Fire for Blasphemy in Bangladesh," South Asia, December 22, 1994.

37. Sofa, *Anupurbik Taslima Nasreen o Ananya Proshongo*, 20. My translation.

38. Swati Ghosh, "History in Black and White," *Statesman*, May 14, 1994.

39. Ibid.

40. West Bengal Hindus, whether in Kolkata or in the United States, often remark to me that I am "like them" (i.e., modern and free thinking) and unlike Bangladeshis who are "tradition-bound and backward."

41. *Dwikhondito* (Kolkata: People's Book Society, 2003).

42. Ibid.

43. Ghosh, "Censorship Myths and Imagined Harms," 451.

44. Ibid.

45. Mamdani, "Good Muslim, Bad Muslim," 774.

46. I am quoting from Priya Kumar's comments at the symposium on obscenity (see note 1).

LAURA BRUECK

At the Intersection of Gender and Caste
Rescripting Rape in Dalit
Feminist Narratives

A DALIT WIDOW victoriously proclaims the brute strength of her
female ancestors and slams a board onto the head of her would-
be attacker, knocking him cold. A young Dalit girl, held cap-
tive and brutalized for two days, suddenly explodes in rage and
slices off her rapist's penis amidst a crowd of stunned onlookers.
These surprising tales constitute what I argue in this essay is a
feminist recuperation of a hegemonic cultural and casteist rape
narrative that regularly imagines Dalit women as silenced and
disempowered victims. It is in this framework that I consider
the narration of sexual violence in various works of contemporary Hindi Dalit short story writing. First, I look at the ways in
which the experience, or threat, of sexual violence has been
rhetorically constructed as constitutive of Dalit women's identities by both Indian Dalit and feminist communities. Next I
consider the strategies by which many leading authors and critics in the Hindi Dalit literary sphere reify sexual violence as a
fundamental aspect of not only Dalit women's identities, but
also as a basic element in the operation of male caste hierarchies;
as a consequence women's subjectivities are entirely erased from
narratives of sexual violence. Finally, I consider the writings of
the Dalit feminist author Kusum Meghwal, particularly those
featuring rape and revenge, as opening up the imaginative possibilities of "the female appropriation of the grammar of physical violence."[1] Throughout I illustrate the centrality of the de-

bates about the social scripting of sexual violence in Dalit literature and literary criticism. Ultimately, this essay points to the complicity of widely disparate forces, both physical and rhetorical, that contribute to the violent appropriation of Dalit women's bodies and the silencing of Dalit women's voices, as well as the emancipatory possibilities offered by the emergence of Dalit women's literary speech to reclaim subjectivity and agency through the imaginative and creative power of narrative.

Debates about the ways in which both anticaste and women's movements in India have located Dalit women precipitated the formation of the National Federation of Dalit Women in 1995, and have remained at the fore of many activist and scholarly discussions. Along with the growing presence of a Dalit women's movement have emerged questions of, on the one hand, the compulsion for Dalit women to talk "differently," or from the perspective of their own experiential authority, and, on the other, the need to develop a "Dalit feminist standpoint" that can be shared by others and that can interrogate overlapping categories of caste, class, ethnicity, and gender.[2] Anupama Rao suggests that "the political empowerment of Dalit and other lower-caste women has posed a strong challenge to Indian feminism. . . . Dalitbahujan feminists critique both anticaste and feminist movements for their particular forms of exclusion."[3] Their alienation both from the anticaste rhetoric of a Dalit movement that perpetuates oppressive patriarchal structures, as well as from an Indian feminist movement that negates caste and class differences in the pursuance of a universal "sisterhood," is what constitutes the particularity of Dalit women's perspectives.

Violence has emerged as the linchpin around which both the experience and *enforcement* of gendered and caste identities revolve. For example, Kalpana Kannabiran and Vasanth Kannabiran argue that caste and gender constitute "twin mediators of oppression," the logic of sexual violence being central to each. Citing numerous high profile cases of sexual assault against Dalit women by upper-caste men, they point to the "mediation of inter-caste relations through a redefinition of gendered spaces," or in other words, the ways in which upper-caste men appropriate Dalit women's bodies as a way to emasculate and control Dalit men. If the " 'manhood' of a caste is defined both by the degree of control men exercise over women and the degree of passivity of women in the caste," then, logically, "the structure of relations in caste society castrates [the Dalit man] through the expropriation of his women." An attack on a Dalit woman is an attack on her entire community, "an assertion of power over all women [and men] in her caste."[4] Sharmila Rege further suggests that Dalit women are rendered "impure" or "lacking in virtue" because economic circumstances make their labor outside the home crucial for survival and thus that the rape of Dalit women may not even be considered rape because of the "customary access" upper-caste men have to Dalit women's sexuality.[5] According to Ruth Manorama, founder and president of the National Federation of Dalit Women, "Certain kinds of violence are traditionally reserved for Dalit women: extreme filthy verbal abuse and sexual epithets, naked parading, dismemberment, pulling out of teeth, tongue, and nails, and violence including murder after proclaiming witchcraft, are *only experienced by Dalit women*. Dalit women are threatened by rape as part of a collective violence by the higher castes."[6]

Sexual violence perpetrated against Dalit women, particularly by upper-caste men as a means of exerting a kind of terrorizing control over an entire community of Dalits, is more often than not an act performed in a public space or within already existing oppressive institutionalized hierarchies. In her recently published *The Caste Question: Dalits and the Politics of Modern India* (2009), Anupama Rao analyzes various narrative reconstructions—those in the legal record of the subsequent court case, and the recollections of survivors and witnesses—of the notorious incident known in popular memory as "Sirasgaon," in which, in a village of the same name in Maharashtra, four Dalit women were forced from their homes, stripped, and publicly beaten and paraded naked as retaliation by a perceived threat against the wife of an upper-caste landowner. Though all of these narrative reconstructions of the event represent it as a case of sexual violence between offenders and victims in individualized circumstances, Rao argues forcefully that sexual violence and caste violence are inherently intertwined since "rape, the stripping and parading of women, and other forms of gendered humiliation reproduce upper caste male privilege" and that in these cases "sexual violence perform[s] a pedagogical function in socializing men and women, Dalit and caste Hindu alike, into caste norms."[7] Therefore, ultimately, "the perverse logic of caste's sexual economy is such that the violation of Dalit women as a matter of right and the violent disciplining of Dalit men are two sides of the same coin."[8]

These perceptions of the collective violence, customary access, and expropriation of women's bodies in the construction and maintenance of

LAURA BRUECK

caste hierarchies make it necessary to examine the rhetorical situating of sexual violence in narrative forms within the cognitive framework of a "rape script," or the social coding that prescribes the semiotics of an act of sexual violence. The idea of rape as a socially scripted interaction has been most thoroughly explored by Sharon Marcus, who defines a rape script as "a framework, a grid of comprehensibility which we might feel impelled to use as a way of organizing and interpreting events and actions" in her development of a theoretical approach to rape prevention.[9] She suggests that a "rape script takes its form from . . . a gendered grammar of violence, where grammar means the rules and structure which assign people to positions within a script. . . . The gendered grammar of violence predicates men as the subjects of violence and the operators of its tools, and predicates women as the objects of violence and the subjects of fear."[10] Marcus attempts to deconstruct the way in which rape is posited as "inevitable" so that the script which codes it as such can be challenged and rewritten rather than taken as something fixed and unchanging.

Many scholars of South Asian feminism have explored Marcus's theory of a rape script in relation to various literary and cinematic narratives to consider how it is either complicated or resisted in the very different contexts of colonial and postcolonial societies. For example, Rajeshwari Sunder Rajan contrasts English fiction that depicts the threat of the rape of English women by Indian men with the way rape is depicted in a "third world women's text." Taking Anuradha Ramanan's Tamil short story "Prison" as an example of the latter, she examines how narrative structure and gender politics both shape the depictions of rape.[11] She suggests that in Ramanan's story the female rape victim "scripts her own narrative," carefully crafting a position of social and economic power by shaming the man who raped her. Conversely, the "first world" texts of British male novelists reify the inevitability and totality of female victimhood; "all that is really left for the raped woman to do is fade away."[12] Sunder Rajan points out those elements that make Ramanan's and other "third world" women's narratives of sexual violence "feminist texts of rape," dominant among them the countering of a narrative determinism that conscripts women into compromised positions of silence and absence.

Considering another rape narrative, produced a decade later, Priyamvada Gopal asks two fundamental questions of Shekhar Kapur's 1994 film *Bandit Queen*, a fictionalized biopic of Phoolan Devi, the former dacoit and politician assassinated in 2001. The film was at the center of a firestorm of debate about the representation of sexual violence, victimization, and agency in mainstream media.[13] Kapur admittedly takes creative license in the way he depicts Phoolan Devi being gang-raped by upper-caste men, acts that were earlier recorded in Mala Sen's book *India's Bandit Queen: The True Story of Phoolan Devi* (1993). Arundhati Roy criticized the film as a Bollywood-style "Rape-'n'-Retribution" drama that is fundamentally exploitive of women, especially in light of both Roy's and the lawyer Indira Jaisingh's claims that Phoolan was reluctant to speak about being raped.[14] Gopal intervenes in the debate by asking whether the repeated depictions in the film of Devi's brutalized body are "symbolic of the vulnerability of all female bodies" and, following this, "if the representation of her victimization is harmful to feminist efforts to recuperate female agency."[15] While sympathetic to the critique of this film by Roy and others, Gopal concludes that *Bandit Queen* "documents the female appropriation of the grammar of physical violence, the interventionary strategy at the heart of Marcus's essay," because Phoolan does not merely inhabit the role of victim but acts retributively against her attackers; thus, while "the female body in this text is certainly vulnerable or 'rapable' [it] is also clearly capable of resistance" because Phoolan refuses to remain solely a victim, but commits an act of extreme violence against her rapists.[16] Gopal argues that the film is most distinctive for its narrative structure and its avoidance of building up to a singular, climactic rape scene, instead representing the layered sexual violence of Phoolan's story along with her transformation into an agent of vengeance.

The *difference* of Dalit literary treatments of rape from such revenge narratives is their explicit mission to put the "sociopolitical practice" of caste oppression at the very heart of their narratives. Unlike a narrative such as *Bandit Queen* that has as its center the sexual exploitation and eventual violent reprise of a lower-caste woman, with what Gopal calls "vague connections" to the intersections of caste, class, and gender oppression, Dalit literature makes those processes central. In the Dalit stories I discuss later, rape becomes merely a structural aspect of the narrative, an element in the backstory. Sunder Rajan suggests that this kind of narrative deferral of rape (which accompanies the ironic absence of the raped woman herself in many male-authored rape stories), is a key element in the creation of a "feminist rape text":

Feminist texts of rape counter narrative determinism . . . in a number of ways: by representing the raped woman as one who becomes a subject through rape rather than merely one subjected to its violation; by structuring a post-rape narrative that privileges chastity and leads inexorably to "trials" to establish it; by locating the raped woman in literalizing instead of mystifying the representation of rape; and, finally, by counting the cost of rape for its victims in terms more complex than the extinction of female selfhood in death or silence.[17]

It is essential to extend the arguments about feminist texts of rape made by Sunder Rajan, Gopal, and others to Dalit literary texts that reproduce, complicate, or rewrite the casteist rape script to explicitly address caste hierarchy as a social problem. These are narratives with the desire for social change at their center, narratives for which the representation of rape and sexual assault is at the service of a "larger" problem.

ERASING WOMEN

Hindi-language Dalit short stories typically follow a uniform pattern. The story begins with some sort of humiliating episode or injustice: an insult, an act of physical assault, a denial of basic services, or a rape of a Dalit woman. The (male) protagonist in the story, who either undergoes or witnesses this traumatic experience, finally breaks through the constraints of his socialization as an "untouchable" and seeks an emotional and political reawakening as a Dalit. Thus the story becomes at once documentary and pedagogical; the "reality" of Dalit experience is "authentically" represented and the possibility of individual and social change is taught by example. Rape figures prominently in Dalit stories as the traumatic and transformative event at their center. In the typical (and typically male-authored) Dalit rape text, a Dalit woman is raped or brutalized, very often in a public space, near the beginning of the story. This structural placement of the rape immediately differentiates these stories from the other narratives of rape I have already discussed. In the colonial-era British novels in which rape figures centrally, Sunder Rajan has pointed out, the act occurs in the middle of the story and is subtly eroticized by both a long narrative buildup and the blurring of the line between rape and seduction.

In Dalit stories of rape, the victim's men (father, brother, husband, sons) typically come to her aid and immediately seek justice. They first look for redress through official institutions of justice such as the police, *panchayat*, or the courts, and when they are rebuffed, they come to the realization that their fate and the recuperation of their pride lies solely in their own hands. This sparks a requisite political awakening and the men find their redress in various ways—violence, shaming, education, or a move away from the village to the city, symbolic of the refusal to participate any longer in a "traditional" feudal village caste hierarchy. The victimized women have little voice and are often left by the wayside as the narrative focus turns toward the male agents of the recuperation of honor.

Thus the dominant pattern of representing rape and sexual violence against women in Dalit literature has been to foreground brutalized Dalit women's bodies as catalysts for revenge narratives enacted by men, thereby fundamentally erasing women from the script, and disallowing them even the subject position of victim. Unlike the eroticization of the female rape victim-avenger at the center of mainstream rape-and-retribution films, or the absence and unspeakability of the raped woman at the heart of British colonial rape narratives, or even the brute radicalization of Phoolan Devi in *The Bandit Queen*, the rape of Dalit women in these stories serves as a catalyst for Dalit *men* in the story to revolt against their upper-caste oppressors. Indeed the very predominance of rape narratives in both Dalit men's creative and testimonial writings underlines the fact that the woman under attack herself is in fact tangential to the rape script.

For example, in Mohandas Naimishray's short story *Apna Gaon* (Our village, 1998), the Dalit girl Chamiya is stripped and paraded naked through the village center in retaliation for both her husband's unpaid debts to the upper-caste Thakur and his audacity in leaving the village to find work in the city, and further as a means of providing a warning to the rest of the Dalit community that they had better not think of challenging the estab-lished caste hierarchy.[18] Here is the opening passage of the story:

Eighty-year-old Hariya heard the commotion and looked outside, blinking. He tried to make out the fuzzy shadows moving in front of his eyes. It was Chamiya, his grandson's wife. There was not a piece of clothing on her body.
    But why was she naked?

LAURA BRUECK

Surprised, he squinted his old eyes even more narrowly.

Nearby stood four of the thakur's thugs. His middle son was also there. Hariya's head lolled. His whole body shook in anger. Hariya was like an old, sick horse who did not move even as the reins continuously slapped his back. His old bones were paralyzed. He looked at the sky with tear-filled eyes. The sky was still there, just like always. He was certain at this moment the sky would fall right here. That the earth would explode. But neither did the sky fall nor did the earth burst open. Dhuliya's main square stood right there where it had always stood. The leaves were not even swaying in the trees. It was completely silent. There was a smell of approaching danger. The language of fear could be read on every leaf. Chamiya was in front and behind her followed the thugs and loafers. The naked march was coming toward him. One of them had stripped her body, but all of the others had exposed their hearts. He heard one of the thugs saying, "We own you bastard chamars, and yet you dare look at us in the eyes?" Now another brute chimed in, "From now on you fuckers shit and piss in your own damn houses!"

Then the thakur's middle son shouted, "We'll force all your daughters to strip just like Chamiya until your heads are fixed!"[19]

The public attack on Chamiya is witnessed by her grandfather-in-law, who is mute, paralyzed by fear and shame. Chamiya too is mute. The other villagers can only peer fearfully through their windows. The only people who speak in these opening paragraphs are the upper-caste attackers, demonstrating their domination of Chamiya's body as symbolic of their vulgar claims of "ownership" over the entire Dalit community. After the sexual assault occurs, she is effectively dropped from the narrative as her husband returns to the village and leads a coterie of Dalit males first to the police station (where they are rebuffed) and then to a community council where other men decide the next course of action.

Likewise, in Ajay Navariya's story *Upmahadvip* (Subcontinent, 2004), the adult male protagonist is haunted by the childhood memory of a village woman's rape after a Dalit wedding ceremony is broken up by a group of upper-caste villagers. He writes of his vague memory: "And to the right of my gaze about ten feet away, from beneath the white *dhoti* of some pandit I saw the two black feet of someone bouncing wildly up and down on the ground, and on the pandit's naked back his fat topknot was swinging back and forth like a snake."[20] The rape victim herself is reduced merely to a fleeting vision of "two black feet," but *his* memory of witnessing the incident is what finally drives the protagonist to return to the village as an adult, with a gun, to exact revenge. Thus, for many Dalit male writers rape individualizes otherwise anonymous Dalit women only to the extent that they are seen to be overcome with a sense of overwhelming shame. Revenge or resistance is unquestionably solely in the hands of Dalit men, thus denying the Dalit woman the identity of either a victim whose own testimony validates her experience, or an agent of her own self-preservation and retribution.

Imaginative adherence to the logic of a casteist rape script is also evident in the perspective of many Dalit literary critics, though their opinions have not gone unchallenged by Dalit feminists. In 2006, at a release party for the book *Premchand: Samant ka Munshi* (Premchand, munshi of feudalism), by the Hindi Dalit literary critic Dharamveer, several Dalit women in the audience stood up in the midst of the author's address and hurled shoes at him in a radical public display. The immediate provocation for his public shaming was Dharamveer's controversial reading of "Kafan," the famed short story of the Indian nationalist era by Munshi Premchand. In his analysis of this story about a Dalit father and son who spend, on a gluttonous feast, the money that has been collected for the funeral shroud of the son's wife, Budhiya (who dies in childbirth in the beginning of the story while the two men do nothing to help), Dharamveer makes the following surprising interpretive claim:

> The whole story would become newly clear if Premchand would have written in the final line of the story this reality of Dalit life that Budhiya was pregnant with the Zamindar's child. That he had raped Buddhiya in the field. Then, those words would shed light on the story like a lamp and we would understand everything. That even while Ghisu and Madhav wished to be able to do more, in fact they could only resist by refusing to call the child their own. That this is the real pain of Dalits—who will say this?—a Dalit or a non-Dalit? This is the reality of Dalit exploitation and oppression—that so often their offspring are not actually their own. Compared to this kind of exploitation, the economic exploitation of Dalits seems so small![21]

LAURA BRUECK

In his book, Dharamveer argues that the true cause of Dalit suffering in modern caste society is the sexual abuse and exploitation of Dalit women ("sex crimes," *yaun-aparadhiya*). This obviously echoes the claims of feminist scholars that the key "difference" in Dalit women's experiences is the constant threat of sexual violence. Yet the intervention of such an interpretative claim into Premchand's story bears a more ominous tone. A generous reading of Dharamveer's interpretation suggests a disheartening commentary about a Dalit male psyche that would readily sacrifice "tainted" Dalit women to preserve its own honor. A more critical reading suggests that Dharamveer believes that if Budhiya were in fact raped by an upper-caste *zamindar*, the callous act of allowing her to die without attempting to help her would have been an understandable and perhaps even laudable act of sociopolitical *resistance* by Ghisu and Madhav.

Several Dalit feminist responses to Dharamveer's argument, published in *Stri Naitikta ka Talibanikaran* (The Talibanisation of feminist ethics), a special issue of the Delhi-based Dalit and Adivasi literary magazine *Yuddhrat Aam Aadmi* (The struggling common man, Ramanika Foundation, 2007), suggest the necessity of reconsidering the notion that the singular differentiating experience of Dalit women's lives is sexual violence, or the threat of sexual violence. Writers such as Anita Bharti, Kusum Meghwal, Pushpa Vivek, and others raise significant questions about the "obsession" of many Dalit writers with narratives of the rape and sexual exploitation of Dalit women. Their fundamental argument is that literature needs to serve as a medium where the *dignity* of Dalit women is restored, rather than as a site for further entrenchment of a casteist rape script that derives its power and meaning from the humiliation and disappearing of Dalit women. They argue that the narrative representation by Dalit women of their own lives is "much more expansive. It's about their education, labor, organization of community rights etc. . . . [S]exual exploitation is *not* the only problem facing Dalit women."[22]

This debate demonstrates the ways in which a new wave of Dalit feminist discourse is working to alter the terms of the social script of the gendered violence of caste. What happens when, as in the case of Dharamveer, the discursive constructions of Dalit consciousness and the "difference" of Dalit women collide to rob Dalit women of agency outside that of allegorical victim of caste oppression? According to Anita Bharti, "How many Dalit writers do we have in front of us now who provide dignity to

Dalit women and give importance to their lives? There are certainly exceptions, but we can count them with our fingers. Usually, in trying to pointlessly become an 'icon' of Dalit literature, they just call [Dalit women] names like buddhiya, devdasi, rakhail. Those who graciously don't do this, slap those who do on their backs."[23]

DALIT WOMEN *WRITE* DIFFERENTLY

Dalit feminists have begun developing alternative expressive spaces in their own literature where they can voice resistance and reimaginations of the norm. In particular, writers such as Bama (writing in Tamil), Baby Kamble, and Urmila Pawar (writing in Marathi), as well as other emerging writers in these and many other languages, continue to challenge the codification of a newly celebrated Dalit literary voice that is overtly masculinist in its orientation toward the Dalit female experience. Nowhere is this more evident than in literary representations of rape and sexual assault against Dalit women.

Feminist writers and critics in the contemporary Hindi Dalit literary sphere are working to rescue Dalit women's bodies from passive manipulation in perpetuating the casteist rape script in which they serve as transactional objects in a power struggle between men. They indicate powerful alternatives to such a scripting, or adherence to a singular "grid of comprehensibility."[24] The Rajasthani writer Kusum Meghwal is one such writer who explores alternative possibilities for female agency. This often takes the form of a woman-centered rape revenge fantasy that allows Dalit women to disrupt the normative social script of sexual assault by refusing to acquiesce to the physically passive role prescribed to them.[25] In these narratives, women exercise both verbal and physical acts of resistance; most important, the psychological liberation that results from their resistance belongs to *them*.

Disruption of the casteist rape script is on display in two short stories, "Mangali" and "Spark" (*Angara*). Meghwal is the founder of the Rajasthan Dalit Sahitya Akademi and the author of several books, including the short story anthology *Jurte Dayitva* (1996); a book-length poetic meditation on the position of women in Indian society, *Is Nari ko Pehechan* (Take a look at this woman, 1998); and a study of the representation of Dalits in mainstream Hindi novels, *Hindi Upanyason Mein Dalit Varg* (Dalit class in

LAURA BRUECK

Hindi novels, 1989). In several of the short stories in her prolific collection, Meghwal reinserts women's subjectivity, both as victims who have actually suffered an attack and are fundamentally changed because of it and as victors who hold the power of retribution in their own hands.

"MANGALI"

In the eponymous story, Mangali is a day laborer whose husband is ill with typhoid. He soon dies. Mangali is left a young widow and does not return to the construction site for a few days after her husband's death. When she does return, the contractor abuses her until she shows him her bangle-less wrists and he realizes she is newly widowed. He is suddenly ingratiating toward her and offers that she can stay for free in the servant quarters of his house. "Innocent by nature," Mangali agrees.

Pretending to be sympathetic and attempting to woo her with small gifts and kindnesses, over the course of a few weeks the contractor begins to make advances toward the unsuspecting Mangali, who Meghwal frequently reminds us is "innocent." In the final scene of the story the rising tension comes to a climax after the contractor makes his desires, and her obligations as a lower-caste woman living in his house, clear:

> The revelation of the contractor's lurid designs caused an explosion. Mangali was made of stronger stuff than he had initially thought. Trembling in anger she replied, "Contractor Sahib I had no idea that this monster was hidden inside you and that with the excuse of helping me through my troubles you have actually brought me here to take advantage of me. But I am telling you firmly that I am a daughter of a *Bhil* woman who, if she gives birth to a child while she is cutting wood in the jungle, she'll cut the umbilical cord herself, lift the child in her arms and go home. So don't try to come any closer or I will cut you like a goat."
>
> The contractor exploded in rage—"Even while living in my home you dare threaten me? Good-for-nothing untouchable bitch! You think you'll remain a chaste woman your whole life? Just who do you think will save you now?" Saying this he swooped toward Mangali and tried to pull her tight in his arms.
>
> Mangali swiftly pushed aside her veil and in a flash lifted a thick

piece of firewood lying by the stove and hit the contractor in the head. The contractor had no clue that there was such a powerful woman hidden inside Mangali. He lost consciousness and fell right there on the spot.

Panting, running in rage like an angry goddess, she arrived at the police station and filed a report against the contractor. As it happened the police took her side. Instead of preying upon Mangali, they offered her protection.

The chief sent two constables with her and gave her a seat in the jeep. They quickly arrived at Mangali's quarters and arrested the unconscious contractor.[26]

The radical about-face of the narrative and of Mangali's character is typical of Meghwal's unique treatment of female protagonists in the face of sexual violence. Throughout the story Mangali plays the stereotypical role of the embattled Dalit woman, struggling against the social forces of poverty, exploitative labor conditions, and the ever-present threat of sexual assault. Her victimization by these forces is compounded by the death of her husband, making her an even more obvious target for social and sexual exploitation. There is nothing to suggest, until the end of the story, her sudden conquest.

Meghwal emphasizes Mangali's status as "victim," repeatedly characterizing her as innocent and trusting, and making it a point throughout the sparse narrative to depict Mangali's submissive demeanor and chastely drawn veil in the presence of the contractor. Perhaps Meghwal is guarding the character of Mangali against criticisms grounded in the widespread masculinist assumption that "improper" women invite rape; but she could also be positioning her protagonist and antagonist as "moral" opposites to underscore the radical revisioning of the story's denouement. Throughout, the reader is also given clues to the contractor's devious motives ("Just a few days later the contractor began to lay a snare for Mangali"; "The innocent Mangali did not notice the contractor's scheme hidden behind his sympathy. As though fattening up a goat for sacrifice, he would feed her *pan* and sweets") while Mangali remains unaware, creating a sense of the inevitability of her impending violation and the repetition of the "traditional" Dalit-woman-as-helpless-victim narrative.

But at the moment of Mangali's delayed realization of the contractor's plot, such narrative determinism is overturned. Meghwal asserts that "Mangali was made of stronger stuff than he"—and admittedly we—"had thought." As Mangali *refuses* to become a raped woman, she becomes the subject of a second, somewhat fantastical narrative in which Meghwal transforms her into the victor. Mangali is in fact able to doubly assert her dominant subjecthood over the contractor, first with the strength of her physical attack, after which "he lost consciousness and fell right there on the spot," and second with the backing of the police, who "as it happened . . . took her side," an event just as unlikely as young Mangali's knocking out the contractor with a single blow. It is also important to note, instead of the Dalit woman, it is Mangali's husband who is effectively disappeared from the plot of the story. While her victimized and submissive status for the bulk of the story is contingent upon her status both as widow and as Dalit woman, her transformation to "angry goddess" at the end of the story breaks out of the circumscriptions of both gender and caste to construct a new, self-scripted social role that rewrites the stereotypical rape script.

For many modern literary and filmic treatments of "deviant" womanhood in India, the centrality of the goddess in various Hindu religious traditions provides a rich mine of narratives and symbols. It is clear that in their repetition and expansion of the goddess trope, Meghwal's stories are conversant with these reclamations of the goddess as a "symbolic resource."[27] Sunder Rajan suggests that because most goddess worshippers come from low castes or even non-Hindu communities, veneration of the goddess is in fact a radical act. She also argues that while "unconventional" women may find "sanction" for their behavior through goddess models, they are never evoked as mainstream role models for girls and women.[28] Kancha Ilaiah extols the goddesses of Dalit worship as "strong wise women" who are examples of neither "delicate femininity" (as Sita) nor antimale violence. The Dalit goddess tradition, in direct contrast to mainstream Hinduism, does not glorify "violence as a positive cultural ethos."[29] But it is, in fact, just this violent potential of the goddess (Hindu or Dalit) that Meghwal evokes. It is precisely Mangali's own *exercise* of violence, and its consequent disruption of the violence that was about to be visited upon her, that makes possible the triumphant ending of the story and the rewriting of the rape script.

In "Angara" (Spark), the female protagonist actually suffers a violent sexual attack before she fights back, exacting her bloody revenge. When the story opens, we see seventeen-year-old Jamuna crying quietly at the threshold of her family's hut while her parents cower inside. Outside a crowd has gathered to jeer and taunt her, calling her a prostitute and cursing her for bringing shame to her family. Jamuna relates her ordeal: a few days earlier, while she was working in the fields, the village thakur's brother and oldest son sneaked up on her. Before she could scream they covered her mouth with a cloth and forced her at knife-point to an abandoned storeroom and "blackened her face" (*munh kala kiya*). They kept her locked in the storeroom for several days, availing themselves of her body at will.

Jamuna explains that she begged them not to rape her. She tried to convince them that as soon as they touched her they would be unclean, and asked how they could entwine their bodies with hers, as though there were no difference between them. "What about your practice of untouchability and casteism?" she challenged them. They cursed her and said, "Keep running your mouth bitch, you can't escape from our grasp now. We'll enjoy you for as long as we want and when we've had enough we'll kill you and drop you in the jungle where you'll be eaten by wolves and vultures."

But one night they both got drunk and she escaped. Now she stands at the threshold of her parents' house, ostracized, with nowhere to go. Her brother, Hira, promises her and both their parents that he will not rest until he has punished the men, restoring her honor (*izzat*). They file a report, but a relative of the thakur's family is a government minister, virtually assuring immunity to Jamuna's attackers, who return to the village waving guns and shouting in the streets that they will shoot anyone who challenges them. When they approach, Hira explodes with rage, cursing the impotent (*napumsak*) police, and attacks the men with an ax. The thakur's son eventually falls to the ground weak and exhausted. In the story's climactic conclusion:

> Wide-eyed, Jamuna was staring at this demonic man who had stolen her honor. Now it was her turn. Like a spark [*angara*] she ran inside and grabbed her scythe from the corner of the hut. Then, that punishment that the government and the police were powerless to give,

she gave. She had her revenge [*pratishodh*]. She sliced off the symbol of Sumer Singh's manhood [*purushatva ke pratik ang*] and threw it far from his body. He was writhing. It was impossible to save him now. Even if he could be saved, his life would be worse than death. The life of a hijra. Now he will never play again with the honor of a poor young untouchable girl. This was the right punishment for him.[30]

This is by far the most graphic example among Meghwal's revenge fantasy narratives, and unique in the fact that Jamuna's dramatic enactment of revenge on the body of her attacker is not for the purpose of preventing her own violation, but truly an act of revenge in its most metaphorical manifestation. This man was the one who "stole her honor" (*abaru/izzat*), and in turn she steals his "manhood" (*purushatvua*), the tool of her own violation. Jamuna has destroyed him, literally and graphically rendering him impotent, putting him in the same defenseless and powerless state in which she was meant to be relegated by his violation of her. Her rape, abduction, imprisonment, and the threat of death, rather than rendering her powerless, empower Jamuna to make a public spectacle of her revenge. Whereas she provided a public spectacle at the beginning of the story—as the silent center of a jeering crowd—at the conclusion she is the subject, rather than the object, of the public performance. A crowd of onlookers watches Jamuna's triumphant dismembering of her rapist, just as a large number of readers will witness the spectacle in its narrative form; thus Jamuna's feat of retaliatory violence is public on two different levels.

Meghwal's stories, in their restoration of subjectivity and agency to Dalit women who suffer sexual assault, act as a kind of alternative public performance in which Dalit women perform fantasy revenge scenarios, performances that allow them to voice both protest and resistance to their upper caste oppressors, or at the very least experience a cathartic release of anger and emotion only possible in the creation of a fantasy revenge narrative. These stories recenter the Dalit woman as subject and de-emphasize the normative scripting of rape as an insult directed at Dalit men. Just as Mangali's husband dies at the beginning of her narrative, Jamuna's brother Hira is ultimately unable to avenge his sister—Meghwal rather scripts the act of vengeance as something that only the Dalit woman, both as victim *and* as subject, can perform.

These revenge fantasy narratives employ specific alternative textual strategies of representation to combat the narrative determinism of the rape script. Central to each is the structural decentering of the rape from its normative role as constitutive of the woman's, and the community's, victimhood. In "Mangali," the rape never happens. "Spark" focuses on what Jamuna does in the aftermath of the rape, suggesting that a woman does not die or disappear after she is violated, but rather continues her life as an autonomous, agentive subject. Before the intrusion of the fantastic in both stories, Meghwal works to build the reader's assumption of the inevitable. Mangali's continued naïveté in the face of the increasing transparency of the contractor's lurid designs builds a feeling of dread in the reader, but then, very suddenly, our own assumptions of what is going to happen are knocked as flat as the contractor himself.

The combination of realism with the sudden intrusion of fantasy fits with the blend of realism and melodrama that is the predominant narrative mode of Dalit literature, but with the difference that the female characters serve as the loci of power and resistance, subverting their normative roles as victims of the rape. Meghwal's revenge fantasy narratives give access not only to the psychic "reality" of rape, but of the psychic *possibility* of protecting oneself from rape, or seeking retaliation after it. Such representations of women's agency in the face of the paralyzing rape script— "fantastical" as they may be in these stories—challenge the very logic on which it operates, that women's bodies are mute vessels upon which the battles of men over caste may be waged. Dalit feminist short stories thus emerge as a space in which women's subjectivity, muted by the oppressive logic of the rape script, can be reclaimed, and open the possibility of such subjectivities to make themselves known in the courts as well as in the streets and in the squares of villages.

Kusum Meghwal stands here as a single example from an increasingly vocal community of Dalit feminist writers who are working, through the publication and dissemination of their narratives, to subvert the hegemony of the casteist rape script as it functions to invest sexual violence against Dalit women by upper-caste men with the all-too-real implications of the social consolidation of caste privilege, the regulation and maintenance of caste boundaries, and the violent objectification of Dalit women based on an overlapping of their gender and caste identities. Further, these women writers struggle against a pervasive masculinist prejudice in the Dalit liter-

LAURA BRUECK

ary sphere, a prejudice whose logic is predicated upon the idea that to represent the particular issues facing Dalit women is somehow to threaten the emergence and consolidation of a unified literary voice of Dalit resistance, a literary voice that is increasingly being recognized and celebrated in both mainstream media and academic scholarship, but one that is coded implicitly as male by the overwhelmingly disproportionate publication of Dalit men's testimonial, fictional, and poetic narratives, both in original-language and translated publications.[31]

I have known Kusum Meghwal since 2001, when I was working on my master's thesis in Udaipur. When I returned to India a couple of years later, this time to Delhi, to research a dissertation on Dalit women writers working in Hindi, I was disappointed to find fewer than I had imagined, and I met with active attempts at dissuading me from my gender-based research focus in almost every conversation I had with magazine editors, book publishers, and Dalit literary, social, and political organizers. In the end I relented and wrote my dissertation on the Hindi Dalit literary sphere more broadly, noting the particular struggles of Dalit women writers to carve out their own rhetorical and social space therein. But I have been heartened in the years since to watch the determined emergence of a powerful coterie of Dalit women writers and activists working in the Hindi sphere, a group of women who frequently collectively pool their voices in women's literary conferences and the publication of "special issues" of Hindi Dalit magazines such as *Yuddhrat Aam Aadmi* and *Apeksha* that focus on women's responses to current debates in the Dalit literary sphere, or the anthologizing of Dalit women's short stories or autobiographical essays. As Kusum Meghwal once explained to me about the desired impact of her stories— that rural, uneducated, disempowered Dalit women might hear them and take strength from them, perhaps imagining alternative twists in the nexus of cultural scripts that govern their lives—Dalit feminist narratives position themselves squarely as texts that have the capacity to intervene and subvert the hegemonic narratives of real life.

NOTES

Works by the following three authors are discussed in this essay: Kusum Meghwal, "Angara" (Spark), in *Dalit Kahani Sanchayan* (Dalit story collection), ed. Ramnika Gupta (Delhi: Sahitya Akademi, 2003), 142–45; *Hindi Upanyason Mein*

Dalit Varg (The Dalit class in Hindi novels) (Jaipur: Sanghi Prakashan, 1989); *Is Nari ko Pehechan* (Recognize this woman) (Jaipur: Shilpi Prakashan, 1998); *Jurte Dayitva* (Udaipur: Siddharth Prakashan Sansthan, 1996); and "Mangali," in *Dalit Mahila Kathakaron ki Charchit Kahaniyan* (Popular stories from Dalit women writers), ed. Kusam Viyogi (Delhi: Sahitya Nidhi, 1997).

Mohandas Naimishray, *Apne Apne Pinjare* (Delhi: Vani Prakashan, 1995); "Apna Gaon" (Our village), in *Awazen* (Voices) (Delhi: Samtāa Prakashan, 1998), 31–63.

Ajay Navariya, "Upmahadvip," in *Patkatha aur Anya Kahaniyan* (Delhi: Vani Prakashan, 2006), 36–46.

1. As Priyamvada Gopal has argued about Shekhar Kapur's 1994 film *Bandit Queen* in Gopal, "Of Victims and Vigilantes."

2. Rege, "Caste and Gender."

3. Rao, *Gender and Caste*, 2.

4. Kannabiran and Kannabiran, "Caste and Gender," 60–63.

5. Rege, "Caste and Gender," 29–30.

6. Quoted in "Background Information on Dalit Women in India," a document prepared and presented by Ruth Manorama upon her receipt of the Right Livelihood Award in 2006, Stockholm, Sweden, at rightlivelihood.org. Emphasis added.

7. Rao, *The Caste Question*, 222, 234.

8. Ibid., 236.

9. Marcus, "Fighting Bodies, Fighting Words," 391.

10. Ibid., 392–93.

11. Sunder Rajan, *Real and Imagined Women*, 64.

12. Ibid., 72.

13. See Gopal, "Of Victims and Vigilantes"; Ghosh, "Deviant Pleasures and Disorderly Women"; Kishwar, "The Bandit Queen"; and Arundhati Roy, "The Great Indian Rape Trick," *Sunday*, August 26–September 3, 1994, 58–64.

14. Indira Jaisingh recounts her and Roy's interactions with Phoolan after the release of the film on July 26, 2001, in Jaisingh, "The Rediff Special," *Rediff*, July 2001, at http://rediff.com/news.

15. Gopal, "Of Victims and Vigilantes," 297–98.

16. Ibid., 307–8.

17. Sunder Rajan, *Real and Imagined Women*, 77.

18. Mohandas Naimishray is the author of several short story collections including *Awazen* (Voices) (1998), and an autobiography, *Apne Apne Pinjare*.

19. Naimishray, "Apna Gaon," 31. The translation of this excerpt and all others from the original Hindi are my own.

20. Navariya, "Upmahadvip," 43.

21. Dharamveer, *Premchand*, 17.

22. Anita Bharti, quoted in Prakash, "Aap Kidhar Hai?," 97.

23. Bharti, "Anyay ke Khilaf," 17.

24. Marcus, "Fighting Bodies, Fighting Words."

25. Ibid.

26. Meghwal, "Mangali," 34.

27. Sunder Rajan, "Real and Imagined Goddesses," 269.

28. Ibid., 270, 272.

29. Ilaiah, *Why I Am Not a Hindu*, 96–97.

30. Meghwal, "Angara," 145.

31. A notable exception to this general state of affairs is the high public profile of the Tamil woman writer Bama. Three of her Tamil books (*Karukku*, *Sangati*, and *Harum-Scarum Saar and Other Stories*) have been translated into English to wide national and international recognition.

ANJALI ARONDEKAR

Subject to Sex
A Small History of the Gomantak Maratha Samaj

THE HISTORICAL FIGURE of the *devadasi*—a compound noun, coupling *deva* or god with *dasi* or female slave; a pan-Indian term, (falsely) interchangeable as sex worker, courtesan, prostitute—has become an established staple, or at least a sought-after staple, of gender studies in India, such that its recovery no longer merits much scholarly suspicion or incredulity. For many scholars, the devadasi archive proffers a different historical script, a much-needed shift in the terms through which genealogies of kinship and culture can be narrated. Devadasis (most prominently in Southern India) have emerged as privileged objects of study, propelled largely by feminist and state efforts to excavate sexual difference in India's past.[1] One of the more generative—as well as underarticulated—consequences of such efforts has been the mobilization of sexuality as the modality through which devadasi futures and pasts can be imagined and interrogated. Rescued from the detritus of history, devadasis, the lost and (falsely) maligned subjects of sexuality, are recast within larger redemptive contexts of artistic and legal empowerment. Such recuperations of the devadasi archive inevitably draw on invocations of pathos and misrecognition; the devadasi is disarticulated from her overidentification (and doomed associations) with sexuality and constituted in the density of other more promising configurations and allegiances such as caste, capital, or religiosities. Even as the analytical costs and limits of eliding the devadasi are emphasized, her coupling with sexuality is continually displaced. In the figure of the devadasi, we thus have a history of sexuality that promises a future only at the expense of its own attenuation.[2]

More broadly, the bruited recuperation of the devadasi illustrates how questions of difference produce moments of critical stress within historical thinking. In the case of the devadasi, we are specifically confronted with sexuality's difference, with the hermeneutical demands placed on histories of sexuality, particularly those that entangle with questions of caste and region, and with the multiple binds and enabling possibilities that result from it. Such an analytical challenge echoes the overall uneasy presence of sexuality within the political and intellectual landscape of contemporary India. To explain, two critical orientations to sexuality appear to currently dominate: the first, a largely progressive and expansive enterprise, rigorously extends the categories that define the idea of sexuality, and the second, a more rights-based project, contracts sexuality onto itself, by returning to static categories of identity and practice. The expansion model (exemplified in the work of feminist and queer historians) recruits the language of past difference to accentuate the coming of sexuality into its own, whereby divergent historical temporalities and subjectivities now exist within a model of a progressive politics. On the other hand, the contracted model (exemplified in the work of legal activists) strategically celebrates a past that externalizes difference and stabilizes sexuality as constitutive of Indian history. Yet, despite their ostensible critical segregation (the former internalizes sexuality's difference, the latter externalizes it), both models partake of a historical positivity where past and present understandings of sexuality accede to a script of teleological similarity. The differences of sexuality's past must be equal to the differences of its present and vice versa.[3]

The recent successful efforts around the repeal of Section 377 of the Indian Penal Code, for example, visibly engage both expansive and contractive readings of sexuality in their attempts to procure rights and privileges for alternative sexualities in India. Section 377, in brief, criminally penalizes what are described as "unnatural offences," to the extent that the said provision criminalizes consensual sexual acts between adults in private. The various petitions filed against Section 377 carefully made their arguments for its repeal by referencing a global lexicon of gay civil rights, alongside a more aggressive attentiveness to local instantiations within the context of postcolonial India.[4] Thus, even as the geopolitical ubiquity of same-sex behavior is acknowledged by the petition's references to evidence from around the world, the emphasis remained on its prevalence and acceptance within a wholly Indian landscape. For instance, the petition pointedly cites excerpts from texts understood as primarily Hindu: the Upanishads, the Gita, the Kama Sutra, and so on, disrupting, quite methodically, the logic of the Hindu Right, whose mobilizations have focused on coupling the sin of sodomy with Islamic bodies and texts.[5] To claim "sodomy" and "same-sex acts" as traditional, as a "historical value," as part of who we essentially are as Indians, is merely to invert the language of historical ontology that fixes even as it tries to shift meaning. In this version, Muslims are no longer the vilified sodomites; instead, we have in place the more traditional and historical stable Hindu avatar. Thus, one set of assumptions pathologizes the ontological connection, while the other affirms it.[6]

In the case of the devadasi, recourse to the historical archive produces a similarly recursive analysis. Put more simply, recuperations of the devadasi are too often simply mimetic and literalizing, their presence materializing subjects of our own historical desire, rather than opening to more complex understandings of sexuality's past(s). Devadasis become figures of radical possibility because they hold out the anachronistic promise of a past fashioned from the desires of the present. I want to emphasize here that such resignifying efforts arise not from some form of bad faith, but from feminism's ethical commitment to difference. Rather, the return to the devadasi requires us to ask how—that is, within which critical and political idioms— histories of sexuality are made visible and what the postcolonial politics of that visibility might now entail. To that end, I want to retool our routinized understanding of the devadasi as something much more than a doomed attachment to sexuality. I want instead to attend to the imaginative possibilities offered by sexuality to provide vibrant accounts of community at the scale of the personal and the political.

My argument here is thus less thesis-driven than a meditation on what there is to learn from a devadasi archive that refuses to settle sexuality into a fixed historicity (something that one is "past") or definitionality (something that accedes to a determinate set of meanings and forms). To do so, I shift regional location and emphases, to focus on a vibrant devadasi

ANJALI ARONDEKAR

community in western India (principally in the states of Goa and Maharashtra): the Gomantak Maratha Samaj. If the restoration of the devadasi has been tethered to forms of paucity, loss, and erasure, the Gomantak Maratha Samaj offers a different possibility by denaturalizing any such presumptive understanding of the devadasi's customary forms, particularly under colonialism. The Gomantak Maratha Samaj was established as a community formation in 1927 in Goa and in Maharashtra, and officially became a charitable institution in 1936. The Samaj continues its activities to this day and has from its inception maintained a community of ten thousand to fifty thousand registered members. Two extraordinary features make this Samaj noteworthy: it is unabashedly celebratory of its devadasi past (and present), and it is the only devadasi community that maintains its own extensive and continuous historical archive. Differing crucially from the more familiar disavowal of sexuality, the Samaj's self-archiving project engages the force of sexuality in all its fractiousness, embodying instead a devadasi community alert to the challenges of its own survival. In engaging with its devadasi past, the Samaj archives (as I demonstrate) only occasionally speak idioms of shame or loss of self; sexuality is seen rather as a place of vitalized self-reform and optimism—even futurity.

In turning to the history of the Gomantak Maratha Samaj, I am equally interested in understanding how the devadasi can be seen as a historiographical conundrum, as a locus of confounding identities between nationalist struggles and reformist efforts in colonial and postcolonial India. Even as the devadasi figure becomes taxonomized and rehabilitated through the passing of the various Contagious Disease Acts (1864, 1866, 1869) and the devadasi Protection Acts (1930, 1932, 1934), what falls away are its differentiated attachments to language, pleasure, and capital formation in a colonial India—attachments that need to be widely understood as multiply colonial—Portuguese, British, and, to some extent, French. Goa, for example, was a Portuguese possession, whose fraught relationship with British India complicated the scripts of colonial expansion and nationalist independence.[7] By linking histories of region, reform, and nationalism, I propose to stress and stretch alternate genealogies for the project of devadasi historiography to raise some of the following questions: What happens when the establishment of antidevadasi laws is read in conversation with the Gomantak Maratha Samaj's couplings of profit and pleasure? What forms of citizenship and subjectivity are being historicized through the figure of the devadasi, even as we recuperate its presence and expand our understanding of the colonial past?

In what follows, I engage two related but distinct reflections on the feminist recuperation of devadasis. First, in the section "Mediating Reform and Revival," I rehearse the established debates around the devadasi question to draw attention to the mutating concepts of reform and revival underwriting these discussions. Indeed, these debates register a series of tensions, most of which collate around the disparity between the formidable presence of the devadasis in the past and their (necessary?) disappearance within contemporary political formations. In the second section, I turn briefly to the emergence and success of the Gomantak Maratha Samaj as an example of a community that places interpretive pressure on such inherited readings of devadasi historiography.

MEDIATING REFORM AND REVIVAL

Recent scholarship on the subject of devadasis in colonial and postcolonial India largely falls into two conceptual domains that move within and against a language of reform and revival.[8] The first grouping largely attends to the devadasi question in terms of the devadasi's special status as artist and ritual specialist, and a treasury of lost cultural skills. Such a focus on the arts is best exemplified in the recent indictment of Rukmini Devi and her approach to the dance form Bharata Natyam. For dance scholars such as Avanti Meduri, Rukmini Devi's concerted brahminization and Sanskritization of the origins of Bharata Natyam erases the key contributions of devadasis to sustaining and enriching the dance form. Meduri argues, for instance, that Rukmini Devi's revival of Bharata Natyam relied on a sanitization of its origins, where devadasi contributions are rescripted within a more nationalist and Orientalist framework. Evacuated of its attachments to sexuality, the "temple dance" of the devadasi becomes instead a chaste, secular form, more easily interpellated into the rhetoric of an emergent postcolonial nation.[9] For Meduri, an appropriate recovery of devadasi influences requires a return to a more corporeal vocabulary within choreographic theory and dance compositions.

The second grouping focuses on discussions of the judicial and legal efforts that disenfranchised devadasis and minimized their claims to cus-

ANJALI ARONDEKAR

tomary law. Here, the focus is largely on a language of rights and restitution, most vigorously embodied by the mushrooming of governmental and nongovernmental organizations devoted to the "upliftment" and reform of devadasis. Within such formulations, the figure of the devadasi is either a "social evil," worthy of rescue, or a victim of sustained societal "superstition, ignorance, and poverty."[10] Let me note here that such formulations are not to be entirely dismissed. There might well be a certain evangelical fervor to such pronouncements of search and rescue but there is also an equal awareness of the responsibility and entanglement of (postcolonial) state apparatuses in the very structures worthy of reform.

Several scholars have remarked on some key misreadings undergirding such arguments in artistic or legal recuperations of the figure of the devadasi. Of particular importance is the fact that nineteenth- and twentieth-century court cases and government documents rarely concurred on their understanding of the term "devadasi," and arbitrarily attached the label to questions of religiosity, culture, and labor. For example, court documents frequently refer to devadasis variously as "dancing girls" or "temple dancing girls." Colonial government and social reformers later broadened the usage of the term "devadasi" to include any and all labor conducted by women within the aegis of a temple and/or deity. Such a capacious usage of the term produced a false unity behind the term, especially as there were significant variations to an understanding of devadasis in regional and community practices and customs. (For example, *bhavin, naikin, jogti, basavi, kasb, mahari, bogam sani, khudikar, aradhini, mogarin*, and *phulkari* are only some of the many differentiated terms that are collapsed within the sign of the devadasi.)[11]

Other mystifications of the devadasi figure included assumptions that the women came solely from the lower castes, or were primarily engaged in illicit sexual labor: a narrative shift, Kay Jordan argues, "from sacred servants" "to profane prostitutes." Loss of royal patronage, declining support from *zamindar* (landlord) families, redistribution of wealth away from the temple, urbanization, and industrialization also contributed to such changes in the status of devadasis.[12] The shift in focus to the question of prostitution, as many scholars have previously documented, partially emerged from the ongoing complex terrain of the "woman question" in colonial India, which was dominated by issues of "social reform" of practices such as sati, age of consent law, reform of law regarding widows, and so on. Such a turn to reforms, feminist historians such as Kumkum Sangari, Lata Mani, and Sudesh Vaid have argued, was further complicated by the fact that reform discourses benefited largely upper-caste women, and that too problematically. That is, the debates between "tradition" and "modernity" that often undergirded the agenda of social reform of women's position routinely overlooked the interests of women themselves. Instead, the terrain of the "woman question" became a battleground for various actors in the confrontation between colonial rule and the indigenous elites.[13] The contentiousness of tradition and the promise of modernity solidly provided the political framework for the devadasi reform debates. Yet, as I demonstrate in the next section, such a framework was unevenly extended to the project of reform for a community like the Gomantak Maratha Samaj.

Feminist historians, such as Janaki Nair, situate devadasi reform alongside wide-ranging (and conflicting) efforts to transform diverse (Hindu-based) family structures and customs into more normative patriarchal family structures, resonant with Victorian models of heterosexual marriage. Central to such mobilizations was of course the salvific discourse on the status of Indian women. For example, Nair contends that colonial criminalization of the matrilineal traditions of the Nayars of Malabar placed the customary marriage of the devadasis outside Hindu law, producing structures of kinship and access that disempowered women. Colonial regulatory practices were aided, she argues, in large part by nationalist efforts to establish legal systems that drew on brahminical norms that further erased devadasi structures from visibility. Such efforts around marriage reform were further complicated by the examples of Nayar marriages that drew precisely upon Nambudiri Brahmin forms that were intrinsically "polygamous" in structure.[14]

Kunal Parker, on the other hand, proposes that colonial courts in India augmented devadasi reform through innovative and often unprecedented translations of the law. Legal norms that previously applied to different castes represented within brahminical taxonomies were extended to include an innovative set of patriarchal norms with respect to the sexual behavior of Hindu women. For example, the devadasi was cast less as a "temple dancing girl," and more as a "Hindu girl" engaging in sexual activities outside marriage. Such a shift from the "tradition" of devadasis to the aberration of their sexual practices allowed the courts to legislate

ANJALI ARONDEKAR

against the devadasis without engaging their more complex functions as repositories of art, culture, and religion. According to Parker, these concerns affected the interpretation of the 1861 Indian Penal Code with reference to the devadasis. By focusing on the prostitution of minors dedicated to temples, Parker suggests that devadasi reform groups rerouted provisions intended to protect minors to nullify adoption by devadasis, and to outlaw any and all dedications of girls to deities. Such a turn to the protection of minors became a crucial part of the judicial reform movement aimed at eliminating devadasis.[15]

Amrit Srinivasan, in her now classic study "Temple 'Prostitution' and Community Reform," in Tamil Nadu, south India, links the devadasi reform debates to the revival of Indian dance and to the rise in communal politics in the early twentieth century. Srinivasan, like Parker and Nair, places devadasi reform squarely alongside questions of judicial and cultural formation. She suggests that males within devadasi communities in the Tanjore district supported devadasi reform and backward caste movements because they resented the property rights afforded devadasis under customary law. For Srinivasan, the language of reform and rehabilitation thus worked to erase an entire community of ritual specialists, with their practices replaced and reinterpreted as "a spiritual discipline for upper-caste women."[16] In the more recent postcolonial context, Lucinda Ramberg, studying devadasis dedicated to Yellamma in Belgaum, Karnataka, builds on Srinivasan's early formulations and situates the differentiated nature of devadasi community and kinship formation against state and NGO efforts to abolish and rehabilitate devadasis. Ramberg, like Srinivasan and Nair, remains convinced that devadasis challenge normative structures of kinship, caste, marriage, and property ownership, making reform efforts subject to simultaneous politics of revival and resurgence.[17]

A key text within such reform/revival debates is Kannabiran's superb translation of Muvalur Ramamirthammal's novel *Dasigal Mosavalai* (Web of deceit), which serves as a meditation on devadasi reform in colonial India. Written in 1936 by a follower of the "self-respect" movement (launched by the social reformer Periyar E. Ramasamy in 1925 to promote reform against the inequalities of a caste-based society) and a reformed devadasi, the novel exemplifies the historical complexities of a community trapped in the transition from tradition to modernity.[18] In part a biography of Muvalur Ramamirthammal, the story revolves around several devadasi figures, their relationship to a young zamindar, and the interventions of his wife to bring her husband back into the fold. The young wife disguises herself as a *dasi*, making the husband believe she is the dasi he has been in love with. The devadasis fall into abject penury, as the wife spirits their wealth away to form the corpus of the Devadasi Abolition Sangam.[19] While there is clearly much more to say about this very dense novel, the novel's "multiple" devadasi voices, S. Anandhi argues, robustly complicate the essentialist demarcations of devadasis within the reform or revival debates. The multiple devadasi characters in the novel alternately advocate for and against devadasi reform, while systematically reminding readers of the need to imagine the devadasi question within a larger nexus of affiliations and allegiances. Thus, for instance, S. Anandhi points to the author's interest in anticaste movements, and Dalit mobilization, particularly in Telugu- and Kannada-speaking areas.[20] While the predominant voice in the movement for devadasi abolition in Tamil areas was that of the self-respect movement, in Telugu areas, the anti-Nautch movement (Nautch is another, distinct type of performance) started even earlier and was firmly located within social purity and later social reform movements that followed a very different trajectory from the self-respect movement.[21]

A SMALL HISTORY OF THE GOMANTAK MARATHA SAMAJ

I turn now to a devadasi community, the Gomantak Maratha Samaj, that repeats and ruptures such inherited languages for scripting the devadasi story. Of significance is the relative paucity of sources on the emergence of devadasis within the Goan context. As a result, many speculative theories abound with respect to devadasi emergence and their consequent effacement within colonial and nationalist historiography. For scholars such as Rosa Maria Perez, there is much confusion around what constitutes a devadasi under Portuguese rule, especially given the variegated and often competing references to *bailadeiras* (dancing girls) and "devadasis" within the largely Catholic Goan sources, including ecclesiastical and administrative documents, travel accounts, essays, literature, and poetry.[22] Central to such formulations is the force of Portuguese conversion campaigns that often collapsed all Hindu ritual practices into a larger arena of excess and eroticism. However, in her rush to rescue devadasis from the detritus of Portuguese colonialism and to return them to their former (Hindu) histories and cultural formations, Perez conveniently glosses over similar atrocities committed against devadasis by Hindu and other indigenous elites.

Curiously, one of the few substantial accounts of the Goan bailadeiras appears not in a Portuguese source, but in an 1851 travelogue by the infamous British spy and ethnopornographer, Sir Richard Burton. Burton's interest in the "beautiful *Bayaderes*" situates them in the famed town of "Seroda" (now Shiroda), within a climate of Portuguese imperial decline and moral excess.[23] These bayaderes are lapsed "high-caste maidens," who interestingly have no ostensible ties to deity or creed. As Burton writes: "Having been compelled to eat beef by the 'tyrannical Portuguese in the olden time,' [they] had forfeited the blessings of Hindooism, without acquiring those of Christianity."[24] Yet Seroda is described as a "Hindoo town" (it remains one still) containing "about twenty establishments, and a total number of fifty or sixty dancing girls," some of whom read and write "Sanscrit shlokas" and speak a "corrupt form of Maharatta called Concanee."[25] Throughout his descriptions of the bayaderes, Burton routinely uses the terms "Bayadere," "Nautch" girl, and "dancing girl" interchangeably, thus effacing the distinctions between the different terms in Goa. "Bayadere" is a term exclusively used to describe Goan "dancing girls," whereas the terms "Nautch" and "dancing girl" function more as British Indian categories covering a range of regions and linguistic cultures.[26]

On the one hand, Burton's account of the Goan bayaderes can be written off as yet another instance of his prurient interest in all things carnal and exotic. On the other hand, his description of these bayaderes could also provide us with a complex prehistory to current understanding of the devadasi question in Goa. Seroda, or Shiroda, was and continues to be one of the central locations for devadasi congregation in colonial and postcolonial India. At the center of this "Hindoo town" lies the temple of Kamakshi, an incarnation of Goddess Parvati, consort of Shiva. By the side of the main temple are shrines dedicated to Shri Shantadurga, Shri Laxmi Narayana, and Shri Rayeshwar. Unlike the noted bayaderes, the devadasis in Shiroda were not known for their dancing skills, but were lauded instead for their prowess as musical *kalavants* (artists). Whether the devadasis of Shiroda were distinct from the bayaderes of Burton's Seroda is of less consequence than their historical entanglement within a diverse range of colonial texts and sources.

Postcolonial references to Goan devadasis rarely engage with the nominal substitution of "devadasi" with more fraught terms such as "Nautch girl" or "dancing girl." Instead, the focus is more on constructing genealogies of caste and labor that fix devadasis within a longer history of brahminic despotism. As the story goes, the Goan Saraswats were historically the primary patrons of the devadasis and devised a structure that demarcated kalavants who were either *ghanis* (singers) or *nachnis* (dancers) or both, *bhavnis* (women who attended to temple rituals) and *fulkars* (flower collectors). Of significance here is that *both* men and women did menial and physical labor on the farmlands of the Saraswat Brahmins and the Mahajans (elders associated with religious institutions) and were named *chede* or *bande*, literally bodies tied to the land. Included within the Goan devadasi structure was also *chadde farjand*, or *frejent*, a Persian term literally meaning "boy" but referring to the sons of unwed women who had sex with their employers. These latter groups of boys were referred to as *deuli* (male members of the Bhavin class) and were situated lower than the kalavants within the devadasi substructures.[27]

According to one theory, Goan devadasis were no different from their counterparts in the Deccan in function and history. Another account provides a different history of enslavement and labor by suggesting that the devadasis were brought to Goa by the migration of Saraswat Brahmins, who came in search of fertile lands and sustenance. The term "Gomantak," for instance, is "the Sankritised toponomic of the state of Goa," and denotes the prosperity of its cattle herds.[28] The irony however is that the region of Goa is geographically and topographically not suited for cattle rearing, and the term clearly references the nomadic Brahmins who came to its shores in search of lands and resources. Within the latter theory of enslavement and labor, devadasis were primarily "chattel," enslaved workers, whose services shifted into regimes of sex and art after their migration into foreign lands.[29]

The earliest official mention of the existence of devadasis as a social group appears in the Goa census of 1904. Of note is the careful demarcation of subgroups within the larger community; the first figure states the number of males recorded under the category and the second states the number of females:

Kalavants 305/420

Devlis 4615/4051

Bhandis (slaves) 3752/4099

Adbaktis (semislaves) 900/1881[30]

The Gomantak Maratha Samaj, the focus of this essay, draws its members from such complex groupings of Goan devadasis, and traces its roots back to the early 1800s. Appearing first as a formal community formation in 1927, the Samaj continues to this day, providing services, scholarships, and outreach to over ten thousand members all over Goa and western Maharashtra. Unlike the well-documented histories of reform of other devadasi communities, particularly those in southern India, this community's story in Portuguese Goa underwent very little transformation and exposure, until the early part of the twentieth century. Kalavants in the Samaj community, unlike the devadasi figurations in southern India, rarely wed deities and were not "prostitutes" in any conventional sense of the word. Rather, these kalavants were mostly female singers, classically trained, placed through ceremonies like *hath-lavne* into companionate structures with both men and women. Only occasionally do we find references to dedications to deities through rituals such as the *shens* ceremony. And even then, the ceremony appears more as a proxy wedding, in which a girl who is to be dedicated to a god or goddess is wed to a (surrogate) groom, always represented by another girl dressed as a man, holding a coconut and a knife.

Portuguese colonial officials also granted Samaj members exemption from antiprostitution laws, primarily because its kalavants remained in structures of serial monogamy, supported by *yajamans*, both male and female, functioning as patrons and partners through the life of the kalavant. Kalavants were also, crucially, sworn to remain in the spatial proximity of temples, whether or not they performed ritual temple roles. One curious feature of such arrangements was that children born to kalavants were often given gender-neutral names, which made inheritance (particularly of land) less judicially contentious, especially after the death of a particular yajaman. With the passage of the antidevadasi bills, many Samaj members gradually made their way to urban spaces like Bombay, in search of work in the newly emergent Hindi film industry. The success of kalavants was not restricted to the arts, but extended to science, literature, and philosophy.[31]

Central to the Samaj's self-definition is its eschewing of any antagonistic relationship to its past. That is, its members are rarely encouraged to nudge their linkages to devadasis into the closet of history; rather, such connections are made public, often ad nauseum, to attest to the community's success and presence in contemporary society. Thus, for example, since its inception in 1927, the Bombay branch of the Samaj has held yearly public functions that celebrate the past and future successes of its members. Such functions routinely draw upon references to devadasi genealogies to attest to the artistic and religious wealth of the community. Initial efforts to organize the community were primarily led by Rajaram Rangoji Paigankar in 1902. Paigankar particularly rallied youth members of the community and staged multiple successful conferences all over Goa and Maharashtra. The belief was that education and caste reform could bring power to the community, not at the expense of erasing past histories, but rather by building on the legacies of the past. Based primarily in Panaji, Shiroda, Malvan, and Bombay, the Samaj championed itself as caste reformist (as it were), describing its shift in name from Gomantak Kalavant Samaj, to Gomantak Maratha Samaj, as a primary indication of its commitment to a progressive pancaste politics. As Kakodkar and Paigankar argue, the leaders of the Samaj deliberately expanded their movement in the 1930s through their inclusion of the word "Maratha" (a term referring to dominant Hindu castes of warriors and peasants) in their self-nominalization.[32] Saraswat scholars of the period often dismiss such an inclusion, arguing that regardless of such attachments, the kalavants were not Marathas.[33]

Yet, as Paigankar argues in his passionate biography, *Mee Khon*, such shifts in identity were radical as they made caste status inherently mobile and accessible, an option previously unavailable to members of the community. Thus, it is crucial to recall that in the early declarations of the *Samaj Sudharak* (the monthly publication of the Samaj), Paigankar and his collaborators strongly emphasize the inclusion of the Deuli community alongside its kalavant members, gesturing to a uniform caste identity for all subgroups under the rubric of the Gomantak Maratha Samaj. A key feature of these early endeavors was the Samaj's concerted commitment to linking its own histories of sexuality and self-fashioning to a larger societal narrative of reform. The very first editorial of *Samaj Sudharak* goes to

ANJALI ARONDEKAR

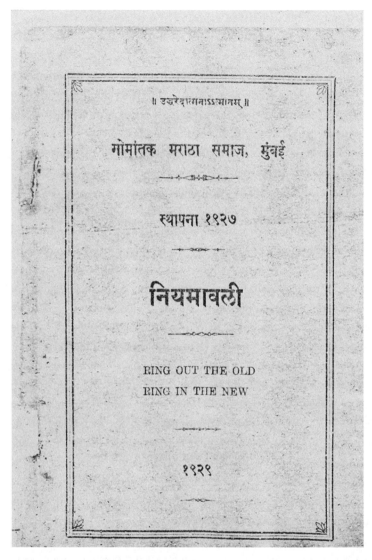

FIGURE 1. Front cover of the first printed constitution (literally, "rule book") of the Gomantak Maratha Samaj (1929). The constitution is archived at the Gomantak Maratha Samaj Society, Mumbai, India, and is published courtesy of the society.

great length to explain why the publication is so loftily called *Samaj Sudharak* and not simply the *Gomantak Maratha Samaj Sudharak*. Entitled "Our Courage," the editorial justifies the choice of title by foregrounding the absence of public debate on questions of sexuality, caste, and tradition, particularly within Marathi-language publications. For the editors, societal reform is impossible without an exposure of such issues, and their goal is to use the experiences of Samaj members to slowly but surely enlighten larger society on these questions.[34]

On the thorny issue of devadasi reform, the early issues of *Samaj Sudharak* are equally invested in understanding how sexuality is made intelligible within such reform efforts. From 1929 to 1948, much discussion focuses on the Samaj's relationship to the devadasi tradition and ways to outlive its past through education and marriage. Yet there appears no easy path to such a story of conventional progress and reform. For at the very time that the abandonment of the devadasi tradition is discussed, there is equally heated discussion on how the question of sexuality is to be managed. The issues raised by multiple contributors range from the inherent vagrancy of brahminical male sexuality and by extension all male sexuality (making the devadasi system inevitable) to more practical concerns of how women were to feed and clothe themselves outside of such established structures. One typical opinion piece (author unknown), entitled "Society, Open Your Eyes," angrily pleads with its readers to acknowledge the dictates of male sexuality. For this writer, the annointment of marriage solves nothing; after all, the men who serve as yajamans to Samaj women are themselves married. Rather, more of the community's men and women need to be educated as to their professional options outside the institution of marriage.[35] Many years later, Suhasini Borkar, one of the few female heads of the Gomantak Maratha Samaj, makes a similar but more complicated contribution to the devadasi debate. In an eloquent speech to its women's group, entitled "Fallen Woman and Wife?," Borkar argues that the women fit neither category since their sexuality is not "fallen" through vice or "entrapped" through marriage. Instead, she calls for a third identification stressing the kalavant woman's sexual independence and skill in the arts.[36] The advertisements accompanying such expressed views raise an equally capacious vista of representation: advertisements for Ambrosia, a "woman's tonic," are placed alongside services offered by tailors specializing in weddings, while movie posters celebrating the participation of Samaj members carry story lines that cast them as unwed mothers or unsung heroines.

By the 1920s or so, many members of Gomantak Maratha Samaj chose to migrate to Bombay, where they could openly pursue their kalavant training, adopt Marathi as their lingua franca, assimilate into society, marry legitimately, and escape the stranglehold of older devadasi histories signified by continued Saraswat condemnation in Goa. An early study on the migration into Bombay and on the rehabilitation of "prostitutes in Bombay" (with a "reference to family background") applauds the positive efforts of the Samaj, and contrasts it sharply with other organizations such as the Association of Tawaifs and Deredars that continue to use the "singing girls" as a "shield" to propagate more "unscrupulous" and unlawful activity. But the study also notes that "the majority of their respondents" are women from Goa, whose mother tongue is Konkani.[37]

However, such upwardly mobile self-descriptions are complicated by the fact that members assumed different caste identities, and were regarded as "other backward castes" in western Maharashtra, and as Saraswat, Prabhus, and Sonars in parts of Goa and Karnataka. For example, many Samaj women maintained coerced and uncoerced monogamous relationships with Brahmin men (and occasionally with lower-caste men). Children born out of such structures were often given caste names not otherwise available to Samaj members. One potential explanation (offered by the Portuguese scholar Rosa-Maria Perez) is that the members of Gomantak Maratha Samaj, "instead of trying to get rid of their stigma, tried to restructure it (during and after colonialism) precisely according to caste components."[38] Thus, there exist in Goa and Maharashtra (and to some extent in Karnataka as well) Samaj members who have Saraswat Brahmin surnames (such as Kakodkar, Welingkar, Shirodkar) acquired primarily through their intimacies with Brahmin men. To this day, the Samaj passionately encourages intercaste, interreligious marriages, and is often referred to as "Bharatatil Ek Aggressar Samaj" (an aggressive community in India) due to the tremendous social progress it has achieved over such a short time.[39]

Such celebratory characterizations of Gomantak Maratha Samaj are echoed in established postcolonial histories of Goa. While the references to the community continually mark it as a "model" of social progress and success, they rarely connect its success to a critique of larger histories of caste and kinship within Goa itself. That is, the story of the Samaj remains a singular history of one community's upliftment, not an interrogation of the foundational (and teleological) processes of subject-formation and citizenship. For Gomantak Maratha Samaj to be termed Bharatatil Ek

Aggressar Samaj, it must make itself intelligible in the very formulations of sexuality and sociality that produced its segregations in the first place. Even less is noted about the community's own return to more conventional structures of gender and sexuality—an area of discussion that lies beyond the scope of this brief essay.[40]

Some final thoughts: My goal here has not been to provide a hagiographical or recuperative reading of the Gomantak Maratha Samaj. To do so would be only to mirror the ideological certainty that characterizes some of the versions of the devadasi story I criticized earlier. Rather, I have highlighted the movement and figuration of sexuality within some of the narratives and histories of the community. There are no efforts within the Samaj archives to disavow the representational burden of its devadasi past; its efforts are focused more on an almost commonsensical understanding of how and what that past signifies. Indeed, what there is most to learn here is the many ways in which the Gomantak Maratha Samaj negotiated its attachment to sexuality, as evidence not of a failed past but rather as promise of future possibilities for social, cultural, and economic success. If the early reform or revival debates around devadasi formation rescue the sign of sexuality either through the language of judicial representation, or the consecration of cultural practices such as dance and music, on the other hand, the claims of a successful devadasi-founded Gomantak Maratha Samaj could produce sexuality as a fulcrum for regional debates on caste, kinship, gender, and beyond. The challenge is to link devadasi histories to a structure of attachments that seemed settled when we first embarked upon this inquiry.

NOTES

1. In Karnataka, for example, the state sponsors multiple projects aimed at the rehabilitation of devadasis. See Joint Women's Programme, "An Exploratory Study on Devadasi Rehabilitation Programme Initiated by Karnataka State Women's Development Corporation and Sc/St Corporation, Government of Karnataka in Northern Districts of Karnataka," report submitted to National Commission for Women, New Delhi, 2001–2.

2. For an excursus on the relationship between sexuality and archival hermeneutics, see Arondekar, *For the Record*.

3. For a related discussion in queer historiography, see Goldberg and Menon, "Queering History," 1608–17.

ANJALI ARONDEKAR

4. "Whoever voluntarily has carnal intercourse against the order of nature with any man, woman or animal shall be punished with imprisonment for life, or with imprisonment of either description for a term which may extend to ten years, and shall also be liable to fine. Explanation: Penetration is sufficient to constitute the carnal intercourse necessary to the offence described in this section. The offence made punishable under this section requires that penetration, however little, should be proved strictly. Thus an attempt to commit this offence should be an attempt to thrust the male organ into the anus of the passive agent. Some activity on the part of the accused in that particular direction ought to be proved strictly. A mere preparation for the operation should not necessarily be construed as an attempt. Emission is not necessary." *Of Unnatural Offences, Section 377, Indian Penal Code* (instituted in 1860, revised 1932, 1968, 1982 and still in effect). See Ranchhoddas and Thakoree, *The Indian Penal Code*.

5. Counteraffidavit, *Naz Foundation v. Govnt. of Delhi, Police Commissioner of Delhi, Delhi State AIDS Control Society, Union of India*, Civil Writ Petition 7455, 2001, 2004.

6. This section distills claims from my recent essay on the repeal of Section 377 and its colonial genealogies; see Arondekar, "Time Corpus."

7. Goa's official liberation came on December 19, 1961, when the Indian Army moved in against the Portuguese garrisons as part of Operation Vijay. Yet this late "liberation" by and into the Indian state did not come without a fair share of controversy and resentment. For many Goan historians and nationalists, Prime Minister Nehru's "soft policy" against the dictatorship of Portuguese rule provided late relief and relegated Goa to an extended state of historical stasis and neglect. See Shirodkar, *Goa's Struggle for Freedom*; Rubinoff, *India's Use of Force in Goa*; and Deora, *Liberation of Goa, Daman, and Diu*.

8. The reference here is to Amrit Srinivasan's well-known essay "Reform and Revival," 1869.

9. Avanthi Meduri, "Nation, Woman, Representation: The Sutured History of the *Devadasi* and Her Dance," Ph.D. dissertation, New York University, 1996.

10. Two classic examples of such efforts are Patil, "Devadasis and Other Social Evils"; and Trivedi, *Scheduled Caste Women*.

11. There is a small and well-recycled set of writings on the cultural history of devadasis in India. Key texts include Kersenboom-Story, *Nityasumangali-Devadasi Tradition in South India*; Kamble, *Devadasi ani Nagnapuja*; Shankar, *Devadasi Cult*; Marglin, *Wives of the God-King*; and Chakraborthy, *Women as Devadasis*.

12. Jordan, *From Sacred Servant to Profane Prostitute*, 1–15. To this day, Jordan's text remains one of the few scholarly attempts to actively bring together the multiple debates within devadasi historiography.

13. See Sangari and Vaid, "Introduction"; and Mani, "Contentious Traditions."

14. Nair, *Women and Law in Colonial India*.

15. Parker, "A Corporation of Superior Prostitutes," 559–663.

16. Amrit Srinivasan, "Temple 'Prostitution' and Community Reform: An Examination of the Ethnographic, Historical and Textual Context of the *Devadasis* of Tamil Nadu, South India," Ph.D. dissertation, Cambridge University, 1984.

17. Lucinda Ramberg, "Given to the Goddess: South Indian *Devadasis*, Ethics, Kinship," Ph.D. dissertation, University of California, Berkeley, with the University of California, San Francisco, 2006.

18. Hodges, "Revolutionary Family Life."

19. Ramamirthammal, *Web of Deceit,* 1–48. The introduction provides a useful context to the regional debates undergirding devadasi reform in the Madras presidency.

20. Anandhi, "Representing *Devadasis.*"

21. Muthulaksmi Reddy was one of the iconic figures in these struggles. In 1927, she advocated an amendment to the Hindu Religious Endowments Act that abolished the granting of land in exchange for service in temples, thus striking at the economic basis of the devadasi system. What is less known is that many devadasis resisted abolitions, and formed groups to oppose the bill and argue against the codification of devadasis as prostitutes and not divinely ordained laborers. See introduction to Ramamirthammal, *Web of Deceit.*

22. Perez, "The Rhetoric of Empire."

23. Burton, *Goa and the Blue Mountains,* 118–35.

24. Ibid., 119.

25. Ibid., 125.

26. See entries for "Bayadere," "Nautch girl," and "Dancing girl" in Yule and Burnell, *Hobson-Jobson.*

27. Archana Kakodkar, "The Portuguese and Kalavants," unpublished paper, 1991. I am grateful to Dr. Kakodkar, senior librarian (retd.), Goa University, for her invaluable help. To this day, she is the only scholar who has worked extensively on cataloguing the history of the Gomantak Maratha Samaj.

28. Sarkar, "Dedication to the Altar," 146.

29. Ibid., 145–51.

30. Figures cited in Mario Cabral e Sa, "Here Lived Batabai: The Story of a Remarkable Clan," *Goa Today,* January 2003, at goacom.org.

31. Archana Kakodkar, "Devadasis of Goa," unpublished paper. While female singers such as Moghubai Kurdikar, Kesarbai Kerkar, Lata Mangeshkar, and Kishori Amonkar remain the best-known members of Gomantak Maratha Samaj, others of note include the first composer of Marathi musical drama, Hirabai Pednekar; the former chief minister of Goa, Shashikala Kakodkar; and Sulochana Katkar, retired president of the Goa Congress.

32. "Marathas" is a collective (and heavily debated) term referring to Indo-Aryan groups of Hindu, Marathi-speaking castes of warriors and peasants hailing largely from the present-day state of Maharashtra. Through their creation of a substantial empire in the late seventeenth and eighteenth centuries, the Marathas occupied a major part of India. Of note here is that the Marathas were known by

the term primarily because their native tongue was mostly but not always Marathi. Thus, the terms "Marathi" people and "Maratha" people are not interchangeable and should not be confused for each other. See Deshpande, *Creative Pasts*.

33. Paigankar, *Mee Khon*.

34. *Samaj Sudharak* (January 1929). All issues of the *Samaj Sudharak* are archived at the Gomantak Maratha Samaj Society building in Mumbai, India. In 2004, the Samaj offices were moved from Gomantak Maratha Samaj Sadan, 345 V.P. Road, Bombay 400004, to Sitladevi Co-op. Housing Society Ltd., 7–16/B Wing, D. N. Nagar, New Link Road, Andheri (W), Mumbai 400053. A partial archive can be found at the Gomantak Maratha Samaj, Dayanand Smriti, Swami Vivekanand Marg, Panaji 403001, Goa. The magazine is still published but is now called *Gomant Shardha*.

35. *Samaj Sudharak* (May 1929).

36. *Samaj Sudharak* (January 1943).

37. Punekar and Rao, *A Study of Prostitutes in Bombay*, 169, 160. For a broader understanding of late-colonial debates on prostitution in Bombay, see Tambe, "Brothels as Families."

38. See Perez, "The Rhetoric of Empire," 141–43.

39. See Kakodkar, "Gomantak Maratha Samaj," 5–16; and Radhakrishnan, *Purushartha*.

40. See Pissurlencar, *The Portuguese and the Marathas*; Priolkar, *Goa Rediscovered*; de Souza, *Essays in Goan History*; Shirodkar, *Goa's Struggle for Freedom*; Danvers, *The Portuguese in India*; Newman, *Of Umbrellas, Goddesses, and Dreams*; and Axelrod and Fuerch, "Flight of the Deities."

V

FEMINISM, SEX WORK, AND THE POLITICS OF SEXUALITY

FIRDOUS AZIM

Keeping Sexuality on the Agenda
The Sex Workers' Movement
in Bangladesh

THE HISTORY OF THE women's movement in Bangladesh can be seen as a struggle to establish women's rights and freedoms within the nation-state, and to confer on women complete democratic status of a citizen. This bland statement is, however, problematic because of the many differences among women themselves, and the limited nature of the struggles mounted by the mainly middle-class organizers of the women's movement in Bangladesh. Feminist struggles everywhere have had to struggle with defining and articulating the ambit of women's rights. The struggles for the establishment of women's rights prove that certain categories of women—such as the poor, or those labeled as deviant or immoral—are kept outside the democratic purview; as Mary Wollstonecraft seems to have realized at the dawn of democratic movements, women always needed to "prove" themselves to be "fit" citizens. Democratic spaces are uneven, and while certain kinds of rights are easy to demand, others have to be framed more carefully. This is especially true if the women asking for rights and recognitions within the state are somehow marginalized. Marginalization may take place for various reasons, such as differences of ethnicity or poverty. For women, being outside the pale of "respectable" structures, such as family and marriage, leads to another kind of marginalization, making access to rights as a citizen even more difficult. As the women's movement today tries to draw a wider and more diverse group of women into a notion of citizenry, the nature of the struggle and the strategies employed have to be rethought and perhaps reconfigured.

This essay illustrates the process by looking at a particular campaign that dominated the women's movement in Bangladesh through the 1990s. Naripokkho is one of the leading women's groups in Bangladesh, and it often describes itself as part of a movement for the realization of women's rights. Based on Naripokkho's experience with the sex workers' movement in Bangladesh, I examine how the discourse on rights helped women to mobilize around the issue of sex work. The issue of sex work was brought to public and political limelight, alliances were drawn and "victories" won, by concentrating on sex workers' status as women and as citizens. While this was felt largely to be an empowering discourse, it is useful to look at what was kept away from the public eye. This history provides us with an opportunity to examine the ways that a rights-based approach helps to forward the cause of women's freedom, as well as the barriers that such an approach encounters, a subject that has been vigorously debated in feminist political theory.[1]

RIGHTS, CITIZENSHIP, AND WOMEN'S MOVEMENTS

In *Inclusive Citizenship: Meanings and Expression*, Naila Kabeer describes how excluded groups seek for an entry into a democratic polity.[2] She points to the values of justice, recognition, and self-determination or the "ability to exercise some degree of control over their lives" as the ones that marginalized groups have identified as markers of inclusiveness.[3] She argues that "solidarity," defined as the "capacity to identify with others and to act in unity with them in their claims for justice and recognition" is "one of the methods by which the struggle for citizenship expresses itself."[4]

It is from within such a notion of democracy that women's groups in Bangladesh continue to seek to gain services, rights, and recognition from the state. The gains, however, cannot be seen as unmixed, and this essay, based on the experience of the sex workers' campaign of the 1990s, debates the values and usefulness of a rights-based approach for a feminist movement.

At this juncture, I would also like to point to the particular situation in which social movements are currently placed in Bangladesh. Citizens' groups as well as a large number of development organizations (NGOs, or nongovernmental organizations) perform multiple roles. Often, they seem to be substituting for government and state functions, especially in the delivery of basic services such as health and education. At other times, they perform the role of pressure groups, holding the government accountable to cater to the rights and needs of its citizens. Yet a third arena of their activity is social mobilization and activism. Regardless of the nature of the NGO, its activities are guided by international donor funding. Hence much of the work of negotiation and forging international and bilateral agreements takes cognizance of this nongovernmental sphere.

The women's movement, comprising fairly divergent types of women's groups, straddles an anomalous ground between these different sectors. Many women's groups are directly involved in service delivery, especially in health and legal aid. At the same time these organizations act as pressure groups, lobbying the government to provide better services, or demanding legal reform. The same groups are part of a larger social movement for rights and a larger democratic space. Given the multiple roles that they occupy, women's groups are increasingly seen as forming an important part of the civil society interventions in the country.

The debates around women's rights, women's status as citizens, and women's ability to choose proliferate in an arena where feminists must oscillate between many tasks. Accordingly, Naila Kabeer has described the arena of women's activism as "fragmented and uneven."[5] The fragmentation is discernible even in the ways that women's groups define or describe themselves. Maheen Sultan and Soheila Nazneen describe how leading women's groups mobilize around issues such as violence against women or women's political participation.[6] It is not only the difference in strategies that are noticeable: what is most interesting is the hybrid nature of the groups themselves.[7] Women's groups, including Naripokkho, underwent a process during the 1990s, largely driven by the then upcoming fourth World Conference on Women, or the Beijing Conference, to register themselves as NGOs, which gave them access to donor funding. At this point in time, groups had to decide whether they would continue to operate as largely voluntary organizations, or enter the more formal arena of donor-funded organizations. However, these groups, including Bangladesh Mahila Parishad and Women for Women, were wary of being subsumed under the aegis of development organizations, as such a move would give rise to doubts about their autonomy.

How the nature of the women's movement changed when women's groups, which had largely functioned as autonomous groups, or sometimes as women's wings of political parties, started registering themselves as funded organizations and started taking funds mainly for research into issues such as violence against women or for the setting up of shelter homes, is a matter of ongoing research and analysis in Bangladesh. Debates within groups such as Naripokkho or Bangladesh Mahila Parishad are heated on this topic, and most such groups emerged from that moment as hybrid organizations, running funded projects and programs, as well as keeping alive the largely autonomous voluntary campaign-based work. However, running funded projects involved large amounts of time, and increasingly campaign work started coming under funded purview. This has had the effect of changing the nature of women's activism in general. Tasks such as influencing policy and making the state accountable have resulted in a greater involvement with the formal structures of the state or the economy, and as a result, issue-based campaign work has been gradually eroded. However, most of these groups have their roots in the nationalist movements of the 1960s and 1970s, and even while they are adjusting to the new regimes of activism and discourse, they have not really shed some of the older ways of organizing. The sex workers' movement had been part of the older structures of the organizations concerned, social activism that can be seen as a relic from the 1970s. But as the donor agencies and funded programs moved into this arena, the emphasis turned to service delivery, and as such, issues of women's sexual rights or the rights of sex workers became subsumed under the needs of a better health delivery system and the emphasis on rights and status was diffused.

The sex workers' campaign, launched in 1991, emerged as a reaction to a threat of eviction from brothels. Naripokkho deployed its "voluntary" or "movement-oriented" wing to combat the threat and announced its solidarity with the sex workers who were struggling to protect themselves against these attacks. The emphasis on rights was felt to be the most effective platform from which to mount sex workers' demands, as well as for Naripokkho to express solidarity with sex workers. Alliance building and creating solidarity was based on a notion of citizens' rights. Ten years after that campaign, while trying to evaluate what was gained from this movement, one of the questions that arises for feminists is whether the campaign had in any way called upon the state to go beyond its established boundaries and accommodate more and "other" women within a notion of citizenry. A critical lens will reveal the limitation of the campaign, which seemed to be mired in a discourse of poverty and exploitation and which could not move the discussion to include issues of sexuality, marginalization, and socially unacceptable practices and spaces. Hence the position of sex workers as "outcasts" remained unaddressed, and therefore unchanged.[8]

In trying to establish themselves as legitimate citizens of the state, sex workers themselves invoked the discourse of rights, drawing the connections of such a discourse with that of responsibilities. They deployed a notion of "worthiness" to prove themselves to be worthy of citizens' rights. Evidence of "citizenship," such as municipal tax papers, was displayed as proof of interactions with the state. Further, personal religiosity was emphasized, to offset the stigma of being "bad" women, along with a reiteration of their participation in the broader religious and charitable life of the community. These activities were highlighted and worked as a special-interest plea. While sex work may be a "degraded" form of work, sex workers did not consider themselves as spiritually or morally separate from their community. However, the mainstream (largely middle-class) women's groups, while building solidarity with sex workers, steered the discussion away from the question of women's sexual identities, instead foregrounding the idea of sex work as part of women's work. The feeling was that it would be easier to voice demands that centered on the right to work and the right to housing. Thus women's groups missed the opportunity to look at women's sexual positioning, even by bringing in the old arguments of prostitution as the flip side of marriage. The chance to bring the issue of women's sexuality to the forefront of the discussion and debate was lost.

The reasons behind this are manifold. The emphasis on broader alliance building made the campaign concentrate on "common" ground, making it wary of stepping into controversial territory such as sexuality. The mainstream women's movement had, so far in its history, concentrated on issues of rights and citizenship, and thus had not developed a vocabulary that could address questions such as women's sexuality, the differences in sexual positioning between men and women, and the relations between different groups of women.

Women's groups were interested in making connections between sex work and women's work in general, and reiterated the oft-voiced demands for greater employment opportunities for women and better working conditions. Such connections were, however, not thought through and therefore were never really established. Thus, sex workers and sex work have not been integrated into the labor discourse, and the struggle for the rights of women workers has not made any links with the rights of women employed as sex workers. Nor has the issue of sex work been included in the discussion of women's labor. As is well known, in Bangladesh the largest number of women are employed in garment factories.[9] Garment factory workers are mainly young and peripatetic. At the time when the sex workers' movement was being forged, the country had not witnessed women garment workers' protests or movements. In recent years, and especially during 2007 and 2008, sporadic protests by garment workers have become noticeable. These protests have concentrated on better pay and working conditions, as discussed in a study by Maheen Sultan.[10] Interventions by women's groups into this largely nonunionized group of women workers (represented by groups such as Kormojibi Nari [Working women]) have made no attempt to expand their ambit to include sex workers. If solidarity was the platform on which the rights of sex workers were being forged, that solidarity has not been visible in labor movements. As a result, sex workers have not been recognized as women workers in campaigns dealing with a variety of female labor.

So far I have dwelt on the strategies of women's groups in Bangladesh during the campaign for the rights of sex workers. I have tried to argue that the campaign may have widened democratic spaces where hitherto excluded groups of women could claim their place as citizens, but that it was fraught with limitations. An examination of the historical background from which the campaign for sex workers' rights emerged may help us understand these better. I have indicated the fragmented and mixed terrain on which social movement activism functions in Bangladesh and which shapes public debates on sexuality. It is within this variegated space that the movements around sex work will have to devise a vocabulary adequate to articulating a wider variety of demands.

NATION MAKING, DEVELOPMENT, AND WOMEN
IN BANGLADESH

Women's groups and movements for women's rights in Bangladesh have historically been linked with the processes of nation making. Narratives of a "glorious" national history have usually elided issues of sexuality and of women's fragile positioning in the national imaginary. However, it is this very same history that opens up different ways of reading women's struggles, especially through a concentration on the participation of women in the 1971 War of Liberation. These liberation narratives have concentrated on the issue of war rape; a very early publication, *Ami Birangona Bolchi* or *The Voices of War Heroines*, had used women's first-person accounts to show the very complex processes through which the war rape victims were accommodated or rejected within the national fabric. Though the state had made a valiant effort to honor these women as heroines, society, family, and official structures of the state proved to be inadequate in the task of including these women in the annals of national history. The first-person narratives collected in *Ami Birangona Bolchi* speak of familial rejection and social ostracism. The author, Nilima Ibrahim, was drawn to collect these interviews when she was horrified on reading in the newspapers that some women were requesting to be "repatriated" along with Pakistani prisoners of war.[11] These stories are an integral part of a feminist historicizing of the war of liberation in Bangladesh.[12]

While the history of Bangladesh's birth opens up spaces for an examination of women, sexuality, and the nation, that of the women's movement in Bangladesh tends to follow a different trajectory because of the fragmentation of the movement that Naila Kabeer has commented on, and the ubiquity of the development discourse within social movements in the country. Women's groups, during their restructuring phase in the 1990s, had to find a niche within the discourse of national development, as this was felt to be the only space within which social movements could make a meaningful contribution. Debates around the process of bringing women into "development" and the economic mainstream start to dominate the agenda from this period. Bangladesh has become a crucible for intervention by development organizations, many of which have concentrated on women. As has already been mentioned, the nongovernmental sector plays a key role in these interventions, and the discourse of women's rights and empowerment is thus heavily influenced by these programs and projects. The development arena is seen as part of national development, where the state and the citizens of the new nation work together for the equal rights and prosperity of its citizens.[13]

The best-known example of a "women and development" program is the Grameen Bank. Critiques of such interventions concentrate on the limitations of the programs rather than on their efficacy with regard to social transformation. However, an article written by Anne-Marie Goetz and Rina Sengupta entitled "Who Takes the Credit? Gender, Power and Control over Loan Use in Rural Credit Programmes in Bangladesh" (1996) questions whether women ever exercise any control over the money that is loaned to them.[14] This article looks at women's agency and decision making, and shows that development interventions, especially in the form of loans to women, do not necessarily lead to women's empowerment and greater agency.

Goetz and Sengupta's critique can be extended beyond the question of economic empowerment to look at whether development interventions in the arena of health, for example, provide women more control over their bodies and sexuality. Population control has been at the forefront in various guises in Bangladesh, ranging from family planning to reproductive health. Bangladesh's interventions in population control and family planning are prominent among the successes claimed by the state. The country has successfully decreased its birth rate (it stands at 1.9 percent annually at the moment), apparently without the sensationally coercive methods used elsewhere in the region, including India. But while the family planning agenda had to, of necessity, center on women's bodies, it did not create any space for discussion of sexuality or a woman's right to choose. Women's groups have at times campaigned against the medical or physical effects of established family planning methods, and raised the question of women's control over their bodies. But there has been a shying away from directly talking about female sexuality and women's control over their sexual choices and practices.[15]

Similarly, movements around violence against women highlight women's vulnerabilities. Women's groups have widened the discussion of violence against women to include an examination of women's position within the family, women's control over decision making, and also state responsibilities in dealing with issues. A series of campaigns by women's groups, while focusing on individual cases of murder, rape, or acid attacks, has led to debates on definitions of violence, as well as its causes and effects. The main issues that emerged have been recorded in an unpublished report by Naripokkho.[16] Rape and sexual harassment have forced the issue of women's sexuality into debates on violence against women. Sexuality did enter the discussion, but was soon subsumed under the discourse of women's vulnerability, leading to demands for safer roads and better policing—a reversal of the "law-and-order" approach that had characterized campaigns against violence in the past.

THE CONTEXT OF THE SEX WORKERS' MOVEMENT

The significance of the movement for sex workers' rights becomes clearer in the light of this history. As I have already outlined, sex workers' campaigns started in response to a series of eviction threats against brothels between 1991 and 1999. Most of the threatened brothels were located in Dhaka and Narayanganj, the latter a river port town situated just outside Dhaka, though some of the campaigning spilled into other areas such as Tangail and Jessore. The brothels in question were old, established institutions from the nineteenth century, situated in port and commercial areas, and had been prominent in the cityscape for more than a century. Sex workers who plied their trade outside brothels were also drawn into the campaign.

The threats to the brothels' existence came from a variety of forces, which were eyeing the commercially desirable lands in which these establishments were located. These included local politicians, such as members of Parliament, and local mosque-based citizens' groups, which formed alliances with names such as Movement against Anti-Islamic Activities. The religious card was played first by those threatening the brothels, with men marching toward brothels after Friday prayers, characterizing the women and their activities as un-Islamic. These scenes of pious men marching on "sinful" women pitted the idea of "free" sex against the morality that is supposed to be embodied by an Islamic society. But the women played their own "Islamic" card, when they talked about how they regularly contributed money to mosques in their area. The brothel residents organized themselves for their own protection and, in a press conference held in April 1991, demanded that the state protect them from these threats.

This was quite a novel step. Sex workers claimed their rights as citizens, and called upon the police to protect them and guard their residences and places of work. Women's groups, such as Naripokkho, joined brothel residents in solidarity with their demands, and at that point the threat of eviction was averted. Similar kinds of threats, however, could not be averted in 1998 and 1999, and, despite all efforts, including winning a court case, women were ejected from their brothels. The movement tried to stick to a legal language of right to abode and a right to work. The legal victory, though largely ineffective, was hailed as a landmark judgment, as women's right to brothels as places of residence was acknowledged. The legal ruling was issued in response to a writ petition filed by 267 women who identified themselves as sex workers, along with 86 human and women's rights organizations. The judgment began by asserting that "prostitution is not illegal under any existing law in Bangladesh." The ruling went on to say that "even while Islam is the state religion, Bangladesh does not follow sharia [Islamic] laws regarding *zinna* [adultery], so accusations brought on that count were not admissible."[17] The rest of the ruling goes on to talk about the sex workers' right to work and abode, and makes the law-enforcing agencies culpable for failing to protect the safety and security of these women. There was a total recognition of sex work as legitimate, and of the duty of state agencies to protect and secure the livelihoods therein.

Until this time the issue of institutionalized sex work had come into public purview in the form of "rescue" work, and rehabilitation was seen as the main mode of redress for women who had been deceived or inveigled into sex work. Such rescue work, in which some women's groups had been involved, had included getting underage girls out of brothels.[18] But now, the focus was on citizens' rights, and the state was asked to provide protection to these women as part of its duty to its citizens. Their position as workers was also highlighted. Changing the nomenclature of the profession from "prostitution" to "sex work" was very deliberate, and brothel workers asserted that they did not live off charity but actually worked for a living. Accordingly, the feminist address to sex workers had to also change from one of opprobrium or pity to that of solidarity as workers and women.

Let us look now at some of the other changes that occurred during the course of the movement. Despite the public recognition resulting from the court ruling, the legal status of sex work or prostitution outside brothels remained vague. Anomalies in the laws that define and regulate sex work within and outside brothels draw public sympathy away from sex workers. Moreover, newspapers and the media are full of horror stories of kidnappings and torture of young girls, and their forcible entry into the sex trade. To this has been added the issue of international trafficking of women and girls. These stories and reports affect the image of the sex trade in the popular imagination, where brothels are viewed as sites of torture and exploitation. The hierarchical nature of sex work has a further effect of vilifying older women or the "madams" of the trade, who, along with pimps and brothel owners, get characterized as villains, about whom sensational horror stories proliferate. International debates also reflect some of these hierarchies, where young Third World women are seen as helpless victims of the sex trade and shown to be completely lacking in the exercise of agency or choice.[19] The campaign had changed the public address inasmuch as positions of moral outrage and sentimental pity were replaced by expressions of solidarity. This was the basis on which "Shanghati" (literally, solidarity)—a loose platform composed of women's groups, human rights groups, and some developmental NGOs—was formed to fight for the rights of sex workers. This platform subsequently led to the formation of sex workers' groups, such as Ulka, which were set up to fight for the rights of their members and to demand health and social services, as well as schooling for their children.[20]

Brothels are interesting and hybrid spaces, being both places of work and domestic spaces. Affective familial functions are carried on here, such as the bearing and rearing of children. As places of work, brothels are perhaps like no other, as sexual acts that are performed here range from the most casual and commercial to the most intimate. Such a mingling of functions throws fresh light on existing notions of work. Sex work can be seen as part of the service sector, as care work, or as entertainment. The coupling of sex and work brought out questions of other uses of sex, when sex is not associated with work but with pleasure.

The campaigns for sex work ideally should have reconsidered the nature of women's work. Sex work or prostitution is often seen as the most obvious form of exploitation of women's bodies. But how and why is it different from other forms of exploitative work? Is it because of the sexual services performed? Paid work is often seen as a pathway for women's empowerment. Is paid sex work then a pathway to empowerment? Does it result in greater autonomy and control over one's body? These questions began to be posed during the course of the campaigns, both publicly in newspapers and media forums, but especially in conversations between sex workers' groups and middle-class women's and human rights groups. Answers to them were never definite, and a firm affirmative to the debate over the legitimacy of sex work was not forthcoming. The issue of an autonomous sphere of female sexuality seemed to lurk behind the scenes, but was never brought to public light. Despite solidarity and the forging of a common platform, sex work continued to be seen by the women's movement and by middle-class feminists as a site of exploitation, not just of women's bodies but also of their work. The forging of links between women involved in other forms of work and sex workers was not attempted. It is only in private conversations—sometimes structured into a workshop format and at others spontaneous and unplanned—that many of the issues that the public campaign failed to highlight began to surface. Despite this, differences—between "us" (activists) and "them" (sex workers)—were not bridged. The most that was achieved was a desire to communicate and talk across this gap. Naripokkho members were fascinated by the sexual freedom that sex workers seemed to enjoy. Publicly, stories of exploitation and control by horrible men proliferated; in private, the conversations tended to be about sexual pleasure and even power. In fact, the lives of middle-class activists appeared by comparison drab and unexciting, controlled and monotonous. These conversations left a feeling of unease among middle-class activists, as the very different trajectories of women's lives tested the notion of solidarity and alliance building. Taking recourse to a language of rights and citizenship drew on previous experiences, but new ways of forming links with other groups of women were not sufficiently explored.

While the campaign developed strategies and agendas based on local experience and understanding, it also made the effort to draw a more international audience. In a letter to Mary Robinson, then the United Nations high commissioner for human rights, attention was drawn to the brothel evictions as a violation of human rights. As shown earlier, existing debates around sex work tended to concentrate on exploitation and even exploitative hierarchies within the sex industry. Naripokkho and other human rights groups largely ignored these hierarchies during the campaign, trying to draw a picture of solidarity among all women. Questions of class and difference were kept outside the public terrain of the campaign.

CONTEMPORARY MOVEMENTS AROUND SEXUALITY
IN BANGLADESH

Where does the sex workers' movement in Bangladesh stand today? As outlined earlier, some brothels were evacuated, and despite court rulings, women have not been able to reoccupy the spaces they were turned out of. Sex workers have formed their own groups, and acquired some recognition and voice in the social movements arena. But other issues have also emerged, changing some of the contours of the rights discourse that the women's movement had opted for. For example, protection from the state had been one of the demands to offset the eviction threats. This was quite ironic, as police harassment is a bane in these women's lives. The demand for state protection thus called on the very entity that threatens them. Other demands included educational opportunities for children and access to health care. This last was quickly translated by groups working with brothel residents to mean protection against AIDS and other sexually transmitted diseases, and newly formed sex workers' groups found it worth their while to become part of the anti-AIDS campaigns in the country. Such an entry into the public health domain, however, has, instead of providing better health services to women, fed into the moral campaign that often singles out sex workers as the carriers of disease. The discourse on women's bodies has thus reshaped itself along the contours of moral hygiene, and the issue of women's health rights is completely overshadowed by this specter of infection and disease.

The AIDS discourse has had other ramifications. One of its effects has been to bring into public purview alternative sexualities. Gay male groups, such as MSM (men having sex with men) or transgendered and *hijra* groups, are important parts of the discourse around sexuality and sex work in Bangladesh today.[21] Here too the emphasis is on two issues—rights and public health. The public health issue seems to predominate, as resources and funds can be garnered more easily for it. Sex workers' groups, for example, have tapped into these resources, and the wider demand for health services is accessed through special programs and projects that cater to "at-risk" groups. The conjuncture between AIDS and the uncovering of different sexualities in Bangladesh has indeed added a new dimension to public health activism. Different forms of sexuality and sexual identities are being increasingly brought under the aegis of AIDS prevention, as is evident from the formation of a center of sexuality and gender rights at the School of Public Health at BRAC University. Research and all activities of the center have to refer to an anti-AIDS agenda if they are to have any form of legitimacy. The new forms of campaigns for greater sexual rights, concentrating on MSMS and hijras, and even sex workers, have deviated from the call for rights and have become more concentrated on health issues. These health services are asked for and provided as social protection. Discussions on sex and sexuality are tolerated only when it is seen as part of an effort to keep the public "safe" from the health hazards of such activities.

It is sad that the demand for rights has become diluted over the years, as the rights demanded ten years ago are far from being realized. Legal recognition has not helped women reoccupy their brothels. Sex work has in the meantime been driven out of the brothels and into other arenas, such as the streets, hotels, and massage parlors. The trade itself has adjusted and reformulated itself to the more peripatetic modes that characterize the contemporary job market. A survey carried out three years after the anti-eviction campaign showed that a large number of brothel residents had transferred to other brothels, mainly outside Dhaka. Out of 112 women respondents, 58 had found work in brothels outside Dhaka, while the others were leading a more nomadic life, constantly changing their locations in the city. They also talked about feeling insecure, having been subject to a larger number of assaults and attacks than they had previously been. None reported a change of profession.[22]

Thus, sex work has become decentralized, informal, and fluid. Ten years on, it will be very difficult to organize a sex workers' rights movement. Different strategies will be needed. A brothel-based movement will no longer have the same kind of impact. For sex workers, other forms of organization, focusing on access to services, have opened up. The rights-based approach of the 1990s, limited though it was, has lost much of its appeal to sex workers, and to add a feminist thrust to the new developments in the arena of sexuality would need a fresh approach. Mainstream feminist groups have in the meantime become more involved in move- ments for greater political representation for women, leaving issues of sexuality to other forms of activism, especially in public health. Women's groups had been trying to change attitudes toward sex work by recognizing the rights of women engaged in the profession, thereby giving them the dignity of citizens. Despite their efforts, other forms of change have oc- curred, and attitudes toward sex work are now colored by the specter of disease, making sex workers more vulnerable and marginalized.

The question that perhaps needs to be posed at this moment is whether the emphasis on rights was the right approach. What was left out because of this emphasis? I have argued here that rights helped us to include the women in a broad arena of citizenship but did not keep in focus the knotted terrain of sexuality. The discussion on sexuality did not go beyond exploitation and delineating areas of work, and the discussion of sex as work. The difficulty of talking about sex and associating it with pleasure in citizens' rights campaigns was highlighted, albeit from a different perspec- tive, in a paper presented at BRAC University in Dhaka in 2007. Tanveer Reza Rouf, talking of the difference between a "gay" man and the category that has emerged as MSM, pointed to the demands of the AIDS discourse that has come to dominate the arena of homosexual activism in the coun- try. The category gay has emerged in contradistinction to the category of homosexual defined by health workers and social scientists, and harks back to a sphere of pleasurable sexual activity.[23] Rouf showed how public dis- courses mask and cloak arenas where sex and sexuality are actually lived out, and the effects that the circumvention of these issues has on the discourse of sexuality as a whole. The distinction helps to shed light on the strategies of circumvention that women's groups adopted in order to in- clude sex workers into the purview of feminist activism. In its engagement with sex workers Naripokkho had discussed issues of sexual pleasure and tried to distinguish or make connections between sex as pleasure and sex as work. In private conversations, there had been an effort to link a middle- class feminist understanding of sex and intimacy with the experiences that sex workers related. This knowledge and sharing were never brought to public view for strategic reasons. Rouf's paper makes a similar distinction between sex as pleasure and sex as work in the separation that is made between "gay" men and the category MSM, pointing to the ways that public discourse separates the pleasurable from the "worthy" and "deserving" or the "needy." This division of the sexual arena helps to cloak, even while bringing into view, and hence processes of ostracism and social stigmatization continue apace. What is needed now is a strategy that would bring excluded discussions into the agenda to broaden notions of freedom and rights.

To conclude, then: the 1990s campaign around sex work is a record of both success and failure. By changing the way that women engaged in sex work enter the arena of civil rights and activism, it laid the ground for a more inclusive citizenry. It also helped to highlight women's sexed position. Its abiding contribution is the public redefinition of sex work as work, and of women engaged in sex work as workers. Ironically, the greatest casualty in the campaign was the issue of sexuality itself. Sex is not merely work or a category that defines and places women in the social spectrum, but a sphere where pleasure is shared and felt, desires are expressed, and dreams are created. So far, it is feminist literary writing that has most consistently tried to open spaces where women's desires can be voiced, where ways of living out our dreams and visions can be opened up. Perhaps the way forward is to translate such writings into the language of campaigns and activism, where notions of citizenry and nationhood can be widened to include the language of desire.

NOTES

1. Menon, *Recovering Subversion.*
2. Kabeer, "The Search for Inclusive Citizenship."
3. Ibid., 5.
4. Ibid., 6.
5. Kabeer, "Subordination and Struggle," 111. Feldman, "Exploring Theories of Patriarchy," also traces the various threads that impinge on a notion of patriarchy within social movements and development practices in Bangladesh.
6. Sultan and Nazneen, "Struggling for Survival and Autonomy."
7. The two main groups being studied by the aforementioned researchers are Naripokkho and Mahila Parishad. The latter is a group that was associated with the Communist Party of Bangladesh in the beginning and emerged out of the students' movements in 1969.
8. Previous writings have taken different positions about the efficacy and lasting impact of the movement. See Huq, "Sex Workers' Struggles in Bangladesh"; and Azim, "Women and Freedom." Huq concentrates on the rights aspect of the cam-

paign, while Azim looks at the broader issue of women's freedom as it is expressed in women's writing, and through women's campaigns for the recognition of sex work.

9. Dependable figures are difficult to come by. The last published survey by the Bangladesh Bureau of Statistics shows that a total of 855,248 women were employed in the garment sector in 2000–2001, while recent newspaper reports state that 80 percent of two million garment workers are women.

10. See Sultan, "Work for Pay and Women's Empowerment," 109–10, for a discussion of the issues and actors involved in campaigns for women workers' rights. It is indeed telling that there is no mention of sex workers' campaigns in this essay.

11. Ibrahim, *The Voices of War Heroines*. The history of rape victims in the 1971 War of Liberation in Bangladesh records the rape of women by Pakistani soldiers. While figures are difficult to verify, the newly formed state had tried to rehabilitate these women as war heroines. The failure of this effort was amply demonstrated when these silenced and largely invisible women came into the public limelight in 1972, when defeated Pakistani soldiers, along with their dependents, were being sent to prisoner-of-war camps in India. Some of these women were opting to go with these soldiers, as they felt that they had no place in Bangladesh.

12. See Akhter, *Talaash*, for a noteworthy example of a novel based on the lives of war heroines or victims of war rape. This is forthcoming (in English translation) as *The Search*, from Zubaan in New Delhi.

13. See Van Schendel, *A History of Bangladesh*, 223.

14. Goetz and Sengupta, "Who Takes the Credit?"

15. Mahmud, "Our Bodies, Our Selves," 185. This article looks at the various forms of control over women's bodies and states that "the control of women's bodies is most succinctly manifest in control over reproduction."

16. Naripokkho, "A Preliminary Survey of Violence against Women in Bangladesh," unpublished report, 1996. This document highlights the issue of domestic violence, and the way that patriarchal control is coercively established at the family level.

17. Sumon, "Tanbazar Ucched, Jounokormider Manoadhikar Rokkharte Aini Lorai." All translations from the Bengali are mine.

18. Newspaper reports from the 1980s tell the story of a court case instituted against older women in the Narayanganj brothel for the kidnapping of a girl named Shab Mehr. Naripokkho protested against this measure as discriminatory to older brothel residents, and this debate may be considered to inaugurate the debate around women involved in sex work in Bangladesh.

19. Doezema, "Ouch!"

20. See Azim, Mahmood, and Shelley, *Phire Dekha*, for a detailed list of the groups involved in the sex workers' campaign, composed mainly of human rights and women's groups.

21. The term "hijra" includes men who adopt a female identity, as well as eunuchs, androgynes, hermaphrodites, or men with genital irregularities.

22. Azim, Mahmood, and Shelley, *Phire Dekha*, 217.

23. Tanveer Reza Rouf, "Class Conflict, Stratification, and the Politics of Negotiating a 'Gay' Identity in Dhaka, Bangladesh," paper presented at the International Workshop on Gender and Sexuality, BRAC University, Bangladesh, July 28–30, 2007.

TOORJO GHOSE

Politicizing Political Society
Mobilization among Sex Workers in Sonagachi, India

DURING A RECENT TRIP to Calcutta, I asked a taxi driver to take me to Sonagachi. He was wary—and justifiably so. The largest red-light area in the city and one of the busiest in Asia, Sonagachi is notorious for its *dalals* (pimps), who swarm taxis coming into the area, trying to secure customers for their sex workers. "To Durbar," I clarified, referring to the collective of sex workers that has been organizing in Sonagachi for more than a decade. The directive worked its usual magic. No directions needed, no questions asked, no problems anticipated. The usual conversation followed—about Durbar's work in Sonagachi, and how much it was appreciated by him, about sexual rights, HIV, and the fight for dignity for sex workers. Nearing our destination, he shouted "Durbar jaachchi [headed to Durbar]" out of the window, which dissipated the onslaught of dalals, allowing us to proceed unmolested. This is Durbar's legacy: its invocation catapults you into a conversation about women's sexual rights, and serves as a passport that ensures safe passage through Calcutta's red-light areas to an address that almost everyone in the area is familiar with.

In his recent articles on economic transformations in India, Partha Chatterjee argues that conceptions of civil society have to be reconfigured in order to understand the vectors of development and democratic transition in the country. Civil society is restricted to the small section of society able to participate in the primitive accumulation of capital while the poor inhabit "political society," where people mobilize around their survival needs and enter into informal negotiations with the state.[1] The state manages claims made by statistically determined "populations of need" in political society so that these populations survive without ever gaining full entry into civil society. "This is a necessary political condition for the continued rapid growth of corporate capital," Chatterjee concludes, since it undermines the "risk of turning them into the 'dangerous classes.'"[2] Nivedita Menon suggests that Chatterjee's notion of a political claims-making sphere separate from civil society is useful in understanding the largely ignored terrain of marginalized and poor women mobilizing in India today.[3] The liberal, rights-based feminist discourse that has marked the women's movement in India situates itself firmly in civil society and its legal processes, eliding the claims, strategies, and issues of women who do not populate this sphere. She argues that Chatterjee's articulation of political society is useful in understanding the mobilization of women hitherto ignored by the liberal feminist movement, *so long as* "it is unhitch[ed] . . . from its link in his argument to the 'welfare function' of government."[4] Chatterjee's conceptual framework, as well as Menon's application of it to the women's movement, raises important questions for Durbar. Does Durbar constitute the type of political society that Chatterjee is talking about? Is its legacy an instantiation of the successful management of claims that constitutes governmentality, or does it necessitate the extension of Chatterjee's concepts to describe the way political society "unhitches" itself from governmentality? Is the gap between political and civil society too wide for marginalized "populations" such as sex workers to cross? What are the implications of the political society–civil society division for conceptualizing the mobilization of women who have been traditionally ignored by the liberal feminist movement, and for their ability to attain the status of a "dangerous class" that can interrupt the workings of bourgeois civil society? In this essay, I grapple with these questions, exploring the implications of Durbar's mobilization for conceptions of civil and political society, and for the contemporary women's movement in India.

Chatterjee argues that we inhabit an era of heightened sensitivity to democratic processes where the marginalized and the poor cannot be entirely ignored.[5] The state responds to the needs of political society through informal quasi-legal initiatives. Governmental technologies of surveillance and categorization reconstitute citizens into populations marked by unmet needs. "Unlike the concept of citizen which carries the ethical consideration of participation in the sovereignty of the State," Chatterjee explains, "the concept of population makes available to government functionaries a set of rationally manipulable instruments for reaching large sections . . . as the targets of their policies."[6] This form of governmentality rests on an "elaborate network of surveillance" through which populations are monitored and their needs identified. Political society members, in turn, take advantage of the state's focus on their survival needs and mobilize around basic issues of sustenance. Chatterjee describes several initiatives where political society confers on itself "the moral attributes of a community" in its engagement with the state, transforming governmentality's statistically determined populations into kinship groups.[7] Often political society succeeds, at least temporarily, in gaining ground through informal arrangements with the state.

Chatterjee's delineation of this space of political claims-making is invaluable in tracing the mobilizational possibilities of marginalized groups operating outside civil society in India. However, driven as it is by the need to illuminate the distinct and innovative political space where claims-making happens, his framework undertheorizes political society's engagement with civil society. His focus on the stranglehold of governmentality's managerial processes curtails the terrain of political society's engagement. The state's atomization of claims into simplistic issues carves out narrow claims-making pathways for governmentality's targets. Simultaneously, his emphasis on political society's informal and utilitarian claims-making calls into question the sustainability of such mobilization, as well as its ability to go beyond the fulfillment of basic survival needs. Chatterjee is ambivalent, perhaps even pessimistic, about political society's ability to mount serious challenges to the corporate capital accumulation enterprise. In describing its mobilizational efforts, he writes that "there is little conscious effort to view these agitations as directed towards a fundamental transformation of the structures of political power, as they were in the days of nationalist and socialist mobilizations."[8] Even when political society succeeds, benefits are evanescent. Describing a colony of squatters near a railway artery in Calcutta, Chatterjee notes that despite having won several concessions from the government in the past, a recent shift in the power balance between political parties has jeopardized its status. Similarly, teachers who have historically been entrusted with crucial roles in mobilizing political society in rural Bengal have had this trust eroded by recent pay hikes initiated by the state government. It "is not a simple story with a happy ending," Chatterjee notes. "No story about political society ever is."[9]

POLITICAL SOCIETY AND THE INDIAN WOMEN'S MOVEMENT

The twin arcs of development and liberalization that Chatterjee engages with have certainly left their imprint on the women's movement. During a period of postindependence silence, women leaders placed their trust in the institutional bodies of the developmental Nehruvian state. However, the period following Nehru's death saw a mushrooming of multiple movements targeting the state.[10] While operating under the discursive frame of addressing the needs of women in poverty, these efforts deployed strategies and targeted issues that bore the imprint of middle-class social and political milieus. Led by educated, middle-class feminists and driven by a Marxist orientation, the movement targeted legal reform, women's participation in the workforce, and other issues that were most relevant to middle-class women.[11]

Economic liberalization brought its own unique challenges for the women's movement. Raka Ray and Mary Katzenstein argue that liberalization's impulse has sparked an "NGO-ification" of civil society wherein nongovernmental organizations operate as proxy agents of the state, providing services and displacing the protest-oriented organizational efforts of women's groups.[12] In examining the mobilization of grassroots women's organizations, Mary John describes the manner in which they were eventually blunted by the state through the withdrawal of resources and the introduction of liberal economic schemes that deflected the oppositional focus of mobilized communities.[13] This period mirrors the conditions of governmentality described by Chatterjee: the management of the needs of women living in poverty through state programs and NGOs, the atomization of a population's demands accompanied by a piecemeal process of addressing survival needs, and the eventual co-optation of mobilized political efforts into governmentality. The question that arises, then, is one of particular interest to the movement and its future: can the dynamics of political society describe the way women organize today, and therefore do the limitations of political society claims-making circumscribe the mobilizational possibilities of grassroots women's organizations like Durbar? Moreover, if informal claims-making is subsumed in the enterprise of managing women's needs through governmentality, can oppositional mobilization still retain a sense of the political? Are women able to respond to the deflection of political claims-making into routinized informal processes? If so, what are the conditions that lead to effective mobilization in political society?

This essay seeks to answer these questions by examining the manner in which Sonagachi's residents mobilized as a community of sex workers. I begin by describing the global and local context of the governmental programs that sought to reduce HIV risk in sex worker communities such as Sonagachi. I then explore the manner in which Sonagachi's sex workers mobilized collective identity as they engaged with these governmental programs. Finally, I reflect on the implications of Durbar's mobilization for political society's engagement with the state and its structures, and for the current trajectory of the women's movement in India.

THE POLITICAL OPPORTUNITY STRUCTURE
OF THE SEX WORKER MOVEMENT

In his work on social movements and collective action, Sidney Tarrow concludes that movements emerge when they are able to seize opportunities that present themselves in the political structural environment; "when institutional access opens, when alignments shift, when conflicts emerge among elites, and when allies become available, . . . challengers find favorable opportunities."[14] The HIV pandemic created a unique opportunity structure for sexuality movements in various parts of the world. In the United States, the gay, lesbian, bisexual, and transsexual (GLBT) community had to mobilize quickly to survive the ravages of what was initially a nameless killer. Cindy Patton notes that mobilization around HIV in the United States in the early 1980s resulted in the establishment of autonomous medical service organizations such as the San Francisco AIDS Foundation and the Gay Men's Health Crisis in New York.[15] By the later 1980s, these had become part of state-funded HIV initiatives in GLBT communities, and influenced how global HIV initiatives were being framed by international bodies such as the World Health Organization.

When HIV started making a significant impact on the Indian health landscape in the early nineties, the overburdened healthcare system in India was ill-prepared to deal with it. However, international support institutions funded by the United States and European countries had already been developed.[16] Supported by generous funding by the World Health Organization, and eventually by the World Bank, the Indian government set up the National AIDS Control Organization (NACO).[17] NACO established several collaborations with other governmental agencies for outreach efforts in populations considered vulnerable to infection, such as sex workers.

State and international agencies play a prominent role in the story of the Sonagachi sex worker community. In 1991, the All India Institute of Physical Hygiene, funded by NACO, the World Health Organization, and a Dutch NGO, initiated HIV education with sex workers in Sonagachi.[18] Aware of the difficulties associated with gaining entry into local communities, Dr. Smarajit Jana, who headed the initiative, used a peer-facilitated education model. He assured the community that unlike other state-led initiatives in the past, the Sonagachi Project did not seek to "rescue" sex workers from their profession. Instead, sex workers were trained as peer educators and went door-to-door in Sonagachi discussing sexual health with brothel residents. Eventually, Dr. Jana and the sex work peer educators formed an independent organization, called Durbar Mahila Samanwaya Committee (now known simply as Durbar), to continue the project and negotiate with the state for more resources.

This, then, was the political opportunity structure confronting the Sonagachi sex workers in the early 1990s. The crisis of the pandemic, coupled with the resources flowing from international civil society institutions into "risky" communities like theirs, allowed them to become visible to the state. The early phase of the Sonagachi intervention vividly illustrates Chatterjee's notions of governmentality and political society mobilization. Sex workers identified by the state as a statistical population vulnerable to HIV were mobilized to work with international and state agencies in formulating a semiformal response to the pandemic. The peer-led initiative introduced by

Dr. Jana allowed sex workers to mobilize around their medical needs. As often happens in governmentality processes, the semilegal status of sex workers was ignored in order to fulfill their immediate need to survive the pandemic. The governmental intervention educated the community about HIV and provided it with much-needed medical resources to combat its spread.

Since the initial initiatives formulated by the state and international agencies were driven by the pressure to manage political society needs, they ran the risk described by Chatterjee of being restricted to informal, short-term governmentality processes. In her account of global efforts to combat the pandemic, Cindy Patton identifies two competing perspectives in the ideological landscape of international HIV initiatives. The first, which she calls a "tropical medicine" orientation, fixes a geographical (tropical) and social (the colonized "other") space to diseases, problematizing them only when they infect European/American bodies.[19] The second perspective is an epidemiological orientation driven by statistical technologies that trace the "vectors" along which diseases spread. While different in form and logic, in actual practice both orientations use HIV to mark difference, demarcate the diseased from the disease-free, and reify categories of power inscribed into colonial and nationalist discourses. Both these strands are braided into a narrative about HIV initiatives in India that was published in the Lancet, one of the leading medical journals:

> HIV prevalence as measured through surveillance of antenatal and sexually transmitted disease clinics is the chief source of information on HIV in India. The factors that influence the Indian epidemic are the size, behaviors, and disease burdens of high-risk groups, their interaction with bridge populations and general population sexual networks, and migration and mobility of both bridge populations and high-risk groups. The interplay of these forces has resulted in substantial epidemics in several pockets of many Indian states that could potentially ignite subepidemics in other, currently low prevalence, parts of the country. The growth of HIV, unless contained, could have serious consequences for India's development.[20]

The passage is infused with what Patton describes as the "vectoriality" of the epidemiological perspective and the segregationary impulses of the tropical discourse: "risk groups" are identified and indicted for spreading the infection while the focus is on surveilling not just the movement of pathogens from bodies, but the movement of bodies themselves. For good measure, these studies tell us who the "risky" bodies are: sex workers, substance users, and gay men. Insofar as the groups are "risky" but not "at risk," there is an assumption that their vulnerability to infection is important only because of their ability to infect low-risk populations. The tropical otherness of those highly vulnerable to HIV infection is highlighted by positioning them on one side of a metaphorical bridge, with the general population occupying the other side. This marking of vulnerable bodies comes with a dire warning: unless "risky" bodies are properly "surveilled" and "contained" from the general population, India's development will be compromised. Here we see how the epidemiological/tropical orientations to HIV management illustrate Chatterjee's contention that governmentality allows modernizing processes to be restricted to the privileged space of civil society.

As one of the model programs in the initiative described in the passage above, the Sonagachi Project as it was initially conceptualized seems to vindicate Chatterjee's and Patton's fears that managerial motivations and othering processes are inextricably inscribed into state and global initiatives. If we were to turn away from Sonagachi at this point, we might be justified in concluding that Chatterjee's conceptual framework provides a complete description of the Sonagachi story. Given the state's desire to segregate targeted populations and thwart larger claims by managing survival needs, the troubling underbelly of HIV's opportunity structure appears to justify Chatterjee's (and Patton's) pessimism regarding these initiatives. However, as we follow Sonagachi's storyline further, we witness the manner in which the political opportunity and grassroots mobilizational structures engage each other and call into question Chatterjee's delineation of political and civil spaces.

In an earlier essay I described the manner in which Sonagachi's sex workers organized themselves and established a collective identity around the claim that sex work was legitimate labor.[21] I draw on the interviews I conducted for that research to describe how organizing around a collective identity helped Durbar's sex workers transform the mobilizational potential of the group, engage strategically with governmental initiatives, and initiate a powerful and sustainable social movement.

Chatterjee argues that kinship ties allow statistically determined populations to engage in the claims-making process as a cohesive collective. As poor women living in a sexually marginalized community, Sonagachi's sex workers were bound together by ties of solidarity embedded in shared experiences. As one Durbar member relates, "I think of . . . Durbar programs as my body parts—as much a part of me as my hands and legs. They are simply inseparable from me. I fight for Durbar the way I fight for myself." In the face of violence, intimidation, and stigma, mobilizing as sex workers became necessary for survival. One worker recalls: "A sex worker in Khidderpore was tortured by local boys. . . . [T]hey burnt her vagina with cigarettes. We went there, set up a stand and protested over a mike continuously until we had them arrested. Our previous organization secretary was harassed in Tollygunge. We organized hunger strikes, held rallies, then surrounded the police station and had those people arrested."

Given that their sense of solidarity has been forged in a crucible of oppression and discrimination, Durbar members are deeply suspicious of institutions outside their own collective. One participant describes her experience at a hospital that helped forge her antipathy toward institutional health care: "I gave birth in Medical College Hospital. After a test, I was declared HIV positive. Afterwards, no one touched me. The nurses would throw the baby on my lap. The baby was kept in a separate room. The hospital authorities killed my baby."

The process of establishing solidarity thus entails inculcating a sense of affiliation with other political society members while casting state and other outside institutions as hostile agents. In particular, building solidarity problematizes the relationship between sex workers and the institutions that manage their medical and social needs. This is a crucial step, given Chatterjee's contention that the expansion of governmental technologies has meant that the developmental state is no longer external to political society. While "in-group" institutions such as community HIV clinics were also part of the governmental technologies mobilized to manage sex workers' HIV medical needs initially, they have had to decouple themselves from state initiatives to a large extent in order to gain legitimacy with the sex worker community. They are now run by clinicians hired by Durbar and employ service providers drawn from Sonagachi's sex work community. The fact that Durbar is able to run these clinics with the help of state and international grants supports Chatterjee's observation about the intertwined relationship between the state and political society. However, Durbar's sex workers compare initiatives and institutions to the metric of past experiences of oppression, separating those initiatives that are *respectful* of the community from those that merely attempt to service it.

Collectively engaging with the social challenges of living as sex workers allows the community to transcend the limited array of needs addressed by medical risk-management initiatives. The logic of solidarity that emerges within the collective is far more variegated than the rationale used by the state to identify a population based on its HIV-related needs. The frames of meaning that emerge in this process anchor the group and the movement to a cause that necessitates affective (rather than merely instrumental) involvement. Moreover, the discourse of solidarity connects Durbar members to the larger societal forces that consign them to political society. Routinely referring to the entire sex work population in India as a kinship group, members transcend the physical boundaries of their neighborhood in building a community for themselves. One member states: "One stick is very feeble. Ten sticks put together have immense strength and can fight back collectively. If the day comes when all the sex workers of India will be part of Durbar, then all will benefit by it. We can demand the rights of the worker, but if I say this alone, then Parliament will not listen to me." This longing for a larger kinship group holds out the possibility of a large-scale mobilizational effort, which has to some degree been realized in Durbar's recruitment of sex workers from all over India. This notion of solidarity significantly expands the concept of kinship described by Chatterjee. Solidarity provides more than a moral justification for cohesion in a group located in a particular geographical space: it lays the foundation for a critique of civil society's institutions and a significant expansion of the mobilizational pool for the group.

NEGOTIATING IDENTITY

The expansion of the claims-making script is fully realized in the manner in which the collective identity forged in the solidarity-establishing narratives described above is deployed, negotiated, and politicized to the outside world. Examining women's movements in Calcutta, Raka Ray notes that they are heavily influenced by Marxist ideologies that have been histori- cally salient in the region. Ray identifies this broader ideology as the master frame of the political field in Calcutta.[22] Durbar draws on the Marxist master frame of compensated labor in formulating its collective action frame. It establishes the narrative that sex work is legitimate work, thereby taking issue with societal forces that stigmatize it and consign it beyond the boundaries of accepted wage-earning. Postulating the central thesis of this frame, one sex worker states: "Why should what I do not be accepted? Through sex work, my children and I can eat, I can pay my house rent. If a lawyer's, teacher's or doctor's job is considered good work, then why not mine? This is also a job. I do my work and earn my bread. I am a worker." Operating within this Marxist interpretive logic, it is not surprising that the "sex work is work" narrative is tethered to the logic of unionizing as *workers*. Right from the beginning of its collectivization process, Durbar members have referred to themselves as a sex workers' union. However, as Ashwini Sukthankar points out in an essay in this volume, the unionizing process is significantly different in Durbar's case. Unlike other trade, and even sex workers', unions, Durbar seeks to include brothel managers. Dur- bar has redefined the boundaries within the unionizing process to include everyone who is directly involved in the sex trade. One worker explains: "We want to work together with people who depend on the sex work industry—the shopkeepers, the madams, the babus [long-term clients]. Many union members are madams. With their help we have been able to stop the exploitation of sex workers by their madams. We have been able to standardize their take from each encounter with clients. We have also formed a babus' union which works against the targeting of customers by the police."

Using the union as a consensus-building device allows Durbar to short- circuit the opposition between sex workers and their managers or clients, targeting instead larger structural agents such as the police and oppressive laws that consign them to the margins of the workforce. This strategy is not without risk: the most repeated criticism of the Durbar model is that it legitimizes the exploitation of brothel owners and madams because of their inclusion in the union. However, Durbar's permeable boundaries highlight the fact that unionizing sex workers is markedly different from unionizing in other trades. The stigma attached to sex work means that managers and consumers have more in common with workers than the agents and processes of normative society whose legal, medical, and cultural discourses seek to maintain the trade's marginality.

The ability to seek common ground with pimps, brothel managers, and clients has allowed Durbar to mobilize sex work communities at a rapid pace. By sending out activists to communities all over the country, and inviting other sex workers into an immersion program in Sonagachi, Durbar has extended its union to forty-nine sex work communities and counts sixty thousand sex workers as active members. It has also organized four national conferences, drawing together thirty thousand sex workers from other parts of India.[23] Its decision in 2007 to form a broader pleasure workers' union is a continued attempt to recover pleasure giving from the margins of respectability.

Championing the cause of disrespected communities has allowed Durbar to build bridges with several other movements that do not have direct links to sex work. Durbar's flexible framing of the unionizing process has enabled it to align with the multiple meaning frames of feminist social movements working with women in poverty. Its fluency in the language of rights and unionization has helped it gain a foothold with the state Communist Party apparatus and the field of feminist organizations in the state. While framing sex work within the rights discourse does annex the discursive space of the established liberal feminist movement in India, Durbar does not appear to be bound by the constrained legal categories and legislative monitoring that accompany this strategy. Whereas liberal feminist legal strategy has sought to bring the private sphere into a public domain monitored by laws and the state, Durbar seeks to *protect* the private sphere from the legal gaze. Its members repeatedly reiterate the point that by asserting their right to work, their goal is to defang laws such as the Immoral Traffic (Prevention) Act, 1956, that allow policing of their activities.[24] Pushing for decriminalization rather than legalization becomes part of a broader strategy of " 'making public' in the sense of questioning life forms and values that have been oppressive to women, rather than 'making public' in the sense of making these issues subject to state and legislative action."[25]

While Durbar has successfully organized under the unionizing and poverty alleviation signs, its story is not complete without examining its role in what Raka Ray and Mary Katzenstein refer to as the third period of feminist mobilization in postindependent India, where the twin impulses of liberalization and globalization have created the NGO- or state-based management process and informal political society.[26] Durbar has eked out a crucial space for itself in the academic-NGO-state institutional nexus that has driven HIV management initiatives in India. Research funding from agencies such as the U.S. National Institutes of Health, the World Health Organization, and the Gates Foundation supports Durbar's programs. Articles in major Western journals and presentations at international conferences have established Durbar's credentials in the global health institutional environment. Durbar's association with the CARE-Saksham project funded by the Bill and Melinda Gates Foundation illustrates the kinds of national and international partners it works with. As part of a national HIV intervention program called the Avahan Project, funded by the Gates Foundation and headed by Ashok Alexander, the son of a notable political leader, Durbar worked closely with organs of the Indian government, the internationally prominent NGO CARE, and academic research institutions such as Yale University in the United States to replicate the Durbar model in a sex work community in southern India. Dr. Jana joined CARE and supervised the implementation of Saksham, while Durbar members traveled to the sex work community to help mobilize women there. Durbar's role in prominent initiatives such as Saksham and Avahan has established its status as the prominent sex worker collective involved in HIV initiatives in India.

Seizing the political opportunity created by the HIV crisis invites its own risks, as both Chatterjee and Patton note; utilizing the resources of the state and global welfare society leaves grassroots organizations vulnerable to being co-opted by governmentality processes, ultimately reifying the othering discourses of global civil society institutions. The diversity of Durbar's funding streams has allowed it to remain relatively independent. The multiple frames it has aligned within its mobilization allow it to tap into a wide range of sources that include funders of HIV interventions, women's poverty alleviation programs, antitrafficking initiatives, and state-sponsored development efforts among sex workers. In addition, its member-generated union fees, small investments in farming businesses, and peer-run banking co-operatives provide modest revenue sources. Durbar has resisted co-optation into governmentality's managerial agenda through the accountability that is brought to bear within its soli-darity networks. Dr. Jana recounts: "When the initial peer [education] group established itself, and wanted autonomy from AIIPH [All India In-stitute of Hygiene and Public Health], people at work were not happy. They wanted control of the project, and the credit. When I supported the peers' attempts to become independent of the state program, people were angry with me—they'd avoid me in the corridors. Eventually I quit AIIPH and started working full time with Durbar." This strategy of decoupling from governmental processes when they drift away from community mo-bilizational goals has endured through the years. Recently, Dr. Jana re-signed his position at CARE, and Durbar has distanced itself from the Saksham project due to disagreements over core ideological issues. Simi-larly, a constant process of negotiation with the state AIDS Control Organi-zation in West Bengal has allowed Durbar to engage with governmental initiatives, without abandoning its larger ideological frames.

POLITICIZING CIVIL SOCIETY

In a sustained movement, realignments in the political opportunity struc-ture present opportunities to mobilize, which if seized upon, create further pathways to transform institutional structures. This interlocking process of double engagement describes the manner in which Durbar was born out of governmentality, but was able to ultimately breach the boundary mark-ing political and civil space. Far from being a story with an uncertain ending, as Chatterjee contends, collective identity formation allows mar-ginalized groups such as sex workers to impose themselves on the public sphere of civil society, subvert governmentality, and ultimately create fur-ther political opportunities that sustain the movement.

CREATING AN "EXPANDED PUBLIC"

The sex worker movement fueled by Durbar's mobilization has had a profound effect on the public sphere. Through the negotiation processes described above, Durbar has put out literature, been written about in numerous scholarly and news articles, performed in major national and international events, mounted huge marches and rallies, and organized major conferences. Its peer-led intervention model has become the gold standard for community-based HIV intervention efforts across the globe. Durbar played a prominent and public role in the creation of a massive advertisement campaign in Calcutta featuring "Bula-di," a matronly animation figure advocating safe sex practices. The HIV initiative in Bengal is synonymous with Durbar's name and, by extension, with sex worker rights.

The conversation I had with the taxi driver who took me to Durbar is evidence of the success with which it has injected itself into the public consciousness. One of the most intriguing results of Durbar's visibility is the rapid growth in the number of middle-class sex workers operating in Sonagachi. A destigmatization of the sex work identity has accompanied Durbar's entry into the popular lexicon, encouraging middle-class women to engage in sex work by day in Sonagachi and go home in the evening to families who are often unaware of the trade they ply. Many of them have joined Durbar, and credit it with bringing about a transformation in their own consciousness about sex work. Their willingness to operate in what has historically been a segregated red-light area is evidence of the blurring of class boundaries, as well as those of civil and political society. The process of what Seyla Benhabib refers to as "making public" the issues surrounding sex work is an unmeasured but critical outcome of Durbar's mobilization.[27]

Chatterjee's conceptualization does not account for the kind of expanded public created by Durbar. There is an assumption that the public sphere is exclusively infused with the desires of the corporate capital accumulation enterprise, and that political society lacks the means to influence it. The failure to account for alterity in the public sphere significantly limits the ability of Chatterjee's notion of governmentality to describe the complex engagement between the state and *politicized* society. Durbar's mobilization has left a significant footprint in the public sphere and allowed it to transcend the circumscribed space of political society. In the mobilizational context of the current women's movement, political impulses are often subsumed into, and therefore blunted by, managerial governmental programs.[28] The reformulation of public discourse on sexuality thus counts as a significant achievement. It also emphasizes the fact that molding the public aesthetic by creating an expanded public sphere *is* an enduring political mode of engagement.

The initial response of the state and international agencies to the HIV needs of sex workers in Sonagachi harnessed the kind of governmental technologies described by Chatterjee. Sex workers were designated a statistically risky population, and the multiple needs of women living in Sonagachi were whittled down to their HIV-related health needs, mostly because as promiscuous carriers of disease, they represented the kind of "dangerous class" that had the potential to arrest the modernizing initiatives of civil society. HIV scholars based in Western institutions were complicit in this campaign. Trained in tropical medicine and epidemiological perspectives, we arrived in India to arrest the movement of pathogens and educate the object of our research in the use of safe-sex practices. But a strange thing happened on the way to Sonagachi: we became part of a process of collective identity formation that preempted our initial initiative. On the first day that I met Bharati De, the sex worker who heads Durbar, she turned to me in front of my English-speaking research colleagues from the United States and said in Bengali, "HIV is a boon for us. Without it, you people would never be interested in the lives of sex workers like us." Durbar has strategically utilized single-issue governmentality initiatives to introduce into the conversation the complex circumstances of life as a sex worker, profoundly transforming the discourse of HIV intervention in the process.

Durbar has worked with scientists to expand epidemiological and tropical perspectives in order to incorporate an understanding of the *structural* issues influencing sexuality in the Sonagachi context. This allowed a new band of scholars to become involved in HIV initiatives in India. Kim Blankenship, who headed the Yale University team that studied the CARE-Saksham implementation of the Durbar model in south India, has been instrumental in developing the concept of *structural* interventions in HIV initiatives. In a seminal article on the subject, she refers to Durbar's efforts in describing how issues such as availability of resources, acceptability of cultural norms, and access to institutional means need to be addressed by structural interventions.[29] The call to reformulate perspectives on HIV intervention has begun to influence the larger community of institutional HIV scholars.[30] While the inclusion of the concept of community-led structural interventions in the global discourse on HIV intervention has been influenced by several factors, the repeated references to Durbar as a model program in articles, books, and conferences on the subject are evidence of the influential role it has played in the transformation.

The government-backed Saksham project's invitation to Durbar to partner with it in ongoing efforts to collectivize sex worker communities in other sites in India is a clear example of the extent to which the original HIV-management programs have been transformed into social movement initiatives. The manner in which Durbar has pushed back on governmental programs helped to reshape them and made a space for itself in the upper echelons of policy formulation; Durbar's example speaks to the possibility that in the presence of the mobilizational context described above, state initiatives do get subsumed into a broader movement. Chatterjee's description of political society operating within the interstices of governmentality explains how political society survives, but not how it imposes its will on state programs, completely subverting their original managerial motivations. I call special attention to this process of engaging with the state's motivations, rather than merely its initiatives. By refocusing the state on structural agents of oppression, amplifying its interventions to routinely include community mobilization efforts around sex work issues and convincing it to incorporate sex workers as equal partners in the formulation of initiatives, Durbar has effectively replaced the managerial impulse in the state's programs with an ideological perspective molded in the movement. This particular engagement with(in) governmentality goes beyond a mere deflection or cooptation of state programs: governmentality is invigorated with transformational potential through a subversion of its original intent. Durbar's mobilization is an example of how "people are learning, and forcing their governors to learn, how they would prefer to be governed."[31]

CREATING POLITICAL OPPORTUNITIES

Sidney Tarrow notes that successful movements not only seize opportunities that present themselves in the political structure, but also create new ones for themselves.[32] Durbar has actively sought to engage members of related social movements, supplying them with a repertoire of actors, strategies, and networks that have helped to constitute new political opportunities. In a conference in 2008, Durbar expanded the field of attendees to include those involved in the entertainment industry. A new cadre of traditional dancers, folk singers, bar dancers, hostesses, and male sex workers who attended the conference now count themselves as participants in the movement. Many of Durbar's seasoned members have relocated to states such as Bihar and Andhra Pradesh to mobilize local sex worker networks. Using the "right to earn a living" frame that emerged out of its movement, Durbar's members have worked with rural peasant communities on issues of land and fishing rights in Bengal.

Perhaps the most intriguing move to create new political opportunities for itself is exemplified by Durbar's decision to secure international funding to resist the trafficking of minors in the sex work industry. Kamala Kempadoo and Jo Doezema note the considerable attention paid by Western feminists to rescuing Third World women from what is assumed to be an involuntary, coerced decision to engage in sex work.[33] By asserting the right to engage in sex work while positioning itself as the guardian of minors in the industry, Durbar is seeking to bridge the divide between coerced and voluntary sex work, create new opportunities of support by targeting new sources of funding, and undermine any contention that it condones involuntary sex work.

The strategic alignment of meaning frames has allowed Durbar to build its constituency and broaden the claims-making field in its engagement with governmental bodies. As Sidney Tarrow notes, this active engagement in the process of creating its own political opportunity structure allows a movement to sustain itself.[34]

THE IMPLICATIONS OF A BROAD-BASED MOBILIZATION

The ability to expand the public sphere, subvert governmentality processes, and create new political opportunities allows political society to impose itself on civil society. Government programs for populations become the site of a double engagement: governmentality, seeking to manage political society claims, also provides opportunities for politicized members of political society to inject subaltern subjectivities into civil society.

While Chatterjee's framework describes some of the processes that are at play in Durbar's story, it stops short of tracing political society's entry into civil space. There is a strong suggestion in his account that this is an unlikely event, a product perhaps of his attempt to differentiate civil from political. Chatterjee is correct in noting that political society mobilizes outside the jurisdiction of civil society structures. He is particularly accurate in describing the initial claims-making processes that emerge out of governmentality: Durbar's movement, after all, was born out of, and actively engaged with, state and international HIV intervention efforts. This is precisely why it is impossible to "unhitch" political society from the state's managerial programs. However, Menon, who calls for such an uncoupling in an attempt to theorize about the mobilization of women outside the purview of civil society, is justified in her unease about Chatterjee's notion of governmentality. His framework does not fully explore the radical possibilities of the political in political society, especially when the latter seeks to bridge the division between civil and political society. To fully describe the mobilizational possibilities that animate Durbar's story, it is necessary to hold out the possibility that on occasion movements like Durbar *civilize* political society (by engaging strategically and successfully with civil society processes) and *politicize* civil society (by injecting civil society with the political discourse born in marginal spaces). This ability to blur the civil/political divide lurks in the reeds of political society. When collective identity mobilization engages with the political opportunity structure in the manner I have described above, political society kicks into high gear, leaving a substantial and enduring trace.

In this expanded understanding of political society, not all mobilization is restricted to informal negotiation with the state. As Durbar's movement demonstrates, claims-making can result in a place at the table in civil society, one that can then be used to trigger large-scale institutional changes. Moreover, contrary to what Chatterjee argues, even extremely marginalized groups within political society can stake their claim in this scenario. In fact, it is the extreme marginalization of sex workers in the face of the HIV pandemic that invited organs of international civil society to move in, ultimately energizing the Durbar movement. The radical possibilities of such mobilization can therefore be embedded in precisely the elements of political society that Chatterjee argues undermine its ability to mount sustainable movements.

The encroachment of political society into civil space exemplified in Durbar's mobilization has important implications for conceptualizing the contemporary women's movement in India. By describing the manner in which marginalized women mobilize outside civil society while influencing its processes and institutions, I have attempted to explore the radical potential of feminist political society. In theorizing the mobilization of women located outside the juridical discourse of middle-class feminism, Menon calls for a conceptual framework that illuminates the duality of invoking liberal feminist referents while also deconstructing them. I submit that Durbar's mobilization is a case study of precisely this process. By framing issues in the language of women's work, rights, exploitation, unionization, and development, Durbar engages with institutions and discourses embedded in legal, Marxist, and neoclassical economic frames of analysis. However, by challenging traditional definitions of these concepts in the manner I have described above, it reformulates these discourses and presents an alternative to liberal feminist mobilizing.

While the example of Durbar may provide impetus to the notion of a systematic, enduring, and widespread oppositional engagement by political society, there are inherent risks involved in formulating a future of resistance based on a deployment of collective strategic identity. As Menon notes, claims of authentic representation, or strategically superior ways of deploying identity, are rooted in notions of "false" consciousness and can elide differences, unleashing their own tyranny.[35] Similarly, strategic engagement with the apparatus of the state and the global welfare system exposes Durbar to the constant threat of being co-opted into the management machinery of governmentality. These may still prove to be limiting conditions for the sustainability of the movement. Whatever the trajectory of the movement from this point on, however, Durbar's success allows us to be ambitious about the impact and endurance of political society. The particularly energized and robust form of political society that emerges out of Durbar's mobilization suggests that an expanded conception of political society may answer Menon's call for a theoretical framework that adequately describes the manner in which marginalized women in India mobilize in the shadows of civil society.

NOTES

1. See Chatterjee, "Democracy and Economic Transformations in India"; Chatterjee, *The Politics of the Governed*; and Chatterjee, "Beyond the Nation?"

2. Chatterjee, "Democracy and Economic Transformations in India," 58.

3. Menon, *Recovering Subversion*, 217–19.

4. Ibid., 217.

5. Chatterjee, "Democracy and Economic Transformations in India," 55.

6. Chatterjee, *The Politics of the Governed*, 55.

7. Ibid., 57.

8. Chatterjee, "Democracy and Economic Transformations," 67.

9. Chatterjee, *The Politics of the Governed*, 67.

10. Ray and Katzenstein, "In the Beginning There Was the Nehruvian State."

11. John, "Feminism, Poverty, and the Emergent Social Order."

12. Ray and Katzenstein, "In the Beginning There Was the Nehruvian State," 10.

13. John, "Feminism, Poverty, and the Emergent Social Order," 132.

14. Tarrow, *Power in Movement*, 81.

15. Patton, *Globalizing AIDS*, 11.

16. Chatterjee refers to the emergence of this global welfare sphere as a new international civil society. "Democracy and Economic Transformations," 55.

17. Basu et al., "HIV Prevention among Sex Workers in India"; Chandrashekharan et al., "Containing HIV/AIDS in India."

18. Basu et al., "HIV Prevention among Sex Workers in India," 845–52.

19. Patton, *Globalizing AIDS*, 34–50.

20. Chandrashekharan et al., "Containing HIV/AIDS in India," 508.

21. Ghose et al., "Mobilizing Collective Identity to Reduce HIV Risk."

22. Ray, "Women's Movements and Political Fields."

23. Chakrabarty, *Influence of Rights-based Approach in Achieving Success*, 1.

24. The Immoral Traffic (Prevention) Act states that sex work is legal, but criminalizes the sharing of any earnings from sex work, in effect criminalizing sex workers who maintain families on their earnings.

25. Menon, *Recovering Subversion*, 13. I do not mean to understate the opposition that Durbar encounters within the trade union community, and from a segment of the feminist antitrafficking movement.

26. Ray and Katzenstein, "In the Beginning There Was the Nehruvian State," 22.

27. Benhabib, "The Generalized and the Concrete Other," 177, cited in Menon, *Recovering Subversion*, 13.

28. John, "Feminism, Poverty, and the Emergent Social Order."

29. Blankenship, Bray, and Merson, "Structural Interventions in Public Health."

30. See, for example, Gupta et al., "Structural Approaches to HIV Prevention." Likewise, several recent requests for grants put out by the National Institutes of Health in the United States emphasize the need for a structural and sociological perspective on HIV interventions.

31. Chatterjee, *The Politics of the Governed*, 78.

32. Tarrow, *Power in Movement*, 81–99.

33. Kempadoo and Doezema, *Global Sex Workers*.

34. Tarrow, *Power in Movement*, 81–99.

35. Menon, *Recovering Subversion*, 233–34.

ASHWINI SUKTHANKAR

Queering Approaches to Sex, Gender, and Labor in India
Examining Paths to Sex Worker Unionism

OVER THE LAST DECADE it has become increasingly common to hear, in an Indian context, articulations such as "sex work is work like any other," or "sex work is work, we demand workers' rights."[1] The underlying formulation—that sex work is work—is predictably contentious outside sex workers' movements, raising objections from those who assert on the contrary that sex work constitutes violence against women or commercialized rape.[2] It has also encountered minor opposition within sex worker movements, with some arguing that the idea runs counter to lived experiences of the men and women in India who sell sexual services and call it *dhanda* (business), invoking entrepreneurship rather than labor.[3] Nevertheless, the slogan has become the dominant paradigm for mobilizing sex workers. At the same time, it has not translated easily into workers' rights–centered organizing strategies. The naming of sex work as work has been at the heart of sex workers joining together as savings and credit societies, self-help groups, cooperatives, and cultural bodies. But only very recently have there been tentative explorations of a trade union space. This essay looks at the emergence of this small handful of sex worker unions.

The three experiments in sex worker unionism addressed here arose in much the same ways as other forms of sex worker organizing: through varying degrees of collaboration between HIV/AIDS NGOs, women's groups, and queer activists. However, national and global forces shifted collectivization efforts to take on the deeper political implications of the claim that "sex work is work," leading sex workers to consider the potential of organizing as workers into a trade union. Understanding the formation of sex workers unions requires not only that we examine a fuller history of activist interventions in sex workers' lives in India, but also a much broader geopolitical context. Thus, the essay begins with a sketch of the international legal and policy debates around sex work. The sex worker unions that are my focus here are deeply rooted in this larger, international dynamic. However, their story is also intrinsically connected to activist debates that were taking place within other groups and movements in very local ways in India. For example, some HIV/AIDS groups began critiquing new funding streams that stifled organizing and protest, and began to consider the potential of member-funded mobilizing. Mainstream trade unions, facing the reality of sex workers' demands for recognition as workers, began grappling with the question of if and how to extend solidarity. I try to indicate the many distinct strands that are bound up in the story of sex worker unions in India, not to suggest that these formations were purely contingent, but rather to highlight the importance of strategic collaborations between advocates across movements confronting sharp shifts in domestic and international policy. Without going to the opposite extreme of suggesting any degree of teleological inevitability to sex worker unionism as a mode of organizing, I propose that the collaborations have also helped bring content and political potential to the "sex work is work" slogan, which otherwise risks being another call for human dignity without a more concrete agenda. Finally, these collaborations must continue to sustain and shape unionism experiments if they are to mature.

APPROACHES AND ATTITUDES TO SEX WORK
THROUGH THE 1990S

Until recently, activist alignments around sex work in India did not mirror the sharp divisions of territory carved out by international groups focused on advocacy, particularly at the United Nations level.

At the international level, the discussion is dominated by two camps: the so-called abolitionists and the antiabolitionists. While abolitionists seek an end to sex work, and understand it to be a thickly networked criminal operation, they perceive sex workers to be victims rather than criminals, arguing that most—especially from the global South—are compelled to join the industry. They argue for the criminalization of clients of sex workers and the rescue and rehabilitation of the sex workers themselves.[4] Antiabolitionists argue for a nuanced distinction between free and forced sex work that would allow individuals in sex work to determine for themselves whether or not they wish to exit. They argue further that the numbers cited by abolitionists who assert that the majority of sex workers are coerced are profoundly suspect. Antiabolitionists state that sex workers have by and large made hard but thoroughly considered choices in order to subsist, rather than being pawns caught in a system of organized crime. They propose that it would be paternalist, antifeminist, and antiworker to seek to rescue them. Antiabolitionists seek the decriminalization or legalization of voluntary sex work, arguing that criminal penalties push an industry underground and render sex workers more vulnerable to poor treatment.[5]

These debates are typically coded within debates on "trafficking"—a concept that at face value has nothing to do with sex work, but rather with the coerced movement of people across borders in order to exploit them. To the extent that sex work is named, the bevy of international agreements have tread a wary line between abolitionist and antiabolitionist positions, keeping silent on the private selling of sexual services while barring what the International Agreement for the Suppression of the "White Slave Traffic" (1904) called "the procuring of women or girls for immoral purposes abroad" or, as the language has evolved over the decades, the "exploitation of the prostitution of others," which generally translates as a prohibition on pimps or other middlemen, and on establishments such as brothels.[6]

Until the 1990s, the international legal frameworks did not occupy center stage for activists addressing sex work in India, whether they came from an abolitionist or antiabolitionist perspective. This was the case, even though the dominant legal framework regulating sex work in India—the Immoral Traffic (Prevention) Act—was itself responsive to India's international obligations pursuant to ratification of a 1949 convention on "the suppression of the traffic in persons and of the exploitation of the prostitution of others."[7] Neither abolitionists nor antiabolitionists agreed philosophically with the central premise of the international agreements—an arbitrary distinction between sex work for private subsistence, on which

ASHWINI SUKTHANKAR

there is silence, and sex work for the profit of others, which is prohibited. However, the principle of distinguishing between sex work for subsistence and sex work for profit was not contested. Activists, particularly feminist activists, either bought into the distinction or refused to challenge it, in order to further goals related to understandings of the state and patriarchy that were common to abolitionists and antiabolitionists alike.

Thus, abolitionist activists did not seek to change the state's permissive attitude toward those engaged in sex work for private subsistence, but rather, through the 1990s, joined with antiabolitionists to attack the state's hypocrisy in stigmatizing and harassing those women, arguing that the growing phenomenon of informal, unprotected labor such as sex work was itself a result of ill-conceived national development policies.[8] Mixed experiences with legal reform proposals, particularly around amendments to the rape law in the early 1980s, where feminists felt co-opted and disappointed with the final outcomes, also contributed to abolitionist activists' reluctance to cooperate with state attempts to eradicate sex work.[9] Meanwhile, antiabolitionists shared with abolitionists an understanding of patriarchy that rendered them reluctant to push aggressively for decriminalizing commercial systems of sex work, given their distaste for existing arrangements where male pimps, relatives, and husbands or lovers often benefited economically from female sex workers.[10] While in principle antiabolitionists favored a system based on consent, experiences with the rape law reform process led them, like abolitionists, to prefer that questions of consent not be adjudicated by the state. Throughout the 1990s, even where abolitionists and antiabolitionists diverged on key issues, such as whether activists should distinguish between sex workers who entered the profession voluntarily and those who were "coerced," both parties were profoundly reluctant to invoke the regulatory or police power of the Indian state.

It is worth contrasting this reluctance with the consensus found at the international level, where distinctions between free and forced entry into sex work have been critical to policy development. A critical issue at the international level with respect to the free/forced distinction has been the treatment of consent in the context of "economic coercion." Antiabolitionists have urged that international regulatory agreements on the entry into sex work should not address those who "voluntarily enter as a result of economic coercion . . . making the best of a bad situation."[11] Abolitionists have urged that economic coercion cannot be distinguished from other forms of coercion because there is no such thing as meaningful consent to engage in sex work. They have sought international treaties requiring that state parties neither legalize nor regulate prostitution and that they commit themselves to punishing all clients as well as rescuing and rehabilitating all women engaged in prostitution.[12]

Meanwhile, activists addressing the Indian state were resistant to aligning themselves with the international divergence in policy prescriptions. Their distrust of the state led to a shared conviction that the free/forced distinction was not the appropriate basis for line drawing at the level of the law. They believed that abolition-inspired "rescue and rehabilitation" would increase harassment, blackmail, and violence by police, and would doom more women to squalid, underfunded, prison-like "shelters." The legalization of sex work and regulation of rules of entry would place women at the mercy of bureaucracy, corruption, and worse.

Thus, activists spoke out against *all* attempted and effected consolidations of state power with respect to sex work, through the 1990s. Some state proposals were abolition-motivated, such as the 1986 amendments to the law, which enhanced police powers to search without a warrant and to hold women in sex work in protective homes.[13] Other contemplated expansions of police powers, however, were articulated in the language of legalization, such as the legislation proposed in the state of Maharashtra in the mid-1990s, which would have required compulsory testing for HIV and the branding of all sex workers who tested positive.[14] So both abolitionists and antiabolitionists tended to support proposals for decriminalization that would, at a minimum, ensure that there were no longer criminal penalties against women engaging in an "act of soliciting" as currently defined by the Immoral Traffic (Prevention) Act.[15]

So, on the one hand, activists who believed that prostitution was a form of violence against women that should be abolished nevertheless proposed self-regulatory boards for adult sex workers as a means of improving conditions in the industry, monitoring for abusive treatment, and preventing the entry of children into sex work.[16] This meant that abolitionists' proposals were in basic agreement with those of ardently antiabolitionist groups such as the Durbar Mahila Samanwaya Committee, a sex worker–led organization in Calcutta, which developed and runs self-regulatory boards.[17] Meanwhile, antiabolitionists supported national social and economic development strategies that would increase alternative employment options for sex workers who left the profession. They also supported the possibility of regional arrangements through bodies such as the South Asian Association for Regional Cooperation that would limit the undocumented movement of persons across the border with Bangladesh or Nepal.[18] Abolitionists and antiabolitionists disagreed in their underlying assumptions about sex work, but not at the level of strategy.

When this fragile agreement on strategy was upended less than a decade ago, abolitionist and antiabolitionist strategies suddenly diverged profoundly because of philosophical dissensions that had existed beneath this apparent consensus. The positions outlined above were, to state the obvious, those adopted by middle-class activists. This is not to take away from the emerging role of sex worker leadership and self-organizing, but to acknowledge that middle-class activists have frequently played a significant role in catalyzing movements through their access to resources of all kinds. The critical question in understanding the alliances that took sex worker politics to the next level are the following: For those activists not engaged in sex work, what was at stake in the sex work debates? How did they understand the significance of sex work within a broader political vision? There are several strands of thinking on these questions.

One of the primary stances of antiabolitionists is that sex workers are, wittingly or unwittingly, the critics of bourgeois morality, and therefore deserve the support of all who would challenge its dominance. Many who subscribe to this position avoid the economics of sex work in deference to a "politics of pleasure and desire," where sex workers become symbols of subversive desire.[19] Similarly, activists will often cite the Hindu devadasis or Mughal mujra dancers in their nostalgia for a real or mythic precolonial sexual freedom where prostitution was a part of religion and culture. While this appears to be an antiabolitionist stance, it has also been used to argue that sex work in its current form is degraded and deracinated—no longer cultural, but commercial.[20]

Other activists articulate a connection between their own condition and that of sex workers. This is apparent among gay and lesbian activists who see sex workers as fellow sexual radicals or marginals—whether equal targets in draconian HIV/AIDS policies with respect to who is considered "high risk" where gay men are concerned, or in terms of reclaiming women's sexual agency where lesbians are concerned, or through an extrapolated connection from the gender and sexuality deviance of hijra or kothi sex workers.[21] Similarly, those campaigning within other realms of sexuality and the law—such as on questions of rape and sexual harassment—either liken the stigmatization of the sex worker to the stigmatization of the rape victim or assert that sexual abuse is one of the main routes through which women enter sex work.[22] Locating all women as "at risk" of violation, and thus of being forced to engage in sex work, is one common means of legitimizing engagement. This type of argument takes a broader form among some feminists, such that the connection between sex workers and "the rest of us" is that sex work is the model for women's condition. Of course, the term "the rest of us" applies to other categories also, prominent among them being that of the worker.

All of these strands of argumentation share a desire to remove the stigma from sex work. They are also characterized by their ability to serve both abolitionist and antiabolitionist projects. Although these arguments are primarily used by activists to legitimize their own involvement in the debate, they are used just as deliberately by activists to delegitimize each other. For example, one abolitionist group, justifying its own work by assigning victim status to sex workers, uses the very same argument to dismiss antiabolitionist stances adopted by autonomous sex worker organizations, arguing that since sex workers are abject, these could not possibly be their own articulations, but must be those of more privileged women, whether activists or madams.[23]

DISARRAY, PARALYSIS, AND CONFLICT
IN THE NEW MILLENNIUM

The violent disruption of the uneasy equilibrium that prevailed among activists in matters of strategy involved two linked phenomena: first, a glut of HIV/AIDS money available for interventions, with increasingly stringent conditions attached to it; second, in reaction to this, attempts to shape sex worker organizing strategies without large funding. These led to considerations of the union framework, which was traditionally resourced through dues collected from individual members. These experiments with nonfunded processes were largely driven by activists with histories in queer, feminist, and working-class politics, as well as an understanding of social movement dynamics outside the NGO framework. To the extent that trade unionists were involved, they were from small independent unions, not from the world of political party–affiliated unions, which dominate the Indian labor scene.

Mainstream trade union expressions of support for sex workers' struggles (through solidarity actions, partnering on strategy, joint protest, etc.) happened almost simultaneously with sex worker unionism itself taking shape. This is unusual in the history of new forms of unionism: it is more common to see relationships between marginalized workers and established union structures developing through the identification of areas of common struggle. To some extent, the prior lack of engagement between sex workers and unions reflects the historic unease between mobilizations of women workers and trade unions outside the sphere of party politics. While there are some links between working-class women's groups and independent unions in sectors such as domestic work, construction work, and agricultural labor, a lack of engagement is by far more common. Mainstream trade unions—typically led by men and focused on the interests of working-class men—often rely on and reinforce distinctions between work and home, or public and private, rarely addressing fault-line issues important to women workers, such as affordable child care, equitable divisions of domestic labor, sexual harassment, and so on. Since the women's movement's engagement with women's work has led primarily toward the informal or unorganized sector, the isolation of sex worker organizing from trade unions was also a product of the dividing lines between organized and unorganized sector worker movements, which survive in spite of a number of principled attempts to develop a shared platform.[24] Obvious sites for bringing a trade union analysis to sex work, such as the Self-Employed Women's Association or unions organizing domestic workers, never developed into solidarity or organizing efforts, perhaps because of discomforts around sexuality that characterized the Gandhian, Marxist, or religious philosophies of the leadership.

The early part of the new millennium saw several dramatic turns at the global and domestic levels, which had profound consequences for sex worker organizing and advocacy in India. The administration of George W. Bush placed new conditions on money channeled through the U.S. Agency for International Development (USAID). Under a clause that came to be known as the "prostitution pledge," each grantee was required to declare that it did not "promote, support or advocate the legalization or practice of prostitution." This was an initial but definitive wedge between anti-abolitionist groups—some of whom, like Durbar, had been recipients of USAID money—and abolitionist groups, who suddenly anticipated rewards for their opposition to prostitution, and penalties for any further strategic alliances with pro–sex work groups.[25]

The same Bush administration also revitalized the capacity of international abolitionist campaigns to have a domestic impact. While the latest international agreement on trafficking had, like its predecessors, not required ratifying states to take a position on sex work, the Bush administration aggressively urged an abolitionist interpretation, arguing that trafficking and sex work were inextricably linked.[26] International abolitionist groups were galvanized, with feminist groups such as Sanctuary for Families and Equality Now joining with the Bush administration in support of the new policy. The administration also initiated a special annual report by the State Department on "trafficking in persons," which, in assessing the measures each country had taken to reduce trafficking, belabored the idea that tolerating sex work meant tolerating trafficking. The administration particularly lauded the approach of Sweden, which in 1999 had opted to decriminalize solicitation, but to impose criminal penalties on clients of sex workers. The so-called Swedish model was hailed as a tremendous step toward recognizing sex workers as victims, and stigmatizing those who sought their services, treating them akin to child molesters and other criminal deviants. Abolitionists were quick to join the Bush administration in praise of Sweden and in putting pressure on other states to consider the Swedish model. India, in particular—as a major site of female migration for economic opportunity and with large, highly visible centers of street- and brothel-based prostitution such as Mumbai's Kamathipura and Calcutta's Sonagachi—had long been a favorite target of antiprostitution hysteria.

Under U.S. pressure, India began to reconsider legislation and policy. In 2005, the Ministry for Women and Child Development proposed amendments to the Immoral Traffic (Prevention) Act that would remove penalties for solicitation. However, it would penalize "sexual exploitation or abuse of persons for commercial purposes or for consideration in money or in any other kind"—language that, while purporting to target only those who sought the sexual services of trafficked persons, was vague enough to apply also to private, consensual transactions between adults. Some groups found this problematic.[27] In Bangalore, Sangama, a sexuality rights NGO founded in 1999 to advocate for and with non-English-speaking queers, had been working with hijra and kothi communities. It noted that its constituency faced multiple penalties under the Immoral Traffic (Prevention) Act and Section 377 of the Indian Penal Code (the antisodomy law), as clients and as sex workers, and urged closer coordination between the struggles to challenge the two laws.

Also in 2005, the deputy chief minister of the state of Maharashtra announced a ban on "dance bars," establishments (primarily in the city of Mumbai) where alcohol was served and women dancers received tips from customers, which they shared with bar owners. The Bharatiya Bar Girls Union, which had been initiated by bar owners in 1996 to oppose the Bombay Shops and Establishment Act's ban on women's employment in hotels after 8:30 P.M., was revived in an effort to challenge the ban.

Through a brief examination of how Durbar, the Bharatiya Bar Girls Union, and mobilizations in Bangalore each sought out the language of unionism, I analyze the development and divergence of strategies among groups supportive of sex work. Choices made in each case implicate a number of issues: HIV/AIDS intervention strategies and the funding that accompanies them; the question of whether it is necessary to talk about "women" and "feminism" when talking about sex work; and debates over how to think about the occupation itself—as livelihood, a profession, a business, a critical component of movements for working-class unity. These debates within pro–sex worker groups were taking place at a time when a large number of abolitionist groups had already chosen to work with USAID, the Indian state, and international "raid and rescue" NGOs, arguing that collaboration with police, prosecutors, state remand homes, legislators, and so on, was not only defensible, but necessary. The vision of an Indian state humbled and compliant on the international stage, and the prospect of massive resources for rescue, rehabilitation, and victim protection had made this shift possible for Indian abolitionists.

Durbar emerged in the early 1990s out of the Sexual Health Intervention Program, a community-based peer-to-peer initiative that addressed the spread of HIV among sex workers in Sonagachi, Calcutta. Currently claiming sixty-five thousand members in the states of West Bengal and Orissa, Durbar is a potent political force. The organization has cast a wide net in seeking alliances, and has consistently articulated and generated strong links between its membership and workers in other sectors. Its experiments in shaping the analogy between sex workers and other workers are worth examining.

Durbar began with the relatively anodyne and apolitical issue of "livelihoods," a word suggestive of mere subsistence, and eliding questions of class. In 1995, the group circulated a "Sex Workers' Manifesto" that urged, in part, that "women take up prostitution for the same reason as they may take up any other livelihood option available to them. Our stories are not fundamentally different from the laborer from Bihar who pulls a rickshaw in Calcutta, or the worker from Calcutta who works part time in a factory in Bombay." Gesturing toward multiple examples of internal labor migration, Durbar sought to dismiss, without overt confrontation, the specter of trafficking, as well as the idea that sex work was somehow "different."[28] Nevertheless, a large number of activist groups resisted and opposed the analogy. Fourteen organizations signed on to a letter reinscribing the distinction, on the basis of the patriarchal domination of women, feminization of poverty, and intimately horrible conditions within which sex workers must work.[29] Other sporadic efforts to emphasize similarities with workers in other low-wage, exploitative sectors were similarly unsuccessful, partly due to the widespread belief that sex work is extremely lucrative.

When Durbar convened a union in 2007, much had changed. The organization had been abruptly defunded by USAID, and had consistently spoken out against the new U.S. policy in both domestic and international forums. It had sought and received expressions of support and material assistance from governments (including that of South Africa and Brazil), civil society organizations around the world (including sex workers' networks), groups of HIV-positive people, and other prominent funders (such as the Bill and Melinda Gates Foundation).

Thus, Durbar's experimentation with the union framework took place against a dramatically altered backdrop. It is hardly surprising that the organization, pressed into a posture of international and domestic defiance and prominence, gave up on the formulation that sex work is not "different" from other livelihoods, instead flaunting the perceived difference before its middle-class support base. At the founding of the Binodini Shramik Union, the charter declared it an "entertainment workers' union," organized around the very un-trade-union-like idea of a right to pleasure. Sexual pleasure and sexual expression as potential alternative organizing principles, as opposed to victimhood and sexual harm, appealed to a large swathe of middle-class queer activists, sex-positive feminists, proponents of artistic and creative freedom, and some part of the general public, both domestic and abroad.

For other allies, the idea represented less the radical convergence of demands for queer-inflected sexual rights and trade union rights than a failure to make any demands at all. Some read the founding documents' failure to explicitly challenge oppressive Indian legislation or critique USAID as a sign that the voice of the union was, ultimately, controlled not by its members, but by the powerful foundations and bilateral agencies that represent the bulk of HIV/AIDS money. Even the Gates Foundation, considered to be extremely sympathetic to sex workers in its HIV/AIDS strategy, allows grantees to educate themselves on the law but does not allow them to participate in legal reform processes.[30]

The New Trade Union Initiative (NTUI), a national federation of independent trade unions, expressed a different dissatisfaction with the formulation in an open letter stating that "'pleasure' is a term in complete conflict with the notion of work and labor."[31] NTUI activists also argued that a "right to pleasure" was problematic in this context, since the pleasure was not the sex workers' but the clients'—and what kind of union organized itself primarily around clients' rights?[32] While acknowledging that sex work is work, and that the right of association must apply, the NTUI letter asserted that there was an "inherent exploitative character" to prostitution. NTUI further critiqued the Durbar's openness to absorbing management and owners as members of the union, objecting to the inclusion of those "actively engaged in extracting the surplus generated by these sex workers." However, even critics have acknowledged privately that, while excluding brothel owners and "management" would appear a basic principle of union organizing, in practice it is much more complicated.

The Bharatiya Bar Girls Union in Mumbai required allies to engage with the realities of collaborating with management in support of workers. The leader of the union, Varsha Kale, a middle-class woman who was not a dancer herself, neither denied the unfair conditions of work imposed by management (with dancers' earnings from customers split 30:70 with the bar owner in some cases) nor the fact that the union's entire budget was underwritten by the bar owners' association. She urged that throughout history, unions had worked with management when an industry was in peril as a result of state action, developing a more confrontational relationship once the danger had passed.[33]

In this case, the industry was confronting a crisis: the state of Maharashtra had announced on August 16, 2005, that establishments serving alcohol would no longer be permitted to employ women as dancers. In conversations with activists supporting the bar dancers, the deputy chief minister, R. R. Patil, acknowledged that there had been direct pressure on Maharashtra from the U.S. Office on Traffic in Persons to close an industry that was seen as a gateway to prostitution, but noted that the ultimate decision had been made purely on grounds of Indian morality.[34] The legislation made an exception for hotels with three or more stars, and other more elite locales, on the grounds that this was necessary to "promote culture" and "boost tourism." This meant that the ban would affect, primarily, the poorest strata of dancers. However, in articulating its challenge, the union chose not to emphasize the class angle or seek solidarity on that basis. It also resisted addressing the global antiprostitution/antitrafficking angle. Instead, it carved out a very particular struggle, stressing that the "bar girls" belonged to traditional dancer and entertainer communities, and were not sex workers. By claiming that the women's occupations were determined by caste and community lineages, the union tacitly rejected the notion that the women were workers, exercising agency to shape their own identities and affiliations.

In seeking supporters, the Bharatiya Bar Girls Union reached out to middle-class women's groups. As Flavia Agnes, a lawyer closely associated with the campaign against the ban, describes, the "victim-oriented feminists" wanted to have little to do with the bar dancers issue. Groups that had emerged through close relationships with queer movements, however, responded to the appeal. Ironically, the very politics of sexuality that drew this particular category of feminist groups to the union's struggle—an understanding of the need to critique monogamy and delink sex from family and the private sphere—resulted in disillusionment. These allies were ultimately alienated by the union's insistence that advocacy focus on the bar dancers' lack of choices, and the implicit rejection of any connection to sex workers. As Agnes noted, "The anti-ban lobby framed its arguments within this accepted 'victim' mould: Single mothers, traditional dancers with no other options. Further, it was important for the antiban lobby to make a clear distinction between the dancer/entertainer and the

ASHWINI SUKTHANKAR

street walker and base the arguments squarely upon the fundamental right to dancing. The [eroticism] inherent in dancing had to be carefully crafted and squarely located within 'Indian traditions' and the accepted norm of 'Bollywood gyrations' and not slip beyond into sexual advances."[35]

The idea of a "fundamental right to dancing" was to some activists—particularly feminists—as potentially problematic a use of rights language as a right to culture, given the lack of interest in the complicated mix of reasons why these women were dancing in the first place. The women's group Forum against the Oppression of Women, in conjunction with the Research Centre on Women's Studies at SNDT University, conducted extensive interviews with bar dancers in 2005. Their research found that most of the dancers were "from communities in which people earn their living as daily wage workers." The researchers radically reframed the issues of choice and community, noting that in this context, "women could either be dancing, earning their living as domestic workers, agricultural laborers and construction workers, or doing piece work or some other form of labor in one of the myriad informal economies functioning in India." The interviews yielded a sense of the particular appeal of dancing: it was more lucrative than the other options, and preferable to direct prostitution because it was legal and somewhat safer.[36]

The union's reliance on "Indian tradition" or an even narrower localism was also implicitly critiqued by the research. The study challenged the union's claim that the majority of dancers were from Maharashtra, finding that no more than 5 percent came from within the state.[37] The researchers' interest in the question reflects a challenge to communalism within India and an engagement with movements throughout South Asia. While mainstream trade unions in India have had some difficulty in challenging nationalism, asserting that the right to form and join a union applies equally to migrants, women's groups in Mumbai had long relied on regional and international solidarity, and were openly dismayed by the Bharatiya Bar Girls Union's equivocation.

But, as noted by Apoorva Kaiwar, an activist with ties to both the women's movement and trade unions, women's groups were ultimately no better able to initiate and sustain a movement of bar dancers than the Bharatiya Bar Girls Union had been. The queer-feminist position on sexuality adopted by the women's groups supporting the dancers was critical to shaping a genuine solidarity with the bar dancers. As Kaiwar noted, however: "It was not a bad idea to talk about sexuality with respect to the bar girls, but it could not be the basis for organizing."[38]

The Karnataka Sex Workers Union, a group originating in the Bangalore region, chose a much more traditional union framework than either Durbar or the Bharatiya Bar Girls Union. It engaged with the public through demonstrations that did not downplay the violence and exploitation that union members experienced, and in doing so focused more on the work than on the sex. The decision of the Karnataka Sex Workers Union echoed Vicki Schultz's formulation, developed with respect to approaches to sexual harassment: organizing around work rather than sex allows for a rejection of the victim/agent dichotomy through a claiming of both.[39] The simultaneous embrace of victimhood and agency is a familiar feature of trade union organizing campaigns: the focus on shared experiences of exploitation, but also the possibility of transforming working conditions through unified struggle, emphasizes the material and the collective rather than the individual and the expressive.

This insistence on addressing exploitation in the sex industry also formed the basis for the Karnataka Sex Workers Union's activist mobilizations around a spate of brothel raids in India. In an analysis of a January 2008 raid on brothels in New Delhi carried out by police in partnership with abolitionist NGOs, the union acknowledged that, while the majority of "rescued" women had entered the occupation voluntarily and had not wanted to leave, there were two instances of women who had been trafficked into the brothel, and the working conditions for all the women were appalling. Nevertheless, it reiterated that as a union it would never replicate the "raid and rescue" model, but would continue to insist that organizing to improve working conditions was the best solution.

The unionization efforts that led to the Karnataka Sex Workers Union had complex relationships with other groups and movements. The efforts were initiated by activists within Sangama, the majority of whom were working-class men and hijras, and a significant percentage of whom were involved in sex work. Through them, a group of female sex workers also were drawn into the NGO.

Sangama's engagements with women's groups were extremely fraught. For some, the underrepresentation of queer women in Sangama was an issue. For others, the alliances between women, men, and hijras in sex work seemed to subsume the particular exploitation of women in sex work. The growing focus on campaigning for the repeal of the sodomy law was seen as inapplicable to women. The move into greater activism around HIV/AIDS was seen by several women's groups as the final betrayal, with many middle-class feminists refusing to believe that it was an issue of importance for queer women. However, this also drew queer men and female sex workers even closer, leading to a collaboration on legal strategy between activists challenging Section 377 and those mobilizing around the Immoral Traffic (Prevention) Act, with the shared argument that effective HIV interventions required that these groups be addressed, not through the operation of criminal law but as essential partners in developing and promoting safer sex practices.

The break from NGOs and the embrace of the possibilities offered by coming together within a trade union were also, interestingly, about HIV/AIDS. Activists connected to Sangama became frustrated with the politics of HIV/AIDS funding. Through regional and international queer, HIV/AIDS, and feminist alliances (including the Network of Sex Work Projects, Women Working Worldwide, conferences on treatment access, and more) activists came into contact with other sex worker groups around the world exploring unionization and nonfunded structures as a strategy to challenge and bypass USAID's policies under the Bush administration. Interlocutors included the Women's Network for Unity in Cambodia, the Asociación de Mujeres Meretrices de la Argentina, and the Sex Worker Education and Taskforce in South Africa. Other funders considered sympathetic to sex workers, such as the Gates Foundation, were also implicated in the critique.

The Karnataka Sex Workers Union also benefited from long debates within the women's movement, and later within queer groups, about nonfunded organizing. Its deep roots in feminist and queer debates also led it away from organizing in tandem with unions affiliated to political parties, instead choosing independent unionism as its model. Thus, the union sought to engage with the New Trade Union Initiative, the emerging federation of politically autonomous trade unions founded in 2005, in spite of the sharply anti–sex work opinions expressed by the federation in the context of the Binodini Shramik Union in Kolkata. However, in part because the Sex Workers Union fashioned itself as a more traditional union, and in part because the New Trade Union Initiative's constitution does not provide for the denial of requests for affiliation from unions that meet certain basic criteria, it has not met substantial opposition from within the federation. For the New Trade Union Initiative, the affiliation has required it to negotiate between the sympathetic inclinations of the federation's leadership and a membership that still—as the aforementioned letter to Durbar indicates—harbors deep discomfort about sharing a platform with sex workers. As Gautam Mody, an officer of the federation, noted, the strategy cannot simply be about asserting straightforward class solidarity. At a global meeting of sex worker unions convened at the World Social Forum in early 2009, he described an incident where an official of a union of traveling sales representatives affiliated to the New Trade Union Initiative asked why there were so many "prostitutes" present at their convention. In his response, Mody pointed out that traveling sales representatives made up a critical core of sex workers' client base, exposing an uncomfortable but visceral potential basis for coming together.[40]

While the sex worker unionization efforts described here emerged through very different relationships to women's movements, queer mobilizations, HIV/AIDS NGOS, and mainstream unionism, it would be a mistake to suggest that these dynamics allow us to predict outcomes in terms of the positioning or philosophy of the union structure that emerges. It would certainly be premature to draw comparisons to mainstream unions in any methodical way, given that experiments in sex worker unionizing are still at such an early stage, and arose in reaction to global phenomena as well as local organizing imperatives. Some unresolved issues, for these three unions, are outlined below, along with a brief outline of ways in which insights from queer-feminist mobilizing in India might provide some ways forward, especially as the need to network globally on the USAID issue recedes under the Obama administration.

Moving toward union democracy, and rank-and-file engagement in shaping the unions' identity and agenda, will be important in the next stages of growth. While the Binodini Shramik Union, like other Durbar projects, is genuinely led by sex workers, it appears to be driven by its leadership. It is hard to point to meaningful decentralization, a second-tier leadership, or participation of a broader membership. The Karnataka Sex Workers Union currently has greater involvement of union members in its decision making, but it is much smaller than the Calcutta union, and it is not obvious that the processes that have sufficed to maintain basic democratic principles among two hundred members—monthly meetings, active dues collection, regular elections—could easily be scaled up to address the needs of an organization a hundred times larger. Grassroots involvement and democratic participation have not *necessarily* been standard characteristics of any of the political formations that inspired these efforts: women's groups, queer struggles, or, for that matter, many mainstream trade unions. To the differing extent to which activists involved in the sex worker unions have maintained ties to social movements, there is, at least, a self-conscious awareness of the need to aspire toward a mass-based politics.

Activists in the Karnataka Sex Workers Union are sensitive to the critique that their union remains small. In response they point out that while other membership organizations may have achieved more in terms of impact on communities and membership numbers, those organizations have not been as intent on staying outside the NGO framework. However, even for the union, the NGO model has not been easy to repress. In the first place, the giant HIV/AIDS NGOs that dominate the Bangalore environment employ some current union members and provide services, in the form of treatment and outreach, to still more. The difficulty in "breaking our [NGO] habit," as one core organizer in the Karnataka Sex Workers Union put it ruefully, has implications for the union's capacity to shape itself in independent directions.[41]

Another form of the NGO, the "community-based organization," has emerged in the sex worker context. Community-based organizations for sex workers are being promoted aggressively by the government and its National AIDS Control Organisation. Some union activists close to sex worker unionization efforts fear that such a model—providing for worker's voice and some self-determination, and requiring no payment of dues in return—can only undermine unions at this stage. The differences between unions and community-based organizations can seem so subtle that first-generation sex worker activists may have a hard time articulating them, or understanding justifications for a union framework. Some union organizers take the long-term view that once funding dries up for HIV/AIDS community-based organizations, the resulting anger will foment unionization. At an as-yet-distant moment of reckoning, sex workers will suddenly arrive at the consciousness that the state is not a benevolent structure, but one interested primarily in its own perpetuation. It is assumed that, at this point, they will be prime targets for an organizing drive.

Other supporters of sex worker unionism, and in particular the Karnataka Sex Workers Union, are unwilling to cede the current moment. They urge that an agreement be negotiated immediately between the NGOs, community-based organizations, and the union on a division of roles and responsibilities: lobbying, direct action, service provision, and legal support. This proposal appears contentious, with some activists suggesting that sex worker mobilization will then be no different from political party structures, where each party claims a satellite "women's wing," trade union, student activist group, lawyers' organization, and so on. According to these critics, unless sex worker unions maintain a healthy distance from other elements of sex worker mobilization, they will lose the ability to openly criticize NGOs as employers, advocates, or service providers.

These debates replicate current tensions in queer and feminist politics regarding the respective roles of NGOs, mass mobilizations, community-based organizations, and individual activists in the work of advocacy and movement building—and in that sense, there is potential for sharing experiences. Inputs from queer groups that have already prioritized organizing outside the realm of identity politics—arguing that campaigns against Section 377 must go beyond "gay dignity" or "gay rights" by shaping common causes with other potential plaintiffs—may also help sex worker unions address critical challenges. Similarly, an open, textured way of thinking about sexuality beyond the "rights and health" framework of NGOs and funders has already helped navigate sex worker unionization efforts beyond the easy slogan of "sex work is work," toward complicated thinking about who stands to profit from that work, how to secure a larger share of the profit for workers, decent working conditions, and so on. These conversations could also help unions confront the strategic choices that lie ahead:

— The rejection of identity politics and "queer only" spaces that has characterized much queer organizing in India has paved the way for unionizing efforts to challenge a central orthodoxy of sex worker organizing: that the goal of organizing must be toward "sex worker only" political spaces. By also mobilizing a trade union history that has consistently recognized the role of middle-class organizers, the Karnataka Sex Workers Union has pressured the mainstream union movement to accept the proposition that unions should proactively organize sex workers, rather than just waiting for sex workers to organize themselves. In doing so, they argue, mainstream unions should draw from experiences organizing other marginal workers: migrants, informal sector workers, home-based workers, or the self-employed. The Binodini Shramik Union presents a different challenge to the "sex worker only" model. By allying itself cheekily with the more elite world of Bollywood performers and high-earning artists, it also stakes a claim on the resources of middle-class supporters.

— It remains an open question whether sex worker unionization efforts will succeed in bringing together the interests of female and male or transgender sex workers in the long term. Activists familiar with the fluidity of transactional sex between men, or between men and hijras, which often occurs in cruising areas, wonder whether male and trans sex workers might not experience the transactions as "alienated work" to the same extent as do female sex workers. If this is indeed the case, then male and trans sex workers, who have shared a platform with women thus far on police harassment and societal stigmatization, may have to be engaged in different ways when it comes to conditions of work.

— Inevitably, the project of unionization implies a relationship to the state, a demand for state recognition of a particular sort. Given that nonfunded mass mobilization was partly a reaction to "antitrafficking" interventions by the state, there is an inherent tension. Experiments in sex worker unionization have been informed by queer and feminist experiences of negotiating toward state proposals for regulation or protection, which have typically been far more contentious than purely oppositional struggles. We have already discussed feminist experiences with the rape law; it is also worth considering the perspective of queer groups in this respect. While they were largely united in their campaign for repeal of the sodomy law, they scrambled to shape a common position in response to the Law Commission's proposal that the rape law, Section 292, be amended to make it gender-neutral, thus equipping it to address sexual violence between men, between women, and of men by women. In the face of the state's claim that it was working to protect "good" gays and lesbians (among others) from "bad" gays, lesbians, and perverted predators of all sexual stripes, queer groups differed sharply on the potential harms and benefits that might result from the state launching into the previously almost unregulated terrain of private, same-sex interactions. With that experience in mind, activists close to sex worker unions have been urging proactive debate on issues that are sure to be pressed by state agencies, labor commissioners, city officials, and others. These include taxation, zoning for brothel- and street-based sex work, state-conducted testing for sexually transmitted infections, and compulsory social security schemes.

— Queer struggles in India have been riven by issues related to class privilege. A sizable subset of activists are unwilling to address the issue at the level of public debate, arguing that open discussion will create divisions that can be taken advantage of by opponents. Similarly, many in sex worker movements object to trade unionism as a model that foregrounds the distinction between brothel management and workers. This is not to say that the dynamic is secret—a sex worker collective, VAMP, openly acknowledges the friction that resulted when brothel owners entered the group: "Gharwalis . . . joined the collective once they realized its influence in the community and started trying to direct it. This created tensions and power hierarchies within VAMP, which have yet to be resolved."[42] It *is* the case, however, that there is no way to subsume this conflict in the union model. With unions moving toward seeking legal status, activists already anticipate the eventual moment where workers will invoke the machinery of the state against brothel owners, on issues that may range from nonpayment of wages to occupational health and safety concerns.

— Queer groups have gradually shifted from rooting their claims for rights within documentations of indigenous histories of same-sex love or gender nonconformity, finding these foundations problematic at best. Similarly, sex worker unions are an indication of a movement's willingness to adopt a critical relationship to tradition. (In this, as with other issues, the Bharatiya Bar Girls Union may well be the exception that emphasizes the validity of the claim.) The Karnataka Sex Workers Union's approach to hijra sex workers was informed by the experiences of queer activists, who realized that organizing as equal partners with hijras would inevitably entail confronting their attachments to the structure of traditional hamams, with their rigid hierarchies and abuses, but also their capacity to provide a sense of identity, belonging, and physical security. Similarly, organizing devadasis (Dalit girls and women dedicated to temple prostitution by their families) requires a politics that goes beyond simple pronouncements on the evils of child prostitution.

ASHWINI SUKTHANKAR

Unions have had to come from an understanding that profound and complicated attachments to a whole caste system are at stake, and resistance to unionization efforts will be many-layered, coming not just from locations of upper-caste entitlement, but also from below.

CONCLUSION

The current global and national realities confronting sex worker unions in India are not the same as those that engendered their initiation. The Delhi High Court recently handed down a decision finding that the sodomy law is unconstitutional to the extent that it criminalizes consensual sex between adults in private.[43] A new U.S. president has signaled some willingness to reconsider the Prostitution Pledge. Reform of the Immoral Traffic (Prevention) Act is no longer an urgent agenda item for the Indian government. It remains unclear, at this preliminary stage, whether sex worker unions in India can possibly navigate the complicated terrain of global and national politics related to prostitution, or powerful funding priorities in HIV/AIDS work, without being co-opted or derailed from the critical issues of building membership, challenging local power structures, and identifying a means of collective bargaining and protest for core workplace issues. It is noteworthy (and troubling) that these small efforts at unionization are already being scrutinized by all sides of the international sex work debates, their flaws and their achievements magnified. The challenge posed by *the idea* of sex workers unions to the victim/agent dichotomy upon which the debates rely appears to be so profound that much rides on the success or failure of the experiment. Thus, sex worker groups in countries facing possible campaigns for Swedish-style legislation beg union activists from India to speak about their experiences at legislative hearings and public meetings all over the world, while on the other hand, abolitionists dismiss them as no more than pimps in another guise.

Meanwhile, a more subdued narrative is at risk of being erased. Sex worker unionism in the Indian context emerged when activists with long histories in a range of different movements connected across delineated comfort zones to bring together their perspectives on sex and work, shaping alternative organizing strategies and structures. Before premature verdicts are written on whether or not sex worker unionism will end or facilitate trafficking, create a resurgence in service sector organizing, or enable the development of a cooperatively run worker-owned sex industry, this smaller story should be given greater attention. Greater support for and a better understanding of the collaborative processes that brought about these attempts at organizing differently may also help ensure their survival.

NOTES

1. Sheree Gomes-Gupta, "Sex Work Is Work Like Any Other," *Daily News and Analysis*, August 12, 2008, at dnaindia.com. Press release from the Durbar Mahila Samanwaya Committee, Calcutta, April 30, 1998.

2. See, for example, interview with Indrani Sinha, founder of Sanlaap, by Asha for Education (Washington, D.C.), April 16, 2005, at ashanet.org.

3. Seshu, "Is Business Work?," 15.

4. See, for example, the campaign website of the international NGO Coalition against Trafficking in Women, at catwinternational.org/campaigns.php.

5. See, for example, the website of the international network Global Alliance against Traffic in Women, at gaatw.org.

6. The International Agreement for the Suppression of the "White Slave Traffic," 18 May 1904, *entered into force* 18 July 1905. The United Nations Protocol to Prevent, Suppress, and Punish Trafficking in Persons, especially Women and Children, supplementing the Convention against Transnational Organised Crime, 2000, *entered into force* 25 December 2003.

7. Convention for the Suppression of the Traffic in Persons and of the Exploitation of the Prostitution of Others, 2 December 1949, *entered into force* 25 July 1951.

8. See, for example, the position espoused by the Calcutta-based NGO Sanlaap in the late 1990s. Sanlaap, "Sex Work Cannot Be Termed Work."

9. For discussions of the rape law reform process, see Kumari, "State's Response to the Problem of Rape and Dowry," 111.

10. See, for example, the "Sex Workers' Manifesto" drafted by the Durbar Mahila Samanwaya Committee for the First National Conference of Sex Workers in India, held November 14–16, 1997, in Calcutta.

11. Jordan, "Commercial Sex Workers in Asia," 528.

12. See, for example, Defeis, "Draft Convention against Sexual Exploitation."

13. The Suppression of Immoral Traffic in Women and Girls Act—the earlier version of the legislation—was amended in the ways indicated, and renamed the Immoral Traffic (Prevention) Act by the Suppression of Immoral Traffic in Women and Girls (Amendment) Act, 1986 (44 of 1986).

14. Maharashtra Protection of Commercial Sex Workers Act, 1994, draft bill.

15. Sanlaap, "Sex Work Cannot Be Termed Work," 1.

16. See, for example, ibid., 14.

17. Kamala Singh and Sankari Das, "Self-Regulatory Boards of Durbar," in the Durbar report, *The Third State Conference of Sex-Workers*, May 27, 2005, 22.

18. "Legalizing Prostitution Is Legalizing Violence," South Asian Agreement for Regional Cooperation press release.

19. Kapur, "Law and the Sexual Subaltern," 21.

20. See Kalpana Kannabiran, Rajeswari Sunder Rajan, and Janaki Nair, cited in Sharma, "The Social World of Devadasis and Prostitutes."

21. This reflects my own experience of debates on sex work in lesbian-feminist spaces such as Lesbians and Bisexuals in Action, Mumbai. See also Kinsuk Roy, "Status of Male Sex Workers in India," a box insert in Sanlaap, "Sex Work Cannot Be Termed Work," 6. *Hijra*: working-class male-to-female transsexuals. *Kothi*: working-class feminine or feminized men who primarily have sex with other men.

22. Haksar, "Human Rights Lawyering," 38; Bagilhole, "Sexual Violence in India," 193.

23. Sanlaap, "Sex Work Cannot Be Termed Work," 4.

24. Examples include the Hind Mazdoor-Kisan Panchayat and the National Centre for Labour, both of which attempted, in the 1990s, to bring together industrial unions and nascent mobilizations in the informal sector.

25. For Durbar's own extended critique of the change in policy, see Ahmad et al., "Of Bush and God and ABC and How the Right-wing Thinks," in *Proceedings of the Third State Conference of Sex Workers* (2005), 18–21.

26. U.S. State Department, at state.gov/g/tip.

27. Draft legislation, section 2(f).

28. "Sex Workers' Manifesto," produced for the first Calcutta conference of sex workers in 1995.

29. Reproduced in Sanlaap, "Sex Work Cannot Be Termed Work," 8.

30. Elavarthi Manohar, "Sexual Minorities and Sex Workers in South India: The Politics of AIDS Funding and Strategies in Organizing," paper presented to the Columbia University Seminar on Sexuality, Gender, Health and Human Rights, New York, November 15, 2007.

31. Leaflet circulated by the New Trade Union Initiative at the Binodini Shramik Union founding conference on February 27, 2007.

32. Conversation with Apoorva Kaiwar, March 26, 2009.

33. Conversation with Varsha Kale, April 15, 2006.

34. Conversation with Flavia Agnes, March 20, 2009.

35. Flavia Agnes, "State Control and Sexual Morality: The Case of the Bar Dancers of Mumbai," paper presented at the Yale University Workshop on Life and Law in South Asia, New Haven, May 11, 2006, 26.

36. Forum against the Oppression of Women and the Research Centre on Women's Studies, "After the Ban," Mumbai, 2005, 3.

37. Ibid., 6.

38. Conversation with Apoorva Kaiwar, March 26, 2009.

39. Schultz, "Reconceptualizing Sexual Harassment."

40. Session on "Trafficking, Migration and Sex Work," held at the "Trade Union Protections for Sex Workers" meeting, Belém, Brazil, January 30–February 1, 2009.

41. Conversation with Elavarthi Manohar, March 19, 2009.

42. Quoted on the website of the AIDS-focused voluntary organization Sangram, which provides administrative support and guidance to VAMP. See "The Struggle to be Human," at http://www.sangram.org/info8.aspx (accessed on July 8, 2010).

43. *Naz Foundation v. Government of NCT of Delhi and Others,* WP(C) No. 7455/2001, 2 July 2009.

VI

FEMINIST CRISIS AND FUTURES

RATNA KAPUR

Hecklers to Power?
The Waning of Liberal Rights and Challenges to Feminism in India

FEMINISM AND FEMINIST activism in India are going through turbulent times. Spirits among the ranks have begun to flag while the promise of revolution fades and feminism faces challenges from within and without. Feminism's dream, to make discrimination on the basis of sexual and gender difference a thing of the past, has not been realized, partly as a result of feminists' unwillingness to surrender certain ideas about sex and gender. Advocates of sexual rights and religious minorities have also eroded the ground on which the movement once stood firm. The waning of the broader emancipatory goals of freedom and hope has also weakened the movement, as has become all too evident in the context of its struggles to reform the law. Critiques of the exclusionary and conservative potential of rights and the liberal project on which they are based have blunted the tools of transformation and left progressive movements, including feminism, rudderless and without a political vision.[1]

The feminist movement in India is heterogeneous, emerging from a broad range of movements based on class, caste, and religion. In this essay, I mainly draw upon the experiences of one strand of the movement, sometimes termed the "autonomous women's movement," which claims to represent all women regardless of class, caste, or religious affiliations.[2] I ex-

plore the possibilities and limitations of the autonomous women's movement as a broad-based, emancipatory movement and discuss how feminists across the political spectrum have frequently sought recourse to law
as one means of securing women's freedoms and emancipation. Law has
not been the exclusive focus of these movements, including the autonomous women's movement, but because it has been an authoritative discourse, my essay centers on legal engagements and their impact.

I begin by setting out some of the primary assumptions on which
feminism in India has been based, focusing on how feminism has constantly negotiated two conflicting goals: realizing its revolutionary cravings
versus establishing its nationalist credentials, which are inevitably nonrevolutionary. This tension emerges from the need to acquire and sustain
legitimacy in India while also carving out a distinct voice in the international arena, where South Asian feminists have operated under the rubric
of Third World feminism.[3] From there, I move to a discussion of the
challenges posed to feminism by sexual and religious minorities and show
how the resulting uncertainties experienced by feminists are symptomatic
of the waning of modernity. I address the implications of such challenges
for feminism before concluding with some reflections on how to recover a
politics of transformation and restore feminism as an intellectually and
politically viable force.

CONTEXTUALIZING FEMINISM IN INDIA

The context of anticolonial nationalism framed early feminism's engagements with the law and the question of women's rights. The focus of early
campaigns on women's education and political participation formed part
of the endeavor to break free of colonial rule and build a strong, independent nation. Although women also expressed the need to eliminate oppressive social practices such as child marriage, there was not an immediate
resort to law. The Age of Consent Bill proposed by colonial authorities at
the end of the nineteenth century, which sought to raise the age of marriage, was viewed as an attempt to undermine native autonomy in the
"private" arena.[4] Such interventions met with fierce resistance from cultural nationalists and social reformers alike.

While feminism was born partly out of the revolutionary zeal of the
anticolonial freedom movement, it did not necessarily emerge as a force

RATNA KAPUR

for radical change.[5] The early twentieth century witnessed the emergence of several all-India women's organizations: the Women's Indian Association (1917), the National Council of Women (1925), and the All India Women's Conference (1927). These organizations were able to usher in a new social and political agenda, which included women's suffrage, a more comprehensive reform of the personal laws, widow remarriage, and the previously contentious issue of child marriage. The latter two issues contributed to the discourse of "women's upliftment," which was used to demand social and economic reforms that would enable a greater public role for women. These organizations used the argument that women's distinctive roles and values as self-sacrificing mothers and dutiful wives could make an important contribution to the public sphere.[6]

The discourse of upliftment of women developed alongside the discourse of gender equality over the course of the twentieth century, a period that was marked by a distinct liberal faith in state institutions and the rule of law.[7] Laws were passed guaranteeing gender equality and special provisions for women in the areas of employment, politics, education, and some aspects of the family law. But such benefits sat in tension with the construction of an ideal of Indian womanhood, which, even within the feminist movement, served to distinguish Indian women from their Western counterparts. Below, I demonstrate how this tension played out in legal campaigns and survived well into the postindependence period. In the late 1980s the autonomous women's movement took up the issue of sexual violence against women in public and private spheres; prominent in the campaign was a demand for the reform of rape law. The feminist protests against rape connected sexual violence against women with the systemic oppression of women. The campaign's attention to police rape and to women as victims was enthusiastically picked up by the media and politicians, and protests spread well beyond the women's movement. With the entry of mainstream politicians, the discourse of the rape campaign began to transform. Politicians spoke with outrage of the increasing attacks on women, and of the shame and dishonor brought on women and their families. Although the feminist campaigns made inroads in revealing the violence experienced by women, they did not alter the discourse within which this violence was condemned. Shame, dishonor, and the notion of woman as victim continued to inform both popular and legal discourse. Ultimately, the reform of the rape provisions met with mixed results.[8]

It did not transform the legal meaning of rape, displace the problematic constructions of consent, or disrupt conservative assumptions about women's sexuality.[9]

The focus on women as victim-subjects has helped the autonomous women's movement retain its anti-Western, nationalist credentials. Feminism in India continues to have a tenuous relationship with nationalism, and has therefore been cast as Western and imperialist at several historical moments.[10] It has been charged with being a product of "decadent Western capitalism . . . based on a foreign culture of no relevance to women in the 'Third World.'"[11] Therefore feminists have adamantly denied allegations of being Western and have sought to establish a distinctively Indian feminism, based on the notion of an authentic Indian woman, one who is routinely a victim of oppression and violence. Any discussion of female choice, especially in sexual matters, has been muted. Sexual pleasure per se has been regarded by many within the women's movement as a foreign contaminant, and something that distinguishes Indian women and culture from the "West."

Thus the women's movement in India has remained simultaneously tied to a revolutionary and a nonrevolutionary sensibility. It continues to invest in an essentialist and conservative notion of Indian culture and womanhood while pursuing the revolutionary enterprise of achieving equality between men and women. This tension continues to inform feminist engagements with the law, which have focused on securing formal equal rights with men without disrupting the dominant cultural, familial, and sexual norms that define Indian womanhood.[12]

The violence against women campaigns and their focus on women's victimization have also been central to South Asian feminism's agenda in the international legal arena, specifically in its advocacy for women's human rights. In the international women's rights arena, South Asian feminism is often dovetailed with Third World feminism, a platform that ostensibly represents the voices of women from the global South, although there is no consensus on exactly who and what it represents.[13] However, Third World feminism has emerged as a political perspective that broadly includes a commitment to achieving formal equality for women and a deep faith in the emancipatory potential of human rights. Third World feminism has found common ground with Western feminism on the issue of violence against women and a focus on the victim-subject. But like

RATNA KAPUR

South Asian feminism, it has steered away from discussing or engaging with sexuality in the international human rights context, regarding advocacy of sexual rights and their association with pleasure and desire as a specific obsession of First World feminism.

A focus on victimization and violence against women helped South Asian feminists to produce an alliance with one stream of Western feminism while consolidating the identity of Third World women as distinct from Western women. While Third World feminism has expanded the horizon of thinking and activism in relation to women's rights, it has also been inward looking. The discourse about the Third World victim-subject was largely shaped by nationalistic and anti-Western thinking, and the project of Third World feminism, however effective in countering the culturally essentialist assumptions of Western feminists about women in the Third World, adopts a position that inhibits it from radically expanding the agenda of feminism in the global South.

EXTERNAL CHALLENGES TO FEMINISM

The revolutionary spirit of feminism has been stymied by the weight of its own history; more recently, it has also been confronted by questions of religious and sexual identity. In India, at a national women's studies conference in the early 1990s, feminist activists and scholars from the Muslim and Christian communities accused the women's movement of being "Hindu"-dominated and protected by its Hindu affiliations, especially in times of civil strife and riots. Many feminists, especially leftists, were apoplectic at this challenge to their secular credentials. The women's movement, with its focus on gender, victimization, and a universal Indian woman's identity, had not adequately addressed issues of religious identity and conflict. It continued to appeal to the discourse of secularism as per se an effective counter to right-wing movements and refused to engage with the politics of religion.

In subsequent years, Hindu-Muslim riots in Mumbai, the victory of the Hindu Right in national elections in 1999, and the slaughter of over a thousand Muslims in Gujarat in 2002 highlighted the need to address minority communities' critiques of feminism. In the aftermath of the Gujarat riots, women's groups participated in nongovernmental investigations of the violence inflicted on Muslims, especially Muslim women. The resulting reports drew attention to the particularly horrific nature of the sexual violence perpetrated against the Muslim community, and argued that such sexual violence and killings of Muslim women constituted genocide under international law.[14] There was also a recognition that rape was used as an instrument for the "subjugation and humiliation" of the minority community.[15] The reports' recommendations focused on international and legal remedies, and on expanding the definition of rape in domestic law.[16] Justice for Muslim women was to be addressed separately from the justice secured for the community as a whole. A reparations tribunal for victims was established to provide compensation for losses or injury suffered, including the impact of sexual assault on women and their families.

These reports revealed a more sophisticated understanding of the nature of the violence inflicted on Muslim women. However, they continued to focus on the victimization of such women, and on providing redress through international legal instruments dealing with genocide and through prosecutions under criminal law at the domestic level. While important, these efforts failed to address the role of the Hindu Right's ideology of Hindutva, which seeks to establish India as a Hindu state, in producing the violence unleashed in Gujarat. With the Muslim cast as "alien" perpetrator and the Hindu as internal victim, the violence inflicted against the Muslim community is justified as an act of self-defense. While the initiatives gave the victims of violence a voice, they did not address this broader discursive context.

While the autonomous women's movement recognizes religious difference, it does not see it as producing conflict between women. The focus remains on the commonality of women's experiences, especially of sexual exploitation and sexual violence. This position argues that all women experience oppression at the hands of patriarchal power, and that power is invariably male. Feminists can then interrogate and critique the practices of religious communities, regardless of their own location, because, as Kumkum Sangari puts it, "all religions are implicated in and enter into the broad process of social legitimation of patriarchies."[17] This shared patriarchal experience is precisely why feminists should not, in Sangari's view, recede "from a secular democratic agenda and from a commitment to common struggles."[18] Ironically, the Hindu Right has also invoked secularism, understood in the Indian context as the formal equality and equal treatment of all religions, to call on Muslims to assimilate into a national

Hindu culture.[19] Any resistance on the part of Muslims and other religious minorities is immediately cast as antinational and antisecular, and as posing a grave threat to the identity and security of the Indian nation. The violence inflicted on Muslims during riots can be justified as self-defense on the part of a Hindu nation that is understood as all-encompassing and tolerant. While the autonomous women's movement has gradually recognized the powerful influence of the Hindu Right, it remains reluctant to surrender or significantly restructure its universal feminist foundations and hence is unable to effectively counter this influence.[20]

Yet another set of challenges to feminism has come from sexual rights advocates in the domestic context, and responses to controversies around questions of sex. In India this challenge has been expressed in the legal contests over the screening of films such as Shekhar Kapur's *The Bandit Queen*, debates about beauty pageants and the hip gyrations and pelvic thrusts of Bollywood cinema, threats by Hindu Right mobs during Valentine's Day celebrations, and protests over the growing visibility of gays, lesbians, sex workers, and other sexual minorities.[21] All of these reflect unease with the increasing publicity of sex and sexuality.[22]

Contemporary debates about sexuality initially erupted over the screening of the 1998 film *Fire*, directed by Deepa Mehta. The story involves the attraction between two beautiful women, Radha and Sita, who are both married to distinctly unappealing men and live together in a joint-family household. Radha and Sita, whose names derive from central female characters in Indian epics, are depicted transgressing every sexual, familial, and cultural norm. This includes trespassing into an "unacceptable" sexual space, or what one reviewer described as "the Indian lesbian scene." The film, and this scene in particular, triggered a national controversy. Attacks on cinema halls screening the film ultimately resulted in the banning of the film in India for a period of time. Civil rights groups, including many feminists, regarded the ban as a fundamental violation of the right to free speech. The Hindu Right read the film as an attempt to convert women to lesbianism, which would lead to the demise of the Hindu family. Gay and lesbian groups challenged the assumption that lesbians did not already exist in Indian culture. They used the film to lobby for the recognition of their rights to sexual identity and the repeal of discriminatory legislation. Some of them suggested that feminist advocates were antipleasure and unwilling to engage with the politics of sexuality for fear of relinquishing the victim-subject through which their distinct "Indian" brand of feminism had been constituted.[23]

Organized movements of sex workers have posed similar challenges to feminists. Some of them have viewed feminists as against sex workers, especially in the context of the nearly universal support by feminists for antitrafficking laws.[24] These laws invariably conflate trafficking with sex work, are deeply moralizing, and continue to constitute sex workers as victims. Sex workers have countered this representation of their work and identities at two levels. First, they have argued for their rights to sexual expression, safe working conditions, livelihood, a family life, adequate health care, and education for their children. Second, through their claims as mothers, entertainers, migrants, and workers they have challenged the dominant cultural, familial, and sexual assumptions about women that inform the law.

Sexual subalterns, including gays, lesbians, and sex workers, argued that feminists were preoccupied with violence and the goals of formal equality, while paying little or no attention to sexual life. Such challenges are significant, but not necessarily revolutionary. It is not yet evident that the sexual rights campaign has taken on board the need to foreground the erotic body and sexual pleasure. The successful campaign against the sodomy provision in the Indian Penal Code has been claimed as a landmark victory for homosexuals in India.[25] Yet, the legal victory has not entirely disrupted the dominant sexual, gender, and familial norms that inform the legal regulation of all sexual subjects—lesbians, to take one instance, are not governed by the legal or public discourse around sodomy.

While feminism and feminist activism appear to be hemorrhaging from internal contradictions and external challenges, they share in the common despair expressed by progressive groups over the loss of a revolutionary dream and emancipatory political vision. The retreat by feminism and the gloom afflicting feminist activists can be framed by despair over the waning of modernity and flagging faith in liberalism as a coherent, progressive project for human emancipation.

THE WANING OF MODERNITY

During the 1990s, there was a gradual professionalization of feminism.[26] The autonomous women's movement was transformed into an NGO community, flush with funds from government and foreign organizations.[27] This shift, combined with the challenges to feminists posed by sexual and religious minorities as well as by lower-caste activists, led to fears that the Indian women's movement was being fragmented.[28] But such developments only partly account for the anxiety and uncertainty over the feminist agenda. The liberal faith in state institutions and law, which was a hallmark feature of the women's movement and integral to the emancipatory dream, has been exposed as exclusive and myopic. While liberal thought is intellectually diverse, I focus on three core attributes of the liberal idea that are now in crisis: first, belief in a progressive and evolutionary narrative of history; second, rights as the basis of freedom; and third, the supremacy of the liberal subject. The fact that feminists have been complicit in aligning with each of these components reveals an inadequate reckoning with the structure and foundational assumptions of the liberal state.

The liberal assumption about a historical progression toward greater freedom, prosperity, and equality is obviously in crisis. The United States, especially under the two-term presidency of George W. Bush, aggressively launched a new age of empire that harks back to older rhetoric by speaking of fighting "crusades" against "evildoers" through its global "war on terror." Combined with neoliberalism, these developments have produced apprehensions on both the right and the left. On the right, strident reactionary voices mourn the loss of the certainties of the past—including family values, moral righteousness, and God—and long for a return to a golden era. The progressive Left and feminists, on the other hand, mourn the loss of a golden era of a cohesive, "truly political" movement.[29]

At the same time, is there a waning of belief in the idea of "rights" as the basis of freedom and emancipation for women? Women's rights activists in India have successfully challenged laws that discriminate against women, and ensured the enactment of laws to prohibit violent practices against women. These demands for "women's rights" and "equal rights" have given the women's movement its political character and signaled some of its successes, even though many reforms have fallen short of what the movement had demanded. But despite the legal victories over the years, the social, political, and economic status of women has shown remarkably little improvement. There is evidence of extensive sexual and physical violence against women—rape, dowry, and domestic violence persist in the face of legislation designed to eliminate these practices. And the list goes on. Women continue to be paid less than men notwithstanding legislation designed to eliminate discrimination in remuneration. They continue to bear the economic costs of childbirth, notwithstanding legislation designed to provide maternity benefits. In fact, there is increasing evidence that the socioeconomic status of women in India, as in other developing countries, is deteriorating. The global economic restructuring of the 1980s and the current phase of neoliberalism have resulted in economic policies that are having a devastating impact on the already precarious social and economic position of women.

The role of law in struggles to improve women's status has been a recurrent problem for feminists concerned with the gap between women's de jure and de facto status. Notwithstanding some incisive work by feminists in this area, the feminist debate on this subject is characterized by an undertheorization of the role of law and rights in the struggle for human emancipation. Law is assumed to be an instrument of either change or oppression, while rights are assumed to challenge oppression and realize freedom. Yet the successful law reform campaigns against rape, sexual harassment, and trafficking have not necessarily afforded women greater freedom, protection from harm, or ensured their rights to sexual autonomy, bodily integrity, and greater mobility. There is a lack of understanding about how rights are contingent on sexual, gender, and cultural stereotypes that inform and are sustained by law.

The third and related crisis is produced by the challenge to the idea of the liberal subject. Liberalism's insistence on a universal human subject that exists independent of social relations has historically coexisted with exclusion and subordination on the basis of class, gender, and racial difference. Struggles for liberty, equality, and freedom within Europe coexisted with the subjugation of Europe's "others" through colonialism and slavery. Even within Europe, gender and class hierarchies shaped the ideology of the ideal liberal subject, who was a white, Christian, heterosexual, propertied male. This history continues to shape the present discourse of liberty, equality, and freedom. There are at least three ways in which "difference" has been addressed in the liberal intellectual tradition and the rule of law: through assimilation, naturalizing difference, and incarcerating or annihilating difference.

In colonial India, the "universal" principles of liberty, equality, and freedom were contingent on the native's ability to conform to the dominant colonial culture.[30] Today, assimilation in postcolonial India is pursued through strict compliance with new legal criteria for citizenship and nationality. A formal approach to equality simultaneously informs both feminists' calls for gender equality and the Hindu Right's demand that Muslims surrender their claims to "special treatment." These pursuits have, at times, adversely affected women who are not "similarly situated."[31] For example, bar dancers, who are Indian citizens, are targeted in the state of Maharashtra as being "outsiders," corrupting and eroding the state's cultural values, and undeserving of rights to livelihood, expression, and mobility. Similarly, Muslim women are routinely portrayed by the Hindu Right as victims of a backward Muslim culture, and by feminists as victims of an overarching patriarchal oppression that cuts across religious differences.[32]

Historically, the legal treatment of colonized peoples and women reflected the liberal assumptions that such persons were morally and intellectually inferior. James Mill, who wrote a six-volume history of India in 1817, declared the country primitive and rude and thus unfit for anything other than despotic rule. His son, John Stuart Mill, who drafted policy documents for the East India Company for thirty-five years, argued that a lack of civilizational maturity warranted the denial of certain rights and liberties to the native. Today, legal campaigns by feminists and others against human trafficking are powered by analogous stereotypes that turn on the portrayal of Third World women as forever falling victim to trafficking, violence, death by culture, and are therefore in perpetual need of rescue by their liberal, feminist sisters.[33] "Rescue missions" have resulted in the "wretched of the earth" ending up in homes for the destitute, juvenile centers, and inadequate government shelters.

Those who refuse to embrace democracy, the rule of law, and human rights are constructed as opponents of these values and undeserving of the protections they oppose. Such opposition justifies the creation of new categories of people, such as enemy combatants or unlawful noncitizens, who are liable to incarceration without due process, elimination, or annihilation because of the threat they pose.[34] The Gujarat riots of 2002 witnessed a near annihilation of Muslim identity in parts of the state, with the razing of mosques, residences, businesses, and an almost sadistic brutality inflicted on Muslim women. In light of their refusal to assimilate, the continued "special treatment" of Muslims was projected as appeasement for those whose loyalty remained suspect and whose allegiance lay elsewhere. Muslims were regarded as occupying zones outside the law, making them legitimate targets for violence. These responses to difference are located in the heartland of the postcolonial liberal democratic state. They are pursued in and through legal discourse to produce distinctions between new nonhumans, lesser humans, and superhumans. They cannot be explained as deviations from an otherwise honorable liberal project by loony right-wing movements, as is sometimes suggested by some feminist scholars. Arguments that poverty, corruption, lack of good governance, and continuing cultural primitiveness have barred liberal values from effectively taking root in South Asian societies only underline the fact that the problem lies within the liberal tradition itself. The rights and freedoms that all good liberals and progressives support, including rights to freedom, liberty, and equal worth, are partly constituted by assumptions about cultural, sexual, racial, and religious superiorities of some people and civilizations, over others.

FEMINIST NOSTALGIA

The despair accompanying this unraveling of the liberal project has elicited two major responses from feminists. The first is an effort to identify what has been lost: the "truly political" aspects of feminism, including feminism's potential to subvert and destabilize dominant values and structures.[35] The period when this vision had the most potential was when the movement was autonomous rather than donor-dependent, on the streets rather than housed in smart offices. It was a period of sisterhood, when self-identified feminists worked for all women. The focus on consciousness raising, mobilization, and public advocacy constituted the political core of the movement, and brought about radical changes such as legal reforms in rape and dowry laws.[36]

Such nostalgia views the modern history of the women's movement through a teleological lens. This history is told as a linear narrative, in terms of "waves," an "evolution," or "development" from the first to the third wave, peaking during the 1970s and 1980s period of the autonomous women's movement.[37] The past becomes a repository of the political vision that the present has lost. That past must be recovered in order for a feminist future to exist. Such temporality can be seen as melancholic lament over the loss of past possibilities and visions that reside in an empty place and time rather than now, in the present.[38] It forecloses a political orientation that looks to future possibilities to provide answers to the current predicament.

This teleological reading of the women's movement also fails to capture the messiness of its history. The autonomous women's movement's self-representation as an authentic feminist voice—broad based, inclusive, and progressive—coupled with its nostalgic longings negates the fact that a cohesive feminist movement has never existed. Even if it had, points of origin are impossible to identify and retrieve. While the cleavages of caste and religion have always been a feature of women's lives and experiences, my focus on the autonomous women's movement draws attention to its reluctance to displace gender as a central category of analysis and more deeply interrogate how such differences have come to be constituted and to engage with the messiness of law and rights, which are sites of discursive struggle over different world visions.[39]

A second and related response of feminists to the current moment of despair is to remain wedded to the idea of modernity as progressive, partly because so much political hope has been invested in it. It is an approach that has been characterized by Wendy Brown as a "Yes I know. But . . ." politics.[40] Critique is suspended out of concern it will create anxiety, fear, and even nihilism. Yet it is difficult to formulate a persuasive argument for returning to the ideals of progress, universality, and free will when these lie so fully exposed in a postcolonial context. Indeed, any serious argument for such a return would in itself be a nihilistic move. It can lead us nowhere.

HECKLERS TO POWER?

If crisis and a sense of despair is indeed the present condition we are in, then where does that leave feminism, let alone progressive politics, in India? Are feminists simply reduced to the status of permanent hecklers to power, neither able to imagine a transformative future nor ever to fully embrace power? What happens when faith in feminism is eroded, when its revolutionary zeal has diminished? I argue that it is better to confront these questions than hark back to a golden past, cling to tattered frameworks, or keep reusing broken tools. Feminism needs to incorporate the insights of postcolonial theory, from which it has hitherto remained distant, not only because such a theory can better capture law's complex and contradictory role in struggles to improve women's social, economic, political, and cultural position, but also because it can provide a productive way out of the current crisis. The distinction between South Asian feminism and what I call "postcolonial feminism" lies in the challenge posed by the latter to the basic assumptions on which the liberal project is based.

In this segment I set out the insights offered by such a postcolonial feminism, which may offer a way out of the current malaise. This will require feminists in India, and elsewhere in South Asia, to move away from their continued hostility to critical theory. This hostility can partly be explained by the history of women's studies in the region. Feminists have viewed women's studies as necessarily aligned with the concerns of women on the ground, and their issues of development and poverty. The emergence of more critical perspectives, it is suggested, has severed this link and foreclosed the possibility of convergence between women's studies and the women's movement.[41] Of course postcolonial theory is not adverse to activism, and itself emerges from the history of the colonial encounter.[42] But it does not subscribe to the call by some activists to abandon the need for "footnotes and references" and simply "think on our feet" in order to attend to the urgency of the current crisis.[43] Rather, it raises epistemological questions that challenge not only the pillars of the liberal project but also the alignment of Indian feminism to this tradition, in particular, in its engagements with law and liberal rights. Such interrogation produces acute fear and anxiety that the category of gender will be destabilized and the future of feminist activism jeopardized. Gender is understood as the crucial category that gives feminism its legitimacy and is the basis for its survival. I want to propose, instead, that feminism needs to move beyond sex and gender, delink itself from its liberal inclinations, and surrender its search for revolution either through an appeal to some authentic past or in some kind of big bang moment. Instead, it needs to take on board the critiques of liberalism, modernity, identity, and law offered by postcolonial theory.[44]

This requires at least four distinct analytical shifts. First, it requires feminism to turn the gaze back on itself, and ask: How has it been implicated in conservative pursuits of gender? How has it reinforced difference

　　　　　　　　　　　　　　　　　　　　　　　RATNA KAPUR

and cultural and gender stereotypes—especially in its engagements with law—and produced or encouraged antiquated responses from feminists, human rights groups, and governments? While Agnes, Menon, and others have unmasked some of these limitations, their proposed solutions are limited—either a capitulation (once again) to liberal reformism, or the recovery of a "subversive politics" through a nostalgic return to a period that was "really political." Such critiques do not resolve the problems of feminist complicity in reinforcing gender and cultural stereotypes, offering protectionist responses to women's rights violations, or encouraging sexual sanitization in pursuit of justice for sexual violence. Nor do they address the question of who is accountable when such interventions do more harm than good. In these approaches, the "virtue" of feminists, armed with good intentions, remains intact whereas a more honest and urgent self-critique is warranted.

Second, we need to understand how feminism operates in and through cultural and historical discourses that regulate and construct gender. Gender is a site of power, and can be invoked equally by seeming opponents to advance their agendas. Historically the discourse of women's rights has been used to advance civilizing missions, and in the contemporary moment it is used to legitimate new kinds of imperialism, such as the bombing of Afghanistan. Gender has been used to resuscitate authentic versions of culture, entrench the public/private divide, and justify protectionist measures. It is this power in the hands of those who use gender that must be understood—not its lack of ability to transform women's lives.

Third, postcolonial theory more generally, and postcolonial feminism in particular, demonstrate the need for a deeper interrogation of the law. The autonomous women's movement has been tied to a modern liberal framework in its engagements with law and legal reform. Postcolonial theory is an analysis that is distinct from theory that regards law simply as a tool of oppression embedded in a grand patriarchal scheme, and it also argues for the need to delink our equation of law with the pursuit of human freedom. It reveals law as a discursive site where different visions of the world are fought out and normative assumptions about gender, sex, and culture are consolidated, universalized, and naturalized. Postcolonial theory allows us to unpack how the universal is produced in Indian law through historically specific processes such as imperialism, and how these processes continue to inform the postcolonial present.[45]

The fourth and final exercise is perhaps the most challenging. So far I have characterized postcolonial feminism as a position that is critical of Western liberalism while avoiding slippages into either a nativist or reformed Marxian stand. Yet postcolonial feminism also clears space intellectually and philosophically to rethink the foundations on which such a critique might be based. This move requires a more thoughtful engagement with philosophical traditions from elsewhere, nonliberal traditions but not illiberal ones. The idea of a nonliberal position being necessarily narrow-minded and illiberal is itself framed within a binary according to which Western liberalism is the norm and illiberalism its opposite. But the world is not constituted within this binary. I conclude with some thoughts on what a conversation between postcolonial feminism and such intellectual and philosophical traditions might offer, highlighting three aspects that will of course require further exploration.

In order to consider whether non-Western philosophical and intellectual traditions can provide metaphysical and ontological moorings for feminist critiques and analysis we must first address two pervasive assumptions: first, that non-Western philosophy is embedded in religious thought; and second, that Western liberalism is free from religious taint. The latter fails to recognize the religious underpinnings of the Western liberal tradition, which has been shaped not only by social, economic, and historical forces, but also by Christianity. At the same time, we need to acknowledge the significant distinction in non-Western traditions between philosophy and religion. Some of these traditions are focused on perception as the sole means of knowledge as distinct from the notion of a "supreme being."[46] Others are immersed in systems of logic, inference, and dialectics that can be traced from well before the Buddha, an agnostic, to Amartya Sen, who traces this tradition of dialectics, debate, and even skepticism in his book *The Argumentative Indian*, which, he concludes, illustrates that everything is open to question.[47] In Sen's book, "culture" is articulated as not necessarily a negative attribute, and as having deeply philosophical and potentially liberating aspects.[48]

These traditions, much like liberal thought, are in no way homogeneous. However, their articulations about the basis of knowledge, the subject, and time challenge some of the central components common to liberal thought. They can assist Indian feminists in several ways in rethinking their political engagements and the understandings of freedom and emancipation that inform these engagements. First, the critique of Western liberal thought requires a larger discursive frame within which to situate the critique, so that we can identify spaces outside the epistemology of the Enlightenment.[49] While postmodernist or post-Enlightenment thinkers have critiqued the basis from which knowledge proceeds, there has been little effort to foreground other modes of thinking or epistemological frameworks on which to situate this critique, especially from non-Western traditions.

Consider, for example, the support of some Indians for the recent Delhi High Court decision confining the application of the law criminalizing sodomy to nonconsensual sex. Does such acceptance indicate the penultimate liberal value of tolerance? Or does it emerge from an acceptance of the metaphysical law of causation, an almost morally patronizing attitude to "leave them alone" because they are "suffering" the results of actions they did in some earlier point of time, time not being defined exclusively in terms of one's life span?[50] Are the sexual choices of individuals and the consequences of these choices considered a part of that law? Or does their acceptance indicate an *advaita* logic based on nondualism, where all manifestations of the self, including sexuality, resolve in the self, and hence the primary struggle rests in bringing about this inner resolution?[51] Or does it rest on a philosophy that suggests that all absolute claims are myopic? These multiple framings are all possible in a context where law and liberal thought do not have the same pervasive, colonizing, and indoctrinating function as in many Western contexts. They cannot be dismissed by the liberal ruse of "irrationality," given that they are neither assertions of belief or faith, but logical and evidenced-based positions.

A second related area where further debate needs to take place concerns the link between the conceptualization of the subject and understandings of freedom and emancipation. The space clearing for such interrogation partly occurs once human freedom is no longer exclusively aligned with the pursuit of more rights and more law. I offer three examples of figures whose subjectivity cannot be captured within a victim/agent divide or their freedom secured simply through the embrace of liberalism, more rights, and more law. When a Muslim woman wears the veil, some feminists address her either exclusively as a victim of false consciousness subordinated to masculine norms, or read her choice to wear the veil as an act of resistance to liberal norms and values. Both of these readings miss how her choice can be linked integrally to her inner emancipation, and her way of being in the world that is simply not captured within the bounds of a liberal imaginary. As Saba Mahmood argues, her choice needs to be understood in terms of the relationship between the external acts and performance of the subject, that is, the wearing of the veil and the cultivation of her inward disposition and emancipation.[52] The veil is a performance that is linked to her desire to be free, and this notion of freedom is linked to a journey inward rather than a movement outward.

Another example is captured in the life of Umrao Jaan, a nineteenth-century Bombay courtesan, or sex worker, who wrote deeply philosophical poetry. In contemporary feminist liberal discourse, she might be regarded as subordinated by male privilege—a truncated, victimized subject, whose liberation lies in the abolition of her profession. Critical theorists might read her as a subversive sexual subject who challenges hegemonic sexual, cultural, and familial norms, though their critique offers no possibility or understanding of freedom. Umrao Jaan is simultaneously a courtesan and a sensitive poet, who earns her money in a *kotha* (brothel). Neither position addresses the fact that her work is not what defines her. What defines her is her poetry. She seeks an internal grounding and liberation through her poetry, which is philosophical and provides her with a reflective space that connects with her inner being.

Another example would be the *hijras*, or eunuchs, of south India. Every year on the full moon day in May they congregate in the south Indian state of Tamil Nadu before a deity, Iravan (who is a son of a warrior prince), to perform the ritual of marriage and claim their status as the brides of Iravan. While they hold beauty pageants, seminars on their social and legal status, and discussions on health matters two or three days before the full moon event, the marriage is the act of supreme power and significance. The event is deeply ritualistic and fervent, in which, like dervishes, they work themselves into a frenzied and altered state of consciousness. It is a space that is freed from the references that govern their ordinary lives. The hijras' subjectivity and agency is not just defined by their sexuality, and their liberation is experienced in and through this more ritualistic, frenzied relationship.

All these figures link understandings of the subject with notions of freedom and liberation that cannot be captured purely within the liberal framework. They are embedded in a metaphysical space that enables a complex articulation of subjectivity and freedom that cannot be reduced to either victimage or performance. Their agency is located in the relationship of these identities and performances with the subject's interior disposition, a relationship that is potentially liberating, but not in the way that the liberal imaginary conceives of liberation. This is a philosophical space, constituted by much more than one's performance or identity. It is constituted by what the subject is; liberation rests in recognizing this "is-ness," rather than in a focus on change through a liberal trajectory and the never-ending pursuit of more rights and law that ultimately fail to deliver on the promise of more freedom. And finally, these examples illustrate that neither history nor time are linear, and that progress means not a march forward but an exercise of going deeper, here and now. Such an exercise entails constant reflection, critique, and debate of the metaphysical grounds on which our arguments are based, without fear of nihilism. It is a pursuit of knowledge that locates the revolution within the subject, where transformation of the world lies within the transformation of the self.

Of course, all these possibilities need to be further elaborated. I am simply suggesting that they can provide the grounds for newly imagining a political position that eschews despair and paralysis, on the one hand, and refuses to surrender to liberal reformism, on the other. I am proposing that such philosophical rethinking can open up two possibilities for feminists. First, it offers the possibility of thinking about freedom and liberation in a way that is not confined to or exclusively aligned with the liberal tradition, especially in the guise of a demand for more rights and more law. Second, such rethinking enables Indian feminists to provide a powerful challenge to the Hindu Right's shallow claims to be the exclusive exponents of "authentic Indian culture," without themselves falling into a culturally nationalist or nativist position.

My critique of feminism in India is intended to be productive, rather than simply pointing out what is wrong with the existing scenario. The arguments in this essay are intended to articulate a different cosmology within which to understand the place of feminism in our world. To remain invested in precisely those categories that feminism seeks to dismantle— that is, sex and gender—is to move away from revolution. Of course we cannot simply emancipate feminism from sex and gender, because these identities are so deeply embedded in the capillaries of power. But we can think in terms of transformation of these categories through a deeper and different engagement with alternative knowledge systems. Ultimately, this engagement is an effort to put some life back into a feminist project in desperate need of resuscitation—to help stage the sorely needed intellectual insurrection in the area of feminist activism and open up the possibility to live and think differently.

NOTES

1. Dietrich, "Loss of Socialist Vision and Options before the Women's Movement"; Krishnaraj, "Challenges before Women's Movement"; Phadke, "Thirty Years on Women's Studies Reflects on the Women's Movement"; Poonacha, "Women's Studies in Indian Universities"; Menon, *Recovering Subversion*; and Kapur and Cossman, *Secularism's Last Sigh?*

2. There are many women's groups affiliated with the major political parties such as the Mahila Congress, the women's wing of the Congress Party; the All India Women's Conference, which developed close links with the Congress Party after independence; the All India Democratic Women's Association, which is linked with the Communist Party of India (Marxist); and the Mahila Morcha (Women's Front), linked with the right-wing Bhatriya Janata Party. The autonomous women's movement's claim to be free from party political affiliations and representing all women and their issues makes it a significant voice in shaping and influencing the way in which feminism has emerged in India. The movement has struggled to distinguish itself at times from party- and state-affiliated organizations as well as donor-dependent organizations by describing themselves as "feminist." However, this appellation has been largely avoided in the public domain for the reasons set out in this essay as well as the historical association of feminism with the colonial power and a nonprogressive political project. The term "autonomy" remains fluid and there is no common consensus as to who it includes or excludes. Saheli, a Delhi-based women's organization founded in the early 1980s, claimed to be a part of the autonomous women's movement on the basis that it was not affiliated to any party or government, nor did it take any funds. Similar claims were made by Jagori (Delhi), Viomochana (Bangalore), and the Forum against the Oppression of Women (Bombay), who also used the term "autonomous" to distinguish themselves from the national women's organizations set up pre- and postindependence. While most of these groups initially came together as voluntary, unregistered, urban-based collectives, in the contemporary period they have also become increasingly institutionalized and donor-funded. At the same time, other issue-based and donor-funded organizations that adopt a "gender" perspective are increasingly staking a claim of belonging to the autonomous women's movement, primarily on the grounds that they remain free of any party affiliations. The fluidity of the term "autonomy" has been captured in the argument that it is a developing concept, and

"viewed more as a process or a state of being one aspires to rather than a set of conditions which, if fulfilled, give an individual or organisation the label of autonomous" (Gandhi and Shah, "Organizations and Autonomy," 338). According to Gandhi and Shah, "there is so far no single definition of autonomy which can be debated, critiqued, questioned. Perhaps this is because the concept has emerged from and is still being developed through political practice" (338). The diminishing scope and identity of the autonomous women's movement as a distinct entity or having a distinct politics partly informs the recent "nostalgic" longing and groping back to the "certainties" of the past that I discuss elsewhere in this essay.

3. I use "South Asia" to indicate countries that are members of the South Asian Association for Regional Co-operations: Bangladesh, India, Maldives, Nepal, Pakistan, Sri Lanka, and, most recently, Afghanistan.

4. Sarkar, "Rhetoric against Age of Consent."

5. The partition of British India in 1947 led to the creation of the separate states of India and Pakistan. In 1971, East Pakistan seceded from Pakistan and became Bangladesh.

6. Forbes, *Women in Modern India*, 64–91; Kumar, *A History of Doing*; Kapur and Cossman, *Secularism's Last Sigh?*, 47–48; and Chaudhuri, *Indian Women's Movement*.

7. Sunder Rajan, *The Scandal of the State*, 31.

8. Agnes, "Protecting Women against Violence?," 20; and Agnes, "Law, Ideology and Female Sexuality."

9. Kannabiran, "A Ravished Justice"; and Menon, *Recovering Subversion*.

10. Gandhi, *Postcolonial Theory*; and Loomba, *Colonialism/Postcolonialism*.

11. Jayawardena, *Feminism and Nationalism in the Third World*, 2.

12. Kapur and Cossman, *Secularism's Last Sigh?*, 19–86.

13. My discussion is confined to the use of "Third World feminism" in international conferences such as the Vienna World Conference on Human Rights (1993), the Beijing Conference on Women (1995), the United Nations International Conference on Population and Development in Cairo (1994), and the Beijing plus Ten Conference, New York (2005).

14. International Initiative for Justice, "Threatened Existence: A Feminist Analysis of the Genocide in Gujarat," in *International Initiative for Justice*, 2003, 117–20, at onlinevolunteers.org; and Concerned Citizens' Tribunal, "Crime against Humanity: An Inquiry into the Violence in Gujarat," 2002, at sabrang.com.

15. Concerned Citizens' Tribunal, "Crime against Humanity."

16. Ibid., 171, 178; and International Initiative for Justice, "Threatened Existence," 117–20.

17. Sangari, "Politics of Diversity," 521.

18. Ibid., 522.

19. Kapur, "Imperial Parody," 79–88.

20. Arya, "Imagining Alternative Universalisms," 328.

21. *Bandit Queen* (1994), directed by Shekhar Kapur, depicted the story of Phoolan Devi, a poor, lower-caste village woman, who was subjected to extraordinary violence at the hands of upper-caste men, the police, and politicians in the state of Bihar. Phoolan subsequently became a feared and elusive outlaw. The scenes of violent rape in the film became the subject of censorship and obscenity challenges; the resultant public controversy recast the film as being primarily about sex rather than violence against poor women.

22. Kapur, *Erotic Justice*, 51–94.

23. Gopinath, *Impossible Desires*; and Kapur, *Erotic Justice*, 85–88.

24. Kempadoo and Dozema, *Global Sex Workers*, 11–12; and Kempadoo, "Women of Color and the Global Sex Trade."

25. *Naz Foundation v. Government of* NCT *of Delhi and Others*, July 2, 2009, Delhi High Court (which declared the sodomy provision in the Indian Penal Code as inapplicable to consensual adult sexual relationships).

26. Menon, *Recovering Subversion*.

27. Kishwar, "A Horror of 'Isms.'"

28. John, "Women's Studies"; and Kalyani Menon-Sen, "The Problem," *Seminar* 505 (September 2001), at indiaseminar.com.

29. John, "Gender, Development, and the Women's Movement," 114.

30. Mégret, "From 'Savages' to 'Unlawful Combatants.'"

31. Kapur and Cossman, *Secularism's Last Sigh?*, 175–86.

32. Ibid., 27–30.

33. Narayan, *Dislocating Cultures*.

34. Mégret, "From 'Savages' to 'Unlawful Combatants.'"

35. Menon, *Recovering Subversion*, 219.

36. Menon-Sen, "The Problem"; and Gangoli, *Indian Feminisms*. This turn to reclaim the past is also a feature of women's wings of left parties. See Dietrich, "Loss of Socialist Vision and Options before the Women's Movement."

37. Chaudhuri, *Feminism in India*, xi–xiv; Gandhi and Shah, *The Issues at Stake*; and Khullar, "Introduction," 17.

38. Brown, *Politics out of History*, 81.

39. Kapur, "Imperial Parody," 79–88.

40. Brown, *Politics out of History*, 15.

41. Desai, "Reflecting Back," 31.

42. Loomba, *Colonialism/Postcolonialism*.

43. Arundhati Roy, "Instant Mix Imperial Democracy," *Outlook*, May 26, 2003, 46–56; and Loomba, Kaul, Bunzl, Burton, and Esty, *Postcolonial Studies and Beyond*, 1–38.

44. Debates about postcolonial theory do not need to be rehearsed here (see, for example, Williams and Chrisman, *Colonial Discourse/Post-Colonial Theory*; Loomba, Kaul, Bunzl, Burton, and Esty, *Postcolonial Studies and Beyond*, 1–38; Mongia, *Contemporary Postcolonial Theory*; Chambers and Curti, *The Postcolonial Question*). My discussion is located within scholarship emerging at the intersection

of postcolonial theory and law. See Baxi, "Postcolonial Legalities"; Darian-Smith and Fitzpatrick, *Laws of the Postcolonial*, 1–14; Guha, *Subaltern Studies*, 135–65; Halder, *Law, Orientalism, and Postcolonialism*; Otto, "Everything Is Dangerous"; and Amin, "Approver's Testimony, Judicial Discourse."

45. Kapur and Cossman, *Secularism's Last Sigh?*, 65–68.

46. Chattopadhyay, *Lokayata and What Is Living and What Is Dead in Indian Philosophy*.

47. Sen, *The Argumentative Indian*.

48. For more examples of these heterogeneous traditions, see Venkata Raman, *Nagarjuna's Philosophy*; Burton, *Emptiness Appraised*; Ganeri and Tiwari, *The Character of Logic in India*; and Giri, *Senkottai Sri Avudai Akkal*.

49. Chatterjee, *The Nation and Its Fragments* and "Postcolonialism and the New Imperialism," 71–93; and Chakrabarty, *Provincializing Europe*, 47.

50. While the law of causation is an integral part of criminal law and is featured in the writings of Western liberal philosophers from Aristotle to J. S. Mill, I refer to the broader philosophical basis for the law of causation found in some Indian philosophical traditions, which underscores all human action. Matilal, *Logic, Language, and Reality*, 311–12.

51. These ideas of nondualism have been expounded by the ninth-century philosopher Adi Sankara. Advaita is an influential part of the Vedanta school of Hindu philosophy.

52. Mahmood, *Politics of Piety*.

MRINALINI SINHA

A Global Perspective on Gender
What's South Asia Got to Do with It?

THE QUESTION THAT ANIMATES my essay is this: what might it
mean to bring a global perspective to gender? The familiar understanding of gender, as having to do with a perceived binary
construction of man and woman, derives, arguably, from a particular historical and geographical context: the modern period
in northwestern Europe and North America. Yet *this* particular
meaning of gender is now not only widely recognized as a "useful category of historical analysis" but also routinely extended,
without any significant modification, to different contexts as the
default understanding of gender.[1] What are the implications of
making a particular conception of gender universal? What does
it mean to extend a parochial, albeit familiar, understanding of
gender to times and places other than those that gave rise to it in
the first place? These are some of the stakes in the desire to
reimagine gender from a global perspective.

The call to reappraise gender from a global perspective might
seem, at first glance, to be somewhat redundant. After all, we
have now had several decades of scholarship on gender focusing
on almost every conceivable area of the world. Moreover, we
now also have a sizable body of scholarship devoted to the potential and specific problems of integrating gender both in the
research and in the teaching of fields such as world and/or
global history. In the wake of this vast body of scholarship on
gender in global contexts, the call to bring a global perspective

to gender might seem somewhat belated: a Johnny-come-lately or a Janaki, as the case may be. Surely a global perspective on gender by now is an imperative rather than a proposition. Let me clarify the stakes by framing my point somewhat differently: while we certainly have a great deal of scholarship on women's and gender history *in* global contexts, we have not learned sufficiently from these contexts to begin to open up the concept of gender itself to different meanings. We must distinguish between merely exporting gender as an analytical category to different parts of the world and rethinking the category itself in the light of those different locations. In other words, what do these different global locations contribute to the meaning of gender *theoretically*?

In raising such questions, I am not alone.[2] Ulrike Strasser and Heidi Tinsman, for example, conclude their essay "Engendering World History" (2005) with a cautionary note: "Given that so many of gender history's analytical categories were first developed for the European context," they write, "how can we make sure that in studying gender systems in other cultures, we do not resort to another form of Eurocentrism, less obvious but more insidious because it is methodological rather than topical?"[3] Afsaneh Najmabadi's talk at the thirteenth Berkshire Conference on the History of Women takes up Strasser and Tinsman's challenge in her own appropriately titled "Beyond the Americas? Are Gender and Sexuality Useful Categories of Historical Analysis?"[4] The analytical project has never been merely about substituting "pure" and "autonomous" non-European alternatives, or "native" categories of analysis, as it were; this, in the wake of the history of European imperialism, would clearly be disingenuous at best. The categories of European political thought, as Dipesh Chakrabarty reminds us, are both indispensable and, ultimately, also inadequate for writing Third World histories.[5] The question, then, is precisely this: how does a global perspective on gender confront the default understanding of gender with its theoretical limits?

A truly global perspective on gender—rather than merely the extension of an a priori conception of gender to different parts of the globe—must give theoretical weight to the particular contexts in which it is articulated. It offers, in lieu of an already known understanding of gender, a radically open conception that derives its meaning from the work it does in particular contexts. This shift in the understanding of gender has implications not only for feminist scholarship but also for feminist practice.

To be sure, the argument for expanding the default understanding of gender has been made before. It has been the particular burden, for example, of a variety of "Third World feminisms" that have insisted on the crisscrossing and mutual constitution of gender with other axes of difference, such as class, race, caste, age, nationality, and sexuality, to name only a few.[6] To be sure, we have been made familiar with the working of gender outside dominant modern European communities; not least, this scholarship has now established the ways in which gender "intersects," and is "mutually constituted," by other axes of difference. Valuable as these challenges have been, they do not dislodge gender, in effect, from its privileged association with the binary relationship of men and women. Insofar as this binary understanding—derived from a specifically modern European context—continues as the essential meaning of gender, however expanded, it does not go far enough. The project of fully taking on board that the history of Europe is not exceptional, and not exceptional, above all, in its supposed universality, calls for a still further denaturalization: that is, we must dare to risk the disassociation of gender from its one-dimensional modern European association with binary sexual difference.

Herein lays the ambition of a global perspective on gender. It takes theoretical cognizance of both the nonmodern articulations and the extra-European locations of gender to throw open the meaning of the concept itself. What if the meaning of gender is not singular, after all? What if, in fact, its meaning is radically contextual? The task, then, is to give theoretical weight to the multiplicity of locations in which gender is articulated. This would entail, at the least, making strange what we still too often assume—man/woman—as the proper referent for gender. Once gender is thus liberated from its unnecessary association with any one parochial history, it becomes newly available for a reinvigorated feminist theory and praxis.

The various critiques that have been made over the years of the routine extension to other times and places of a very local and particular conception of gender—*local*, as Jeanne Boydston reminds us, to the cultures of the modern United States and Western Europe—offer useful signposts along the way of thinking gender anew.[7] Here it may be worth revisiting the controversial arguments made by the Africanists Ifi Amadiume and Oyeronke Oyewumi. To be sure, there is something defensive, and even, perhaps, unquestioningly essentialist, in the logic of their claim: that gender is so hopelessly compromised by its particular European constitution as to have no relevance for understanding social relations in precolonial Africa. Oye-wumi's 1997 book, *The Invention of Women: Making African Sense of Western Gender Discourse*, offered what is, perhaps, the most developed version of this case. She argued on the basis of her study of the Oyo-Yoruba in western Nigeria that the category woman in European society had no equivalent among the Yoruba; and, indeed, that gender was totally absent from precolonial Yoruba society, where the central organizing principle of social relations was not gender but seniority.[8] Notwithstanding the numerous critiques of her position, it is still possible, without wholly embracing her claim of an unbridgeable gulf between the allegedly gender-obsessed Europeans, on the one hand, and a supposedly gender-free Oyo-Yoruba, on the other, to take on board Oyewumi's central challenge: that is, that modern European-derived gender categories cannot be translated uncritically to understand the social complexities of very differently constituted societies.

Certainly there is other contemporaneous scholarship on Africa that, while using gender analytically, has demonstrated what an illuminating lens it can still be for understanding the organization of power relations in that continent whether in the colonial or in the precolonial periods; but some of the most exciting and innovative work of this type has also followed Oyewumi, at least halfway. In many of these works, for example, age and class figure so prominently in the constitution of gender identities that they allow us to question the relevance of the understanding of gender predominantly in terms of the male-female binary. As Andrea Cornwall notes in a recent review of gender-scholarship on Africa, "The transmutability of gender identities in Africa and the range of relational subject positions taken up by women and men in everyday life reveal a range of identities and identifications that undermine attempts to limit their frames of reference."[9] The power of this observation does not derive from evidence of the exotic, if by-now-familiar, existence of multiple genders and of multiple sexes. Nor does it derive merely from a theoretical commitment to the poststructuralist deconstruction of that staple of second-wave feminist theorizing: the sex-gender system.[10] Instead, it is rather precisely in the nonexotic ordinary character of the daily practices of gender, the "range of subject positions taken up by women and men in everyday life," that the implications of this scholarship are potentially so devastating to a unitary (and modern European) understanding of gender as part of a sex-gender schema.

The opportunity to rethink gender comes not necessarily from a theoretical commitment to poststructuralism, but from the intransigent refusal of empirical material to fit a predetermined concept of gender. Some of the anthropological and historical work on Africa has demonstrated the stark gap between a modern European understanding of gender and gender's field of operation; the sheer range, in short, of identifications open to men and women in their everyday lives. This scholarship suggests that women and men, in different places and at different times, have been constituted in relation to a whole range of different forces and not primarily, and definitely not necessarily, only in relation to one another.[11] The emphasis here may seem unsettling: the unmooring of gender itself from its natural link to a binary construction of men and women. The cumulative effect of some of the Africa-centered scholarship has been precisely to draw attention away from a priori meanings of gender to gender's "logic of practice" (in Pierre Bourdieu's terms) in different contexts.[12]

The larger point, however, is not merely the predictable one of contrasting theoretical abstractions with the immediacy of practice. It is, rather, about deriving the theoretical abstractions and the conceptual categories—in this case, the concept of gender—from the empirical material itself.[13] It suggests nothing less than a refusal to foreclose the meaning of gender on the basis of a limited, and limiting, parochial history of the concept in modern Europe. And its potential lies in the possibility of more robust histories of the concept in Europe as elsewhere. Men and women, this line of thinking suggests, are historically and discursively constructed not necessarily only in relation to one another, but also in relation to a variety of other categories, including dominant formulations of the political and social spheres, which are themselves subject to change.[14] This much, at least, has acquired widespread, though certainly not universal, lip service in feminist scholarship. However, the logical implications of this insight—the impossibility of a pregiven meaning of gender or of determining how men and women are constituted in advance of concrete analysis—have been repeatedly, and pointedly, ignored even in some theoretically sophisticated scholarship on gender. Hence, once again, more often than not, a Eurocentric conception of gender emerges by default as the essential meaning of gender; and this predictable and a priori modern European

MRINALINI SINHA

conception crops up, as such, in scholarship on all time periods and on all parts of the world. Under the circumstances, it is only when the empirical material simply resists being shoehorned into preexisting categories that the radical openness of gender as a category of analysis, or its continued capacity to surprise, becomes partly visible. This is precisely why historical and anthropological scholarship on gender in different parts of the world and in different eras has been so useful to think with.

The examples of a deliberate and self-conscious challenge to gender's typical frame of reference in feminist scholarship thus especially deserve our attention. In her 2005 book, *Women with Moustaches and Men without Beards: Gender and Sexual Anxieties of Iranian Modernity*, and in pointed reflections both in the book and elsewhere, Afsaneh Najmabadi comments extensively on the process of writing the book and of the journey of discovery it entailed.[15] The process involved *unlearning* many of the unspoken certitudes about gender with which she had approached her project initially. A chance encounter with a wealth of visual material from the period of the Qajar dynasty in Iran led her to go back and read her sources differently. While looking at paintings of heavy-browed women with moustaches and of slim-waisted beardless young men—called *amrads*—she discovered that male and female ideals of beauty were remarkably similar early in this period. Najmabadi deduces evidence of two *different* gender regimes in this encounter. She thus refuses to read *retroactively* the figure of the amrad, or the beardless adolescent male, who was the object of male desire; that is, as effeminate or a feminized deviation of masculinity. The amrad, as she demonstrates instead, belonged to a different logic of gender in which the point of reference for masculinity was not femininity but an adult male masculinity. Here was an understanding of gender in which *all* gender categories were understood in relation to adult manhood. Such an alternative perspective effectively estranges the prevailing notion of gender.

This initial "discovery" prompted Najmabadi to look at her sources differently and to notice in them a story for which she had not been quite prepared: the gradual "heterosocialization" of gender and of sexual relations—accompanied by the shift to a binary male-female understanding of gender—in the making of an Iranian modernity in the nineteenth and early twentieth centuries. "Thinking of gender as man/woman," Najmabadi concludes, "turned out to be a very modern imperative."[16] Najmabadi's contribution, indeed, forces us to reconsider the a priori assumptions about gender that we still too often bring to understanding the social practices in sites away from its particular and parochial enunciation among dominant modern European communities. It offers, at least, the possibility of radically destabilizing our commonly held assumptions about gender through identifying persisting traces of alternative gender regimes as well as by acknowledging the belated and *contingent* nature of the arrival of the taken-for-granted binary understanding of gender.

Once the concept of gender is liberated from its hitherto artificial tethering to a singular geographical location and historical trajectory, it becomes visible as the radically open concept that is suggested by a global perspective. Such a provocation has considerable bearing on giving theoretical cognizance to the particular iterations of gender. This, in turn, has the potential of opening up the fields of feminist scholarship and of feminist praxis anew. The implications of this shift in perspective may be illustrated through some examples from South Asia. Judith Walsh's enormously generative book *Domesticity in Colonial India: What Women Learned When Men Gave Them Advice* (2004), when read against the grain, illustrates the limits of shoehorning the colonial Indian material within an inherited paradigm of gender. Walsh's book explores the Bengali-language incarnation of what is often recognized to be a very nineteenth-century international genre: the domestic manual.[17] Her discussion of Bengali domesticity is especially apposite for my purposes because of its self-consciously global framing. This "global" framing, as I show, both enables and disables some of the most thoughtful and pointed contributions of the book.[18]

Walsh frames her analysis of the Bengali-language domestic manuals through the lens of "global domesticity": that is, the transnational circulation of ideas and practices of home and family life. She situates the preoccupations of the Bengali manuals—with such things as systematization, economy, efficiency, and order—alongside similar concerns in other examples of the genre from Britain and the United States. The book thus includes consideration of the famous manual of English domestic life, *Mrs. Beeton's Book of Household Management* (1861), the contributions of the nineteenth-century American domestic diva, Catherine Beecher, as well as Flora Annie Steel and Grace Gardiner's guide for British women in India, *The Complete Indian Housekeeper and Cook* (1888). Walsh is certainly right to note that these British and American texts, especially in their claims to civilizational and national superiority, are not merely the "internal" products of European culture, but, importantly, are "shaped by the civilizing mission of colonialism, now returned home to educate others."[19] Walsh's brief foray into British and American domestic manuals serves to complicate any easy characterization of the transnational ideas about home and family life as simply "European" (that is, as internal to, or exclusively of, Europe).

However, the methodological maneuvers of the book do not always keep up with such moments of insight. For example, Walsh ends up pulling her punches on the global provenance of the notions of domesticity. She slips back too quickly into the more conventional view: that the "ideas on home and family life [that] became naturalized in this period as a transnational hegemonic discourse on domestic life" were, in fact, "European."[20] To be sure, Walsh's focus in the book is not on the deconstruction of the self-contained European provenance of British and American domestic manuals, which form only a minor part of her subject matter. However, this slippage—between the logical conclusions arising out of the empirical information and the dominant interpretive frames used to make sense of them—is symptomatic of a problem that confronts even avowedly global scholarship: the continued persistence of existing European-derived conceptual paradigms even in the context of an expanded global unit of analysis.

This has some unintentional consequences. Walsh draws our attention to an important difference between the Euro-American and Bengali domestic manuals. Unlike the former, the overwhelming majority of the texts in this genre in the Bengali-language were written by men. (This was not necessarily the case for other indigenous languages; so, as Walsh reminds us, one of the earliest Marathi language domestic manuals was penned by a woman.) The Bengali anomaly, Walsh explains, was the result of the smaller number of educated and literate Bengali women in the first half of the nineteenth century during the heyday of the domestic manual. However, as she also notes, albeit in passing, when a greater number of educated and literate Bengali women emerged later in the century, they were not as attracted to the domestic manual as a genre compared to other genres. This suggests the possibility, at least, that there may be more to the predominantly male authorship of the Bengali manuals than merely the shortage of women writers in Bengal. Might the predominantly male-authored Bengali manuals be indicative of a significant difference between the Euro-

American and Bengali contexts of domesticity? Even the possibility of this line of enquiry is foreclosed, however, when the Bengali manual is too readily assimilated into a global narrative that has both already identified the domestic manual as a women's genre and assumed a certain fixity to gender as the perceived sexual differences between men and women.

Walsh's own material, however, takes us a long way down the road of teasing out the outlines of an alternative logic at work. For example, Walsh usefully draws our attention to the particular ideological work of the Bengali manuals. The latter, according to Walsh, mediate the shift in the locus of authority within the Bengali family, from an extended family where authority was dispersed across several family elders, including women elders, to a dyadic marital unit where familial authority rested less ambiguously on the shoulders of the young husband. The strategies for negotiating this shift in the manuals, as she demonstrates, were as varied as the manuals themselves. Some authors emphasize a companionate model for the relationship between husband and wife; others stress wifely devotion over all other family obligations; and still others, while partaking in the changes, are decidedly conflicted about them or are openly misogynist. What emerges from this discussion, albeit only implicitly, is the importance of the domestic as the site for the construction of a new masculine identity defined in opposition to elders, both men and women, in the family.[21] One of the many contributions of Walsh's study—fully attentive to the quirky details as well as to the particular ideological burdens of her texts—is to leave no doubt that the Bengali domestic manual, as such, was no mere "derivative" product: it was, neither more nor less than its Euro-American counterpart, part of a global process whose manifestations were undoubtedly uneven in different locations. By the same logic, Walsh's contextual Bengali material also suggests the possibility of pushing her analysis still further: that is, to recognize that a Euro-American conception of gender, understood in the binary terms of man/woman, might not at all be adequate for the ideological work of gender in the Bengali-language domestic manuals.

Consider for a moment how a revised conception of gender—one that in fact takes the Bengali material seriously in a theoretical sense—might raise a very different set of questions about the gender work of the Bengali manuals than the ones arising typically from the Euro-American manuals. What if—as hinted in Walsh's own contextual analysis of the manuals—a binary relationship between men and women does not structure the politics of gender in the Bengali-language manuals? What too if the domestic manual was not automatically identified with the fashioning, or, indeed, self-fashioning, of women? The Bengali-language manuals, freed from such a priori assumptions, might indicate an alternative possibility: that is, the genre serves precisely in the fashioning of a new masculine gender identity constructed in opposition to family elders.

The ability to recognize an alternative politics of gender at work, to acknowledge variety in the modes of the constitution of masculinity and femininity, rests on a willingness to abandon the binary man-woman structure of gender and all that comes with it. By this logic, moreover, Walsh's difficulty in finding traces of women's agency in the Bengali manuals extends beyond the fact that the manuals were written overwhelmingly by men. Her efforts are further complicated by the binary assumption of gender that accords the primacy of the man-woman opposition as the constitutive condition for the agency of women qua women. The Bengali manuals, with their emphasis on constituting the conjugal unit of husband and wife against the larger extended family, do not yield so easily to a conception of women's agency more suited to Euro-American domestic manuals in which the modern husband-wife dyad has already been naturalized. They suggest, instead, that the traces of a new agency for women qua women might be found paradoxically *within*, and through, the conjugal unit itself: that is, in opposition to extended kinship relationships rather than in any simple opposition to men.

By this same logic, moreover, the most telling aspect of the gender politics of the Bengali manuals might not be a question of women's agency after all. One intriguing aspect of nineteenth-century colonial Indian discourses on domesticity—as distinct, say, from both Euro-American and precolonial discourses on domesticity in the region itself—is the narrowing and progressive identification of the domestic sphere with men and masculinity.[22] The domestic, in fact, emerges in the context of colonial Indian conditions as a preferred site for the self-constitution of men qua men. The heavily male-authored Bengali manuals may be indicative of more than just the belatedness of modern education for women in Bengal. In the world of the Bengali domestic manual, Bengali men were being produced *as* men in opposition to finely graded familial hierarchies rather than in a simple binary opposition to women. The alternative foundations for the gender identities of "men" and "women" in nineteenth-century Bengal, as suggested in the Bengali-language domestic manuals, create an opening for radically rethinking the politics of gender in the region.

The delinking of gender in South Asia from the man-woman binary has been, for a variety of reasons, pioneered by the scholarship on men and masculinities. In the first place the scholarly attention on masculinity as a gender identity in South Asia did not arise in the context of binary sexual difference, but in the context of colonizer-colonized relations. Here Ashis Nandy's remarkable 1983 book on the psychology of colonialism, despite its reliance on purportedly natural and monolithic conceptions of British versus Indian masculinity, was a pioneering contribution.[23] My own 1995 book on the use, and the reuse, of the idea of the "effeminate Bengali" both by British officials and by Bengali elites was both enabled by, and conceived broadly within, this tradition of the studies of colonialism, even though, at the same time, it was also interested in the various other indigenous vectors of power that crisscrossed colonial categories in the late nineteenth century.[24] Since then, the scholarship on masculinity in relation to multiple forms of power, from colonialism to the more contemporary politics of Hindutva in India, has grown exponentially.[25] This burgeoning field has put pressure on the commonsense about gender that still informs by default much of the gender scholarship in South Asia.

The field of masculinity studies in South Asia, like elsewhere, has undergone something of a renaissance associated with what R. W. Connell identifies as the "ethnographic moment."[26] The new ethnographically oriented studies have dual implications. On the one hand, they go a long way in demonstrating the sheer diversity of masculinities within South Asia as well as in uncovering a range of different sites—the agricultural field, the workplace, the street, the cinema, literature, to name just a few—for the constitution and performance of different masculinities.[27] Moreover, and in keeping with the earlier work in this field, the masculinities that are explored here are shown to be constructed in relation to generation, class, caste, and religious identity rather than to women in any simple way. On the other hand, however, the newer ethnographic turn also comes with some significant silences that limit its usefulness for a theoretical reconsideration of the concept of gender. There is, for example, a certain residual tendency in this scholarship of reproducing an unproblematic relationship between men and masculinity, without addressing the *contingent* mapping

MRINALINI SINHA

of masculinity onto male bodies in the first place.[28] As such, more con-textual and better-grounded studies of men and masculinities in the region have been enormously productive for a more robust feminist politics. At its best, however, finely grained ethnographic studies also have theoretical significance.

Take the emergence of the category of MSM, or men who have sex with men. The category itself migrated from the vocabulary of grassroots orga-nizations working in South Asia, like the Naz Foundation International, into the vocabulary of international agencies. MSM was designed to capture the multiplicity of frameworks for sexual behavior that did not fit within the standard framework of sexual orientation or gender identity. In this case, the scrupulous attention to the pattern of sexual behavior on the ground in South Asia produced a conceptual breakthrough: the birth of a new category, MSM, to capture the realities on the ground. By taking theo-retical cognizance of gender's myriad "logics of practice," this shift in perspective opens up the category itself to contextual analysis instead of assuming the meaning of gender in advance.

This kind of reorientation of conceptual categories can have enormous implications for feminist politics and it is here that I turn to a fuller discussion of the potentially productive relationship between the kind of global approach to gender that I have been arguing for and its relationship to feminist praxis. Take, for example, the debates over the contemporary challenges to mainstream feminism in India. These debates too often rely on facile comparisons of the crisis of Indian feminism with a superficially similar trajectory undergone by a white Euro-American feminism. My own recent study, informed by an attempt to think against the constraints of a preexisting and monochromatic conception of gender, suggests a very different history of early Indian feminism and, by extension, of its contem-porary crisis.[29] The interwar period saw the spectacular public emergence of a new politics of women qua women in colonial India. The new gender identity of Indian women, in this case, emerged not in opposition to men but in opposition to the collective identity of communities, defined by religion, caste, ethnicity, and so on, which had formed the typical building block of colonial Indian society. Hitherto the symbolic burden of rep-resenting the identity of the respective communities had fallen on the women of the communities; the latter thus jealously guarded the right to control "their" women. Women, self-constituted as such, emerged out of the stifling embrace of communities in the interwar period to constitute a dramatic new public identity. The far-reaching implications of this development, however, have been hitherto obscured by a conventional binary discourse of gender within which this moment of arrival for early Indian feminism appears as less spectacular and is found to be wanting in comparison with Euro-American feminism. Rather than apprehend the nexus of woman/community as a rich site for the struggles of early Indian feminism, what one sees is simply the lack of a fully formed feminist sensibility according to a Euro-American model based on a conception of gender rooted in the man/woman binary.

Yet in India—unlike in Europe and North America—the gender identity of women, under the transitional conditions of the interwar period, carried an extraordinary political valence. The Indian woman, as the subject of a new feminist politics, became, against the collective community rights of the ex-colonial subject, the paradigmatic figure for the individualized rights of the future Indian citizen. And it was thus that the specifically feminist articulation of women qua women became the prerequisite for the critical transition that took place in India in the 1920s and 1930s: from a cultural to a political nationalism directed toward a nation-state in the making. This particular history of the making of women as a public constituency in colonial India, and the recruitment of this new woman as the paradigmatic subject of rights in the future nation-state of India, however briefly, weighs heavily on the contemporary dilemmas and contradictions that confront feminism in India.

The reliance on a priori understandings of gender has done a certain disservice to appreciating fully the potential and pitfalls of this history of early Indian feminism. Until recently, for example, scholarly accounts of the Child Marriage Restraint Act of 1929, the first piece of social reform legislation in colonial India that was enabled in large part by the efforts of autonomous all-India women's organizations themselves, failed to note its crucial significance: the first, and since then also the only, uniform law on marriage that cut across separate religious personal laws affecting marriage for different religious communities in India to be applicable universally.[30] To be sure, the 1929 legislation was a penal and not a civil measure; but it carried enormous symbolic significance as the first uniform law on marriage. The act enabled Indian feminists to put into circulation a different kind of liberalism—an agonistic liberal universalism that was defined both

MRINALINI SINHA

with, and against, classical European liberalism—to underwrite the revised new political nationalism of late colonial India. The fact that subsequently efforts to substitute separate religious personal laws with a uniform civil code have gained little traction, even in postindependent India, tells us something about both the possibilities and the limitations of the interwar moment in which the politics of Indian feminism came into its own.

By the 1930s, for example, the feminist movement in India was already deeply divided over the terms of women's political representation in the proposed new colonial constitution for India. To be sure, the competing sides in the debate made their arguments in language made familiar by parallel debates among feminists in Europe and North America: that is, they grounded their claims on the competing foundations of women's equality with, and difference from, men. Yet this classical liberal paradox of Euro-American feminists is not what informed feminist debates over women's political representation in India. Indian feminists were caught in a very different paradox that was rooted in their investment in an agonistic liberal universalism: the simultaneous disavowal, and constitution, of collective communal identities in the claims made on behalf of women. The very conditions that had once enabled women, as in the campaign for the Child Marriage Restraint Act of 1929, to constitute themselves as distinct from the collective identities of distinct religious communities, confronted Indian feminists now with impossible choices. The outcome of the constitutional wrangling of the 1930s was the return, willy-nilly, of women as symbols once again of reconstituted group identities. The dilemmas for a contemporary politics of women cannot merely draw on superficial comparisons with the trajectory of feminisms elsewhere; it needs precisely to engage with the particular legacy of early Indian feminism.

Interestingly, both the possibility of a uniform civil code and the question of women's political representation have reemerged as subjects of controversy for Indian feminism today, but their interwar genealogy remains largely misunderstood.[31] The point is not merely to register continuities, but to understand better the very particular dynamics that have informed the legacy of the gender politics of women in India. The constitutive contradictions of Indian feminism, despite some superficial similarities, have been quite different from those made familiar by a dominant Euro-American feminism.[32] While it might be tempting to see the contemporary problem for Indian feminists to accommodate adequately various kinds of "difference," within women and within feminism, in terms of the challenges that black or "Third World" feminism has posed for white Euro-American feminism, this would, in effect, be a misdiagnosis. Only by breaking loose from received notions of gender does it become possible to register the peculiarities of early Indian feminism and to reflect on its legacy for contemporary feminist debates in India. By the same token, this same conceptual move also helps to cut through invocations of a routinized conception of gender that have blunted its once radical and subversive edge. Nivedita Menon identifies two distinct trajectories for the term "gender" in the contemporary political landscape in India. On the one hand, the politics of caste and sexuality have widely deployed gender as an analytical category in ways that challenge "women" as the subject of feminist politics. On the other hand, in state developmental discourses, gender is used as a synonym for "women." The result, as Menon notes, has been both to dissolve and domesticate women as the subject of feminist politics.[33] If gender is to continue to serve a robust feminist politics, then feminists need to start with putting the term itself under interrogation.

The larger point is more than just an insistence on the multiplicity: the innumerable range of particularities that typically mark the manifestations of gender in different places and in different times. Rather, it is to insist that the empirical workings of gender—in all its variety—has a broader theoretical point to make: the need for a radically open conception of gender that decisively exceeds the unacknowledged and surreptitious way in which its use in feminist analysis is still too often reduced or folded back—"in the last instance," as it were—into a reassuring and familiar binary: the dichotomous understanding of male and female.

To return, then, to the question with which we began: to bring a global perspective to gender means to give theoretical cognizance to the multiple contexts in which it appears. This has potential, to be sure, for democratizing our concepts and analytical categories—like that of gender—in the project of recasting a Eurocentric historiography. But, more important, it has potential for raising a new and different set of questions about a past whose full import for the present has still to be realized. This has implications not only for better feminist scholarship but also, ultimately, for a more potent feminist praxis that is shaped by, and responsive to, the peculiarities of its own histories.

The significance for feminist practice of taking theoretical cognizance of the local and the empirical is, at least, threefold. It cautions against false analogies between different historical formations. It also serves as a corrective to the hubris of much contemporary politics, which, in sublime ignorance of the past, not only naturalizes the present but limits the possibilities of the future. And, finally, it opens the door for a feminist politics of the future that is not hemmed in by the conceptual constraints of its past, but whose concepts and strategies are flexible enough to respond to changing conditions. My argument is not premised on attributing any special qualities to the areas grouped recently under the label of South Asia. Rather, in my argument "South Asia," as both a particular and an ambiguous geopolitical entity, serves as a telling reminder that the multiple locations of feminist scholarship and of feminism have both a substantive and a theoretical contribution to make. We elide this at the expense of a feminist politics that requires dense contextual analysis to remain both relevant and critical. Feminism's future as a radical project may lie precisely in a scrupulous accounting, both contextually and conceptually, of the particular locations of its multiple iterations.

NOTES

1. The reference, of course, is to Joan Wallach Scott's pioneering essay "Gender: A Useful Category of Historical Analysis." For Scott's own discomfort with the routinized invocations of gender, see her "Some More Reflections on Gender and Politics"; and, more recently, see Scott, "Unanswered Questions," her response to the "American Historical Review Forum: Revisiting 'Gender': A Useful Category of Historical Analysis."

2. For various iterations of my own attempt to think through this question, see Mrinalini Sinha, "Reflections from the Scholarship on India" (round-table panel, "Gendering Trans/National Historiographies: Similarities and Differences in Comparison," at the Berkshire Women's History Conference, June 2005); "How to Bring a Global Perspective to Gender?" (paper presented at the American Historical Association annual conference, January 2008); "Beyond Europe: Working with Gender, Masculinity, and Women" (paper presented at the University of North Carolina–Duke workshop series "What Is the Future of Feminist/Gender History," February 2008); comment, at the conference "South Asian Feminisms: Gender, Culture, Politics" (University of Pennsylvania, March 2008); and the Asian Studies Lecture (Northern Arizona University, March 2009). I am grateful to the organizers and to the audience at these events for giving me an opportunity to pursue these questions. My biggest debt, however, is to Srimati Basu, Ania Loomba, and Ritty

Lukose for pushing me to clarify my arguments and for insisting that I stay with this argument even when I was ready to give up in frustration.

3. Strasser and Tinsman, "Engendering World History," 164. Also see Najmabadi, "Beyond the Americas?"; and Boydston, "Gender as a Question of Historical Analysis."

4. Najmabadi, "Beyond the Americas?"

5. Chakrabarty, *Provincializing Europe.*

6. I use the term "Third World feminisms" in its politically expansive, but not necessarily homogenizing, sense to include feminisms of women of color within Europe and North America as well as the feminism of women outside these areas; see Mohanty, Torres, and Russo, *Third World Women and the Politics of Feminism*; and Sandoval, *Methodology of the Oppressed.*

7. See Boydston, "Gender as a Question of Historical Analysis."

8. Oyewumi, *The Invention of Women.* Also see Amadiume's *Male Daughters Female Husbands.*

9. Cornwall, *Readings in Gender in Africa*, 13. My attention was drawn to this point by Heike Becker, "Review of Andrea Cornwall, ed., *Readings in Gender in Africa*," *H-SAfrica, H-Net Reviews*, April 2006, at http://h-net.org. See also Cole, Manuh, and Miescher, *Africa after Gender?*

10. See Butler, *Gender Trouble.*

11. For one example, see Becker, "Let Me Come to Tell You."

12. The reference here, of course, is to Pierre Bourdieu's classic *Outline of a Theory of Practice.*

13. For an example of this kind of theorizing—where the empirical details themselves generate the theory that is utilized to make sense of them—in the context of South Asian material, see Pollock, *The Language of the Gods in the World of Men.* My reading of Pollock's theoretical strategy is indebted to Gould, "How Newness Enters the World."

14. See, for example, Riley, *"Am I That Name?"*

15. Najmabadi, *Women with Mustaches* and "Beyond the Americas?"

16. Najmabadi, "Beyond the Americas," 14.

17. Walsh, *Domesticity in Colonial India.*

18. In this dicussion, I am drawing from my review of Walsh, *Domesticity in Colonial India* and *How to Be the Goddess of Your Own Home, Indian Economic and Social History Review* 44, no. 4 (2007): 547–51.

19. Walsh, *Domesticity in Colonial India*, 116.

20. Ibid., 2.

21. For hints that domesticity in nineteenth-century colonial India might operate in a different register than its Euro-American counterpart, see Sangari and Vaid, *Recasting Women*; Sarkar, *Hindu Wife, Hindu Nation*; and Chatterjee, *Unfamiliar Relations.*

22. To be sure, the domestic sphere was an equally important site for the construction of bourgeois masculinity in Britain; see Tosh, *A Man's Place.* But the

making of an autonomous "domestic" sphere became crucial in very different ways for indigenous middle-class claims to masculinity in colonial India; see Chatterjee, "Colonialism, Nationalism, and the Colonized Woman," "The Nationalist Resolution of the Women's Question," and *The Nation and Its Fragments*. Also see Sarkar, *Hindu Wife, Hindu Nation*.

23. Nandy, *The Intimate Enemy*.

24. Sinha, *Colonial Masculinity*.

25. For some examples, see Chowdhury, *The Frail Hero and Virile History*; Banerjee, *Make Me a Man!*; and Basu and Banerjee, "The Quest for Manhood."

26. See Connell, "Masculinities and Globalization."

27. For some examples, see Chopra, Osella, and Osella, *South Asian Masculinities*; and Srivastava, *Sexual Sites, Seminal Attitudes*. For my review of these books, see *Biblio* 10, nos. 1–2 (January–February 2004): 32–33; and *Indian Economic and Social History Review* 43, no. 4 (2006): 528–33.

28. For a discussion of this issue, see Sinha, "Giving Masculinity a History."

29. I am summarizing the argument from Sinha, *Specters of Mother India*.

30. For some recent, albeit belated, recognition of the 1929 act as a uniform law cutting across communities, see Sinha, *Specters of Mother India*; and Arya, "The Uniform Civil Code."

31. For the context of this contemporary discussion, see Sunder Rajan, "Women between Community and State"; and Nivedita Menon, "Reservation for Women: 'Am I That Name?,'" June 12, 2009, on the Kafila blog, at http://kafila.org.

32. I am tempted here to quote the famous line of the eighteenth-century theologian and philosopher Joseph Butler: "Everything is what it is, and not another thing."

33. Menon, "Sexuality, Caste, Governmentality."

Bibliography

Abu-Lughod, Lila. "Introduction: Feminist Longings and Postcolonial Conditions." In *Remaking Women: Feminism and Modernity in the Middle East*, ed. Lila Abu-Lughod. Princeton: Princeton University Press, 1998.

Agamben, Giorgio. *Remnants of Auschwitz: The Witness and the Archive*. New York: Zone Books, 2002.

———. *State of Exception*. Chicago: University of Chicago Press, 2005.

Agarwal, Bina. *Structures of Patriarchy: State, Community, and Household in Modernising Asia*. New Delhi: Kali for Women, 1988.

Agnes, Flavia. "Law, Ideology, and Female Sexuality: Gender Neutrality." *Rape Law* 37, no. 9 (2002): 844–47.

———. "Protecting Women against Violence? Review of a Decade of Legislation, 1980–1989." *Economic and Political Weekly* 25, no. 17 (April 1992): ws 19–33.

———. "Women's Movements in a Secular Framework: Redefining the Agendas." In *Women's Studies in India: A Reader*, ed. Mary E. John, 501–8. New Delhi: Penguin, 2008.

Agnes, Flavia, Neera Agarkar, and Madhushree Dutta. *The Nation, the State and the Indian Identity*. Calcutta: Samya, 1996.

Ahluwalia, B. K. *Shivaji and Indian Nationalism*. Delhi: Cultural Publishing House, 1984.

Ahmad, Anwara, Mithu Sarkar, and Amritrajit Saha. "Of Bush and God and ABC and How the Right-wing Thinks." In *Proceedings of the Third State Conference of Sex Workers*, 18–21. Kolkata: Durbar, 2005.

Akhter, Shaheen. *Talaash*. Dhaka: Mowla Brothers, 2004.

A'la Maududi, Abul. "Al Amr bil Marouf wa Nahin An al Munkir." In *Tafhimat*. Lahore: Islamic Publishers, 1968.

———. *Purdah and the Status of Woman in Islam.* Translated by Al-Ashari. Lahore: Islamic Publications, 2004.

Alam, Muzaffar. *The Languages of Political Islam: India, 1200–1800.* Chicago: University of Chicago Press, 2004.

Ali, Azra Asghar. *The Emergence of Feminism among Indian Muslim Women, 1920–1947.* Delhi: Oxford University Press, 2000.

Alvarez, Sonia. "Advocating Feminism: Latin American Feminist NGO 'Boom.'" *International Feminist Journal of Politics* 1 (1999): 181–209.

Amadiume, Ifi. *Male Daughters Female Husbands: Gender and Sex in an African Society.* London: Zed Books, 1987.

Amin, Samir. *Unequal Development.* New York: Monthly Review Press, 1976.

Amin, Shahid. "Approver's Testimony, Judicial Discourse: The Case of Chauri Chaura." In *Subaltern Studies V: Writings on South Asian History and Society*, ed. Ranajit Guha, 166–202. New Delhi: Oxford University Press, 1987.

Anandhi, S. "Representing *Devadasis*: 'Dasigal Mosavalai' as a Radical Text." *Economic and Political Weekly* 26, nos. 11–12 (March 1991): 739–46.

Arasanayagam, Jean. "Numerals." In *Reddened Water Flows Clear.* London: Forest Books, 1991.

Ardener, Shirley, Leela Dube, and Eleanor Leacock. *Visibility and Power: Essays on Women in Society and Development.* Delhi: Oxford University Press, 1986.

Arendt, Hannah. *On Revolution.* New York: Penguin, 1977.

Aretxaga, Begona. *Shattering Silence: Women, Nationalism, and Political Subjectivity in Northern Ireland.* Princeton: Princeton University Press, 1997.

Arondekar, Anjali. *For the Record: On Sexuality and the Colonial Archive in India.* Durham: Duke University Press, 2009.

———. "Time Corpus: On Sexuality, Historiography, and the Indian Penal Code." In *Comparatively Queer*, ed. Jarrod Hayes and William Spurlin, 153–72. New York: Palgrave, 2010.

Arredonda, Gabriela F., Aída Hurtado, Norma Klahn, Olga Nájera-Ramírez, and Patricia Zavella. *Chicana Feminisms: A Critical Reader.* Durham: Duke University Press, 2003.

Arunima, G. *There Comes Papa: Colonialism and Transformation of Matriliny in Malabar c. 1850–1940.* Hyderabad: Orient Longman, 2003.

Arya, Lakshmi. "Imagining Alternative Universalisms: Intersectionality and the Limits of Liberal Discourse." In *Theorising Intersectionality and Beyond: Social Inequality, Justice and the Politics of Subjectivity*, ed. D. Cooper, D. Herman, E. Grabham, and J. Krishnadas, 326–51. London: Routledge and Cavendish, 2008.

———. "The Uniform Civil Code: The Politics of the Universal in Postcolonial India." *Feminist Legal Studies* 14 (2006): 293–328.

Asad, Talal. *Formations of the Secular: Christianity, Islam, and Modernity.* Stanford: Stanford University Press, 2003.

——. *On Suicide Bombing*. New York: Columbia University Press, 2007.

Asia Watch and Physicians for Human Rights. "The Human Rights Crisis in Kashmir: A Pattern of Impunity." July 1, 1993, http://www.hrw.org/en/reports/1993/07/01/human-rights-crisis-kashmir.

Axelrod, Paul, and Michelle A. Fuerch. "Flight of the Deities: Hindu Resistance in Portuguese Goa." *Modern Asian Studies* 30, no. 2 (May 1996): 387–421.

Azim, Firdous. "Women and Freedom." *Inter-Asia Cultural Studies* 3, no. 3 (October 2002): 395–405.

Azim, Firdous, Mahbooba Mahmood, and Selina Shelley. *Phire Dekha* [Looking back]: *Nari Adhikar, Manabadhikar o Joinokorbider Lorai*. Dhaka: Shanghati, 2002.

Azim, Firdous, Nivedita Menon, and Dina Siddiqi, eds. "South Asian Feminisms: Negotiating New Terrains." Special issue of *Feminist Review* 91 (2009).

Bachetta, Paola. *Gender in the Hindu Nation: RSS Women as Ideologists*. New Delhi: Women Unlimited, 2003.

——. "Hindu Nationalist Women Imagine Spatialities/Imagine Themselves: Reflections on Gender Supplemental Agency." In *Right Wing Women: From Conservatives to Extremists around the World*, ed. Paola Bacchetta and Margaret Power, 43–56. London: Routledge, 2002.

——. "Communal Property/Sexual Property: On Representations of Muslim Women in a Hindu Nationalist Discourse." In *Forging Identities: Gender, Communities, and the State*, ed. Zoya Hasan, 188–225. Delhi: Kali for Women, 1994.

Bagilhole, Barbara. "Sexual Violence in India: 'Eve-teasing' as Backlash." In *Sexual Harassment: Contemporary Feminist Perspectives*, ed. Celia Kitzinger and Alison M. Thomas, 188–98. Buckingham, U.K.: Open University Press, 1997.

Bakshi, S. R., and Sri Kant Sharma. *The Great Marathas*. New Delhi: Deep and Deep Publications, 2000.

Balibar, Etienne. *Masses, Classes, Ideas*. New York: Routledge, 1994.

Banerjee, Sikata. *Make Me a Man! Masculinity, Hinduism, and Nationalism in India*. Albany: State University of New York Press, 2005.

——. *Warriors in Politics: Hindu Nationalism, Violence, and the Shiv Sena in India*. Boulder: Westview Press, 2000.

Banerjee, Sukanya, Angana P. Chatterji, Lubna Nazir Chaudhry, Manali Desai, Saadia Toor, and Kamala Visweswaran. "Engendering Violence: Boundaries, Histories, and the Everyday." *Gendered Violence in South Asia: Nation and Community in the Postcolonial Present*. Special issue of *Cultural Dynamics* 16, nos. 2–3 (2004): 125–40.

Barlow, Tani E. "Globalization, China, and International Feminism." *Signs: Journal of Women in Culture and Society* 26, no. 4 (2001): 1286–91.

——. "Introduction: On 'Colonial Modernity.'" In *Formations of Colonial Modernity in East Asia*, ed. Tani Barlow, 1–20. Durham: Duke University Press, 1997.

Barthakur, Sheila, and Sabita Goswami. "The Assam Movement." In *A Space within the Struggle: Women's Participation in People's Movements*, ed. Ilina Sen, 213–28. New Delhi: Kali for Women, 1990.

Bastian, Sunil. "Foreign Aid, Globalisation, and Conflict in Sri Lanka." In *Building Local Capacities for Peace: Rethinking Conflict and Development in Sri Lanka*, ed. Markus Mayer, Darini Rajasingham-Senanayake, Yuvi Thangarajah, 1332–51. New York: Macmillan, 2003.

——. *The Politics of Foreign Aid in Sri Lanka: Promoting Markets and Supporting Peace*. Colombo: International Centre for Ethnic Studies, 2007.

Basu, Amrita. *Women's Movements in Global Perspective*. Boulder: Westview Press, 1995.

Basu, Ishika, et al. "HIV Prevention among Sex Workers in India." *Journal of Acquired Deficiency Syndrome* 36, no. 3 (2004): 845–52.

Basu, Subho, and Sikata Banerjee. "The Quest for Manhood: Masculine Hinduism and Nation in Bengal." *Comparative Studies of South Asia, Africa, and the Middle East* 26, no. 3 (2006): 476–90.

Baxi, Upendra. "Postcolonial Legalities." In *A Companion to Postcolonial Studies*, ed. Henry Schwarz and Sangeeta Ray, 540–55. London: Blackwell, 2000.

——. "The Second Gujarat Catastrophe." *Economic and Political Weekly* 37, no. 34 (August 24–30, 2002).

Baxter, Craig. *Bangladesh: From Nation to a State*. Boulder: Westview Press, 1998.

Baykan, Aysegul. "Politics, Women, and Postmodernity: Women between Fundamentalism and Modernity." In *Theories of Modernity and Postmodernity*, ed. B. S. Turner, 136–146. London: Sage, 1990.

Becker, Heike. " 'Let Me Come to Tell You': Loide Shikongo, the King, and Poetic License in Colonial Ovamboland." *History and Anthropology* 16, no. 2 (2005): 235–58.

Benhabib, Seyla. "Feminism and Postmodernism: An Uneasy Alliance." In *Feminist Contentions: A Philosophical Exchange*, ed. Seyla Benhabib, Judith Butler, Drucilla Cornell, and Nancy Fraser, 17–34. London: Routledge, 1995.

——. "The Generalized and the Concrete Other: The Kohlberg-Gilligan Controversy and Feminist Theory." In *Feminism as Critique*, ed. Seyla Benhabib and Drucilla Cornell, 77–95. Cambridge: Polity Press, 1987.

Benhabib, Seyla, Judith Butler, Drucilla Cornell, and Nancy Fraser. *Feminist Contentions: A Philosophical Exchange*. London: Routledge, 1995.

Bharti, Anita. "Anyāy ke Khilāf—Laṛnā hī Naitiktā Hai." *Yuddhrat Aam Aadmī*, no. 87 (2007): 16–18.

Bhasin, Kamla, Ritu Menon, and Nighat Said Khan. *Against All Odds: Essays on Women, Religion, and Development in India and Pakistan*. New Delhi: Kali for Women, 1994.

Bhatia, Manjeet, Deepali Bhano, and Nirmalya Samanta. *Gender Concerns in South Asia: Some Perspectives*. Jaipur: Rawat Publications, 2008.

Bhattacharjee, Anannya. "Habit of Ex-nomination: Nation, Woman, and the Indian Immigrant Bourgeoisie." *Public Culture* 5, no. 1 (Fall 1992): 19–44.

———. "Immigrant Dreams and Nightmares: South Asian Domestic Workers in North America in a Time of Global Mobility." In *Trans Status Subjects: Gender in the Globalisation of South and Southeast Asia*, ed. Sonita Sarkar and Esha Niyogi De, 289–307. Durham: Duke University Press, 2002.

———. "Migration and Organising: Between Periphery and Centre." In *Learning/Work: Turning Work and Lifelong Learning Inside Out*, ed. Linda Cooper and Shirley Walters, 142–53. Cape Town: Human Sciences Resource Council Press, 2009.

———. "A Slippery Path: Organising Resistance to Violence against Women." In *Dragon Ladies: Asian American Feminists Breathe Fire*, ed. Sonia Shah, 29–45. Boston: South End Press, 1997.

Bhave, Y. G. *From the Death of Shivaji to the Death of Aurangzeb: The Critical Years*. New Delhi: Northern Book Centre, 2000.

Biyanwila, Janaka. "Sri Lanka: Contradictions for Women in Labour Organizing." In *Women and Labour Organizing in Asia: Diversity, Autonomy, Activism*, ed. Kaye Broadbent and Michele Ford, 66–83. New York: Routledge, 2009.

Blackburn, Stuart. "Life Histories as Narrative Strategy: Prophecy, Song, and Truth-Telling in Tamil Tales and Legends." In *Telling Lives in India: Biography, Autobiography and Life History*, ed. David Arnold and Stuart Blackburn, 203–26. Bloomington: Indiana University Press, 2004.

Blankenship, Kim, Sarah Bray, and Michale Merson. "Structural Interventions in Public Health." *AIDS* 14, Suppl. 1 (2000): S11–21.

Blee, Kathleen. "Becoming a Racist: Women in Contemporary Ku Klux Klan and Neo-Nazi Groups." *Gender and Society* 10, no. 6 (December 1996): 680–702.

Bosco, Fernando. "The Madres of Plaza de Mayo and Three Decades of Human Rights Activism: Embeddedness, Emotions, and Social Movements." *Annals of the Association of American Geographers* 96, no. 2 (2006): 342–65.

Bourdieu, Pierre. *Outline of a Theory of Practice*. Cambridge: Cambridge University Press, 1977.

Boydston, Jean. "Gender as a Question of Historical Analysis." *Gender and History* 20, no. 3 (November 2008): 558–83.

Brass, Paul. *Language, Religion and Politics in India*. Cambridge: Cambridge University Press, 1974.

Brown, Wendy. *Edgework: Critical Essays on Knowledge and Politics*. Princeton: Princeton University Press, 2005.

———. *Politics out of History*. Princeton: Princeton University Press, 2001.

——. *States of Injury: Power and Freedom in Late Modernity*. Princeton: Princeton University Press, 1995.

Buchanan, Allen. *Justice, Legitimacy, and Self-Determination: Moral Foundations for International Law*. New York: Oxford University Press, 2007.

Burton, David F. *Emptiness Appraised: Critical Study of Nagarjuna's Philosophy*. London: Routledge, 1999.

——. *Goa and the Blue Mountains, or, Six Months of Sick Leave*. Berkeley: University of California Press, 1991.

Butalia, Urvashi. *The Other Side of Silence: Voices from the Partition of India*. New Delhi: Viking Books, 1998.

Butler, Judith. "Contingent Foundations: Feminism and the Question of 'Post-modernism.'" In *Feminists Theorise the Political*, ed. Judith Butler and Joan Scott, 3–21. New York: Routledge, 1992.

——. *Gender Trouble: Feminism and the Subversion of Identity*. New York: Routledge, 1990.

——. *Precarious Life: The Power of Mourning and Violence*. London: Verso, 2004.

——. *Undoing Gender*. New York: Routledge, 2004.

Carby, Hazel. "White Woman Listen! Black Feminism and the Boundaries of Sisterhood." In *The Empire Strikes Back: Race and Racism in 70s Britain*, 212–35. London: Hutchinson, 1982.

Chakrabarty, Dipesh. *Provincializing Europe: Postcolonial Thought and Historical Difference*. Princeton: Princeton University Press, 2000.

Chakrabarty, I. *Influence of Rights-based Approach in Achieving Success in HIV Program and in Improving the Life of Sex Workers*. Kolkata: Durbar Mahila Samanwaya Committee Press, 2004.

Chakraborthy, Kakolee. *Women as Devadasis: Origin and Growth of the Devadasi Profession*. New Delhi: Deep and Deep Publications, 2000.

Chakravarti, Uma, and Nandita Haksar. *The Delhi Riots: Three Days in the Life of a Nation*. New Delhi: Lancer International, 1997.

Chambers, Iain, and Lidia Curti. *The Postcolonial Question*. New York: Routledge, 1996.

Chandrashekharan, Padma, et al. "Containing HIV/AIDS in India." *Lancet Infectious Diseases* 6 (2006): 508–21.

Chatterjee, Indrani. *Unfamiliar Relations: Family and History in South Asia*. New Delhi: Permanent Black, 2004.

Chatterjee, Partha. "Beyond the Nation? Or Within?" *Economic and Political Weekly* 4, no. 11 (January 1997): 30–34.

——. "Beyond the Nation? Or Within?" *Social Text* 53 (1998): 57–69.

——. "Colonialism, Nationalism, and Colonialized Women: The Contest in India." *American Ethnologist* 16, no. 4 (November 1989): 622–33.

——. "Democracy and Economic Transformations in India." *Economic and Political Weekly* 43, no. 16 (April 2008): 53–62.

——. *The Nation and Its Fragments: Colonial and Postcolonial Histories*. Princeton: Princeton University Press, 2007.

——. "The Nationalist Resolution of the Women's Question." *Postcolonial Discourses: An Anthology*, ed. Gregory Castle, 151–66. Oxford: Blackwell Publishers, 2001.

——. "On Civil and Political Society in Post-colonial Democracies." In *Civil Society: History and Possibilities*, ed. Sudipta Kaviraj and Sunil Khilnani, 165–78. Cambridge: Cambridge University Press, 2001.

——. *The Politics of the Governed: Reflections on Popular Politics in Most of the World*. New York: Columbia University Press, 2004.

——. "Postcolonialism and the New Imperialism." In *The Present as History: Critical Perspectives on Contemporary Global Power*, ed. Nermeen Shaikh, 71–93. New York: Columbia University Press, 2007.

Chatterjee, Piya. *Women, Labor, and Post/Colonial Politics on an Indian Plantation*. Durham: Duke University Press, 2001.

Chatterjee, Piya, Manali Desai, and Parama Roy. *States of Trauma: Gender and Violence in South Asia*. New Delhi: Zubaan, 2009.

Chatterji, Angana P. *Violent Gods: Hindu Nationalism in India's Present; Narratives from Orissa*. Gurgaon: Three Essays Collective, 2009.

Chatterji, Angana P., Parvez Imroz, et al. *Militarization with Impunity: A Brief on Rape and Murder in Shopian, Kashmir*. Srinagar: International People's Tribunal on Human Rights and Justice in Kashmir, 2009.

Chatterji, Lola. *Woman, Image, Text: Feminist Readings of Literary Texts*. Delhi: Trianka, 1986.

Chattopadhyay, Debiprasad. *Lokayata and What Is Living and What Is Dead in Indian Philosophy*. New Delhi: People's Publishing House, 1976.

Chaudhry, Lubna. "Reconstituting Selves in the Karachi Conflict: Mohajir Women Survivors and Structural Violence." *Cultural Dynamics* 16, nos. 2–3 (2004): 259–90.

Chaudhuri, Maitrayee. *Feminism in India*. New Delhi: Kali for Women and Women Unlimited, 2004.

——. *Indian Women's Movement: Reform and Revival*. Delhi: Radiant Publishers, 1993.

Chaudhuri, Nupur, and Margaret Strobel. *Western Women and Imperialism*. Bloomington: Indiana University Press, 1992.

Chenoy, Anuradha. *Militarism and Women in South Asia*. New Delhi: Kali for Women, 2002.

Chopra, Radhika, Caroline Osella, and Filippo Osella. *South Asian Masculinities:*

Contexts of Change, Sites of Continuity. New Delhi: Kali for Women and Women Unlimited, 2004.

Chowdhury, Indira. *The Frail Hero and Virile History: Gender and the Politics of Culture in Colonial Bengal*. Delhi: Oxford University Press, 1998.

Cole, Catherine M., Takyiwaa Manuh, and Stephan F. Miescher. *Africa after Gender?* Bloomington: Indiana University Press, 2007.

Connell, R. W. "Masculinities and Globalization." *Men and Masculinities* 1, no. 1 (July 1998): 3–23.

Connelly, William. *Political Theory and Modernity*. Madison: University of Wisconsin Press, 1986.

Cook, Michael. *Commanding Right and Forbidding Wrong in Islamic Thought*. Cambridge: Cambridge University Press, 2000.

Coomaraswamy, Radhika. "Mission to Bangladesh, Nepal, and India on the Issue of Trafficking in Women and Girls." Addendum to "Report of the Special Rapporteur," *Integration of the Human Rights of Women and the Gender Perspective: Violence against Women*. New York: United Nations Econmic and Social Council, Commission on Human Rights, 2001.

Coomaraswamy, Radhika, and Dilrukshi Fonseka. *Peace Work: Women, Armed Conflict, and Negotiation*. New Delhi: Women Unlimited, 2004.

Coomaraswamy, Radhika, and Nimanthi Perera-Rajasingham. *Constellations of Violence: Feminist Intervention in South Asia*. Colombo: International Centre for Ethnic Studies, 2008.

Cornwall, Andrea. *Readings in Gender in Africa*. Bloomington: Indiana University Press, 2005.

Crenshaw, Kimberlé. "Mapping the Margins: Intersectionality, Identity Politics, and Violence against Women of Color." *Stanford Law Review* 43, no. 6 (July 1991): 1241–99.

——. "Whose Story Is It, Anyway? Feminist and Antiracist Appropriations of Anita Hill." In *Racing Justice, Engendering Power*, ed. Toni Morisson, 402–36. New York: Pantheon Books, 1992.

Daniel, E. Valentine. *Charred Lullabies: Chapters in an Anthropography of Violence*. Princeton: Princeton University Press, 1997.

Danvers, Frederick Charles. *The Portuguese in India: Being a History of the Rise and Decline of Their Eastern Empire*. London: W. H. Allen, 1896; reprint 1966.

Darian-Smith, Eve, and Peter Fitzpatrick. *Laws of the Postcolonial*. Ann Arbor: University of Michigan Press, 1999.

Das, Samir Kumar. "Ethnicity and Democracy Meet When Mothers Protest." In *Women in Peace Politics*, ed. Paula Bannerjee, 54–77. New Delhi: Sage, 2008.

Davies, Tony. "Unfinished Business: Realism and Working-Class Writing." In *The British Working-Class Novel in the Twentieth Century*, ed. Jeremy Hawthorne, 125–36. London: Edward Arnold, 1984.

Davis, Angela. "Reflections on Post–September 11 America: An Interview with Angela Y. Davis." In *Policing the National Body: Race, Gender, and Criminalization*, ed. Jael Silliman and Anannya Bhattacharjee, 325–28. Boston: South End Press, 2002.

de Alwis, Malathi. "Ambivalent Maternalisms: Cursing as Public Protest in Sri Lanka." In *The Aftermath: Women in Post-war Reconstruction*, ed. Meredeth Turshen, Sheila Meintjes, and Anu Pillay, 210–24. London: Zed Books, 2001.

——. "Critical Costs: Negotiating Feminism 'At Home.'" *Inter-Asia Cultural Studies Journal* (October 2002): 493–500.

——. "Feminism." In *A Companion to the Anthropology of Politics*, ed. David Nugent and Joan Vincent, 121–34. Oxford: Blackwell, 2004.

——. "The 'Language of the Organs': The Political Purchase of Tears in Sri Lanka." In *Haunting Violations: Feminist Criticisms and the Crisis of the "Real,"* ed. Wendy Hesford and Wendy Kozol, 195–216. Champaign: University of Illinois Press, 2000.

——. "Millennial Musings on Maternalism." *Asian Women* 9 (December 1999): 151–69.

——. "Moral Mothers and Stalwart Sons: Reading Binaries in a Time of War." In *The Women and War Reader*, ed. Lois Lorentzen and Jennifer Turpin, 254–71. New York: New York University Press, 1998.

——. "Motherhood as a Space of Protest: Women's Political Participation in Contemporary Sri Lanka." In *Appropriating Gender: Women's Activism and the Politicization of Religion in South Asia*, ed. Amrita Basu and Patricia Jeffrey, 185–202. London: Routledge, 1998.

de Alwis, Malathi, and Kumari Jayawardena. *Embodied Violence: Communalising Female Sexuality in South Asia*. New Delhi: Kali for Women, 1998.

Deeb, Lara. *An Enchanted Modern: Gender and Public Piety in Shi'i Lebanon*. Princeton: Princeton University Press, 2006.

Defeis, Elizabeth F. "Draft Convention against Sexual Exploitation." In *Women and International Human Rights Law: Volume 2*, ed. Kelly Askin and Dorean Koenig, 333–48. New York: Transnational Press, 1999.

de Mel, Neloufer. *Militarizing Sri Lanka: Popular Culture, Memory, and Narrative in the Armed Conflict*. New Delhi: Sage, 2007.

——. *Women and the Nation's Narrative*. Lanham, Md.: Rowman and Littlefield, 2001.

de Mel, Neloufer, and Selvy Thiruchandran. *At the Cutting Edge: Essays in Honour of Kumari Jayawardena*. Delhi: Women Unlimited, 2007.

Deora, Man Singh. *Liberation of Goa, Daman and Diu*. New Delhi: Discovery, 1995.

Desai, Neera. "Reflecting Back: Forging Ahead Issues before Women's Studies." In *Between Tradition, Counter Tradition, and Heresy: Contributions in Honour of*

Vina Muzumdar, ed. Lolita Sarkar, Kumud Sharma, and Leela Kasturi, 31–46. New Delhi: Rainbow Publications, 2002.

Deshpande, Prachi. *Creative Pasts: History, Memory, and Identity in Western India.* New York: Columbia University Press, 2006.

De Souza, Teotonio. *Essays in Goan History.* New Delhi: Concept, 1989.

Dharamveer. *Premchand: Sāmant ka Munshi.* Delhi: Vāni Prakāshan, 2005.

Dietrich, Gabriele. "Loss of Socialist Vision and Options before the Women's Movement." *Economic and Political Weekly* 38, no. 43 (October 2003): 4547–54.

——. "Women and Religious Identities in India after Ayodya." In *Against All Odds: Essays on Women, Religion, and Development from India and Pakistan*, ed. Kamla Bhasin, Nighat Said Khan, and Ritu Menon, 35–59. Delhi: Kali for Women, 1994.

di Leonardo, Micaela. "Morals, Mothers, and Militarism: Antimilitarism and Feminist Theory." *Feminist Studies* 11, no. 3 (Fall 1985): 599–617.

Doezema, Jo. "Ouch! Western Feminists' 'Wounded Attachment' to the 'Third World Prostitute.' " *Feminist Review* 67, no. 1 (Spring 2001): 16–38.

Doniger, Wendy. *The Implied Spider: Politics and Theology in Myth.* New York: Columbia University Press, 1999.

Duff, James Grant. *History of the Marathas.* Bombay: Times of India Press, 1873.

Dunham, David, and Sisira Jayasuriya. "Equity, Growth, and Insurrection: Liberalisation and the Welfare Debate in Contemporary Sri Lanka." *Oxford Development Studies* 28, no. 1 (2000): 97–110.

Eagleton, Terry. *Literary Theory.* Minneapolis: University of Minnesota Press, 1983.

Elshtain, Jean Bethke. "On Beautiful Souls, Just Warriors, and Feminist Consciousness." In *Women and Men's Wars*, ed. Judith Stiehm, 341–48. Oxford: Pergamon Press, 1983.

——. *Women and War.* New York: Basic Books, 1987.

Engineer, Asghar Ali. *The Gujarat Carnage.* New Delhi: Orient Longman, 2003.

Engle, Karen. " 'Calling in the Troops': The Uneasy Relationship among Women's Rights, Human Rights, and Humanitarian Intervention." *Harvard Human Rights Journal* 20 (2007): 189–226.

——. "Feminism and Its (Dis)contents: Criminalizing Rape in Wartime Bosnia and Herzegovina." *American Journal of International Law* 99, no. 4 (October 2005): 778–816.

Enloe, Cynthia. *Does Khaki Become You? The Militarization of Women's Lives.* Boston: South End Press, 1983.

Esposito, John L. "Introduction: Modernizing Islam and Re-Islamization in Global Perspective." In *Modernizing Islam: Religion in the Public Sphere in Europe and the Middle East*, ed. John L. Esposito and François Burgat, 1–16. London: Hurst, 2003.

BIBLIOGRAPHY

Feldman, Allen. *Formations of Violence: The Narrative of the Body and Political Terror in Northern Ireland*. Chicago: University of Chicago Press, 1991.

Feldman, Shelley. "Exploring Theories of Patriarchy: A Perspective from Contemporary Bangladesh." *Signs* 16, no. 4 (Summer 2001): 1097–27.

Fernandes, Leela. *Producing Workers: The Politics of Gender, Class, and Culture in the Calcutta Jute Mills*. Philadelphia: University of Pennsylvania Press, 1997.

Fisher, Jo. *Mothers of the Disappeared*. Boston: South End Press, 1989.

Forbes, Geraldine. *Women in Modern India*. Cambridge: Cambridge University Press, 1996.

Foucault, Michel. *The Birth of Biopolitics: Lectures at the Collège de France, 1978–1979*. New York: Palgrave Macmillan, 2008.

——. *Discipline and Punish: The Birth of the Prison*. New York: Pantheon Press, 1979.

——. "Nietzsche, Genealogy, History." In *Language, Counter-Memory, Practice: Selected Essays and Interviews by Michel Foucault*, ed. Donald F. Bouchard, 139–64. Ithaca: Cornell University Press, 1977.

——. "Politics and the Study of Discourse." In *The Foucault Effect: Studies in Governmentality*, ed. Graham Burchell, Colin Gordon, and Peter Miller, 53–72. Chicago: University of Chicago Press, 1991.

——. *Power/Knowledge*. New York: Pantheon Press, 1980.

——. "The Statement and the Archive." In *The Archaeology of Knowledge and the Discourse on Language*, 77–131. New York: Pantheon Press, 1972.

Franke, Katherine. "Gendered Subjects of Transitional Justice." *Columbia Journal of Gender and Law* 15, no. 3 (2006): 813–28.

Fraser, Nancy, and Axel Honneth. *Redistribution or Recognition? A Political-Philosophical Exchange*. London: Verso, 2003.

Fujio, Christy. "From Soft to Hard Law: Moving Resolution 1325 on Women, Peace, and Security across the Spectrum." *Georgetown Journal of Gender and the Law* 9, no. 1 (2008): 215–36.

Gandhi, Leela. *Postcolonial Theory: A Critical Introduction*. New Delhi: Oxford University Press, 1998.

Gandhi, Nandita, and Nandita Shah. *The Issues at Stake: Theory and Practice in the Contemporary Women's Movement in India*. New Delhi: Kali for Women, 1992; New York: Routledge, 1999.

——. "Organizations and Autonomy." In *Gender and Politics in India*, ed. Nivedita Menon, 299–342. Delhi: Oxford University Press, 2001.

Ganeri, Jonardon, and Heeraman Tiwari. *The Character of Logic in India: Bimal Krishna Matilal*. Oxford: Oxford University Press, 2000.

Gangoli, Gitanjali. *Indian Feminisms: Law, Patriarchies, and Violence in India*. London: Ashgate, 2007.

Gedalof, Irene. *Against Purity: Rethinking Identity with Indian and Western Feminisms*. London: Routledge, 1999.

Ghose, Toorjo, et al. "Mobilizing Collective Identity to Reduce HIV Risk among Sex Workers in Sonagachi, India: The Boundaries, Consciousness, Negotiation Framework." *Social Science and Medicine* 67 (2008): 311–20.

Ghosh, Shohini. "Censorship Myths and Imagined Harms." In *Sarai Reader: Crisis/Media*, ed. Sarai Media Lab, 447–54. New York: Autonomedia, 2004.

——. "Deviant Pleasures and Disorderly Women: The Representation of the Female Outlaw in Bandit Queen and Anjaam." In *Feminist Terrains in Legal Domains: Interdisciplinary Essays on Women and Law in India*, ed. Ratna Kapur, 150–183. Delhi: Kali for Women, 1996.

Ginsberg, Faye. *Contested Lives: The Abortion Debate in an American Community*. Berkeley: University of California Press, 1998.

Giri, S. N. *Senkottai Sri Avudai Akkal*. Tapovanam: Chennai, 2002.

Glenn, Evelyn Nakano. *Unequal Freedom: How Race and Gender Shaped American Citizenship and Labor*. Cambridge: Harvard University Press, 2002.

Goetz, Anne-Marie, and Rina Sengupta. "Who Takes the Credit? Gender, Power and Control over Loan Use in Rural Credit Programmes in Bangladesh." *World Development* 24, no. 1 (1996): 44–63.

Goldberg, Jonathan, and Madhavi Menon. "Queering History." *PMLA* 120, no. 5 (2005): 1608–17.

Gonsalez, Juan. *Harvest of Empire: A History of Latinos in America*. New York: Penguin Books, 2000.

Goodhand, Jonathan. *Aid, Conflict, and Peacebuilding in Sri Lanka*. London: Conflict, Security, and Development Group, 2001.

Gopal, Priyamvada. "Of Victims and Vigilantes: The Bandit Queen Controversy." In *Signposts: Gender Issues in Post-Independence India*, ed. Rajeshwari Sunder Rajan, 293–331. New Brunswick: Rutgers University Press, 2004.

Gopinath, Gayatri. *Impossible Desires: Queer Diasporas and South Asian Public Cultures*. Durham: Duke University Press, 2006.

Gordon, Ruth. "Saving Failed States: Sometimes a Neocolonialist Notion." *American University Journal of International Law and Policy* 12 (1997): 953–59.

Gould, Rebecca. "How Newness Enters the World: The Methodology of Sheldon Pollock." *Comparative Studies of South Asia, Africa, and the Middle East* 28, no. 3 (2008): 533–57.

Grewal, Inderpal, and Caren Kaplan. "Postcolonial Studies and Transnational Feminist Practices." *Jouvert: A Journal of Postcolonial Studies* 5, no. 1 (Autumn 2000). http://english.chass.ncsu.edu/jouvert/v5i1/grewal.htm (accessed May 15, 2011).

——. *Scattered Hegemonies: Postmodernity and Transnational Feminist Practices*. Minneapolis: University of Minnesota Press, 1994.

Guha, Ranajit. *Subaltern Studies, Vol. 5: Writings on South Asian History and Society.* Delhi: Oxford University Press, 1987.

Gunaratna, Punyani, trans. *A Review of Free Trade Zones in Sri Lanka,* ed. Sunila Abeyesekera, 18–19. Ja-Ela: Dabindu Collective, 1997.

Gunasinghe, Newton. "Politics of Ethnicity and Religion." In *Selected Essays,* ed. Sasanka Perera, 172–208. Colombo: Social Scientists' Association, 1996.

Gupta, Dipankar. *Nativism in a Metropolis: The Shiv Sena in Bombay.* New Delhi: Manohar, 1982.

Gupta, Geeta, et al. "Structural Approaches to HIV Prevention." *The Lancet* 37, no. 2 (2008): 764–75.

Haase-Dubosc, Danielle, Mary John, Marcelle Marini, Rama Melkote, and Susie Tharu. *French Feminism: An Indian Anthology.* New Delhi: Sage, 2003.

Haksar, Nandita. "Human Rights Layering: A Feminist Perspective." In *Engendering the Law: Essays in Honour of Lotika Sarkar,* ed. Amita Dhanda and Archana Parasher, 71–88. Lucknow: Eastern Book Company, 1999.

Haldar, Piyel. *Law, Orientalism, and Postcolonialism: The Jurisdiction of the Lotus-Eaters.* London: Routledge, 2008.

Halley, Janet, Prabha Kotiswaran, Hila Shamir, and Chantal Thomas. "From the International to the Local in Feminist Legal Responses to Rape, Prostitution/Sex Work and Sex Trafficking." *Harvard Journal of Law and Gender* 29, no. 2 (2006): 336–423.

Hassan, Zoya. *Forging Identities: Gender, Communities and the State in India.* Boulder: Westview Press, 1994.

"Hasuna" [Letter]. *Dabindu* 15, no. 2 (2000): 7.

Helms, Elissa. "Women as Agents of Ethnic Reconciliation? Women's NGOs and International Intervention in Postwar Bosnia-Herzegovina." *Women Studies International Forum* 26, no. 1 (January–February 2003): 15–33.

Hensman, Rohini. "Feminism and Ethnic Nationalism in Sri Lanka." *Journal of Gender Studies* 1, no. 4 (1992): 501–6.

Hewamanne, Sandya. *Stitching Identities in a Free Trade Zone.* Philadelphia: University of Pennsylvania Press, 2008.

Hewamanne, Sandya, and James Brow. "If They Allow Us We Will Fight: Strains of Consciousness among Women Workers in the Katunayake Free Trade Zone." *Pravada* 6, no. 11 (2001): 19–23.

Hinton, Alexander L. *Annihilating Difference: The Anthropology of Genocide.* Berkeley: University of California Press, 2002.

Hobsbawm, Eric. "Introduction: Inventing Traditions." In *The Invention of Tradition,* ed. Eric Hobsbawm and Terence Ranger, 1–14. Cambridge: Cambridge University Press, 1983.

Hodges, Sarah. "Revolutionary Family Life and the Self Respect Movement in

Tamil South India, 1926–49." *Contributions to Indian Sociology* 39, no. 2 (2005): 251–77.

Honig, Bonnie. "Toward an Agonistic Feminism: Hannah Arendt and the Politics of Identity." In *Feminists Theorise the Political*, ed. Judith Butler and Joan Scott, 215–35. New York: Routledge, 1992.

Hoole, Rajan, et al. *The Broken Palmyrah*. Claremont, Calif.: Sri Lanka Studies Institute, 1990.

Hossain, Sara. " 'Apostates,' Ahmadis, and Advocates: Use and Abuse of Offences against Religion in Bangladesh." In *Warning Signs of Fundamentalisms*, 83–97. London: Women Living under Muslim Laws Publications, 2004.

Hull, Gloria T., Patricia Bell Scott, and Barbara Smith. *But Some of Us Are Brave: All the Women Are White, All the Men Are Black: Black Women's Studies*. New York: Feminist Press at CUNY, 1993.

Human Rights Watch. "Abdication of Responsibility: The Commonwealth and Human Rights." October 1, 1991. http://www.hrw.org/en/node/78772.

——." 'Everyone Lives in Fear': Patterns of Impunity in Jammu and Kashmir." September 11, 2006. http://www.hrw.org/en/reports/2006/09/11/everyone-lives-fear.

——. "India's Secret Army in Kashmir." May 1, 1996. http://www.hrw.org/en/reports/1996/05/01/india-s-secret-army-kashmir.

——. " 'With Friends Like These': Human Rights Violations in Azad Kashmir." September 20, 2006. http://www.hrw.org/en/reports/2006/09/20/friends-these.

Huq, Jahanara, Hamida Begum, Khaleda Salahuddin, and S. Rowshan Qadir. *Women in Bangladesh: Some Socio-Economic Issues*. Dhaka: Women for Women, 1983.

Huq, Shireen. "Sex Workers' Struggles in Bangladesh: Learning from the Women's Movement." *Sexuality Matters*, IDS Bulletin 7, no. 5 (October 2006): 134–37.

Ibrahim, Nilima. *The Voices of War Heroines [Ami Birangana Bolchi]*. Dhaka: Jagrata Prakashani, 1998.

Ilaiah, Kancha. *Why I Am Not a Hindu*. Calcutta: Samya, 2002.

Ivekovic, Rada, and Julie Mostov. *From Gender to Nation*. Ravenna, Italy: Longo Editore Ravenna, 2002.

Jackson, Michael. *The Politics of Story-telling: Violence, Transgression, and Inter-Subjectivity*. Copenhagen: Museum Tusculanum Press, 2002.

Jalal, Ayesha. *Democracy and Authoritarianism in South Asia: A Comparative and Historical Perspective*. Cambridge: Cambridge University Press, 1995.

——. "The Religious and Secular in Pre-colonial South Asia." *Daily Times*, April 21, 2002.

Jamal, Amina. "Feminist 'Selves' and Feminism's 'Others': Feminist Representations of Jamaat-e-Islami Women in Pakistan." *Feminist Review* 81 (2005): 52–73.

——. "Gendered Islam and Modernity in the Nation-Space." *Feminist Review* 91, no. 1 (2009): 9–28.

———. "Transnational Feminism as Critical Practice: A Reading of Feminist Discourses in Pakistan." *Meridians* 5, no. 2 (2005): 57–82.

Jashn-e-Azadi [How we celebrate freedom]. DVD. Directed by Sanjay Kak. New Delhi: Octave Communications Production, 2007.

Jayawardena, Kumari. *Ethnic and Class Conflicts in Sri Lanka*. Madras: Kaanthalakam, 1987.

———. *Feminism and Nationalism in the Third World*. London: Zed, 1986.

———. *The Rise of the Labor Movement in Ceylon*. Durham: Duke University Press, 1972.

———. "Time to Mobilise for Women's Liberation." *Lanka Guardian* 8, no. 7 (August 1985): 16–17, 24.

———. "The Women's Movement in Sri Lanka, 1985–1995." In *Facets of Change: Women in Sri Lanka, 1986–1995*, 396–407. Colombo: Centre for Women's Research, 1995.

Jayawardena, Kumari, and Malathi de Alwis. "The Contingent Politics of the Women's Movement." In *Women in Post-independence Sri Lanka*, ed. Swarna Jayaweera, 245–77. Delhi: Sage, 2002.

Jeffrey, Patricia, and Amrita Basu. *Appropriating Gender: Women's Activism and Politicized Religion in South Asia*. New York: Routledge, 1997.

Jeganathan, Pradeep. "A Space for Violence: Anthropology, Politics, and the Location of a Sinhala Practice of Masculinity." In *Community, Gender, and Violence*, ed. Partha Chatterjee and Pradeep Jeganathan, 37–65. New York: Columbia University Press, 2000.

———. " 'Violence' as an Analytical Problem." *Nethra* 2, no. 4 (1998): 7–47.

John, Mary E. *Discrepant Dislocations: Feminism, Theory, and Postcolonial Histories*. Berkeley: University of California Press, 1996.

———. "Feminism, Poverty and the Emergent Social Order." In *Social Movements in India: Poverty, Power, and Politics*, ed. Raka Ray and Mary Fainsod Katzenstein, 107–34. Lanham, Md.: Rowman and Littlefield, 2005.

———. "Gender, Development, and the Women's Movement: Problems for a History of the Present." In *Signposts: Gender Issues in Post-Independence India*, ed. Rajeshwari Sunder Rajan, 100–124. New Delhi: Kali, 1999.

———. *Women's Studies in India: A Reader*. New Delhi: Penguin, 2008.

———. "Women's Studies: Legacies and Futures." In *Between Tradition, Counter Tradition and Heresy: Contributions in Honour of Vina Muzumdar*, ed. Lolita Sarkar, Kumud Sharma, and Leela Kasturi, 47–62. New Delhi: Rainbow Publications, 2002.

John, Mary E., and Janaki Nair. *A Question of Silence? The Sexual Economies of Modern India*. New Delhi: Kali for Women, 1998.

John, Mary E., and Tejaswini Niranjana. "Mirror Politics: 'Fire,' Hindutva, and Indian Culture." *Economic and Political Weekly* 34, nos. 10–11 (March 1999): 581–84.

Jordan, Ann. "Commercial Sex Workers in Asia: A Blind Spot in Human Rights Law." In *Women and International Human Rights Law*, ed. Kelly Askin and Dorean Koenig, vol. 2, 525–85. New York: Transnational Press, 2000.

Jordan, Kay. *From Sacred Servant to Profane Prostitute: A History of the Changing Legal Status of the Devadasis in India, 1857–1947*. New Delhi: Manohar, 2003.

Joshi, Rama, and Joanna Liddle. *Daughters of Independence: Gender, Caste, and Class in India*. Delhi: Kali for Women, 1986.

Kabeer, Naila. *The Power to Choose: Bangladeshi Women and Labor Market Decisions in London and Dhaka*. London: Verso, 2000.

——. "The Quest for National Identity: Women, Islam and the State." *Feminist Review* 37 (Spring 1991): 38–58.

——. "The Search for Inclusive Citizenship: Meanings and Expressions in an Interconnected World." In *Inclusive Citizenship: Meanings and Expressions*, ed. Naila Kabeer, 1–27. London: Zed Books, 2005.

——. "Subordination and Struggle: Women in Bangladesh." *New Left Review* 168 (1988): 95–121.

Kakodkar, Harikishan. "Gomantak Maratha Samaj: Bharatatil Ek Aggressar Samaj." *Diamond Jubilee Celebration Issue*, ed. Harikishan Kakodkar and Parvatkar. Bombay: Gomantak Chapkana, 1987.

Kamble, Uttam. *Devadasi ani Nagnapuja*. Bombay: Lokvangmaya Gruh, 1988.

Kannabiran, Kalpana. "A Ravished Justice: Half a Century of Judicial Discourse on Rape." In *De-Eroticising Assault: Essays on Modesty, Honour, and Power*, ed. Kalpana Kannabiran and Vasanth Kannabiran, 104–69. Calcutta: Stree, 2002.

Kannabiran, Kalpana, and Vasanth Kannabiran. "Caste and Gender: Understanding Dynamics of Power and Violence." In *De-Eroticizing Assault: Essays on Modesty, Honour, and Power*, ed. Kalpana Kannabiran and Vasanth Kannabiran, 55–67. Calcutta: Stree, 2002.

Kaplan, Caren, Norma Alarcon, and Minoo Moallem. *Between Women and Nation: Nationalisms, Transnational Feminisms, and the State*. Durham: Duke University Press, 1999.

Kaplan, Temma. "Female Consciousness and Collective Action: The Case of Barcelona, 1910–1918." *Signs* 7, no. 3 (Spring 1982): 545–66.

Kapur, Ratna. *Erotic Justice: Law and the New Politics of Postcolonialism*. London: Glasshouse, Routledge; New Delhi: Permanent Black, 2005.

——. "Imperial Parody." *Feminist Theory* 2, no. 1 (2001): 79–88.

——. "Law and the Sexual Subaltern: A Comparative Perspective." *Cleveland State Law Review* 48, no. 1 (2000): 15–23.

——. "Normalizing Violence: Transnational Justice and the Gujarat Riots." *Columbia Journal of Gender and Human Rights* 15, no. 3 (2006): 885–927.

——. *Subversive Sites: Feminist Engagements with Law in India*. New Delhi: Sage, 1995.

Kapur, Ratna, and Brenda Cossman. *Secularism's Last Sigh? Hindutva and the (Mis)Rule of Law.* New Delhi: Oxford University Press, 2002.

Karim, Lamia. "Demystifying Micro-Credit: The Grameen Bank, NGOs, and Neoliberalism in Bangladesh." *Cultural Dynamics* 20, no. 1 (March 2008): 5–29.

Katzenstein, Mary Fainsod. *Ethnicity and Equality: The Shiv Sena Party and Preferential Policies in Bombay.* Ithaca: Cornell University Press, 1979.

Katzenstein, Mary Fainsod, Uday Mehta, and Usha Thakkar. "The Rebirth of the Shiv Sena in Maharashtra: The Symbiosis of Discursive and Institutional Power." In *Community Conflicts and the State in India,* ed. Amrita Basu and Atul Kohli, 215–38. Delhi: Oxford University Press, 1998.

Kazi, Seema. *Between Democracy and Nation: Gender and Militarization in Kashmir.* New Delhi: Women Unlimited, 2009.

Kearney, Robert. "The Marxist Parties of Ceylon." In *Radical Politics in South Asia,* ed. Paul R. Brass and Marcus F. Franda, 401–39. Cambridge: MIT Press, 1973.

Kempadoo, Kamala. "Women of Color and the Global Sex Trade: Transnational Feminist Perspectives." *Meridians: Feminism, Race, Transnationalism* (2001): 28–51.

Kempadoo, Kamala, and Jo Doezema, eds. *Global Sex Workers: Rights, Resistance, and Redefinition.* New York: Routledge, 1998.

Kennedy, David. "The International Human Rights Movement: Part of the Problem?" *Harvard Human Rights Journal* 15 (2002): 101–25.

Kersenboom-Story, Saskia C. *Nityasumangali-Devadasi Tradition in South India.* New Delhi: Motilal Banarasidas, 1987.

Key, Ellen. *The Century of the Child.* New York: G. P. Putnam and Sons, 1909.

Khan, Nyla Ali. *Islam, Women, and Violence in Kashmir: Between India and Pakistan.* New Delhi: Tulika Books, 2009.

Khan, Shahnaz. "'Zina' and the Moral Regulation of Pakistani Women." *Feminist Review* 75 (2003): 75–100.

Khan, Shivananda. "Culture, Sexualities, and Identities: Men Who Have Sex with Men in India." *Journal of Homosexuality* 40 (2001): 99–115.

——. "Males Who Have Sex with Males in South Asia—A Kothi Framework." *Pukaar* (Newsletter of the NAZ Foundation International) 31 (October 1, 2000): 12–13, 22–23.

Khan, Shivananda, and Omar Khan. "The Trouble with MSM." *American Journal of Public Health* 96 (2006): 765–66.

Khullar, Mala. "Introduction." In *Writing the Women's Movement: A Reader,* ed. Mala Khullar, 1–43. New Delhi: Zubaan-Kali, 2005.

Kishwar, Madhu. "The Bandit Queen." *Manushi* (September–October 1994): 34–37.

——. "A Horror of 'Isms': Why I Do Not Call Myself a Feminist." In *Feminism in India,* ed. Maitrayee Chaudhuri, 26–51. New Delhi: Kali for Women and Women Unlimited, 2004.

———. "Women in Gandhi." *Economic and Political Weekly* 23, no. 41 (October 1988): 2131–32.

Kishwar, Madhu, and Ruth Vanita. *In Search of Answers: Indian Women's Voices from Manushi: A Selection from the 1st 5 Years from a Feminist Magazine.* London: Zed Books, 1984.

Kleinman, Arthur. "The Violences of Everyday Life: The Multiple Forms and Dynamics of Social Violence." In *Violence and Subjectivity,* ed. Veena Das, Arthur Kleinman, Mamphela Ramphele, and Pamela Reynolds, 226–41. Berkeley: University of California Press, 2002.

Kovacs, Anja. "You Don't Understand, We Are at War!: Refashioning Durga in the Service of Hindu Nationalism." *Contemporary South Asia* 13, no. 4 (2004): 373–88.

Koven, Seth, and Sonya Michel. *Mothers of a New World: Maternalist Politics and the Origins of the Welfare State.* New York: Routledge, 1993.

Krishnaraj, Maithreyi. "Challenges before Women's Movement in a Changing Context." *Economic and Political Weekly* 38, no. 43 (October 2003): 4536–45.

Kumar, Radha. *The History of Doing: Illustrated History of Movements for Women's Rights and Feminism in India, 1800–1990.* New Delhi: Zubaan, 2009.

Kumari, Ved. "State's Response to the Problem of Rape and Dowry." In *Women and Law: Contemporary Problems,* ed. Lotika Sarkar and B. Sivaramayya, 104–28. New Delhi: Vikas Publishing House, 1994.

Laclau, Ernesto, and Chantal Mouffe. *Hegemony and Socialist Strategy: Towards a Radical Democratic Politics.* London: Verso, 1985.

Laine, James W. *Shivaji: Hindu King in Islamic India.* New York: Oxford University Press, 2003.

Lamb, Alastair. *Incomplete Partition: The Genesis of the Kashmir Dispute, 1947–1948.* Hertingfordbury, U.K.: Roxford Books, 1997.

Lane-Poole, Stanley. *Aurangzeb.* Oxford: Clarendon Press, 1893.

Lang, Sabine. "The NGOization of Feminism." In *Transitions, Environments, Translations: Feminisms in International Politics,* ed. Joan W. Scott, Cora Kaplan, and Debra Keates, 101–20. New York: Routledge, 1997.

Lewis, Reina, and Sara Mills. *Feminist Postcolonial Theory: A Reader.* New York: Routledge, 2003.

Lifton, Robert Jay. *Death in Life: Survivors of Hiroshima.* Chapel Hill: University of North Carolina Press, 1967.

Loomba, Ania. *Colonialism/Postcolonialism.* London: Routledge, 2005.

———. "Dead Women Tell No Tales." *History Workshop Journal* 36 (Autumn 1993): 209–27.

Loomba, Ania, Suvir Kaul, Matti Bunzl, Antoinette Burton, and Jed Esty. *Postcolonial Studies and Beyond.* Durham: Duke University Press, 2005.

Lukose, Ritty. *Liberalization's Children: Gender, Youth, and Consumer Citizenship in Globalizing India*. Durham: Duke University Press, 2009.

Lynch, Caitrin. "The 'Good Girls' of Sri Lankan Modernity: Moral Orders of Nationalism and Capitalism." *Identities* 6, no. 1 (1991): 55–89.

Mackinnon, Catherine A. "Rape, Genocide, and Women's Human Rights." In *Mass Rape*, ed. A. Stiglmeyer. Lincoln: University of Nebraska Press, 1993.

Mahmood, Saba. *Politics of Piety: The Islamic Revival and the Feminist Subject*. Princeton: Princeton University Press, 2005.

Mahmud, Simeen. "Our Bodies, Our Selves: The Bangladesh Perspective." In *Mapping Women's Empowerment: Experiences from Bangladesh, India, and Pakistan*, ed. Firdous Azim and Maheen Sultan, 181–206. Dhaka: University Press Limited, 2010.

Mamdani, Mahmood. "Good Muslim, Bad Muslim: A Political Perspective on Culture and Terrorism." *American Anthropologist* 104, no. 3 (2002): 766–75.

——. "Making Sense of Political Violence in Postcolonial Africa." *Identity, Culture, and Politics* 3, no. 2 (December 2002): 1–24.

Manchanda, Rita. "Maoist Insurgency in Nepal: Radicalizing Gendered Narratives." *Cultural Dynamics* 16, nos. 2–3 (2004): 237–58.

——. *Women, War, and Peace in South Asia: Beyond Victimhood to Agency*. New Delhi: Sage, 2004.

Mani, Lata. "Contentious Traditions: The Debate on Sati in Colonial India." In *Recasting Women: Essays in Colonial History*, ed. Kumkum Sangari and Sudesh Vaid, 88–126. New Delhi: Kali for Women, 1989.

——. "Cultural Theory, Colonial Texts: Reading Eyewitness Accounts of Widow Burning." In *Cultural Studies*, ed. Lawrence Grossberg, Cary Nelson, and Paula Treichler, 392–408. New York: Routledge, 1992.

Mankekar, Purnima. *Screening Culture, Viewing Politics: An Ethnography of Television, Womanhood, and Nation in Postcolonial India*. Durham: Duke University Press, 1999.

Marcus, Sharon. "Fighting Bodies, Fighting Words: A Theory and Politics of Rape Prevention." In *Feminists Theorize the Political*, ed. Judith Butler and Joan Wallach Scott, 385–403. London: Routledge, 1992.

Marglin, Frédérique Apffel. *Wives of the God-King: Rituals of Devadasi of Puri*. Delhi: Oxford University Press, 1985.

Marx, Karl. "Theses on Feuerbach." In *The Marx-Engels Reader*, ed. Robert Tucker, 143–45. New York: Norton, 1978.

Matilal, Bimal Krishna. *Logic, Language, and Reality: Indian Philosophy and Contemporary Issues*. New Delhi: Motilal Banarsi Dass, 1997.

Maunaguru, Sitralega. "Gendering Tamil Nationalism." In *Unmaking the Nation: The Politics of Identity and History in Sri Lanka*, ed. Pradeep Jeganathan and Qadri Ismail, 157–73. Colombo: Social Scientists Association, 1995.

Mbembe, Achille. *On the Postcolony*. Berkeley: University of California Press, 2001.

McAuley, Chrissie. *Women in a War Zone: Twenty Years of Resistance*. Dublin: Republican Publication, 1989.

McCormick, Adrienne. "The Women's Studies, Area, and International Studies Curriculum Integration Project at Thirteen Institutions." In "Internationalizing the Curriculum," *Women's Studies Quarterly* 26, nos. 3–4 (Fall–Winter 1998).

Mégret, Frédéric. "From 'Savages' to 'Unlawful Combatants': A Postcolonial Look at International Humanitarian Law's Others." In *International Law and Its Others*, ed. Anne Orford, 265–318. Cambridge: Cambridge University Press, 2006.

Menon, Nivedita. *Recovering Subversion: Feminist Politics beyond the Law*. Urbana: Permanent Black/University of Illinois Press, 2004.

——. "Sexuality, Caste, Governmentality: Contests over 'Gender' in India." *Feminist Review* 91 (February 2009): 94–112.

Menon, Ritu. "Do Women Have a Country?" In *From Gender to Nation*, ed. Rada Ivekovic and Julie Mostov, 43–62. Ravenna, Italy: Longo Editore Ravenna, 2002.

Menon, Ritu, and Kamala Bhasin. *Borders and Boundaries: Women in India's Partition*. New Delhi: Kali for Women, 1998.

Merry, Sally. *Human Rights and Gender Violence: Translating International Law into Local Justice*. Chicago: University of Chicago, 2006.

Mies, Maria. *Women and Indian Patriarchy*. Delhi: Concept, 1980.

Minault, Gail. *The Khilafat Movement: Religious Symbolism and Political Mobilization in India*. New York: Columbia University Press, 1982.

Mitchell, Timothy. "The Stage of Modernity." In *Questions of Modernity*, ed. Timothy Mitchell, 1–34. Minneapolis: University of Minnesota Press, 2000.

Mitter, Swasti. *Common Fate Common Bond: Women in the Global Economy*. London: Pluto Press, 1986.

Mohanty, Chandra. *Feminism without Borders: Decolonizing Theory, Practicing Solidarity*. New Delhi: Zubaan, 2003.

——. "Under Western Eyes: Feminist Scholarship and Colonial Discourses." *Feminist Review* 30 (Autumn 1988): 61–102.

Mohanty, Chandra, and Jacqui Alexander. *Feminist Genealogies, Colonial Legacies, Democratic Futures*. New York: Routledge, 1997.

Mohanty, Chandra, Lourdes Torres, and Ann Russo. *Third World Women and the Politics of Feminism*. Bloomington: Indiana University Press, 1991.

Mohanty, Manoranjan. "On the Concept of 'Empowerment.'" *Economic and Political Weekly* 30, no. 24 (June 1995): 1434–38.

Mongia, Padmini. *Contemporary Postcolonial Theory: A Reader*. London: Oxford University Press, 1996.

Morris, David. "About Suffering: Voice, Genre, and Moral Community." In *Social Suffering*, ed. Arthur Kleinman, Veena Das, and Margaret Lock, 25–46. Berkeley: University of California Press, 1997.

Moser, Caroline N. O., and Fiona Clark. *Victims, Perpetrators, or Actors?: Gender, Armed Conflict, and Political Violence.* New Delhi: Zed Books, 2001.

Mouffe, Chantal. "For a Politics of Democratic Identity." Lecture given at the Globalization and Cultural Differentiation seminar, March 19–20, 1999, MACBA-CCCB. http://macba.es/antagonismos/english/09_04.html.

Mufti, Aamir. "The Aura of Authenticity." *Social Text* 18, no. 3 (2000): 87–103.

Mukeherjee, Meenakshi. *Realism and Reality: The Novel and Society in India.* Delhi: Oxford University Press, 1985.

——. *Twice-Born Fiction; Themes and Techniques of the Indian Novel in English.* New Delhi: Heinemann, 1971.

Mukherjee, Nayanika. "Gendered Embodiments: Mapping the Body-Politic of the Raped Woman and the Nation in Bangladesh." *Feminist Review* 88, no. 1 (April 2008): 36–53.

——. " 'Remembering to Forget': Public Secrecy and Memory of Sexual Violence in Bangladesh." *Journal of the Royal Anthropological Institute* 12, no. 2 (June 2006): 433–50.

Mumtaz, Khawar, and Farida Shaheed. *Women of Pakistan: Two Steps Forward, One Step Back?* Lahore: Vanguard, 1987.

Nair, Janaki. "The Troubled Relationship of Feminism and History." *Economic and Political Weekly* 43, no. 43 (October 2008): 57–65.

——. *Women and Law in Colonial India: A Social History.* New Delhi: Kali for Women, 1996.

Najmabadi, Afsaneh. "Beyond the Americas? Are Gender and Sexuality Useful Categories of Historical Analysis?" *Journal of Women's History* 18, no. 1 (2006): 11–21.

——. "Feminism in an Islamic Republic: Years of Hardship, Years of Growth." In *Islam Gender and Social Change*, ed. Yvonne Yazbeck Haddad and John L. Esposito, 59–84. New York: Oxford University Press, 1998.

——. *Women with Mustaches and Men without Beards: Gender and Sexual Anxieties of Iranian Modernity.* Berkeley: University of California Press, 2005.

Nandy, Ashis. *The Intimate Enemy: Loss and Recovery of Self under Colonialism.* Delhi: Oxford University Press, 1983.

Narayan, Uma. *Dislocating Cultures: Identities, Traditions, and Third World Feminism.* London: Routledge, 2006.

Nasr, Seyyed Vali Reza. *Mawdudi and the Making of Islamic Revivalism.* New York: Oxford University Press, 1996.

Nasrin, Taslima. *Dwikhondito* (Divided in two). Kolkata: People's Book Society, 2003.

——. *Lajja* (Shame). Dhaka: Pearl Publsihers, 1993.

——. *Nirbachita Kolam* (Selected writings). Kolkata: Anando Publishers, 1993.

Navarro, Marysa. "The Personal Is Political: Las Madres de Plaza de Mayo." In *Power and Popular Protest: Latin American Social Movements*, ed. Susan Eckstein, 241–58. Berkeley: University of California Press, 1989.

Navlakha, Gautam. "Invoking Union: Kashmir and Official Nationalism of 'Bharat.'" In *Region, Religion, Caste, Gender, and Culture in Contemporary India*, ed. T. V. Sathyamurthy, 64–106. Delhi: Oxford University Press, 1996.

——. "Jammu and Kashmir: Winning a Battle Only to Lose the War?" *Economic and Political Weekly* 43, no. 45 (November 2008): 43–49.

Needham, Anuradha Dingwaney, and Rajeshwari Sunder Rajan, eds. *The Crisis of Secularism in India*. Durham: Duke University Press, 2007.

Nesiah, Vasuki. "From Berlin to Bonn: Militarization and Multilateral Decision-Making. *Harvard Human Rights Law Journal* 17 (Spring 2004): 75–98.

——. "The Princely Imposter: Stories of Law and Pathology in the Exercise of Emergency Powers." In *Emergency Powers in Asia: Exploring the Limits of Legality*, ed. Victor Ramraj and Arun Thiruvengadam, 121–46. Cambridge: Cambridge University Press, 2010.

——. "The Specter of Violence That Haunts the UDHR." *Maryland Journal of International Law* 24 (2009): 135–54.

Nesiah, Vasuki, and Alan Keenan. "Human Rights and Sacred Cows: Framing Violence and Disappearing Struggles." In *From the Margins of Globalization: Critical Perspectives on Human Rights*, ed. Neve Gordon, 261–95. Lanham, Md.: Lexington Books, 2004.

Newman, Robert. *Of Umbrellas, Goddesses, and Dreams: Essays on Goan Culture and Society*. Mapusa: Other India Press, 2001.

Nilufer, Gole. *The Forbidden Modern: Civilization and Veiling*. Ann Arbor: University of Michigan Press, 1996.

Niranjana, Tejaswini, and Mary E. John, eds. "Feminisms in Asia." Special issue of *Inter-Asia Cultural Studies* 3, no. 3 (October 2002).

Oldenburg, Veena. *Dowry Murder: The Imperial Origins of a Cultural Crime*. New York: Oxford University Press, 2002.

Olsen, Tillie. "I Want You Women Up North to Know." In *Writing Red*, ed. Charlotte Nekola and Paula Rabinowitz, 179–81. New York: Feminist Press, 1987.

Otto, Dianne. "Everything Is Dangerous: Some Poststructural Tools for Rethinking the Universal Knowledge Claims of Human Rights Law." *Australian Journal of Human Rights* 5, no. 1 (1999). http://www.austlii.edu.au/au/journals/AJHR/1999/1.html.

Oyeronke, Oyewumi. *African Women and Feminism: Reflecting on the Politics of Sisterhood*. Trenton: Africa World Press, 2003.

——. *The Invention of Women: Making African Sense of Western Gender Discourse*. Minneapolis: University of Minnesota Press, 1997.

Oza, Rupal. *The Making of Neoliberal India: Nationalism, Gender, and the Paradoxes of Globalization*. New York: Routledge, 2006.

Paigankar, Rajaram. *Mee Khon*. Vols. 1 and 2. Margao: Gomantak Chapkhana, 1969.

Parker, Kunal. "'A Corporation of Superior Prostitutes': Anglo-Indian Legal Conceptions of Temple Dancing Girls, 1800–1914." *Modern Asian Studies* 32, no. 3 (1998): 559–633.

Parmar, Pratibha, and Valerie Amos, "Challenging Imperial Feminism." *Feminist Review* 17 (Autumn 1984): 3–19.

Patil, B. R. "Devadasis and Other Social Evils." *Social Defence* 34 (1973): 24–33.

Patton, Cindy. *Globalizing AIDS*. Minneapolis: University of Minnesota Press, 2002.

Pawar, Urmila. *The Weave of My Life*. Kolkota: Stree Press, 2008.

Pawar, Urmila, and Meenakshi Moon. *We Also Made History*. New Dehli: Zubaan, 2004.

Perera, Sasanka. "Spirit Possessions and Avenging Ghosts: Stories of Supernatural Activity as Narratives of Terror and as Mechanisms of Coping and Remembering." In *Remaking a World: Violence, Social Suffering, and Recovery*, ed. Veena Das, Arthur Kleinman, Margaret Lock, Mamphela Ramphele, and Pamela Reynolds, 157–200. Berkeley: University of California Press, 2001.

Perera, Sonali. "Rethinking Working-Class Literature: Feminism, Globalization, and Socialist Ethics." *differences* 19, no. 1 (Spring 2008): 1–31.

Perera-Rajasingham, Nimanthi, Lisa Kois, and Rizvina Morseth de Alwis. *Feminist Engagements with Violence: Some Contingent Movements from Sri Lanka*. Colombo: International Centre for Ethnic Studies, 2007.

Perez, Rosa Maria. "The Rhetoric of Empire: Gender Representations in Portuguese India." *Portuguese Studies* 21 (Autumn 2005): 126–34.

Petchesky, Rosalind. *Abortion and Women's Choice: The State, Sexuality, and Reproductive Freedom*. Boston: Northeastern University Press, 1984.

Peto, Andrea. "Who Is Afraid of the 'Ugly Women'?: Problems of Writing Biographies of Nazi and Fascist Women in Countries of the Former Soviet Block." *Journal of Women's History* 21, no. 4 (Winter 2009): 147–51.

Phadke, Shilpa. "Thirty Years On Women's Studies Reflects on the Women's Movement." *Economic and Political Weekly* 38, no. 43 (October 2003): 4567–76.

Pissurlencar, S. S. *The Portuguese and the Marathas: Translation of Articles of the Late Dr. Pandurang Pissurlencar's Portugueses e Maratas in Portuguese Language*. Bombay: State Board for Literature and Culture, 1975.

Pollock, Sheldon. *The Language of the Gods in the World of Men: Sanskrit, Culture, and Power in Premodern India*. Berkeley: University of California Press, 2006.

Poonacha, Veena. "Women's Studies in Indian Universities: Current Concerns." *Economic and Political Weekly* 38, no. 26 (June–July 2003): 2653–58.

Prakash, Ved. "Aap Kidhar Hai?" *Yuddhrat Aam Aadmi* 87 (2007): 96–99.

Priolkar, A. K. *Goa Re-discovered*. Self-published, 1967.

Punekar, S. D., and Kamala Rao. *A Study of Prostitutes in Bombay (With Reference to Family Background)*. Bombay: Lalwani Publishing House, 1962.

Radhakrishnan, Smitha. "Examining the Global Indian Middle Class: Gender and Culture in the Silicon Valley/Bangalore Circuit." *Journal of Intercultural Studies* 29, no. 1 (February 2008): 7–20.

Radhakrishnan, Waman. *Purushartha*. Panjim: Rajhauns, 1998.

Rahman, Shahidur. "Bangladesh: Women and Labour Activism." In *Women and Labour Organizing in Asia: Diversity, Autonomy, Activism*, ed. Kaye Broadbent and Michele Ford, 84–99. New York: Routledge, 2009.

Rai, Mridu. *Hindu Rulers, Muslim Subjects: Islam, Rights, and the History of Kashmir*. Delhi: Permanent Black, 2004.

Rajasingham-Senanayake, Darini. "Between Reality and Representation: Women's Agency in War and Post-Conflict Sri Lanka." *Cultural Dynamics* 162, no. 3 (2004): 141–68.

Ramamirthammal, Muvalur. *Web of Deceit: Devadasi Reform in Colonial India*. Translated by Kalpana Kannabiran and Vasanth Kannabiran. New Delhi: Kali for Women, 2003.

Ranchhoddas, Ratanlal, and Dhirajlal Keshavlal Thakoree. *The Indian Penal Code*. 27th ed. Nagpur: Wadhwa, 1992.

Rankin, Katherine. "Governing Development: Neoliberalism, Microcredit, and Rational Economic Woman." *Economy and Society* 30, no. 1 (February 2001): 18–37.

Rao, Anupama. *The Caste Question: Dalits and the Politics of Modern India*. Berkeley: University of California Press, 2009.

——, ed. *Gender and Caste (Issues in Contemporary Indian Feminism)*. New Delhi: Kali for Women, 2003.

Ray, Raka. *Fields of Protest: Women's Movements in India*. Minneapolis: University of Minnesota Press, 1999.

——. "Women's Movements and Political Fields: A Comparison of Two Indian Cities." *Social Problems* 45 (1998): 21–36.

Ray, Raka, and Mary Katzenstein. "In the Beginning There Was the Nehruvian State." In *Social Movements in India: Poverty, Power and Politics*, ed. Raka Ray and Mary Katzenstein, 1–31. Lanham, Md.: Rowman and Littlefield, 2005.

Razack, Sherene. "The 'Sharia Law Debate' in Ontario: The Modernity/Premodernity Distinction in Legal Efforts to Protect Women from Culture." *Feminist Legal Studies* 15, no. 1 (2007): 3–32.

Rege, Sharmila. "Caste and Gender: The Violence against Women in India." In *Dalit Women: Issues and Perspectives*, ed. P. G. Jogdand, 18–36. New Delhi: Gyan Publishing House, 1995.

——. *The Sociology of Gender: The Challenge of Feminist Sociological Knowledge*. New Delhi: Sage, 2003.

——. *Writing Caste/Writing Gender: Narrating Dalit Women's Testimonies*. New Delhi: Zubaan, 2006.

Riaz, Ali. "Constructing Outraged Communities and State Responses: The Taslima Nasreen Saga in 1994 and 2007." *South Asia Multidisciplinary Academic Journal* 2 (2008): 1–20.

——. "Taslima Nasrin: Breaking the Structured Silence." *Bulletin for Concerned Asian Scholars* 27 (1995): 21–27.

Riley, Denise. *"Am I That Name?": Feminism and the Category of "Women" in History.* Minneapolis: University of Minnesota Press, 1988.

Robinson, Francis. *Islam and Muslim History.* New Delhi: Oxford University Press, 2000.

Rosa, Kumudhini. "The Conditions and Organisational Activities of Women in Free Trade Zones: Malaysia, Philippines, and Sri Lanka, 1970–1990." In *Dignity and Daily Bread,* ed. Sheila Rowbotham and Swasti Mitter, 73–99. London: Routledge, 1994.

——. "Strategies of Organisation and Resistance: Women Workers in Sri Lankan Free Trade Zones." *Capital and Class* 45 (1991): 27–35.

Rouse, Shahnaz. "Gender, Nationalism(s), and Cultural Identity." In *Embodied Violence: Communalizing Women's Sexuality in South Asia,* ed. Kumari Jayawardena and Malathi de Alwis, 42–70. New Delhi: Kali for Women, 1996.

——. *Shifting Body Politics: Gender, Nation, and State in Pakistan.* New Delhi: Women Unlimited, 2004.

Roy, Arundhati. *Field Notes to Democracy: Listening to Grasshoppers.* New Delhi: Haymarket Books, 2009.

Roy, Kinsuk. "Status of Male Sex Workers in India." In Sanlaap, "Sex Work Cannot Be Termed Work," *Gender-Just Laws Bulletin* 1, no. 3 (October 1998): 6. Delhi: India Centre for Human Rights and Law.

Roy, Olivier. *Globalized Islam: The Search for a New Ummah.* New York: Columbia University Press, 2004.

Roy, Srila. "The Ethical Ambivalence of Resistant Violence: Notes from Postcolonial South Asia." *Feminist Review* 91 (2009): 135–53.

——. "Melancholic Politics and the Politics of Melancholia: The Indian Women's Movement." *Feminist Theory* 10, no. 3 (2009): 1–17.

Rubinoff, Arthur G. *India's Use of Force in Goa.* Bombay: Popular Prakshan, 1971.

Ruddick, Sara. "Maternal Thinking." *Feminist Studies* 6, no. 2 (Summer 1980): 342–67.

——. *Maternal Thinking: Towards a Politics of Peace.* Boston: Beacon Press, 1989.

——. "Women of Peace: A Feminist Construction." In *The Women War Reader,* ed. Lois A. Lorentzen and Jennifer Turpin, 213–26. New York: New York University Press, 1998.

Sa'di, Ahmad H., and Lila Abu-Lughod. *Nakba: Palestine, 1948, and the Claims of Memory.* New York: Columbia University Press, 2007.

Said, Edward. *Orientalism*. New York: Pantheon Press, 1994.

Samarath, Anil. *Shivaji and the Indian Movement: Saga of a Living Legend*. Bombay: Somaiya Publication, 1975.

Sandoval, Chela. *Methodology of the Oppressed*. Minneapolis: University of Minnesota Press, 2000.

Sangari, Kumkum. "Politics of Diversity: Religious Communities and Multiple Patriarchies." In *Women's Studies in India: A Reader*, ed. Mary E. John, 515–23. New Delhi: Penguin, 2008.

Sangari, Kumkum, and Sudesh Vaid. "Introduction." In *Recasting Women: Essays in Colonial History*, ed. Kumkum Sangari and Sudesh Vaid, 1–26. New Delhi: Kali for Women, 1989.

——. *Recasting Women: Essays in Colonial History*. New Delhi: Kali for Women, 1989.

Sangathana, Stree Shakti. *"We Were Making History": Life and Stories of Women in the Telengana People's Struggle*. Delhi: Kali for Women, 1989.

Sanlaap. "Sex Work Cannot Be Termed Work." In *Gender-Just Laws Bulletin* 1, no. 3 (October 1998): 1–9. Delhi: India Centre for Human Rights and Law.

Saradamoni, Kunjulekshmi. *Finding the Household: Conceptual and Methodological Issues*. New Delhi: Sage, 1992.

——. *Matriliny Transformed: Family Law and Ideology in Twentieth Century Travancore*. New Delhi: Sage, 1999.

Sarkar, Jadunath. *Shivaji and His Times*. London: Sangam, 1992.

Sarkar, Rameshchandra. "Dedication to the Altar: The *Devadasi* Tradition in Goa." In *Goa: Cultural Patterns*, ed. Saryu Doshi, 140–55. Bombay: Marg Publication, 1983.

Sarkar, Tanika. *Hindu Wife, Hindu Nation: Culture, Religion, and Cultural Nationalism*. New Delhi: Permanent Black, 2001.

——. "Rhetoric against Age of Consent: Resisting Colonial Reason and Death of a Child-Wife." *Economic and Political Weekly* 4 (September 1993): 1869–78.

——. "Semiotics of Terror: Muslim Children and Women in Hindu Rashtra." *Economic and Political Weekly* 37, no. 28 (July 2002): 2872–6.

——. "The Woman as Communal Subject: The Rashtrasevika Samiti and the Ramjanmabhoomi Movement." *Economic and Political Weekly* (August 1991): 2057–62.

Sarkar, Tanika, and Urvashi Butalia. *Women and the Hindu Right: A Collection of Essays*. New Delhi: Kali for Women, 1995.

——. *Women and Right-Wing Movements: Indian Experiences*. London: Zed Books, 1996.

Sarkaria, Mallika Kaur. "On Trial: Human Rights in Kashmir." *Harvard Kennedy School Review* 9 (2009): 59–64.

Sarker, Sonita, and Esha Niyogi De. *Trans-Status Subjects: Gender in the Globalization of South and Southeast Asia*. Durham: Duke University Press, 2002.

Schirmer, Jennifer. "The Seeking of Truth and the Gendering of Consciousness: The Comadres of El Salvador and the Conavigua Widows of Guatemala." In *"Viva": Women and Popular Protest in Latin America*, ed. Sarah Radcliffe and Sallie Westwood, 30–64. London: Routledge, 1993.

——. " 'Those Who Die for Life Cannot Be Called Dead': Women and Human Rights Protest in Latin America." *Feminist Review* 32 (Summer 1989): 3–29.

Schmitt, Carl. *The Concept of the Political*. Trans. George Schwab. Chicago: University of Chicago Press, 1996.

Schreiner, Olive. *Women and Labour*. London: Virago, 1978.

Schultz, Vicki. "Reconceptualizing Sexual Harassment." *Yale Law Journal* 107, no. 6 (1998): 1683–805.

Scott, Joan Wallach. "Gender: A Useful Category of Historical Analysis." *American Historical Review* 91 (1986): 1056–61.

——. "Some More Reflections on Gender and Politics." In *Gender and the Politics of History*, ed. Carolyn G. Heilbrun and Nancy K. Miller, 199–222. New York: Columbia University Press, 1988.

——. "Unanswered Questions." *American Historical Review* (December 2008): 1422–29.

Sen, Amartya. *The Argumentative Indian: Writings on Indian History, Culture, and Identity*. London: Penguin, 2006.

——. "Reflecting on Resistance: Hindu Women 'Soldiers' Remember the Birth of Female Militancy." *Indian Journal of Gender Studies* 13, no. 1 (February 2006): 1–35.

——. *Shiv Sena Women: Violence and Communalism in a Bombay Slum*. London: Hurst, 2007.

Sen, Ilena. *A Space within the Struggle: Women's Participation in People's Movements*. New Delhi: Kali for Women, 1990.

Sen, Surendra Nath. *Foreign Biographies of Shivaji*. Calcutta: K. P. Bagchi, 1977.

Seshu, Meena, and Shohini Ghosh. "Selling Sex—Work, Business, or a Profession?" *Plainspeak: Talking about Sexuality in South and Southeast Asia* 1 (October 2005): 12–15.

Setalvad, Teesta. "The Woman Shiv Sainik and Her Sister Swayamsevika." In *Women and Right-Wing Movements: Indian Experiences*, ed. Tanika Sarkar and Urvashi Butalia, 223–44. Delhi: Kali for Women, 1996.

Shankar, Jogan. *Devadasi Cult: A Sociological Analysis*. New Delhi: Ashish Publishing House, 1990.

Sharma, Aradhana. *Logics of Empowerment: Development, Gender and Governance in Neoliberal India*. Minneapolis: University of Minnesota Press, 2008.

Sharma, Karuna. "The Social World of Devadasis and Prostitutes." *Journal of International Women's Studies* 9, no. 1 (November 2007): 297–310.

Sheth, Pravin. *Indians in America: One Stream, Two Waves, Three Generations.* Jaipur: Rawat Publications, 2001.

Shirodkar, Prakashchandra Pandurang. *Goa's Struggle for Freedom.* Delhi: Ajanta, 1988.

Shiva, Vandana. *Staying Alive: Women, Ecology, and Survival in India.* Delhi: Kali for Women, 1988.

Shohat, Ella. "Area Studies, Transnationalism, and the Feminist Production of Knowledge." *Signs* 26, no. 4 (Summer 2001): 1269–72.

——. *Taboo Memories, Diasporic Voices.* Durham: Duke University Press, 2006.

——. *Talking Visions: Multicultural Feminism in a Transnational Age.* Cambridge: MIT Press, 1998.

Siddiqi, Dina. "In the Name of Islam? Gender, Politics, and Women's Rights in Bangladesh." *Harvard Asia Quarterly* 10, no. 1 (Winter 2006): 1–13.

——. "Taslima Nasreen and Others: The Contest over Gender in Bangladesh." In *Women in Muslim Societies: Diversity within Unity*, ed. Herbert L. Bodman and Nayereh Tohidi, 205–27. Boulder: Lynne Riener Publishers, 1998.

Siddiqi, Dina, and Malathi de Alwis. *Feminist Activism in the 21st Century: Challenges and Prospects: Report of South Asian Feminist Meeting, July 25–29, 2006, Negombo, Sri Lanka.* New Delhi: Sangat, 2006.

Simpson, John, and Jana Bennett. *The Disappeared and Mothers of the Plaza.* New York: St. Martin's Press, 1985.

Sinha, Mrinalini. *Colonial Masculinity: The "Manly Englishman" and the "Effeminate Bengali" in the Late Nineteenth Century.* Manchester: Manchester University Press, 1995.

——. "Giving Masculinity a History: Some Contributions from the Historiography of Colonial India." *Gender and History* 11, no. 3 (November 1999): 445–60. Reprinted in *Gender and History*, ed. Leonore Davidoff, Keith McClelland, and Eleni Varikas, 27–42. Oxford: Blackwell, 2000.

——. *Specters of Mother India: The Global Restructuring of an Empire.* Durham: Duke University Press, 2006.

Smith, Wilfred Cantwell. *Islam in Modern History.* New York: New American Library, 1957.

Sofa, Ahmad. *Anupurbik Taslima Nasreen o Ananya Proshongo.* Dhaka: Student Ways, 1995.

Spelman, Elizabeth. *Fruits of Sorrow: Framing Our Attention to Suffering.* Boston: Beacon Press, 1997.

Spivak, Gayatri Chakravorty. "Can the Subaltern Speak?" In *Marxism and the Interpretation of Culture*, ed. Cary Nelson and Lawrence Grossberg, 271–313. Urbana: University of Illinois Press, 1988.

——. *In Other Worlds: Essays in Cultural Politics*. London: Routledge, 2006.

——. "Righting Wrongs." In *Human Rights, Human Wrongs: The Oxford Amnesty Lectures 2001*, ed. Nicholas Owen, 164–227. Oxford: Oxford University Press, 2003.

——. "Three Women's Texts and a Critique of Imperialism." *Critical Inquiry* 12, no. 1 (1985): 243–61.

"Sri Lankan Mothers' Front Plans to Hold Mass Rally." *Island*, February 9, 1991.

Srinivasan, Amrit. "The Devadasi and Her Dance." *Economic and Political Weekly* 20, no. 44 (November 2, 1985): 1869–76.

Srivastava, Sanjay. *Sexual Sites, Seminal Attitudes: Sexualities, Masculinities, and Culture in South Asia*. New Delhi: Sage, 2004.

Steinson, Barbara. " 'Mother Half of Humanity': American Women in the Peace and Preparedness Movements in World War I." In *Women, War, and Revolution*, ed. Carol Burkin and Clara Lovett, 259–84. New York: Holmes and Meier, 1980.

Strange, Carolyn. "Mothers on the March: Maternalism in Women's Protest for Peace in North America and Western Europe, 1900–1985." In *Women and Social Protest*, ed. Guida West and Rhoda Lois Blumberg, 209–24. Oxford: Oxford University Press, 1990.

Strasser, Ulrike, and Heidi Tinsman. "Engendering World History." *Radical History Review* 91 (Winter 2005): 151–64.

Stri Nirmana. Rattanapitiya: C.R.C. Press, 1988.

Suleri, Sara. "Woman Skin Deep: Feminism and the Postcolonial Condition." *Critical Inquiry* 18 (Summer 1992): 756–69.

Sultan, Maheen. "Work for Pay and Women's Empowerment: Bangladesh." In *Mapping Women's Empowerment: Experiences from Bangladesh, India, and Pakistan*, ed. Firdous Azim and Maheen Sultan, 95–119. Dhaka: University Press Limited, 2010.

Sultan, Maheen, and Soheila Nazneen. "Struggling for Survival and Autonomy: Impact of NGO-ization on Women's Organizations in Bangladesh." *Development* 52, no. 2 (June 2009): 193–99.

Sumon, Hussain Shahid. "Tanbazar Ucched, Jounokormider Manoadhikar Rokkharte Aini Lorai" [Tanbazar eviction and the legal battle for the rights of sex workers]. In *Phire Dekha: Nari Adhikar, Manabadhikar o Joinokorbider Lorai* [Looking back: women's rights, human rights and sex workers' struggles], ed. Firdous Azim, Mahbooba Mahmood, and Selina Shelley, 198–202. Dhaka: Shanghati, 2002.

Sunder Rajan, Rajeshwari. *The Lie of the Land: English Literary Studies in India*. New Delhi: Oxford University Press, 1992.

——. *Real and Imagined Women: Gender, Culture, and Postcolonialism*. London: Routledge, 1993.

———. *The Scandal of the State: Women, Law, and Citizenship in India*. Durham: Duke University Press; New Delhi: Permanent Black, 2003.

———. "Women between Community and State: Some Implications of the Uniform Civil Code Debates in India." *Social Text* 65 (Winter 2000): 55–82.

Swerdlow, Amy. "Female Culture, Pacifism, and Feminism: Women Strike for Peace." In *Current Issues in Women's History*, ed. Arina Angeran et al., 109–30. London: Routledge, 1989.

Takakhav, N. S. *Life of Shivaji*. New Delhi: Rishabh Publishers, 1998.

Tamang, Seira. "Civilising Civil Society: Donors and Democratic Space in Nepal." *Himal South Asia* 16, no. 7 (2003): 14–24.

———. "Legalizing State Patriarchy in Nepal." *Studies in Nepali History and Society* 5, no. 1 (2000): 127–56.

Tambe, Ashwini. "Brothels as Families: Reflections on the History of Bombay's Kothas." *International Journal of Feminist Politics* 8, no. 2 (June 2006): 219–42.

Tambiah, Stanley. *Leveling Crowds: Ethnonationalist Conflicts and Collective Violence in South Asia*. Berkeley: University of California Press, 1996.

Tarrow, Sidney. *Power in Movement: Social Movements and Contentious Politics*. New York: Cambridge University Press, 1994.

Taylor, Diana. *Disappearing Acts: Spectacles of Gender and Nationalism in Argentina's "Dirty War."* Durham: Duke University Press, 1997.

Tejani, Shabnum. *Indian Secularism: A Social and Intellectual History, 1890–1950*. Bloomington: Indiana University Press, 2008.

Tharu, Susie. *Subject to Change: Teaching Literature in the Nineties*. New Delhi: Orient Longman, 1998.

Tharu, Susie, and Ke Lalita. *Women Writing in India*. New York: Feminist Press, 1993.

Toor, Sadia. "Moral Regulation in a Postcolonial Nation-State: Gender and the Politics of Islamization in Pakistan." *Interventions: International Journal of Postcolonial Studies* 9, no. 2 (July 2007): 255–75.

Torab, Azam. *Performing Islam: Gender and Ritual in Iran*. Vol. 4 of *Women and Gender: The Middle East and the Islamic World*. Leiden, Netherlands: Brill, 2007.

Tosh, John. *A Man's Place: Masculinity and the Middle-Class Home in Victorian England*. New Haven: Yale University Press, 1999.

Trivedi, Harshad R. *Scheduled Caste Women: Studies in Exploitation with Reference to Superstition, Ignorance, and Poverty*. Delhi: Concept Publishing, 1977.

Utvik, Bjorn Olav. "The Modernizing Force of Islam." In *Modernizing Islam: Religion in the Public Sphere in Europe and the Middle East*, ed. John L. Esposito and François Burgat, 43–67. London: Hurst, 2003.

Van Schendel, Willem. *A History of Bangladesh*. Cambridge: Cambridge University Press, 2009.

Venkata Raman, K. *Nagarjuna's Philosophy*. New Delhi: South Asian Books, 1993.

Visweswaran, Kamala. *Fictions of Feminist Ethnography*. Minneapolis: University of Minnesota Press, 1994.

Walsh, Judith E. *Domesticity in Colonial India: What Women Learned When Men Gave Them Advice*. New Delhi: Oxford University Press, 2004.

——. *How to Be the Goddess of Your Own Home: An Anthology of Bengali Domestic Manuals*. New Delhi: Yoda Press, 2005.

Weerakoon, Batty R. *The Evolution of Labor Law in Sri Lanka: Tea Plantation to Free Trade Zone*. Colombo: Ceylon Federation of Labor, 1986.

Weiss, Anita M. "Implications of the Islamization Program for Women." In *Islamic Reassertion in Pakistan: The Application of Islamic Laws in a Modern State*, ed. Anita M. Weiss, 97–115. Syracuse: Syracuse University Press, 1986.

Weizman, Eyal. *Hollow Land: Israel's Architecture of Occupation*. London: Verso, 2007.

White, Hayden. *The Content of the Form: Narrative Discourse and Historical Representation*. Baltimore: Johns Hopkins University Press, 1987.

Williams, Patricia. *The Alchemy of Race and Rights*. Cambridge: Harvard University Press, 1992.

Williams, Patrick, and Laura Chrisman. *Colonial Discourse/Post-Colonial Theory*. New York: Columbia University Press, 1994.

Wirsing, Robert. *Kashmir in the Shadow of Rivalries in a Nuclear Age*. New York: M. E. Sharpe, 2003.

Women's Initiative. "Women's Testimonies from Kashmir: 'The Green of the Valley Is Khaki.' " In *Speaking Peace: Women's Voices from Kashmir*, ed. Urvashi Butalia, 82–95. New Delhi: Kali for Women, 2002.

Yami, Hisila. *People's War and Women's Liberation in Nepal*. Kathmandu: Janadhwani Publications, 2007.

Yule, Henry, and A. C. Burnell. *Hobson-Jobson: The Anglo-Indian Dictionary (1886)*. Ware, U.K.: Wordsworth Editions, 1996.

Zaman, Muhammad Qasim. *The Ulama in Contemporary Islam: Custodians of Change*. Princeton: Princeton University Press, 2002.

Zawilski, Valerie. "Saving Russia's Sons: The Soldiers' Mothers and the Russian-Chechan Wars." In *The Military and Society in Post-Soviet Russia*, ed. Stephen Webber and Jennifer Mothers, 228–40. Manchester: Manchester University Press, 2005.

Zia, Afiya Shehrbano. "The Reinvention of Feminism in Pakistan." *Feminist Review* 91, no. 1 (2009): 29–46.

Contributors

FLAVIA AGNES is a legal scholar and feminist activist based in Mumbai. She is the cofounder and co-coordinator of MAJLIS, a legal and cultural resource center for women and children. Her publications include *State, Gender, and the Rhetoric of Law Reform* (1995) and *Law and Gender Inequality: The Politics of Women's Rights in India* (1999).

ANJALI ARONDEKAR is an associate professor of feminist studies at the University of California, Santa Cruz. Her research engages the poetics and politics of sexuality, colonialism, and historiography in South Asia. She is the author of *For the Record: On Sexuality and the Colonial Archive in India* (2009) and has published in GLQ, *Journal of Asian Studies, Interventions, Victorian Studies, Feminist Studies*, and the *Journal of the History of Sexuality*.

FIRDOUS AZIM is a professor of English at BRAC University in Dhaka, Bangladesh. She is also a member of Naripokkho, a women's activist group, and is actively engaged in women's liberation issues. Her publications include *The Colonial Rise of the Novel* (1993), *Infinite Variety: Women in Society and Literature* (1994), and *Galpa: Short Stories by Bengali Women* (2005).

ANANNYA BHATTACHARJEE is the international organizer, based in India, for Jobs with Justice. Her work focuses on the effect of corporate-led globalization on labor practices, and current projects include an initiative to build solidarity between American and Indian workers. Her publications include *Policing the National Body: Sex, Race, and Criminalization* (2002), coauthored with Jael Silliman and Angela Yvonne Davis.

LAURA BRUECK is an assistant professor of Hindi literature in the Department of Asian Languages and Civilizations at the University of Colorado, Boulder. Her research is on modern and contemporary Hindi literature, with a particular focus on literatures of resistance. She is currently completing a book titled *Writing Resistance: The Rhetorical Imagination of Hindi Dalit Literature.*

ANGANA P. CHATTERJI is a professor of social and cultural anthropology at the California Institute of Integral Studies. She is the author of *Violent Gods: Hindu Nationalism in India's Present* (2009), and co-convener of the International People's Tribunal on Human Rights and Justice in India-administered Kashmir.

MALATHI DE ALWIS is a sociocultural anthropologist and teaches in the Faculty of Graduate Studies, University of Colombo. She has published widely on nationalism, humanitarianism, memorializing, suffering, and social movements. Her most recent publication is the book (coedited with Eva-Lotta Hedman) *Tsunami in a Time of War: Aid, Activism, and Reconstruction in Sri Lanka and Aceh* (2009).

TOORJO GHOSE is an assistant professor and postdoctoral fellow at the University of Pennsylvania's School of Social Policy and Practice. His research examines how social movements influence healthcare provision for sex workers and homeless substance users in India, Haiti, and the United States.

AMINA JAMAL is an assistant professor of sociology at Ryerson University in Toronto, Canada. Her work explores the interrelationships among women, religion, citizenship, modernity, transnational feminism, and the Pakistan nation-state. She is writing a book on the cultural and political activism of Jamaat-e-Islami women in Pakistan.

RATNA KAPUR is the director of the Centre for Feminist Legal Research, New Delhi, and is on the faculty of the Geneva School of Diplomacy and International Relations. She is currently a visiting professor of law at Yale Law School. Her publications include *Erotic Justice: Law and the New Politics of Postcolonialism* (2005) and most recently *Makeshift Migrants and Law: Gender, Belonging, and Postcolonial Anxieties* (2010).

LAMIA KARIM is an associate professor of anthropology at the University of Oregon, Eugene. She researches globalization, gender, human rights, and social movements. Her book *Microfinance and Its Discontents: Women in Debt in Bangladesh* was published in 2011. She is currently conducting research on the Asian Highway and women survivors of acid violence in Bangladesh.

ANIA LOOMBA is Catherine Bryson Professor of English at the University of Pennsylvania, and is affiliated with the Departments of Comparative Literature, South Asian Studies, Women's Studies, and Asian-American Studies. Her publications include *Gender, Race, Renaissance Drama* (1989, 1992); *Colonialism/Postcolonialism* (1998, 2005), and *Shakespeare, Race, and Colonialism* (2002); coedited volumes include *Postcolonial Studies and Beyond* (2005) and *Race in Early Modern England: A Documentary Companion* (2007).

RITTY A. LUKOSE is an associate professor at the Gallatin School, New York University. Her research engages cultural and political theory and gender, globalization, feminism, and anthropology in South Asia. She is the author of *Liberalization's Children: Gender, Youth, and Consumer Citizenship in Globalizing India* (2009) and has published in *Cultural Anthropology, Journal of Social History,* and *Social Analysis.*

VASUKI NESIAH is an associate professor at New York University. She researches and teaches the law and politics of international human rights, with a focus on transitional justice. Nesiah has written on international human rights, humanitarianism, feminist theory, comparative law, and postcolonial theory for a variety of journals and edited volumes.

SONALI PERERA is an assistant professor of English at Hunter College of the City University of New York. She teaches courses in postcolonial literature and theory, feminist theory, Marxist theory, and globalization studies. Her research interests include traditions of internationalism and literary radicalism from the global South, including parts of India and Sri Lanka. Her book *All That Is Present and Moving: Working-Class Writing in the Age of Globalization* is forthcoming from Columbia University Press.

ATREYEE SEN is Research Council United Kingdom Fellow at the Centre for Interdisciplinary Research in the Arts, University of Manchester. She is an urban anthropologist with a research interest in microcultures of political violence. She is the author of *Shiv Sena Women: Violence and Communalism in a Bombay Slum* (2007) and coeditor of *Global Vigilantes: New Perspectives on Justice and Violence* (2008).

MRINALINI SINHA is a professor of history at the University of Michigan. Her publications include *Colonial Masculinity: The "Manly Englishman" and the "Effeminate Bengali" in the Late Nineteenth Century* (1995), *Specters of Mother India: The Global Restructuring of an Empire* (2006), and *Selections from Katherine Mayo's "Mother India"* (2000).

ASHWINI SUKTHANKAR is a lawyer who works on issues of international labor rights, transnational labor regulation, and sex work with a number of international organizations and trade unions. Her publications include the collection *Facing the Mirror: Lesbian Writing from India* (1999).

Index

Malathi de Alwis, 13

Mangali (Kusam Meghwal), 235–37, 240–41

Mani, Lata, 5–6, 250

Manipur, 12

Manorama, Ruth, 226, 241

Maoists, 12–13, 131

Marathas, 256, 262n.32. *See also* Maharashtra

Marcus, Sharon, 8, 227

Marx, 131, 172

Masculinity, 266, 366–37

Masood, Kausar, 64, 66–67

Maternal agonism, 167, 175. *See also* Maternalism; Mothers' Front

Maternalism, 19, 163, 164, 176; in Latin America, 177n.29; mobilization in Sri Lanka and, 164–65. *See also* Mothers' Front

Matrimonial litigation, 41

Maududi, Maulana, 57, 62, 68; Islamic revivalism and, 60, 61, 62

Media, 41–44, 47–48

Meduri, Avanti, 248

Mee Khon, 256

Meghwal, Kusum, 18, 224, 233–41

Mehr, 39

Mehta, Deepa, 339

Menike, K. G. Jayasundera, 109

Menon, Nivedita, 101, 169, 172–73, 286, 303–4, 347, 370

Merry, Sally, 141, 154–55

Metcalf, Barbara, 59–60

Michel, Sonya, 164

Migrant labor, 129–34

Migration, 117–18, 121, 131; identity formation and, 132–33; politics and, 118, 133; social movements and, 122

Militarization, 2, 3, 5, 12–13, 19, 90; in Kashmir, 21, 181–82, 185–87, 190–91, 193–94, 196, 197; in Sri Lanka, 12, 107, 146. *See also* War

Mill, John Stuart, 343

Ministry for Women and Child Development, 314

Modernity, 44: civil society and, 173; colonialism and, 172; Indian feminism and, 334, 340, 345; Iranian, 361; Islam and, 54–55, 61–62, 69, 71; tradition vs., in devadasi reform debates, 248–52, 260; transnational, 141; Uniform Civil Code and, 44–46

Mody, Gautam, 321

Mohanty, Chandra, 14, 125

Mohtasib (ombudsman), 63, 66–67

Monogamy, 44, 45, 255, 318

Motherhood, 164; martial, 75, 85; Sinhala-Tamil women's political alliance and, 175; as space of protest, 154. *See also* Mothers' Front

Mothers' Front, 20, 154, 158n.13, 165–7, 177n.26

Mouffe, Chantal, 132, 162

Mrs. Beeton's Book of Household Management, 362–63

MSM (men having sex with men) groups, 279, 280, 367

Mujra dancers, 311

Multicultural feminism, 23, 24, 29n.46

Multiculturalism, 24

"Mulu Bara Janathava Matha" (The Entire Weight Lies upon the People), 115n.26

Musharraf, Pervez, 63

Muslim(s), 9, 343–44: communalism of, and British colonialism, 61; Hindus and, 47, 92, 206; Kashmiri, 184, 187, 193–94; Mahila Aghadi and, 87, 92; male sexuality and, 211; reformists, 60–61; as socio-political category, 61. *See also* Muslim women

Muslim feminists, 54–55, 58, 71. *See also* Bangladesh; Pakistan

Muslim Personal Law Board, 35–36

Muslim separatism, 61

Muslim women, 9–10, 19, 33–34, 37, 38–40, 41–44, 47, 48, 50–51, 54, 56, 57–58, 343, 349–50. *See also* Jamaat-e-Islami (Jamaat)

Muslim Women's Act, 9, 35–39, 40, 41, 44

"My Mothers Story" (Taslima Nasreen), 215–16

Mytho histories, 85–86, 87; of Shivaji and Shiv Sena women, 80, 86. *See also* Shivaji

Nahonnate, 214

Naimishray, Mohandas, 230

Nair, Janaki, 4, 15, 250, 251

Najmabadi, Afsaneh, 7, 357, 361

Najma Bibi: case of, 42–43

Nanayakkara, Vasudeva, 177n.26

Nandy, Ashish, 366

Narco analysis, 192

Nari (*Woman*; Humayun Azad), 216

Naripokkho, 17, 215, 222n.30, 268, 269, 270, 275, 276, 278, 281, 282n.7, 283n.18. *See also* Bangladesh

Nasr, Seyyed Vali Reza, 62

Nasreen, Taslima, 18, 19, 205–21, 221n.1, 222n.17, 222n.22

National AIDS Control Organization (NACO), 290, 323
National Centre for Labour, 329n.24
National Council of Women, 335
National Federation of Dalit Women, 225, 226
Nationalism, 4, 8, 10, 334–35
Nation-state, 1, 3, 14; feminist scholarship and, 8–9, 11; gender and, 4; making of, and Islam, 55, 56, 58, 65, 67, 69. *See also* Postcolonial nation state
Nautch girls, 253, 254
Navariya, Ajay, 231
Nava Sama Samaja Pakshaya, 177n.26
Naxalbari, 120
Naxalites, 131
Nayars, 250
Naz Foundation International, 367
Nazneen, Soheila, 269
Nepal, 1, 11, 149, 152
Nesiah, Vasuki, 16, 19, 101
Network of Sex Work Projects, 321
New Trade Union Initiative (NTUI), 317, 321
New York, 121–23
NGOization: of civil society, 288; of Dabindu collective in Sri Lanka, 98, 102, 104, 106; private sector and, 149–50; of women's groups in Sri Lanka, 13, 20, 149, 150
NGOs, 20, 101, 269, 290, 324; in Bangladesh, 209, 269–70, 273–74; CARE, 297, 298, 300, 301; feminist politics and, 13; International Alert, 143–44, 145; Karnataka Sex Worker's Union and, 323, 324; in Sri Lanka, 100, 102. *See also* NGOization
Nijera Kori, 215
Nirmal Nagar: slum area of, 80
Nisr, Atiya, 64, 67
Nondualism, 349, 355n.51
Northern Mothers' Front, 165. *See also* Mothers' Front
Norway, 139

Operation Sadhbhavana, in Kashmir, 182
Oral histories, 26n.15, 76. *See also* Storytelling
Organization of Parents and Family Members of the Disappeared, 177n.26
Organization/movement building, 133–34
Oyewumi, Oyeronke: gender study in Yoruba society and, 358

Paigankar, Rajaram Rangoji, 256
Pakistan, 1, 8, 11, 12, 19, 54–56, 58–59, 65–66,

69, 183, 198n.8; feminists in, 3, 5, 10, 55–57, 70–71. *See also* Jamat-e-Islami
Parker, Kunal, 250–51
Partition: of India, 5, 11, 206, 353n.5
Parvez, Khurram, 181, 186, 197, 199n.19
Paternalistic feminism, 124–25
Patriarchy, 4, 16, 34, 309; militarization and, 90, 193; Muslim woman and, 9–10, 41; religion and, 338; sexuality and, 211–12
Patton, Cindy, 289, 291–92, 297
Pawar, Urmila, 234
Peace activism: in Sri Lanka, 3, 8, 20, 162–63, 167–68, 170–71, 175. *See also* Mothers' Front
Peltier, Leonard, 119, 134n.1
Perera, A. C., 107
Perera, Sasanka, 92
Perera, Sonali, 13–14, 16, 20
Perez, Rosa Maria, 252, 258
Peto, Andrea, 78
Phoolan Devi, 227–28, 230, 354n.21
Pimps, 277, 285, 296, 308, 309, 327
Political, the: concept of, 8, 171–73; Derrida's notion of "constitutive outside" and, 163; Mouffe's definition of, 162; politics and, 162–63
Politics, 170; the political and, 162–63
Political society, 17, 173, 287, 291, 303; civilization of, 303; civil society vs., 17, 172–73, 285–88, 297–98, 301–3; claims-making process and, 286–87, 293–94, 303; concept of, 286; Durbar and, 286, 303; engagement with state and, 287–88; feminists and, 303–4; governmentality and, 286, 287, 293–94, 301, 303; Indian women's movement and, 288–89; mobilization of, 286, 287; public sphere and, 299
Populations, 287
Portrait of a Textile Worker (Terese Agnew), 98–99, 113n.4
Portuguese colonialism, 252–53
Postcolonial feminism, 4, 6, 7, 346; law and, 347; Western liberalism and, 348
Postcolonial nation-states, 6–7, 8, 11–12, 368
Postcolonial theory, 7, 346–47
Prevention of Terrorism Act: in Sri Lanka, 146
Prophet Muhammad, 216
Prostitution pledge, 313–14, 327
Public sphere, 298–99; private space vs., Islamist interpretation of, 65–66
Pupathi, Annai, 165

ANIA LOOMBA is Catherine Bryson Professor of English at the University of Pennsylvania. She is the author of *Shakespeare, Race, and Colonialism* (2002), *Colonialism–Postcolonialism* (1998), and *Gender, Race, Renaissance Drama* (1989). She edited, with Suvir Kaul, Matti Bunzl, Antoinette Burton, and Jedy Esty, *Postcolonial Studies and Beyond* (2005) and, with Martin Orkin, *Post-Colonial Shakespeares* (1998).

RITTY A. LUKOSE is an associate professor at the Gallatin School of Individualized Study at New York University. She is the author of *Liberalization's Children: Gender, Youth, and Consumer Citizenship in Globalizing India* (2009).

Library of Congress Cataloging-in-Publication Data
South Asian feminisms : contemporary interventions /
Ania Loomba and Ritty A. Lukose, eds.
p. cm.
Includes bibliographical references and index.
ISBN 978-0-8223-5165-8 (cloth : alk. paper)
ISBN 978-0-8223-5179-5 (pbk. : alk. paper)
1. Feminism—South Asia. I. Loomba, Ania. II. Lukose, Ritty A.
HQ1735.3.S657 2012
305.420954—dc23   2011030983